Rethinking Social Inquiry

Ricks

Will find recollection
of our years at CASBS,
and appreciation of
your ongoing role at

R SF. David

Rethinking Social Inquiry

Diverse Tools, Shared Standards

EDITED BY HENRY E. BRADY AND DAVID COLLIER

ROWMAN & LITTLEFIELD PUBLISHERS, INC.
Lanham • Boulder • New York • Toronto • Oxford

ROWMAN & LITTLEFIELD PUBLISHERS, INC.

Published in the United States of America
by Rowman & Littlefield Publishers, Inc.
A wholly owned subsidiary of The Rowman & Littlefield Publishing Group, Inc.
4501 Forbes Boulevard, Suite 200, Lanham, MD 20706
www.rowmanlittlefield.com

P.O. Box 317, Oxford OX2 9RU, UK

British Library Cataloguing in Publication Information Available

Library of Congress Cataloging-in-Publication Data

Rethinking social inquiry : diverse tools, shared standards / edited by Henry E. Brady and
    David Collier.
        p.   cm.
    Includes bibliographical references and index.
    ISBN 0-7425-1125-1 (cloth : alk. paper) — ISBN 0-7425-1126-X (pbk. : alk. paper)
    1. Social sciences—Research. 2. Social sciences—Methodology. I. Brady, Henry E.
II. Collier, David, 1942–
    H62.R4646   2004
    300'.72—dc22

                                                                2004008240
Printed in the United States of America

⊖™ The paper used in this publication meets the minimum requirements of American
National Standard for Information Sciences—Permanence of Paper for Printed Library
Materials, ANSI/NISO Z39.48-1992.

To the memory of
Esther Meyers Berins and
Myrtle Cochue Brady,
mothers and grandmothers extraordinaires

And to our students at Berkeley,
who never cease to challenge and
stimulate our thinking.

Brief Contents

Detailed Contents

Figures and Tables

Figures

Tables

Preface

Crafting good social science research requires diverse methodological tools. Such tools include a variety of qualitative and quantitative approaches: small-N and large-N analysis, case studies and structural equation modeling, ethnographic field research and quantitative natural experiments, close analysis of meaning and large-scale surveys. Yet diverse tools are not enough. Without shared standards, social science can lose its way. Shared standards help ensure that the application of these tools leads to meaningful conceptualization and measurement, interpretable causal inferences, and a better understanding of political and social life.

We come to the enterprise of editing this volume with different methodological starting points, yet with the joint conviction that our approaches converge in major respects. Henry E. Brady, who is primarily a quantitative survey researcher, repeatedly finds that he must come to grips with interpreting the meanings conveyed in survey responses and with comprehending the qualitative complexity of the political behavior he studies in various national contexts. David Collier, who is primarily a qualitative comparativist, recognizes that it is sometimes productive to quantify concepts such as corporatism and democracy, the historical emergence of labor movements, and the international diffusion of policy innovations. Our joint teaching and extensive discussions have reinforced our commitment to diverse tools, as well our conviction that we share basic standards for evaluating their use.

This concern with diverse tools and shared standards provides the framework for the present volume. Within that framework, a central focus is on a major scholarly statement about the relationship between quantitative and qualitative methods—Gary King, Robert O. Keohane, and Sidney Verba's book, *Designing Social Inquiry* (hereafter *DSI*). *DSI* is deservedly influential and widely read, in part because it offers an accessible statement of the analytic position that we call "mainstream quantitative methods."[1] The book likewise makes the important claim that quantitative methods can solve many problems faced by qualitative researchers.

Notwithstanding *DSI*'s major contribution, we have misgivings about important parts of the book's argument. First of all, *DSI* does not adequately address basic weaknesses in the mainstream quantitative approach it advocates. The book does not face squarely the major obstacles to causal assessment routinely encountered in social science research, even when sophisticated quantitative techniques are employed. *DSI*'s treatment of concepts, operationalization, and measurement is also seriously incomplete.

Further, we disagree with the claim that *DSI* provides a general framework for "scientific inference in qualitative research," as the authors put it in the book's subtitle. The book's failure to recognize the distinctive strengths of qualitative tools leads the authors to inappropriately view qualitative analysis almost exclusively through the optic of mainstream quantitative methods.

We are convinced that the perspective offered by ideas drawn from what we call "statistical theory"[2]—in contrast to *DSI*'s perspective of mainstream quantitative methods—provides a more realistic approach to evaluating qualitative tools. Statistical theory sometimes points to valuable justifications for practices of qualitative researchers that *DSI* devalues. We therefore consider not only how qualitative research can be justified in its own terms, but also the idea of statistical rationale for qualitative research.

Our project began with the idea of reprinting several insightful review essays focused on *DSI*, which we had intended to bring together as a small volume with some opening and concluding observations of our own. As sometimes happens with book projects, this one expanded greatly, and the newly written material constitutes well over half the text.[3] The book includes an entire chapter that summarizes *DSI*'s recommendations (chap. 2), as well as two substantial concluding chapters (chaps. 12 and 13), an appendix, and a glossary.

---

[1]We define mainstream quantitative methods as an approach based on regression analysis, econometric refinements on regression, and the search for statistical alternatives to regression models in contexts where specific regression assumptions are not met.

[2]We understand statistical theory as a broad, multidisciplinary enterprise concerned with reasoning about evidence and inference. Important scholars in the tradition of statistical theory have expressed considerable skepticism about the application to observational data of the regression-based methodology identified with mainstream quantitative methods.

[3]Acknowledgment of permission to reprint copyrighted material is presented at the end of this book.

Especially in a book with multiple authors, the reader may find it helpful to be able to locate quickly the overall summaries of the arguments. These are found in the first part of chapter 1 (pp. 3–14); pp. 44–50 at the end of chapter 2; and pp. 264–66 at the end of chapter 13, as well as chapters 12 and 13 more broadly. The second part of chapter 1 provides a chapter-by-chapter overview of the volume. The glossary defines key concepts: the core definition is presented in the initial paragraph of each entry, and additional paragraphs are included for concepts that require more elaboration.

We wish to acknowledge our intellectual debt to the many people who have contributed to this project. It has been an enormous pleasure to work with Jason Seawright, whose immense contribution is reflected in the coauthorship of five chapters and the glossary. His mastery of methodological and statistical issues, combined with a remarkable command of substantive agendas, has made him an exceptional collaborator. David A. Freedman of the Berkeley Statistics Department has been a paragon of collegiality, again and again providing new ideas, specific suggestions about the text, and outstanding commentary on broader methodological issues. We also thank the other authors of the chapters within the book for their participation in the project.

David Collier's earlier book, *The New Authoritarianism in Latin America* (1979), which sought to systematically organize a substantive and methodological debate in comparative social science, provided a model for the structure of the present volume, and also for the spirit of constructive criticism that animates it. Correspondingly, renewed thanks are due to two colleagues who played a special role in shaping that earlier book: Louis W. Goodman and the late Benjamin A. Most.

We extend our gratitude to Christopher H. Achen and Larry M. Bartels, whose breadth of vision, elegant approach to methodological problems, and simple good sense have helped to stimulate our thinking about the importance of research design and the use of techniques appropriate to the task at hand. Neal Beck, Alexander L. George, Giovanni Sartori, J. Merrill Shanks, Paul Sniderman, and Laura Stoker have also been key colleagues in discussions of methodological and substantive issues.

Our work on this project convinces us again that institutional context matters. The strong commitment of the Berkeley Political Science Department to methodological and analytic pluralism encouraged us to write this book. At the national level, we have been inspired by the initiative and enterprise of a younger cohort of scholars who have reinvigorated efforts to bridge qualitative and quantitative methods, and some of whom have played a key role in forming the Consortium for Qualitative Research Methods (CQRM), and also the Organized Section on Qualitative Methods of the American Political Science Association. At the potential risk of omitting key names, we would especially mention, among these younger scholars, Andrew Bennett, Bear Braumoeller, Michael Coppedge, David Dessler, Colin Elman, John Gerring, Gary Goertz, Evan Lieberman, James Mahoney, Gerardo L. Munck, Andreas Schedler, and David Waldner.

Several people have made an unusually large contribution through providing either very extensive substantive suggestions or sustained assistance in coordinating the manuscript: Robert Adcock, Michelle Bonogofsky, Maiah Jaskoski, Diana Kapiszewski, Sebastián Mazzuca, Reilly O'Neal, Sara Poster, and Sally Roever.

We also received insightful comments from Michael Barzelay, Andrew Bennett, Mark Bevir, Taylor Boas, George Breslauer, Christopher Cardona, Jennifer Collier, Ruth Berins Collier, Stephen Collier, Michael Coppedge, Rubette Cowan, David Dessler, Jorge Dominguez, Paul Dosh, Ralph Espach, Sebastián Etchemendy, Andrew Gould, Kenneth Greene, Ernst Haas, Peter Houtzager, William Hurst, Simon Jackman, Jonathan Katz, Jeewon Kim, Peter Kingstone, Daniel Kreider, Lien Lay, James Mahoney, Scott Mainwaring, Walter Mebane, Geraldo L. Munck, Guillermo O'Donnell, Wagner Pralon, Charles Ragin, Jessica Rich, Eric Schickler, Carsten Schneider, Taryn Seawright, Jasjeet Sekhon, Wendy Sinek, Jeffrey Sluyter-Bultrao, Alfred Stepan, Laura Stoker, Tuong Vu, Michael Wallerstein, and Alexander Wendt.

Excellent feedback was likewise provided by colleagues who attended presentations on the project at the Kellogg Institute, University of Notre Dame; the Departments of Political Science at Columbia University and at the University of Minnesota; the Institute of Development Studies, London School of Economics; and meetings of the American Political Science Association, the Midwest Political Science Association, the Western Political Science Association, the Institute for Qualitative Research Methods at Arizona State University, the Political Methodology Society, and the Southern California Political Behavior Seminar.

Bruce Cain, Director of the Berkeley Institute of Governmental Studies, has been very supportive throughout the project. Gerald C. Lubenow and Maria A. Wolf of the Berkeley Public Policy Press, and also Jennifer Knerr of Rowman and Littlefield, provided untiring assistance with issues of manuscript preparation and editing. The project received financial support from the Survey Research Center, the Department of Political Science, the Institute of International Studies, and International and Area Studies, all at the University of California, Berkeley.

Henry Brady was supported during 2001–2002 as a Hewlett Fellow (98–2124) at the Center for Advanced Study in the Behavioral Sciences, as well as through a grant (2000–3633) from the William and Flora Hewlett Foundation. Jason Seawright's work on the project was funded by a National Science Foundation Graduate Research Fellowship.

Henry E. Brady
David Collier
Berkeley, California

PART I

Introduction

CHAPTER 1

Refocusing the Discussion of Methodology

Henry E. Brady, David Collier, and Jason Seawright

Mainstream Quantitative Methods, Qualitative Methods, and Statistical Theory

The quest for shared standards of methodology and research design is an abiding concern in the social sciences. A recurring tension in this quest is the relationship between quantitative and qualitative methods. This book aims to rethink the contribution of these alternative approaches and to consider how scholars can most effectively draw on their respective strengths.

One view of the relation between quantitative and qualitative methodology is provided by what we call "mainstream quantitative methods," an approach based on the use of regression analysis and related techniques for causal inference. Scholars who champion this approach often invoke norms identified with these tools to argue for the superiority of quantitative research, sometimes suggesting that qualitative research could be greatly improved by following such norms more closely. These scholars in effect propose a quantitative template for qualitative research. In doing so, they have made some valuable suggestions that qualitative researchers would do well to consider.

Qualitative methodologists,[1] for their part, have raised legitimate concerns about the limitations of the quantitative template. Some qualitative analysts are dubious that the quantitative approach provides the only appropriate model for qualitative analysis. Others consider the quantitative template entirely inappropriate. Still others argue that the qualitative approach has strengths often lacking in quantitative studies and that quantitative analysts have much to learn from the qualitative tradition.

Yet another perspective on quantitative and qualitative methods is provided by ideas drawn from what we call "statistical theory." In contrast to mainstream quantitative methods, these ideas reflect a long history of skepticism about applying the assumptions behind regression analysis and related tools to real-world data in the social sciences.[2] This methodological approach sometimes advocates alternative techniques that allow researchers to draw more limited inferences based on fewer untested assumptions. According to this perspective, it is by no means evident that conventional quantitative tools are more powerful than qualitative tools.

Indeed, it is possible to draw on statistical theory to provide what may be thought of as a "statistical rationale" for many standard practices of qualitative research. This does *not* involve an admonition that qualitative analysts, in designing research, are expected to prove theorems in order to demonstrate that they have adopted the right methods. Rather, this rationale provides other kinds of insight into the analytic contribution of qualitative methods. A basic theme of this volume is that many qualitative research practices can be justified both on their own terms, and on the basis of this statistical rationale.

---

[1]We understand qualitative methods as encompassing partially overlapping approaches such as the case-study method, small-N analysis, the comparative method, concept analysis, the comparative-historical method, the ethnographic tradition of field research, interpretivism, and constructivism. For many purposes, the quantitative-qualitative distinction may be disaggregated. In chapter 13 and the glossary, we propose four component dimensions: level of measurement, number of cases, whether explicit statistical tests are employed, and what we call thick versus thin analysis. Yet the simple quantitative-qualitative dichotomy offers a heuristic distinction that productively structures much of the current discussion.

[2]The tradition to which we refer grows out of debates among statisticians on causal inference in experiments and observational studies. It may be dated to Karl Pearson's 1896 critique of G. Udny Yule's causal assessment, based on a regression analysis of observational data, of the relation between welfare policy and poverty in Britain (Stigler 1986: 351–53, 358). For a recent statement about this debate, see Freedman (1999). In addition to work within the discipline of statistics, we consider this tradition to encompass studies in the fields of econometrics, psychometrics, and measurement theory that, like Pearson's critique, explore the foundations of inference. We would also include methodological contributions by some scholars in political science and sociology whose work stands outside of the basic regression framework.

Overall, a meaningful discussion of methodology must be grounded in the premise that strengths *and* weaknesses are to be found in both the qualitative and quantitative approaches. Regarding the weaknesses, as Brady (55–56 this volume) puts it, qualitative researchers are perhaps "handicapped by a lack of quantification and small numbers of observations," whereas quantitative researchers may sometimes suffer from "procrustean quantification and a jumble of dissimilar cases." The most productive way to reconcile these two approaches is not through the unilateral imposition of norms, but rather through mutual learning.

The Debate on *Designing Social Inquiry*

In the present volume, we explore the relationship between quantitative and qualitative methodology through an extended discussion of a book that exemplifies the approach of mainstream quantitative methods: *Designing Social Inquiry: Scientific Inference in Qualitative Research* (hereafter *DSI*), by Gary King, Robert O. Keohane, and Sidney Verba.

DSI's Contribution

DSI has emerged as one of the most influential statements ever published on the relationship between quantitative and qualitative methods. The book is based on the tacit assumption that quantitative, large-N researchers have superior tools for solving many problems of methodology and research design, compared to their qualitative counterparts. Accordingly, *DSI* seeks to make such tools accessible to qualitative analysts, so as to help them design better research. While the premise is, in effect, the superiority of quantitative methods, the goal is to build bridges. The authors take seriously the idea that we should seek a common language for framing issues that arise in all forms of inquiry, and their effort to articulate the shared concerns of quantitative and qualitative research is a valuable contribution.

DSI's wide influence also stems from the systematization of quantitative methods that it offers. Although framed as an extended set of recommendations for qualitative researchers, the book is based on ideas drawn from the mainstream quantitative framework. In the course of summarizing these ideas, *DSI* offers numerous specific recommendations about different steps in the research process: for example, defining the research problem, specifying the theory, selecting cases and observations, testing descriptive and causal arguments, and subsequently retesting and refining the theory. In sum, *DSI*'s reach is broad and its practical advice abundant.

At the most general level, by focusing scholarly attention on problems of research design, *DSI* aims to improve the practice of social science, understood as a collective effort to describe and explain political and social phenomena. *DSI* characterizes this collective effort as being concerned with descriptive and causal inference, a term which may seem alien to some qualitative researchers. However, as Charles Ragin emphasizes (124 this volume), "there is no necessary wedge separating the goal of 'inference'—the key concern of quantitative approaches— from the goal of making sense of cases—a common concern of qualitative approaches." The term "inference" can thus be seen as one specific label for a shared objective that spans diverse traditions of research.

DSI has had as great an impact, in terms of encouraging analysts to think about research design, as any book in the history of political science. The book is widely read in other fields as well, and it has exercised a salutary influence on many different branches of qualitative research. Even qualitative analysts who strongly disagree with *DSI* have adopted terms and distinctions introduced in the book. In addition, the concern of qualitative analysts with defending their own approach vis-à-vis *DSI* has pushed these scholars toward a more complete systematization of qualitative methods. In this and other ways, *DSI* has been strikingly successful in achieving its basic goal of encouraging researchers to think more carefully about methodological issues.

Finally, the authors of *DSI* deserve praise for their willingness to participate in an ongoing dialogue that is helping to advance this methodological discussion. In their response (reprinted as chapter 11 below) to a 1995 symposium on their book in the *American Political Science Review*, they observe that, "although our book may be the latest word on research design in political science [as of its publication in 1994], it is surely not the last" (182 this volume).

Where Do We Go from Here?

The present volume extends this methodological debate. We take as a point of departure a number of basic concerns about *DSI*'s framework.

In our view, *DSI* gives insufficient recognition to well-known limitations of mainstream quantitative methods. The book does present a useful discussion of assumptions that underlie regression analysis. Yet *DSI* does not devote adequate attention to a key statistical idea: regression analysis specifically relies on the difficult-to-test assumption that the model being estimated is correct. For this reason, estimating a regression model with empirical data does not fully test the model. Relatedly, *DSI* places strong emphasis on evaluating uncertainty. Yet the book fails to acknowledge that significance tests are designed to evaluate *specific* kinds of uncertainty, and that the common practice of employing them as a *general-purpose* tool for estimating uncertainty extends these tests beyond the uses for which they were intended.

Against this backdrop, *DSI* goes too far in advocating the perspective of mainstream quantitative methods as a foundation for research design and qualitative inquiry. We are convinced that this perspective provides an excessively narrow understanding of the research process. More specifically, along with being too confident about the strengths of quantitative tools, the book gives insufficient recognition to the contributions of qualitative tools. *DSI* overemphasizes the strategy of increasing the number of observations, and it overlooks the different kinds of observations and the different ways that data are used in quantitative and qualitative research. The book is inattentive to the risk that increasing the N may push scholars toward an untenable level of generality and a loss of contextual knowledge. It overstates its warning against post hoc hypothesis formation and standard practices of disciplined inductive research. Relatedly, it neglects the fact that econometric writing on "specification searches" has sought to systematize inductive procedures. Finally, *DSI* occasionally refers to trade-offs, yet the book does not acknowledge that they must be a basic concern in designing research.

We want to be clear about what these criticisms do and do not amount to. They do not amount to a rejection of the basic enterprise of striving for a shared vocabulary and framework for both quantitative and qualitative research. Indeed, we are strongly committed to the quest for a common framework. While we have great respect for scholars who explore epistemological issues, we worry that such concerns may sometimes unnecessarily lead researchers and students to take sides and to engage in polemics. Thus, we share *DSI*'s (4–5) view that quantitative and qualitative methods are founded on essentially similar epistemologies.

Correspondingly, the present volume is certainly not meant to widen the gap between the qualitative and quantitative approaches by identifying profound and obdurate differences. Indeed, we would argue that the differences are less deep-seated than is sometimes believed. To the extent that differences do exist, however, we take the normative position that a basic goal in work on methodology is to overcome these differences. We should seek a shared framework allowing researchers using diverse analytic techniques to develop evidence that is convincing to analysts of differing methodological persuasions. This larger body of mutually accepted evidence can, in turn, contribute to finding better answers to the substantive questions that drive social research.

Tools and Standards

As we suggest in the subtitle of this book, while analysts have diverse tools for designing, executing, and evaluating research, it is meaningful to seek shared standards for employing such tools. These shared standards can facilitate recognition of common criteria for good research among scholars who use different tools. Methodological pluralism and analytic rigor can be combined.

By tools we mean the specific research procedures and practices employed by quantitative and qualitative researchers. Some tools are highly systematized and have elaborate technical underpinnings. Examples of such tools are regression analysis, structural equation modeling, factor analysis, tests of statistical significance, and probability theory. Increasing the number of observations is a research tool repeatedly advocated by *DSI*. Other tools include qualitative research practices such as within-case analysis, process tracing, procedures for avoiding conceptual stretching, qualitative validity assessment, and strategies for the comparison of matching and contrasting cases. Methods of data collection are also tools: for example, public opinion research, focus groups, participant observation, event scoring, archival research, content analysis, the construction of "unobtrusive measures," and the systematic compilation of secondary sources. At various points in the text, we have introduced summary tables that provide an overview of the different tools being discussed, and many tools are also discussed in the glossary.

The chapters in the present volume devote considerable attention to various methodological tools that *DSI* undervalues or overlooks. The following paragraphs enumerate five broad methodological literatures with which many of these tools are identified. Some correspond to standard practices of qualitative researchers; others are derived from statistical theory.

1. *Logical and Statistical Foundations of Causal Inference.* A large body of research on the logical and statistical foundations of causal inference expresses considerable skepticism about causal inference based on observational data. This literature points to the need for more robust approaches than those advocated in mainstream quantitative methodology.

2. *Concepts.* Research on concepts, concept formation, and the evolution of concepts in the course of research makes it clear that sustained attention to conceptual issues is an indispensable component of research design. The insights of this literature suggest that the limited advice that *DSI* does give on working with concepts in fact points in the wrong direction.

3. *Measurement.* A major literature located in the fields of mathematical measurement theory and psychometrics provides researchers with systematic guidance for measurement. This literature emphasizes, for example, the contextual specificity of measurement claims, reinforcing the conviction of many political scientists that knowledge of context and care in bounding the generality of research findings must be a central concern in research design. Such guidance is lacking in *DSI*.

4. *Causal Inference in Case Studies.* A long tradition of writing has explored tools and strategies of causal inference in case studies: for example, process tracing and other forms of within-case analysis; the deliberate selection of "most-likely," "least-likely," and "deviant" cases; and, in the comparative case-study tradition, the methods of agreement and difference. *DSI* seeks to subsume these tools within its own framework, based on the norms of large-N quantitative analysis. The case-study literature in effect turns *DSI*'s argument on its head, suggesting that (a) the practice of causal inference in qualitative research is viable on its own terms, and (b) inference in quantitative research can sometimes be improved through the use of tools strongly identified with the qualitative tradition.

5. *Bayesian Inference.* Ideas from Bayesian inference—which have come to be more extensively utilized by political science researchers in the years since the publication of *DSI*—are valuable for addressing many research tasks discussed in the present volume, including making inferences from a small N, evaluating hypothesized necessary and/or sufficient causes, and incorporating contextual knowledge in quantitative analyses. Bayesian ideas are also useful for estimating uncertainty in these situations, and they provide an important alternative to the methods recommended by *DSI*, which extend ideas closely linked to statistical tests well beyond their intended application. Even when scholars do not employ formal Bayesian statistical analysis, Bayesian ideas about prior and posterior distributions provide valuable research heuristics.

Through focusing on tools drawn from these diverse areas of methodology, as well as on more conventional quantitative tools, we seek to lay a stronger foundation for an integrated approach to the design and execution of research.

All research tools, both qualitative and quantitative, must be subject to critical evaluation. Correspondingly, scholars should seek shared standards for assessing and applying these tools. Relevant standards must include attention to basic trade-offs that arise in conducting research. Once we acknowledge that not all analytic goals can be achieved simultaneously—Przeworski and Teune's trade-offs among accuracy, generality, parsimony, and causality are a famous example (1970: 20–23)—then it is easier to move toward a recognition that alternative methodological tools are relevant and appropriate, depending on the goals and context of the research.

Neither qualitative nor quantitative analysts have a ready-made formula for producing good research. We are convinced that the wide influence exercised by *DSI* derives in part from the book's implicit claim that, if scholars follow the recommendations in the book, it is relatively straightforward to do good quantitative research; as well as the explicit argument that qualitative researchers, to the degree possible, should apply the quantitative template.[3]

In fact, it is difficult to make causal inferences from observational data, especially when research focuses on complex political processes. Behind the apparent precision of quantitative findings lie many potential problems concerning equiva-

---

[3]*DSI* does briefly note the limitations of quantitative research. The book states that "[i]n both quantitative and qualitative research, we engage in the imperfect application of theoretical standards of inference to inherently imperfect research designs and empirical data" (7; see also 8–9). However, in the eyes of many critics, *DSI* does not follow through on these words of caution, instead going too far in extending the norms of quantitative analysis to qualitative research. Further, *DSI*'s statements on the pages just cited are closely linked to its arguments about estimating error, and *DSI* is far more confident than we are about the viability of error estimates in quantitative research, not to mention in qualitative research. See, for example, Bartels's discussion of assessing measurement error (72–73 this volume), as well as the discussion in chapter 13 (234–35 this volume) focused on the misuse of significance tests.

lence of cases, conceptualization and measurement, assumptions about the data, and choices about model specification such as which variables to include. The interpretability of quantitative findings is strongly constrained by the skill with which these problems are addressed. Thus, both qualitative and quantitative research are hard to do well. It is by recognizing the challenges faced in both research traditions that these two approaches can learn from one another.

Scholars who make particular choices about trade-offs that arise in the design of research should recognize the contributions of those who opt for different choices. For example, let us suppose that a scholar has decided, after careful consideration, to focus on a small N to carry out a fine-grained, contextually sensitive analysis that will facilitate operationalizing a difficult concept. A large-N researcher should, in principle, be willing to recognize this choice as legitimate.

At the same time, the small-N researcher should recognize that the advantages of focusing on few cases must be weighed against the costs. These costs include, for example, foregoing large-N tools for measurement validation and losing the generality that might be achieved if a wider range of cases is considered. In short, researchers should recognize the potential strengths and weaknesses of alternative approaches, and they should be prepared to justify the choices they have made.

Toward an Alternative View of Methodology

Building on these themes, the present volume develops alternative arguments about the appropriate balance between the quantitative and qualitative traditions, and about research design and methodology more broadly.[4] Here are some key steps in these arguments.

1. *In the social sciences, qualitative research is hard to do well. Quantitative research is also hard to do well. Each tradition can and should learn from the other.* One version of conventional wisdom holds that achieving analytic rigor is more difficult in qualitative than in quantitative research. Yet in quantitative research, making valid inferences about complex political processes on the basis of observational data is likewise extremely difficult. There are no quick and easy recipes for either qualitative or quantitative analysis. In the face of these shared challenges, the two traditions have developed distinctive and complementary tools.

    a. *A central reason why both qualitative and quantitative research are hard to do well is that any study based on observational (i.e., nonexperimental) data faces the fundamental inferential challenge of eliminating rival explanations.* Scholars must recognize the great divide between experiments and observational studies. Experiments eliminate rival explana-

---

[4]While issues of descriptive inference are a recurring theme in the following chapters (see, e.g., 23–25, 202–9 this volume), the focus here is primarily on causal inference.

tions by randomly assigning the values of the explanatory variable to the units being analyzed. By contrast, in all observational studies, eliminating rival explanations is a daunting challenge. The key point, and a central concern of this book, is that quantitative and qualitative observational studies generally address this shared challenge in different ways.

2. *Mainstream quantitative methodologists sometimes advocate the quantitative approach as a general template for conducting research. By contrast, some statistical theorists question the general applicability of the conventional quantitative approach.* Strong advocacy of the quantitative template is found in many disciplinary subfields. Yet it is essential that political scientists—and scholars in other fields as well—take a broader view and reflect more deeply on the contributions and limitations of both qualitative and quantitative methods. A valuable component of this broader view draws on ideas from statistical theory.

   a. *One recurring issue regarding the tradition of advocacy based on the quantitative template concerns how much scholars can in fact learn from findings based on regression analysis, as well as their capacity to estimate the degree of uncertainty associated with these findings.* For regression results to be meaningful, analysts must assume, as noted earlier in this chapter, that they have the correct statistical model to begin with. Empirical data analysis may provide some insight into the plausibility of this assumption, yet such analysis does not fully test the assumption. Another key idea identified with the quantitative template concerns the capacity to estimate uncertainty. Unfortunately, in some areas of research, standard practice in the use of significance tests extends their application to evaluating forms of uncertainty that they were not designed to assess.

   b. *Another issue regarding the quantitative template is the recurring recommendation that researchers can gain inferential leverage in addressing rival explanations by increasing the number of observations—in the conventional sense of increasing the N. Yet this advice is not always helpful, in part because it may push scholars to compare cases that are not analytically equivalent.* Although adding new observations is frequently useful, adding observations from a different spatial or temporal context or at a different level of analysis can extend the research beyond the setting for which the investigator can make valid inferences. While some scholars might be concerned that this focus on context leads researchers toward a posture of excessive particularism, concern with context is in fact a prerequisite for achieving descriptive and causal inference that is valid and rigorous.

3. *In making choices about increasing leverage in causal inference, and to address the concerns just noted, scholars should recognize the contributions of different kinds of observations.* It is productive to distinguish between two quite distinct uses of the term "observation," one drawn from the quantitative

tradition, the other from the qualitative tradition. Examples of these two types are presented in the appendix (see also 252–64 this volume).

a. *Data-set observations.* These observations are collected as an array of scores on specific variables for a designated sample of cases, involving what is sometimes called a rectangular data set. Missing data are an obstacle to causal inference based on data-set observations; it is therefore valuable that the data set be complete. Data-set observations play a central role not only in quantitative research, but also in qualitative research that is based on cross-case analysis.

b. *Causal-process observations.* These observations about context, process, or mechanism provide an alternative source of insight into the relationships among the explanatory variables, and between these variables and the dependent variable. Causal-process observations are sometimes less complete than data-set observations, in the sense that they routinely do not constitute a full set of scores across a given set of variables and cases. The strength of causal-process observations lies not in breadth of coverage, but depth of insight. Even one causal-process observation may be valuable in making inferences. Such observations are routinely used in qualitative research based on within-case analysis, and they can also be an important tool in quantitative analysis.

c. *These two types of observations have contrasting implications for maintaining an appropriate scope of comparison.* A focus on increasing the number of data-set observations, either at the same level of analysis or in subunits at a lower level of analysis, can yield major analytic gains, but it can also push scholars toward shifts in the domain of analysis that may be counterproductive. By contrast, the search for additional causal-process observations may occur within the original domain.

4. *Methodological discussions could benefit from stronger advocacy from the side of the qualitative template, and all researchers should consider carefully some long-standing methodological priorities that derive from the qualitative perspective.* The qualitative template can make important contributions to broader methodological agendas. For example:

a. *Knowledge of cases and context contributes to achieving valid inference.* To expand on the earlier argument (2b and 3c), analytic leverage can derive from a close knowledge of cases and context, which can directly contribute to more valid descriptive and causal inference. This knowledge sensitizes researchers to the impact of cultural, economic, and historical settings, and to the fact that subunits of a given case may be very different from the overall case. In other words, knowledge of context provides insight into potentially significant factors that are not among the variables being formally considered. In this sense, it helps us to know what is hidden behind the assumption "other things being equal," which is in turn crucial for the causal homogeneity assumption that is a requisite for valid causal inference. As discussed in this volume, such contextual knowledge is also crucial for measurement validity. Leverage derived from detailed knowledge of cases and context is closely connected to the idea of causal-process observations just discussed. Such knowledge is invaluable in both quantitative and qualitative research.

b. *Inductive analysis can play a major role in achieving valid inference and generating new ideas. Induction is important in both qualitative and quantitative research.* Mainstream quantitative researchers are sometimes too quick in dismissing the contribution to scholarly knowledge of inductive analysis and of the retesting of hypotheses against the same set of cases, on occasion evoking the traditional mandate to avoid "post hoc" hypothesis reformulation and theory testing. Yet even in technically advanced forms of statistical estimation, quantitative researchers routinely test alternative specifications against a given set of data (i.e., specification searches) and on this basis seek to make complex judgments about which specification is best. This iterated refinement of models and hypotheses constitutes a point of similarity to the inductive practices that are perhaps more widely recognized in qualitative research. Inductive procedures play a role in both traditions, and developing norms that guide and systematize these procedures for causal inference should be a basic concern of methodology.

c. *These arguments add up to a view of methodology in which qualitative research has a major role.* The norms and practices of qualitative research deserve, in their own terms, serious attention in broader discussions of methodology. Further, ideas drawn from qualitative methodology can improve quantitative practices by addressing weaknesses in the quantitative approach.

5. *The contribution of qualitative methods can be justified both from within the qualitative tradition itself, and from the perspective of statistical theory.* Greater attention to qualitative methods can be justified, first of all, by the lessons that qualitative analysts learn from their own research. Many qualitative practices can also be justified on the basis of arguments drawn from statistical theory. Among the goals of this volume are to develop what may be thought of as a statistical rationale for qualitative research and to explore specific ways in which statistical theory can improve both qualitative and quantitative analysis. This perspective is very different from that of much writing in the tradition of mainstream quantitative methods, which seeks to subordinate qualitative research to the quantitative template.

6. *If both qualitative and quantitative methods are to play important roles as sources of norms and practices for good research, scholars must face the challenge of adjudicating between potentially conflicting methodological norms.* Such adjudication requires recognition of a basic fact and a basic priority.

a. *Research design involves fundamental trade-offs.* Methodological advice needs to be framed in light of basic trade-offs among: (a) alternative goals of research, (b) the types of observations researchers utilize, and (c) the diverse tools they employ for descriptive and causal inference. A methodological framework that does not centrally consider trade-offs is incomplete.

b. *Scholars should develop shared standards.* A basic goal of methodology should be to establish shared standards for managing these trade-offs. Shared standards can become the basis for combining the strengths of qualitative and quantitative tools.

These arguments form the basis for the ideas presented throughout this volume. The remainder of this introduction provides an overview of the chapters that follow.

Overview of the Chapters

This book seeks to advance this methodological debate by building on the discussion stimulated by King, Keohane, and Verba's *Designing Social Inquiry*. We bring together a number of previously published statements in this discussion—some presented basically in their original form, others extensively revised[5]—along with two introductory chapters, two concluding chapters that draw together different strands in this debate, and an appendix. The glossary defines basic terms, with a core definition presented in the first paragraph of each entry; for certain terms, subsequent paragraphs elaborate on the definition. The book is divided into five parts: an introduction (chaps. 1–2), Critiques of the Quantitative Template (chaps. 3–6), Qualitative Tools (chaps. 7–9), Linking the Quantitative and Qualitative Traditions (chaps. 10–11), and Diverse Tools, Shared Standards (chaps. 12–13).

Introduction

Following the present introductory chapter, David Collier, Jason Seawright, and Gerardo L. Munck (chap. 2) provide a detailed summary of the methodological recommendations offered by *DSI*, thereby framing the discussion developed later in the book. Chapter 2 focuses on the definition of scientific research, the treatment of descriptive and causal inference, and the assumptions that underlie causal inference. The chapter then synthesizes *DSI*'s recommendations by formulating a series of guidelines for the design and execution of research. Although *DSI* does not present most of its methodological advice in terms of explicit rules,

---

[5]The relationship of each chapter to previously published material is explained in the acknowledgment of permission to reprint copyrighted material at the end of this volume.

much of its argument can productively be summarized in this manner. Chapter 2 concludes by offering an initial assessment of *DSI*'s framework.

Critiques of the Quantitative Template

How useful is the quantitative template as a guide for qualitative research? This question is addressed in chapters 3–6. It merits emphasis that these chapters praise *DSI* for presenting mainstream ideas of quantitative inference in a minimally technical manner; for offering many useful didactic arguments about how qualitative analysts can improve their research by applying simple lessons from statistics and econometrics; and for making genuine contributions to the field of methodology. At the same time, however, these chapters reconsider and challenge some of *DSI*'s basic arguments.

"Doing Good and Doing Better: How Far Does the Quantitative Template Get Us?" by Henry E. Brady (chap. 3) argues that *DSI* does not adequately consider the foundations of causal inference in quantitative research, and that the book does not properly attend to conceptualization and measurement. Regarding causal inference, Brady suggests that *DSI* pays insufficient attention to the challenges faced in research based on observational, as opposed to experimental, data. Specifically, the book fails to discuss how theory and preexisting knowledge can justify the key assumption that underlies causal assessment with observational data, that is, the assumption that conclusions are not distorted by missing variables. Concerning the second theme, Brady finds that *DSI* ignores major issues of concept formation and basic ideas from the literature on measurement. This latter body of work shows that quantitative measurement is ultimately based on qualitative comparisons, suggesting a very different relation between quantitative and qualitative work than is advocated by *DSI*.

"Some Unfulfilled Promises of Quantitative Imperialism" by Larry M. Bartels (chap. 4) suggests that *DSI*'s recommendations for qualitative researchers exaggerate the degree to which quantitative methodology offers a coherent, unified approach to problems of scientific inference. *DSI* classifies research activities that do not fit within its framework as prescientific, leading the authors to a false separation between (a) producing unstructured knowledge and "understanding," and (b) making scientific inferences. Bartels is convinced that unstructured knowledge and understanding are a necessary part of inference. Likewise, in Bartels's view, *DSI* claims to have solutions to several methodological problems that neither its authors nor anyone else can currently solve. These include the challenge of estimating the uncertainty of conclusions in qualitative (and even quantitative) research; distinguishing between the contribution made by qualitative evidence and quantitative evidence in analyses that employ both; assessing the impact of measurement error in multivariate analysis; and multiplying observations without violating the causal homogeneity assumption. According to Bartels, the fact that leading practitioners in political science cannot adequately address these problems suggests that they may be the most important issues currently pending for further research on methodology.

"How Inference in the Social (but Not the Physical) Sciences Neglects Theoretical Anomaly" by Ronald Rogowski (chap. 5) argues that *DSI* underestimates the importance of theory in the practice of research. *DSI*'s rules about case selection and the number of cases needed to support or challenge a theory reflect this inattention. In fact, following *DSI*'s rules would lead scholars to reject as bad science some of the most influential works in the recent history of comparative politics. Single-case studies are particularly useful in challenging already-existing theories, if these theories are precisely formulated; yet *DSI* claims that a single case cannot discredit a scientific theory. Rogowski suggests that if the analyst employs theory that is both powerful and precise, carefully constructed studies that examine anomalous cases can be invaluable, notwithstanding *DSI*'s warnings about selection bias.

"Claiming Too Much: Warnings about Selection Bias," by David Collier, James Mahoney, and Jason Seawright (chap. 6), examines contending perspectives on this form of bias. Recent methodological statements, including *DSI*, argue that qualitative, case-study research focused on extreme cases on the dependent variable is vulnerable to devastating error due to selection bias. The chapter first notes the skepticism that various scholars have already expressed about these warnings. It then presents an illustrative discussion of selection bias as a problem in regression analysis, using this discussion as a point of departure for considering bias in qualitative research. The authors distinguish between qualitative research based on cross-case analysis, as opposed to within-case analysis. They argue that whereas cross-case analysis is subject to selection bias, within-case analysis is in a much stronger position to avoid selection bias, because it relies on causal-process observations that provide very different tools for inference from those of regression analysis. The authors conclude that the strong warnings about selection bias therefore do indeed claim too much. Correspondingly, these warnings inappropriately devalue qualitative research based on within-case comparison.

Qualitative Tools

The basic analytic tools of quantitative researchers are reasonably well understood. By contrast, qualitative tools are less well codified and recognized. What are these tools? The third part of the book presents a survey of qualitative techniques and discusses how they can be integrated into the broader practice of social inquiry.

"Tools for Qualitative Research" by Gerardo L. Munck (chap. 7) provides a new inventory of research methods used by qualitative investigators. Munck argues that *DSI*, in recommending procedures for qualitative analysis, undervalues tools long employed in the qualitative tradition. He focuses on procedures for defining the universe of cases, selecting cases for study, measurement and data collection, and causal assessment. In undertaking the first three tasks, qualitative researchers place much greater emphasis than *DSI* on close knowledge of cases, concern with context, and issues of validity. With regard to causal assessment, Munck argues that qualitative researchers often hypothesize a distinctive model of causation that calls for different tools of inference. Further, qualitative researchers depart from *DSI*'s framework in that they routinely adopt a more interactive view of the relation between hypotheses and data.

"Turning the Tables: How Case-Oriented Research Challenges Variable-Oriented Research" by Charles C. Ragin (chap. 8) observes that *DSI*, along with scholars such as Goldthorpe and Lieberson, have evaluated case-oriented, comparative research from the perspective of large-N, variable-oriented research and have found it lacking. Ragin "turns the tables" and evaluates large-N, quantitative research by the standards of case-oriented work. He focuses on a series of specific research tasks that he believes are more effectively addressed in case-oriented research than in large-N, variable-oriented inquiry: (1) constituting cases through the iterated refinement of concepts and observations, thus allowing scholars to establish the domain of cases relevant to a particular investigation; (2) framing causal assessment through a focus on positive cases, in which the outcome to be explained does in fact occur; (3) delineating negative cases that provide appropriate comparisons and contrasts with these positive cases; (4) analyzing multiple paths to the same outcome, that is, multiple conjunctural causation; and (5) accounting for nonconforming cases. Case-oriented scholars use flexible analytic frames that can be modified in light of the insight into cases they gain in the course of their research. Ragin points out that this aspect of the case-oriented approach makes it especially well suited for concept formation and theory development.

"Case Studies and the Limits of the Quantitative Worldview" by Timothy J. McKeown (chap. 9) argues that the logic of research underlying conventional quantitative approaches like that of *DSI* has unflattering implications for case studies and for other qualitative research strategies. Because *DSI*'s perspective cannot make sense of several aspects of case-study research, such as the attention sometimes given to findings derived from a single case, the book casts doubt on the value of case studies. McKeown presents examples of successful research that are not easily accommodated within *DSI*'s perspective, and he provides an alternative methodological framework for thinking about such case-study work. A central component of McKeown's framework draws on an important branch of statistical theory—that is, Bayesian inference.

Linking the Quantitative and Qualitative Traditions

Given that the qualitative and quantitative traditions have distinctive strengths, how can they best be combined? The fourth section offers two perspectives on this challenge. "Bridging the Quantitative-Qualitative Divide" by Sidney Tarrow (chap. 10) offers valuable suggestions for linking quantitative and qualitative research. Qualitative analysis is better suited than quantitative research for process tracing, for exploring the tipping points that play a critical role in shaping long-term processes of change, and for providing more nuanced insight into findings derived from quantitative investigation. Quantitative analysis, in turn, can frame and generalize the findings of qualitative studies. In Tarrow's view, the most valuable interaction between the two research traditions occurs when scholars "triangulate" among alternative methods and data sources in addressing a given research problem.

"The Importance of Research Design" by Gary King, Robert O. Keohane, and Sidney Verba (chap. 11) is reprinted from the 1995 symposium on *Designing Social Inquiry*, published in the *American Political Science Review*. Chapter 11 should be understood as the authors' interim response to the ongoing debate about linking the quantitative and qualitative traditions. Because it was written in 1995, it does not take into account all the arguments in the present volume, though it does make reference to arguments presented here by Rogowski, Tarrow, and Collier, Mahoney, and Seawright—and to arguments advanced in some other chapters.

King, Keohane, and Verba underscore central themes in *DSI* and clarify certain key ideas. The authors argue that the fundamental challenge for both quantitative and qualitative analysis is good research design. King, Keohane, and Verba agree with Rogowski on the importance of theory, although they emphasize that telling people how to theorize is not their goal. Perhaps most significantly, they argue that "much of the best social science research can combine quantitative and qualitative data, precisely because there is no contradiction between the fundamental processes of inference involved in each" (183 this volume). All researchers, whether quantitative or qualitative, need to understand and utilize the same logic of inference.

King, Keohane, and Verba go on to explore and illustrate two related themes: the idea of science as a collective enterprise, which they discuss in relation to well-known books of Arend Lijphart and William Sheridan Allen; and problems of addressing selection bias, which they illustrate by reference to books by Peter Katzenstein and Robert Bates. Finally, the chapter proposes that Tarrow's arguments about "triangular conclusions" provide a valuable unifying idea that brings together the diverse perspectives on methodology under discussion.

Diverse Tools, Shared Standards

The final part of the book synthesizes and extends the debate on quantitative and qualitative methods. We argue that, precisely because researchers have a diverse set of methodological tools at their disposal, it is essential to seek shared standards for the application of these tools.

"Critiques, Responses, and Trade-Offs: Drawing Together the Debate," by David Collier, Henry E. Brady, and Jason Seawright (chap. 12), integrates and evaluates this methodological discussion. In a further effort to bridge the quantitative-qualitative divide, chapter 12 reviews four critiques of *DSI* offered in chapters 3–9 of the present volume and formulates responses that draw on ideas derived from statistical theory. Two of the critiques concern the challenge of doing research that is important and the issue of probabilistic versus deterministic models of causation. For these topics, the statistical response calls for a synthesis that combines elements of *DSI*'s position and the critique. For other parts of the debate—on conceptualization and measurement, and on selection bias—statistical arguments emerge that more strongly reinforce the critique of *DSI*. The final part of this chapter explores the idea that trade-offs are inherent in research design and develops the argument that the search for shared standards necessarily poses the challenge of managing these trade-offs.

The final chapter offers some broader conclusions about tools for causal inference. "Sources of Leverage in Causal Inference: Toward an Alternative View of Methodology," by David Collier, Henry E. Brady, and Jason Seawright (chap. 13), focuses on the fundamental challenge of eliminating rival explanations and making good causal inferences. This chapter formulates several methodological distinctions that help bring into sharper focus the relationship between the quantitative and qualitative traditions and, more specifically, the contrasts in how they deal with causal inference. A further goal of this discussion is to explore the implications of the distinction between data-set observations and causal-process observations. The chapter argues that this distinction offers a more realistic picture of the contributions to causal inference of both quantitative and qualitative tools—and of how these differing contributions can be integrated. The appendix at the end of this volume, "Data-Set Observations versus Causal-Process Observations: The 2000 U.S. Presidential Election," by Henry E. Brady, illustrates the leverage that can be derived from causal-process observations.

Taken together, the arguments developed in this volume lead us to reflect on the expanding influence in social science of increasingly technical approaches to method and theory. We advocate an eclectic position in response to this trend. While it is essential to recognize the powerful contribution of statistically and mathematically complex forms of method and theory, simpler tools are sometimes more economical and elegant, and potentially more rigorous. Scholars should carefully evaluate the strengths and weaknesses of these diverse tools in light of existing knowledge about the topic under study, and with reference to broader shared standards for descriptive and causal inference and for refining theory. This eclectic approach is the most promising avenue for productive decisions about research design.

CHAPTER 2

The Quest for Standards:
King, Keohane, and Verba's *Designing Social Inquiry*

David Collier, Jason Seawright, and Gerardo L. Munck

Scholars turn to methodology for guidance in conducting research that is systematic, rigorous, and cumulative. *Designing Social Inquiry: Scientific Inference in Qualitative Research*, by Gary King, Robert O. Keohane, and Sidney Verba (hereafter *DSI*), has commanded wide attention because it forcefully and articulately provides such guidance. With clarity of exposition and many examples, the book presents an extended set of practical recommendations for the design and execution of research. In conjunction with *DSI*'s goal of providing a new framework for qualitative research, the book offers an important synthesis of what we will call mainstream quantitative methods. *DSI* therefore constitutes a general statement about methodology, and this fact helps account for the wide attention it has deservedly received.

The present chapter provides an overview of *DSI*. We first introduce three fundamental ideas in *DSI*'s view of methodology: (1) the criteria for scientific research; (2) the concept of inference—a term used in the title of the book and central to *DSI*'s exposition; and (3) the assumptions that justify causal inference.

The second part of this chapter adopts a different approach to summarizing *DSI*'s framework by presenting it in terms of a set of guidelines for conducting research. *DSI* does not explicitly synthesize its recommendations as an overarching set of rules,[1] yet we believe these guidelines provide a summary that plays a constructive role in focusing the discussion.

Finally, the conclusion to the chapter anticipates the debate in the remainder of the present volume, noting both points of convergence and areas of substantial divergence vis-à-vis the perspective presented by *DSI* (see table 2.2 toward the end of this chapter).

In this summary of *DSI*'s arguments, we occasionally provide examples of our own. At certain points, as with the discussion of conditional independence, we offer a somewhat more elaborate presentation than *DSI*, given that these are topics to which we return later in the present volume. Nevertheless, the intent of the chapter, except for the conclusion, is to present *DSI*'s framework.

Scientific Research, Inference, and Assumptions

Three central components of *DSI* are its treatment of scientific research, inference, and assumptions. In relation to prior discussions of these topics, *DSI*'s goal is not primarily to present new ideas. However, as a set of recommendations designed specifically for qualitative researchers, *DSI*'s treatment of these topics is innovative and deserves careful attention.

Scientific Research

DSI argues that social science ought to be good *science*. To that end, the book presents a careful definition of what makes research scientific. Some readers may find *DSI*'s insistence on the idea of science jarring and this framing of goals too narrow. Yet these goals are in fact of broad relevance. How, then, does *DSI* define scientific research? First of all, such research always seeks to make *inferences*, "attempting to infer beyond the immediate data to something broader that is not directly observed" (8). The idea of inference is of such importance in *DSI*'s methodological approach that it is explored in detail in the next section of this chapter.

Next, scientific research makes its procedures *public*. Researchers should report how they select cases, gather data, and perform analysis. This is necessary if the scholarly community is to judge the quality of the research and the plausibility of its conclusions. If analysts do not report how they conduct their research, then "[w]e cannot evaluate the principles of selection that were used to record observa-

---

[1]Munck's (1998) review essay on *DSI* was the first effort to summarize the book in terms of a complete set of rules. Subsequently, Epstein and King (2002) adopted this approach in their long essay, "The Rules for Inference." The recommendations in their essay are quite similar to those in *DSI*, except that they give more attention to the tasks of defining the universe of cases and building a tradition of publicly available data sets.

tions, the ways in which observations were processed, and the logic by which conclusions were drawn" (8).

Moreover, researchers must view their conclusions as inherently *uncertain*. "A researcher who fails to face the issue of uncertainty directly is either asserting that he or she knows everything perfectly or that he or she has no idea how certain or uncertain the results are" (*DSI* 9). Neither measurement nor theory in the social sciences is ever perfect and complete. According to *DSI*, scientific research requires scholars to acknowledge this fact and to estimate the degree of uncertainty in their inferences.

The final characteristic of scientific research is that findings are judged in light of the *method* employed, because, as *DSI* (9) argues, the content of science is the method. In other words, scientific findings should not be accepted or rejected according to the authority of the researcher, or in light of whether they correspond to the particular results preferred by a given investigator. Rather, the credibility of the methods employed should be a central criterion in evaluating research findings.

These criteria present a simple, reasonably straightforward basis for distinguishing scientific research from other kinds of intellectual pursuits.

Inference

The idea of inference is a major component of *DSI*'s methodological framework. Indeed, *DSI* views "inference"—in the sense of drawing larger conclusions on the basis of specific observations—as a foundation of social science. The book (34) treats inference in broad terms, stating that "[i]nference, whether descriptive or causal, quantitative or qualitative, is the ultimate goal of all good social science." *DSI* develops this idea in extended discussions of descriptive inference (chap. 2) and causal inference (chaps. 3–6).[2]

Descriptive Inference

In *DSI*'s view, descriptive inference entails three tasks. First, it encompasses the idea of generalizing from a sample to a universe of cases, as routinely occurs in public opinion research. The researcher establishes the universe and the sample,

---

[2]The relation between description and explanation is complex, as is clear in the discussion below of the contrast between the systematic and random components of phenomena. Even so, description versus explanation remains a fundamental heuristic distinction, both in *DSI* and in the present volume. At the simplest level, description addresses the question of "what?" and explanation addresses the question of "why?" Also, as noted in chapter 1 above (5–6 this volume), although the ideas of descriptive and causal "inference" may seem nonstandard to some readers, they can be viewed as convenient labels for the ubiquitous research task of moving from specific observations to more general ideas.

analyzes the cases included in the sample, and makes inferences about the universe on the basis of the sample (e.g., *DSI* 70–71).

Second, descriptive inference encompasses inferences from observations to concepts. Analysts are rarely interested in reporting raw facts. Rather, they seek to describe political institutions, social structures, ideologies, and other complex phenomena. As conceptualized by social scientists, these phenomena are never directly observable: no one has ever *seen* an entire "social structure." Scholars observe certain facts, often at only one point in time, that are relevant to the complex idea of a social structure, that presumably persists over time. They must therefore make inferences from these particular facts to the broader idea of a social structure. Hence, "[d]escriptive inference is the process of understanding an unobserved phenomenon on the basis of a set of observations" (*DSI* 55).

A third aspect of descriptive inference, which is strongly emphasized by *DSI*, is the more complex issue of separating the "systematic" and the "random" components of any phenomenon. *DSI* (43) argues that descriptive inference inherently involves simplification, and one productive form of simplification can be to focus description on the systematic component of the phenomenon that the researcher seeks to explain.

Although in practice the separation of the systematic and random components may be difficult to achieve, it is important to see why this can be a useful idea. The rationale for this distinction depends on making a link between descriptive inference and causal inference. The systematic component of a phenomenon is understood as that which is explained by an accepted causal model; the random component is that which is not (60, 63).[3]

DSI points to alternative views of this random component. In one view, the world is inherently probabilistic. Thus, "[r]andom variation exists in nature and [in] the social and political worlds and can never be eliminated" (59). Another view rejects the idea that the world is inherently probabilistic, contending instead that what appears to be random "is only that portion of the world for which we have no explanation" (59). In other words, causation is deterministic, and what appears to be random is simply the facet of reality that is explained by variables not yet included in the relevant model, or is due to measurement error.

DSI illustrates this distinction with the example of fluctuations in the vote for a given party within a particular electoral district (55). The vote for this party may vary over time in part due to factors that are truly random. Alternatively, it might vary due to specific events that are outside the conventional explanatory concerns of political scientists—for example, variations in the weather, or some accidental occurrence such as the use of ballots that voters find confusing. In either case, an

---

[3]*DSI* (60) presents this idea by taking as a point of departure the supposition that the researcher lacks any prior knowledge of causal patterns: "[W]e begin any analysis with all observations being the result of 'nonsystematic' forces. Our job is then to provide evidence that particular events or processes are the result of systematic forces."

analyst may wish to generate a description of the party's vote share from which these fluctuations are removed. A common way of accomplishing this is to take an average of the party's vote share across several elections, on the assumption that the random fluctuations will cancel one another out (58).

Of course, variation that falls outside the focus of one explanatory framework or theory may be a central concern for another theory. Correspondingly, a description based on a careful separation of systematic and random components that is well suited to one theory may be less appropriate to another theory. Notwithstanding this limitation, the possibility of such separation raises the important idea that analytically productive description may isolate that part of a phenomenon that we really seek to explain. More broadly, it serves as a useful reminder to researchers that the facts do not "speak for themselves." Rather, they are interpreted from some theoretical perspective.

DSI considers description a fundamental part of the social scientific enterprise, and the book warns that in research contexts where causal inference is unusually difficult, analysts should sometimes be satisfied with careful descriptive inference (44–45; also 34, 75 n. 1). Nonetheless, *DSI* pays greater attention to causal inference, arguing that the best description is organized as a collection of evidence that evaluates a causal claim (46–49). It is therefore hardly surprising that the larger part of *DSI*'s focus is on research designed to test causal hypotheses.

Causal Inference

DSI's treatment of causation follows in the tradition of Neyman (1990 [1923]), Hodges and Lehmann (1964), Rubin (1974, 1978), and Holland (1986), who developed a counterfactual understanding of causation.[4] According to this account, the idea that "X causes Y" in any given unit of analysis raises the hypothetical question of how the outcome on Y would have differed if X had not occurred in that unit. Given that it is impossible to observe both the occurrence and nonoccurrence of X for any given unit at one point in time, causal inference involves comparing something that did occur with something that did not occur. This is the source of what Holland and *DSI* (79, 82) call the "fundamental problem of causal inference," that is, the problem that causal inference implicitly depends on a comparison with something that did not occur.

Using this counterfactual view of causation, *DSI* (76–82) hypothetically posits the existence of two parallel universes, exactly alike in every way except for one. Taking the example of a dichotomous independent variable, we might find that in one of these two universes, the unit being studied has a positive score on the hypothesized cause and thus receives the "treatment." In the other universe, the hypothesized cause does not occur in the unit being studied: it is a "control." The

---

[4]This approach is reviewed in more detail on 31–36 below, in the discussion of conditional independence.

causal effect of the explanatory variable is the difference in the outcome between the two parallel universes.

This definition helps researchers in reasoning about causation as an abstract concept. It serves to clarify why scholars do indeed face a fundamental problem of causal inference: out of the two observations of a given case needed to directly assess a causal effect, researchers can, in the real world, only make one. Either a case gets the treatment, or it does not. In observational studies, analysts cannot even choose which of these two universes to observe, because they cannot manipulate the independent variable. Some kind of inference is necessary to overcome this fundamental problem; hence, causal inference is the only way to appraise causation. When this understanding of causation is applied in observational studies, analysts seek to approximate these hypothetical comparisons through real-world comparisons among observed cases. A central component of *DSI*'s advice focuses on how to carry out these real-world comparisons.

Making Inferences: Quantitative Tools and Analytic Goals

DSI's recommendations can usefully be summarized in terms of the tools the book proposes, and in light of the goals it seeks to pursue with these tools. *DSI* draws heavily on regression analysis, econometrics, and other standard techniques of quantitative methodology (table 2.1). These include basic methods for describing quantitative data, such as means and variances, and, very crucially, the use of regression analysis for causal assessment. Regression analysis in the social sciences relies on quantitative tools of parameter estimation (i.e., estimating the coefficients associated with each independent variable), and generally also on significance tests (which address uncertainty due to sampling error or other forms of randomness in the model). In discussing causal inference from a regression perspective, *DSI* implicitly draws on these statistical techniques. Increasing the number of observations is frequently recommended as a basic tool for enhancing inferential leverage in empirical tests (i.e., achieving higher levels of statistical significance). Finally, *DSI* employs tools of probability theory, such as expected value and variance of the estimator. *DSI*'s tools are designed for use with quantitative data, and the book's fundamental advice to qualitative analysts is to use procedures in their own research that make a parallel contribution to valid inference. Although the chapters below debate whether it is in fact possible to implement this recommendation, there is not the slightest question that this advice has extended the analytic horizon of qualitative researchers.

With regard to *DSI*'s broader analytic agenda, within the framework of what we will call the book's "overarching goals" of achieving valid descriptive and

Table 2.1. Quantitative Tools Employed in *Designing Social Inquiry*

Tools	Comments
Means and Variances	Means and variances are the basis for other tools discussed below.
Regression Analysis	Regression analysis is *DSI*'s basic tool for causal inference from empirical data (e.g., 95–97, 121–22, 130–32, 168–72). Parameter estimation and significance tests, as used in regression analysis, provide a major part of the statistical basis for *DSI*'s discussion of causal inference.
Increasing the N	*DSI* repeatedly advocates increasing the number of observations as the best way to enhance the inferential leverage of empirical tests (e.g., 19, 23–24, 29–31, 46–49, 52, 67, 99, 117–18, 120–21, 123, chap. 6.).
Probability Theory	Many of *DSI*'s "Formal Analysis" text boxes (e.g., 97–99, 166–68, 184–85) evaluate the variance and bias of different estimators by applying tools of probability theory.

causal inference, a central focus is on "intermediate goals," which provide a justification for the use of these quantitative tools in pursuit of the overarching goals. Two major intermediate goals are avoiding bias and minimizing the variance of estimators in order to achieve higher levels of statistical significance.[5] Analysts should seek to avoid bias, potential sources of which include systematic measurement error (155–57), selection procedures that are correlated with the dependent variable—including procedures that may cause selection bias (128–37), missing explanatory variables (168–76), and endogeneity, that is, the problem that the outcome variable or the error term influences the explanatory variables (185–96). Researchers should also minimize the variance of their estimators by excluding irrelevant explanatory variables (182–85) and by reducing nonsystematic measurement error (157–68). In addition to reducing variance, which maximizes the precision of the inferences that can be drawn from a given data set, *DSI* recommends increasing leverage by creating data sets that have greater inferential power. Additional intermediate goals are summarized in the guidelines below. *DSI*

---

[5]*DSI* uses the term "efficiency" to refer to the goal of minimizing estimator variance. However, the technical definition of efficiency in statistics is somewhat different, so we have used this more general phrase in the text. *DSI* does not explicitly defend its preference for lower-variance estimators in terms of statistical significance, but this is the most obvious interpretation.

thus builds on the tools of mainstream quantitative methods to propose a series of procedures for achieving valid inference in qualitative research.

DSI does not simply present these tools and goals in a mechanical fashion, but at various points considers how some of them intersect with concerns that derive from the qualitative tradition. For example, although researchers can avoid some types of selection bias through random sampling, the book recognizes that in small-N research, random sampling may create as many problems as it solves (124–28). Within the framework of nonrandom sampling, *DSI* is careful to avoid a piece of clichéd advice that is often evoked in discussions of selection bias—that is, "do *not* select on the dependent variable." Instead, *DSI* argues that scholars who, for good reason, avoid random sampling and *do* select on the dependent variable should choose cases to reflect the full range of variation on that variable (141).[6]

Assumptions

DSI discusses the assumptions routinely employed to justify causal inference. Some scholars may think of these as "quantitative" or "statistical" assumptions. However, *DSI* (93) argues that these assumptions should not be understood narrowly as relevant only for quantitative analysis. Rather, assumptions are important for any study, whether quantitative or qualitative, that seeks to make the kind of inferences discussed in the previous section.

DSI urges researchers to "make the substantive implications of [their assumptions] extremely clear and visible to readers" (91). This advice is valuable because inferences depend on the assumptions that produce them, and a somewhat different set of assumptions can generate radically divergent inferences. This is one of the reasons why—as noted in chapter 1 above—it is hard to do really good quantitative research, just as it is hard to do really good qualitative research. *DSI* consequently advises researchers to justify their assumptions with theory and empirical evidence to the greatest extent possible (91). Yet *DSI* recognizes that it is often difficult to establish such justifications (93, 95).

Causal homogeneity, independence of observations,[7] and conditional independence are three major assumptions that *DSI* views as essential for causal inference.[8] These assumptions focus researchers' attention on three interrelated tasks:

---

[6]This corresponds to the second meaning of "selecting on the dependent variable" discussed in the glossary.

[7]This assumption is not treated in the same pages as the other two (*DSI* 91–97), yet it is likewise important (222–23).

[8]We would add that somewhat modified versions of these assumptions do also permit causal inference. For example, independence of observations can be weakened, as in time-series analysis, where autocorrelation often arises. However, even the modified

analyzing an appropriate set of cases; considering how cases and observations can influence each other in a way that may affect causal inference; and selecting variables appropriately and modeling the relations among them.

Causal Homogeneity

The assumption of causal homogeneity[9] states that "all units with the same value of the explanatory variables have the same expected value of the dependent variable" (*DSI* 91). In other words, the outcomes for all the cases in the analysis must be produced by one causal model; after controlling for the values of the included independent variables, every case must have the same expected value on the dependent variable.[10]

Discussions of causal homogeneity are motivated by the concern that a given form of a causal model may only be appropriate to a particular domain of cases. If the model is extended to further cases, the researcher may have to make it more complex to accommodate distinctive causal features of those cases. Hence, this assumption is concerned with the relation between our causal ideas and the cases on which we focus.

In the statistical literature on causation (e.g., Rubin 1974; Holland 1986), a stronger version of the causal homogeneity assumption is presented, which Rubin and Holland call "unit homogeneity." According to this version of the assumption, different units are presumed to be *fully identical* to each other in all relevant respects except for the values of the main independent variable. This strong version is sufficient to allow causal inference without the assumption of conditional independence discussed below, but it is extremely unlikely that this strong homogeneity assumption will ever hold in the social sciences.

However, the weaker version of causal homogeneity that we discuss in this section, which allows units to differ from each other but requires that the causal parameters in the analyst's model be constant across all units, is more plausible and plays an important role in causal inference.

Though *DSI* occasionally makes reference to the stronger version of this assumption,[11] much of its discussion invokes the weaker version.[12] *DSI* refers to both

---

assumptions must, in fact, have the same basic properties as the assumptions discussed here.

[9]*DSI* refers to this assumption as "unit homogeneity," as we explain below.

[10]Two points should be made here. First, the "expected value" refers not to the value that one should anticipate for every case being analyzed, but rather to the average value across many hypothetical replications of each case. Second, *DSI* notes that one way to meet the causal homogeneity assumption is through the related assumption of "constant causal effects" (92–93).

[11]*DSI* (91) defines unit homogeneity as being met if "the expected values of the dependent variables from each unit are the same when our explanatory variable takes on a particular value" (italics omitted). In this quote, the reference to multiple dependent vari-

versions of this assumption as "unit homogeneity." However, in labeling the weaker version of the assumption, which is much more central to *DSI*'s overall framework, we find the term "causal homogeneity" more useful, both because it distinguishes this concept from the more rigorous standard of unit homogeneity and because it calls more explicit attention to the need for all cases to share the same causal model.

Specifically, if the causal homogeneity assumption is not met, and a researcher analyzes the data as if it were, the inference will be a misleading average that lumps together differences among subgroups of cases. This average may not adequately represent the pattern of causation in any given case. For example, it has been argued that among advanced industrial countries, in some national contexts the more highly paid workers are more class conscious, whereas in other national contexts they are less class conscious (Przeworski and Teune 1970: 26). If researchers simply average these two findings, they may find no relationship, resulting in a misleading conclusion. The appropriate solution would be to analyze the two groups of countries separately. Researchers would thus address causal heterogeneity by recognizing that causal processes are different between the two groups of countries, and by assuming that they are similar within each group. In regression analysis, this can sometimes be accomplished by introducing an interaction term that includes a dummy variable. In qualitative comparison, separate comparisons can be employed for the two groups. The fact that causal heterogeneity can thus be overcome by using a more complex model underscores a key point: causal homogeneity is not simply a property of the data, but of the data in relation to a particular causal model.

Independence of Observations

Another assumption concerns the independence of observations, that is, the idea that for each observation, the value of a particular variable is not influenced

---

ables for each unit invokes the Rubin-Holland framework for causality, and this clearly should be read as a reference to the strong version of unit homogeneity.

[12]*DSI* (91) alternatively defines unit homogeneity as "the assumption that all units with the same value of the explanatory variables have the same expected value of the dependent variable." This statement, which refers only to the observed value of the dependent variable for each unit, does not invoke more complex statistical ideas of causation. Therefore, it would seem that it should be read as referring to the weaker version of unit homogeneity, involving constancy of causal parameters. This weaker version is also more compatible with *DSI*'s (93) claim that "[t]he notion of unit homogeneity . . . lies at the base of all scientific research." In the Rubin-Holland framework, much scientific research specifically does not employ the unit homogeneity assumption, turning instead to alternatives such as randomization, conditional independence, and "ignorable treatment assignment." Hence, *DSI*'s statement should be read as referring to the weaker assumption, and we therefore use the label "causal homogeneity" in discussing their arguments.

by its value in other observations and therefore provides new information about the phenomenon in question (222–23).[13] If independence of observations is not met, this does not necessarily bias the causal inference. However, it does reduce the amount of new evidence gained from each additional observation, thereby increasing the variance associated with an inference.

For some readers, a familiar alternative label for this assumption, which is appropriate for discussing cross-sectional analysis, is "independence of cases." However, this same assumption plays a major role in time-series analysis, in which the researcher analyzes multiple observations over time for each "case." Hence, the broader idea of independence of multiple observations for the same case becomes a central issue, and it is therefore useful to employ this more general label.

An example of this problem in time-series analysis is found in the literature on advanced industrial countries that explores the impact of corporatism and partisan control of government on economic growth. Scholars who had been working with an N of twelve to fifteen countries sought to achieve a major increase in the N by combining cross-sectional and time-series analysis, focusing on the period 1967–1984 (Alvarez, Garrett, and Lange 1991). However, subsequent research argued that prior results had been based on an incorrect assumption about the independence of observations. Consequently, the estimates of standard errors were too low, yielding excessive confidence in the conclusions. Revised estimates, based on a recognition of interdependence among observations—both among countries and within countries over time—supported some of the findings of the 1991 study, but cast doubt on others (Beck et al. 1993; Beck and Katz 1995; Kittel 1999).

Of course, the nonindependence of observations can also be viewed *not* as a methodological problem, but as a substantive topic—that is, as causation that occurs through processes of diffusion. However, within the framework of most work in regression analysis, it is indeed a methodological problem.

Conditional Independence

DSI's final major prerequisite for causal inference with observational data is the assumption of conditional independence, or, to give it a more complete name, conditional independence of assignment and outcome. We present this assumption by first returning to the counterfactual definition of causation noted above, from which the idea of conditional independence emerges, and then by offering two examples to make clear the importance of this assumption. Our presentation here will be more detailed than for the other two assumptions, given that this third assumption is particularly important to the discussion later in the present volume (240–44).

---

[13]Unlike the other two assumptions discussed in this chapter, the assumption of independence of observations is also important for descriptive inference.

According to the counterfactual understanding of causation, causal inference consists of comparing (a) the value of the outcome variable (Y_t with "t" for treatment) for a particular case when that case is exposed to a treatment, with (b) the value of the outcome variable (Y_c with "c" for control)[14] for the same case when that case is not exposed to the treatment. Y_t and Y_c are thus two different variables that reflect the outcomes a case will experience on the dependent variable, according to whether the independent variable, conceptualized as an experimental treatment, is present or absent.[15]

The causal effect of the treatment for a given case is the difference between the two variables for the case: $Y_t - Y_c$. However, to restate the fundamental problem of causal inference discussed above, it is impossible to simultaneously observe Y_t and Y_c for any particular case. The value of one variable may be observed, but the value of the other is necessarily hypothetical. Consequently, it is impossible to compute $Y_t - Y_c$. Hence, in practice, causal inference seeks to replicate this hypothetical comparison by making real-world comparisons across (hopefully) similar units, some of which are exposed to the treatment and some of which are not.

When a real-world comparison is employed, the quality of the resulting causal inference depends on how cases are "assigned" to the treatment group and to the control group. Two issues are important here. First, a question of terminology: In observational studies, researchers do not actually assign cases to treatment and control groups. However, what we refer to as assignment does take place; it is carried out by social and political processes over which the researcher usually has no control.

The second issue, which is vital to the quality of causal inference, concerns the relationship between the assignment process and the outcome variables, Y_t and Y_c. The key question here is whether the cases are assigned in such a way that those in the treatment category have the same average values on both Y_t and Y_c as the cases in the control category. In other words, is the average of Y_t across the cases exposed to the treatment equal to the average of Y_t across the cases in the control group? Is this also true for Y_c?

If the answers to these questions are "yes," then the standard of independence has been met,[16] and the researcher will be able to make a good inference about the

---

[14]We follow here the Rubin-Holland notation of "t" and "c," which is also employed in chapter 13 below. In chapter 3 below, where Brady presents his direct commentary on *DSI,* he follows the book's notation, which is based on *DSI*'s running example: "i" for "incumbent" and "n" for "nonincumbent."

[15]In this discussion, the independent variable may be dichotomous; alternatively, the treatment and control may reflect two different values on a continuous variable.

[16]To be more precise, what is discussed here as independence is *mean* independence. Likewise, conditional independence as discussed here is actually *mean* conditional independence. For a discussion of these distinctions, see Stone (1993). Finally, the text above neglects two important, although somewhat narrow, technical issues: (a) whether there is

causal effect of the treatment by comparing the observed Y_t among the cases given the treatment with the observed Y_c among the cases assigned to the control. The underlying logic here is that, if independence of assignment holds, any difference between the treatment group and the control group must be due to the treatment—because all other relevant factors are balanced between the two groups. If, on the other hand, cases are assigned in such a way that those in the treatment group tend to have a different Y_t or Y_c than the cases in the control group, then causal inference will be biased. For example, if cases with a high value of Y_t are more likely to enter the treatment group than cases with a lower value of Y_t, the researcher will probably overestimate the causal effect of the treatment.

Independence of assignment is a strong condition, and it is rarely plausible in an observational study. Observational studies often employ an assumption of *conditional* independence, which serves to justify causal inference even though the treatment and control groups initially do not have the same hypothetical average values on Y_t and Y_c. Suppose a variable (which we shall call Z) identifies subgroups of cases, within which independence of assignment does hold, and among which it does not hold. Then controlling for Z by comparing Y_t and Y_c within subgroups allows researchers to make unbiased inferences from the observational data. By stratifying in this manner, the standard of conditional independence is met.[17] In fact, because Y_t and Y_c cannot both be directly observed, the researcher never knows with certainty that their average values are equal. But in principle, the introduction of the appropriate control can make them equal, and hence yield conditional independence. In practice, achieving appropriate statistical control may involve more than one control variable (Z_i to Z_n), and multivariate techniques are needed to introduce these multiple controls. For convenience, we will use the label Z to refer to one or more controls.

Given the importance of introducing control variables, the two words in this label, "conditional independence," thus bring together two essential ideas. (a) It is best for inference that assignment to the treatment and control groups be independent of the two outcome variables Y_t and Y_c. Correspondingly, the full name of the assumption is "conditional independence of assignment and outcome." (b) When independence does not hold, researchers can, in principle if not in practice,

---

a broader population from which the cases under investigation are a sample; and (b) whether the *expected* means of Y_t and Y_c, rather than the observed means, are in fact equal. The equality of the expected means is actually the key condition for mean independence and, if control variables have been introduced, for mean conditional independence.

[17]Regression analysis depends on related assumptions about causation, such as the specification assumption discussed in chapter 13. For most purposes, these assumptions may be seen as similar, in that they both focus attention on the potential problem of missing variable bias. However, it is important to remember that alternative analytic tools (e.g., regression versus stratification) depend on assumptions that sometimes differ in important ways.

make inferences *as if* assignment were independent of Y_t and Y_c by statistically controlling for, or "conditioning" on, Z.

Conditional independence can be established if the appropriate statistical controls are introduced, removing the effect of an assignment process that does not meet the standard of independence. The assumption of conditional independence is thus addressed by employing with observational data the procedure of *statistical* control, as a substitute for the *experimental* control that is achieved through random assignment.

The effort by scholars to satisfy conditional independence by introducing the appropriate control can be illustrated with a well-known example of spurious correlation. In the United States, political participation is lower for African Americans and Latinos than for whites. In other words, if we hypothetically think of "nonwhite" as the treatment condition, and "white" as the control condition, individuals "assigned" to be African American and Latino have an average rate of participation, or average Y_t, that is lower than the average rate of participation, or average Y_c, among people "assigned" to be white. The lower participation rate of the first two groups provides an appropriate basis for descriptive inference (i.e., describing their levels of participation), but it is problematic as a basis for causal inference. It does not necessarily follow that being African American or Latino causes citizens to participate less. Rather, membership in these two groups is correlated with other factors, such as education and income, that could explain lower participation rates. These other factors serve the role of identifying salient subgroups among the cases; hence these other factors may be equivalent to the variable Z in the discussion above. When these other factors are controlled for, thus making it more plausible that conditional independence is satisfied, "neither being African American nor being Latino has a direct impact" on participation (Verba, Schlozman, and Brady 1995: 442).

In other words, after conditioning on—that is, controlling for—Z, these authors conclude that the average value of Y_t is in fact about the same as the average value of Y_c. It is not being African American or Latino that reduces the political activity of individuals within these groups. That apparent causal relation is spurious, and other factors such as low education or low income account for the lower rate of participation. Once the effect of these other factors is removed statistically, the underlying causal relationship emerges.

A second example illustrates the point that the conditional independence assumption is hard to meet when analysts cannot identify, or cannot measure, the variable or set of variables that must be controlled for. Consider the question of whether the *size* of revolutionary movements (independent variable) affects their *success* in overthrowing an existing regime (dependent variable). As Goldstone (1991: 137) emphasizes, because the personal cost of participating in an unsuccessful revolutionary movement can be high, many individuals will only join revolutionary movements that are seen as having at least some probability of defeating the regime. This evaluation obviously depends on the perceived strength of both the revolutionary movement and the regime. Specifically, the probability that a revolutionary movement will grow in size (which corresponds to the treatment) depends in part on the particular characteristics of the national regime that individuals evaluate in judging the relative strength of that regime. Yet the strength of the regime *also* plays a key, direct role in influencing the likelihood that the regime will fall, which is the outcome being explained.

Thus, due to these regime characteristics, those countries most susceptible to revolution may be most likely to face large revolutionary movements, and are in effect assigned to the treatment group. In this discussion, characteristics of the national regime are an instance of the variable Z above. Contrasts in these characteristics group together regimes that differ in the degree to which they are perceived as weak. Perceptions of weakness are, in turn, correlated: (a) with the likelihood of regime collapse, given a strong insurgent movement, or Y_i; and (b) with potential insurgents' decisions to rebel, which, when aggregated, constitutes the treatment. Unless these regime characteristics are included in the analysis and controlled for, researchers will overestimate the importance of popular participation in revolutionary opposition movements for causing regime collapse—given that greater popular participation is more likely when the chance of regime collapse is high.[18]

To meet the assumption of conditional independence, the researcher would need to collect data on these characteristics that adequately capture their role in influencing both the size of revolutionary movements and the likelihood of regime collapse. Yet collecting these variables and adequately controlling for them is doubtless more difficult than it is for the education variable in the prior example. The researcher would have to collect enough information about regime characteristics to arrive at the same evaluations and judgments that potential revolutionaries

---

[18]This problem can arise regardless of whether the researcher takes a more structural or a more actor-centered view of revolution. One interpretation of this causal pattern could be that the perception of these revolutionary actors is an intervening variable that links these regime characteristics to the revolutionary outcome, involving an actor-centered and potentially "agental" explanatory perspective. Another interpretation views regime characteristics as direct, structural causes of revolution. For example, according to Chehabi and Linz (1998), under sultanistic regimes a poorly institutionalized, personalistic military is a critical structural factor in regime breakdown. Although the perception of the military on the part of revolutionary and regime actors may have some importance, this weakness of the military is seen, in its own right, as a critical causal factor. The point here is not to adjudicate between a structural and actor-centered perspective, but rather to show that, from either perspective, failure to satisfy conditional independence may interfere with causal inference. Whether the structural weakness in the military causes revolution directly, or primarily through the perceptions of state and popular actors, varying degrees of regime strength can still confound our attempts to estimate the impact of popular participation on revolution.

make about the strength of the regime. Hence, the idea of conditional independence is crucial here, but it is difficult to meet this assumption.

Overall, the idea of conditional independence uses the counterfactual definition of causation to provide a logical framework for reasoning about the critical task of controlling for rival explanations in causal inference.

To summarize the discussion of these three assumptions, *DSI*'s goal is to underscore the idea that they are important to all researchers, and not just quantitative analysts. In all observational studies, causal inference never relies exclusively on the actual data, but also on assumptions about the political and social processes we are studying. It is evident that not only *DSI*'s discussion of these assumptions, but also the book's treatment of inference and the definition of scientific research, involve a perspective that is far more familiar to quantitative than to qualitative researchers. However, *DSI* is strongly committed to the idea that these issues are of equal relevance to both traditions. Even a scholar who disagrees with *DSI* must recognize that the book makes a fundamental contribution by pushing a broader range of researchers to grapple with these questions.

Guidelines: Summarizing *DSI*'s Framework

This section adopts a different approach to synthesizing *DSI* by presenting many of the book's more specific methodological recommendations as a set of guidelines. These guidelines are largely concerned with what we refer to in chapter 1 as intermediate goals, focusing on procedures for linking specific quantitative tools to the overarching goals of valid descriptive and causal inference. The guidelines help to make clear how *DSI*'s broad ideas, summarized in the present chapter, inform the book's treatment of specific decisions about research design.

We organize the guidelines in terms of a research cycle (figure 2.1): defining the problem, specifying the theory, selecting cases and observations, carrying out descriptive and causal inference, and retesting and reformulating the theory. The final step completes this cycle by bringing the researcher back to the step of theory specification, and potentially also to redefining the research problem (see dashed arrow in the figure). Although research routinely moves through a series of ordered steps such as this, what is learned at each step certainly may lead to revisiting prior steps or jumping forward to subsequent steps. Hence, one could in fact place many more arrows in the diagram.

These guidelines are, of course, our summary of *DSI*'s arguments. *DSI* makes periodic reference to "rules" for research (e.g., 6–7, 9), and the book presents five specific rules for constructing causal theories (99–114). However, the book does not synthesize its recommendations in terms of an overall set of rules or guidelines.[19] Each of the guidelines presented below is introduced as a brief,

---

[19]See note 1 above.

Figure 2.1. Steps in the Research Cycle: A Framework for Summarizing *Designing Social Inquiry*

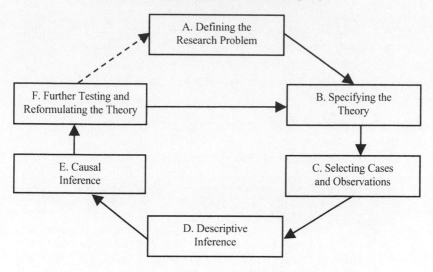

Note: Solid arrows show the main links among steps in the cycle. Choices made at any one step can, of course, potentially affect any other step. This is reflected, for example, by the placement of a dashed line from F to A, in addition to the solid line from F to B.

self-explanatory phrase. For some of the guidelines, we spell out the idea in greater detail, often drawing on quotations from *DSI*. In all cases, specific page references are provided.

DSI states that "[a]ny meaningful rules admit of exceptions. . . . We seek not dogma, but disciplined thought" (7). Correspondingly, we do not want to give the impression that *DSI*'s framework consists of rigid rules. Rather, we seek to bring together systematically the large number of specific recommendations offered by the book, as a means of demonstrating both the scope of these recommendations, and *DSI*'s relative emphasis on different methodological issues.

A. Defining the Research Problem

1.   *Address a problem that is important in the real world* (15).

2. *Contribute to a scholarly literature.* Contribute to "an identifiable scholarly literature by increasing the collective ability to construct verified scientific explanations of some aspect of the world" (15, 16–17).[20]

3. *Modify or abandon a topic that cannot be refined into a research project that permits valid inference* (18).

B. Specifying the Theory

4. *Construct falsifiable theories.* "[C]hoose theories that could be wrong" (19; also 100).
    a. *Strengthen falsifiability by choosing a theory that maximizes observable implications* (19).
    b. *Strengthen falsifiability by being concrete.* "Theories that are stated precisely and make specific predictions can be shown more easily to be wrong and are therefore better" (20, 109–12).

5. *Build theories that are logically consistent.* "[I]f two or more parts of a theory generate hypotheses that contradict one another, then no evidence from the empirical world can uphold the theory" (105).

6. *Increase leverage by explaining more with less.* Explain "as much as possible with as little as possible" (29).
    a. *Increase leverage through parsimony.* "[M]aximize leverage by limiting the number of explanatory variables" (123).
    b. *Increase leverage by explaining more observable outcomes.* "State theories in as encompassing [a way] as feasible" (113), and "list all possible observable implications of [the main] hypothesis that might be observed in [the] data or in other data" (30).

C. Selecting Cases and Observations

7. *Distinguish between cases and observations.* "Cases" are understood as the broader units, that is, the broader research settings or sites within which analysis is conducted; "observations" are pieces of data, drawn from those research sites, that form the direct basis for descriptive and causal inference (52–53, 117–18, 217–18).

8. *Focus on the range of variation relevant to the theory.* Select cases among which the dependent variable in fact exhibits "the variation [researchers] wish to explain" (108). It is thus important not merely to have variation on the de-

---

[20]The italics in many quotations have been omitted.

pendent variable, but that this variation capture the contrasts addressed by the theory.

9. *Construct a determinate, rather than an indeterminate, research design by including a sufficient number of observations.*[21] Avoid an indeterminate research design from which "virtually nothing can be learned about the causal hypotheses" because the researcher has "more inferences to make than implications observed" (118, 119; also 116, 120, 178–79, 213–17, 228). In the face of an insufficient number of observations, scholars can:

   a. *Address indeterminacy by increasing the number of observations—either through changing the dependent variable, or through focusing on subunits* (24, 47, 120, 217–28).

   b. *Address indeterminacy by gaining leverage from strong theory.* If the number of observations is insufficient, "limited progress in understanding causal issues is nevertheless possible, *if* the theoretical issues with which [researchers] are concerned are posed with sufficient clarity and linked to appropriate observable implications" (179).

   c. *Address indeterminacy by situating observations within a larger research program.* Even "a single observation can be useful for evaluating causal explanations if it is part of a research program. If there are other single observations, perhaps gathered by other researchers, against which it can be compared, it is no longer a single observation" (211, 129 n. 6).

10. *Seek causal homogeneity.* Causal homogeneity[22] is "the assumption that all units with the same value of the explanatory variables have the same expected value of the dependent variable" (91, 116).

11. *Avoid selection bias.* Selection bias poses important "dangers" (116), in that it can invalidate both causal inference (129–32) and descriptive inference (135). One important source of such bias is the failure of the sample to reflect the full range of variation on the dependent variable. The random selection of cases is a standard means for avoiding important forms of selection bias, yet in small-N research this may not be appropriate (126).

12. *Select cases nonrandomly in small-N analysis.* Random selection in small-N research can too easily fail to capture the full range of variation on the variables of interest. "Usually, selection must be done in an *intentional* fashion, consistent with . . . research objectives and strategy" (139). This recommendation is relevant both for descriptive (135) and causal (129–32) inference.

---

[21]A determinate research design also requires the absence of perfect multicollinearity. This likewise involves the issue of having enough observations, in that a sufficiently large N can help overcome multicollinearity. See no. 30 below.

[22]Regarding definitions of causal homogeneity versus unit homogeneity, see the glossary.

With reference to causal inference, *DSI* suggests the following standards for nonrandom selection:

a. *Avoid selecting a set of observations in which either the independent or dependent variable is constant.* "[T]he causal effect of an explanatory variable that does not vary cannot be assessed . . . " (146). Researchers "can also learn nothing about a causal effect from a study which selects observations so that the dependent variable does not vary" (147; also 108–9, 129, 148–49). "The cases of extreme selection bias—where there is by design no variation on the dependent variable—are easy to deal with: avoid them!" (130).

    i. *In selecting observations on either the independent or dependent variable, ensure that these observations encompass sufficient variation on this variable.* For example, when selecting on the dependent variable, "select observations with particularly high and particularly low values . . . " (129, 141, 147–49).

    ii. *To address the problem of a no-variance design, seek variance by situating observations within a larger research program* (146–47).

b. *Selecting simultaneously on both the independent and dependent variables can pose a grave problem.* "The most egregious error is to select observations in which the explanatory and dependent variables vary together in ways that are known to be consistent with the hypothesis that the research purports to test" (142).

13. *If observations are not independent from one another, recognize that this reduces the certainty of the findings; researchers may also address the causes of this interdependence.* When observations are not fully independent of each other, "each new [observation] does not bring as much new information to bear on the problem as it would if the observations were independent of one another. . . . [W]hen dealing with partially dependent observations . . . be careful not to overstate the certainty of the conclusions. . . . [C]arefully analyze the reasons for the dependence among the observations" (222).

D. Descriptive Inference

14. *Description requires inference.* Description in social science research must be understood not as the process of collecting unmediated facts, but rather as involving inferences from observations to the broader ideas and comparisons around which the research is organized (chap. 2).

15. *Recognize the similarity between quantitative or formal work and "interpretation," as compared to the full complexity of reality.* "[T]he difference between the amount of complexity in the world and that in the thickest of descriptions is still vastly larger than the difference between this thickest of descriptions and the most abstract quantitative or formal analysis" (43).

16. *Extract analytically relevant features from the uniqueness of cases* (42). "All phenomena, all events, are in some sense unique. . . . The real question . . . [is] whether the key features of social reality that we want to understand can be abstracted from a mass of facts" (42).

17. *Know the context.* "Where possible, analysts should simplify their descriptions only after they attain an understanding of the richness of history and culture. . . . [R]ich, unstructured knowledge of the historical and cultural context of the phenomena with which they want to deal in a simplified and scientific way is usually a requisite for avoiding simplifications that are simply wrong" (43).

18. *Good description is better than bad explanation.* In research contexts in which good causal inference is difficult, it may be preferable to stick to carefully executed descriptive inference (44; also 34, 45, 75 n. 1, 178–79).

19. *Study observable concepts.* "[C]hoose observable, rather than unobservable, concepts wherever possible" (109). "Attempting to find empirical evidence of abstract, unmeasurable, and unobservable concepts will necessarily prove more difficult and less successful than for many imperfectly conceived specific and concrete concepts" (110).

20. *In general, avoid typologies and classifications, except as preliminary heuristic devices.* "[C]onstructs such as typologies, frameworks, and all manner of classifications, are useful as temporary devices [for] collecting data. . . . However, in general, we encourage researchers *not* to organize their data in this way" (48).

21. *Use valid indicators.* "Validity refers to measuring what we think we are measuring" (25). Among the issues that arise in striving for validity is the need to "use the measure that is most appropriate to [the researcher's] theoretical purposes" (153).

22. *Use reliable data-collection procedures that, if applied again, would produce the same data* (25).

23. *Estimate measurement error.* "Since all observation and measurement . . . is imprecise," researchers should "estimate the amount of [measurement] error . . . " (151); "qualitative researchers should offer uncertainty estimates in the form of carefully worded judgments about their observations" (152).

24. *Separate the systematic and random components of phenomena.* "[O]ne of the fundamental goals of [descriptive] inference is to distinguish the systematic component from the nonsystematic component of the phenomena" being studied (56). Thus, analytically productive description may seek to isolate the systematic component, as it is this component that researchers really seek to explain.

E. Causal Inference

25. *Causal assessment requires inference.* Causation is not observed directly. Rather, causation is inferred on the basis of data and assumptions (chap. 3).

26. *Demonstrate, to the extent possible, that the assumptions underlying causal inference are met in a given context of research.* Assumptions such as causal homogeneity, conditional independence, and the independence of observations "can and should be justified" to the greatest extent possible on the basis of insights derived from prior research and knowledge of the research setting (91).

27. *Use theory to select appropriate explanatory variables and avoid "data mining."* "Without a theoretical model, [researchers] cannot decide which potential explanatory variables should be included in [the] analysis." "[W]ork toward a theoretically motivated model rather than 'data mining'. . . ." In other words, researchers should not simply run "regressions or qualitative analyses with whatever explanatory variables [they] can think of" (174).

28. *Avoid missing variable bias by including all relevant explanatory variables.* "[S]ystematically look for omitted control variables and consider whether they should be included in the analysis" (172). If a given variable is correlated with both the dependent variable and an explanatory variable, then failure to include it will bias the causal inference (170). The following three steps can help avoid missing variable bias:
    a.   *First, list potentially relevant explanatory variables* (174).
    b.   *Second, control for relevant explanatory variables* (174).
    c.   *Third, in estimating the main causal effect, do not control for intervening variables.* "[I]n general, [researchers] should not control for an explanatory variable that is in part a consequence of [the] key explanatory variable" (174).

29. *Minimize the variance of estimators by excluding irrelevant variables.* Do not "collect information on every possible causal influence . . ." (182, italics omitted) because "[t]he inclusion of irrelevant variables can be very costly" (183). While the best solution to the problem of "many variables, small N" is to collect more observations, "if this is not possible, researchers are well-advised to identify irrelevant variables" (184) and exclude them from the analysis.

30. *Avoid an indeterminate research design due to multicollinearity.*[23] Avoid a research design in which two or more of the explanatory variables are so highly correlated that it is impossible to separate their causal effects (119). The proposed solution to this problem is to:

---

[23]A determinate research design also requires a sufficient number of observations. See guideline 9 above.

a. *Address multicollinearity by collecting additional observations.* "[S]earch for observable implications at some other level of analysis" (123), which can give more leverage in differentiating the causal effects of highly correlated explanatory variables.

31. *Avoid endogeneity.* "A very common mistake is to choose a dependent variable which in fact causes changes in [the] explanatory variables. . . . [T]he easiest way to avoid [this mistake] is to choose explanatory variables that are clearly exogenous and dependent variables that are endogenous" (107–8; also 94, 185). Five solutions to endogeneity are:

    a. *Address endogeneity by careful selection of observations.* "[W]e can first translate a general concern about endogeneity into [a concern about] specific potential sources of omitted variable bias and then search for a subset of observations in which these sources of bias could not apply" (193).

    b. *Address endogeneity by transforming it into an omitted variable problem.* "By transforming [a research] problem in this way, scholars [can] get a better handle on the problem since they [can] explicitly measure this omitted variable and control for it . . . " (190).

    c. *Address endogeneity by disaggregating the dependent variable.* "[R]econceptualize the dependent variable as itself containing a dependent and an explanatory component. . . . The goal of this method of avoiding endogeneity bias is to identify and measure only the dependent component of [the] dependent variable" (188–89).

    d. *Address endogeneity by disaggregating the explanatory variable.* "[D]ivide a potentially endogenous explanatory variable into two components: one that is clearly exogenous and one that is at least partly endogenous. . . ." Then use "only the exogenous portion of the explanatory variable in a causal analysis" (193).

    e. *Address endogeneity by correcting the biased inference.* "[E]ven if [researchers] cannot avoid endogeneity bias, [they] can sometimes improve . . . inferences after the fact by estimating the degree of bias. At a minimum, this enables [them] to determine the direction of bias, perhaps providing an upper or lower bound on the correct estimate" (188).

32. *Estimate and, if possible, correct for selection bias.* "[I]f selection bias is unavoidable, [researchers] should analyze the problem and ascertain the direction and, if possible, the magnitude of the bias, then use this information to adjust [their] original estimates in the right direction" (133). If they "know there is bias but cannot determine its direction or magnitude . . . [researchers should] at least increase the level of uncertainty [they] use in describing [their] results" (199; also 128–37, 168–82).

F. Further Testing and Reformulating the Theory

33. *Report research procedures, thereby allowing other analysts to evaluate and replicate the findings.* "Only by reporting the study in sufficient detail so that it can be replicated is it possible to evaluate the procedures followed and methods used" (26; also 8, 23, 51).

34. *Test the theory with data other than that used to generate the theory* (46). The original data can be used to test a new implication of a theory, "as long as the implication does not 'come out of' the data but is a hypothesis independently suggested by the theory or a different data set" (30).

35. *The theory should generally not be reformulated after analyzing the data.* "Ad hoc adjustments in a theory that does not fit existing data must be used rarely . . . " (21).
    a. *If the theory is reformulated by making it more restrictive, retest it with new data.* If a theory is modified after analyzing the data, researchers "can make the theory less restrictive (so that it covers a broader range of phenomena and is exposed to more opportunities for falsification), but [they] should not make it more restrictive without collecting new data to test the new version of the theory" (22, italics omitted).

Anticipating the Discussion of *DSI*'s Framework

Subsequent chapters in the present volume provide alternative perspectives on quantitative and qualitative methods, making central reference to the framework offered by *DSI*. This final section of chapter 2 anticipates the assessment presented in the following chapters.[24] As can be seen in table 2.2, we organize the discussion with reference to specific guidelines. Some aspects of *DSI*'s framework evoke agreement, whereas for others there is disagreement.

I. Areas of Convergence

a. *Broad Convergence.* The chapters in this volume strongly endorse the overall goal of developing shared standards for descriptive and causal inference. This convergence once again calls attention to the contribution made by *DSI* in focusing scholarly attention on such standards.

b. *Specific Points of Convergence.* Many of *DSI*'s suggestions are not challenged or reevaluated. The recommendation to move beyond the uniqueness of

---

[24]Whereas the last section in chapter 1 above summarizes the arguments chapter by chapter, the organization here is thematic.

Table 2.2. Anticipating the Debate on *Designing Social Inquiry*

Evaluation of *DSI*'s Contribution and Selected Examples Drawn from Guidelines Presented in Chapter 2	Examples of Relevant Chapters in the Present Volume
I. Areas of Convergence	
a. Broad Convergence. Consensus on importance of standards for good descriptive and causal inference.	All Chapters
b. Specific Points of Convergence. Consensus that *DSI* offers much valuable advice with direct practical application in social science research (2, 3, 4, 5, 7, 12, 12b, 14, 16, 25, 31b/c/d, 33).	All Chapters
II. Areas of Divergence	
a. Extensive Treatment of Causal Inference, but Insufficient Attention to Its Logical Foundations. Greater attention needed to adequately address the obstacles faced in causal inference based on observational data (10, 26, 28, 29, 31, 31a/b/c/d/e, 32).	Brady, Bartels, Ragin, McKeown, Chapter 13
b. Important Issues Are Noted, but Seriously Neglected. Valuable advice is discussed briefly, but this advice must play a far more central role in research design (8, 9b/c, 12a–ii, 17, 21, 22).	Brady, Rogowski, Collier, Mahoney, and Seawright, Ragin, McKeown
c. Regarding Key Advice, Practical Application May Not Be Feasible. Some advice may be hard to apply, not only in qualitative, but even in quantitative, research (13, 18, 23, 26, 28c, 31).	Brady, Bartels, Munck, McKeown, Chapter 13
d. Idea of Trade-Offs Is Mentioned, but Not Recognized as a Central Issue. Trade-offs among methodological goals must be a central concern in designing research (4a, 6b, 9, 9a, 11, 12a, 19, 27, 30a, 31, 34, 35, 35a).	Brady, Bartels, Rogowski, Collier, Mahoney, and Seawright, Munck, Ragin, Tarrow, Chapter 12, Chapter 13
e. Independent Contribution of Qualitative Tools Is Undervalued. Qualitative analysts have developed valuable tools that must to a greater degree be taken seriously on their own terms (1, 10, 13, 15, 17, 21, 22, 24, 30, 31).	Rogowski, Collier, Mahoney, and Seawright, Munck, Ragin, McKeown, Tarrow, Chapter 13, Appendix

cases by extracting analytically relevant features (guideline no. 16 above) articulates a fundamental priority in social science research. *DSI*'s suggestion to distinguish between cases and observations (no. 7) and the discussion of descriptive and causal inference (nos. 14, 25) have given some qualitative researchers a useful new vocabulary. As noted earlier in this chapter, part of the advice about selection bias is quite nuanced, in that *DSI* recognizes the importance of nonrandom sampling in the context of small-N research. Rather than offering the excessively limiting recommendation that scholars should not select on the dependent variable, the book suggests how sampling on the dependent variable is best carried out (no. 12). Replicability (no. 33) is certainly a widely held goal in the social sciences,[25] and other areas of agreement likewise emerge, as indicated in the table.

II. Areas of Divergence

In a number of other areas, the authors in the present volume raise questions about *DSI*'s recommendations.

a.   *Extensive Treatment of Causal Inference, but Insufficient Attention to Its Logical Foundations. DSI* is on the right track in pushing analysts to consider the assumptions that constitute the logical foundations of inference. However, the book's presentation of methodological norms falls short in helping scholars include the right variables, exclude the wrong ones, and more generally design their research and specify their models appropriately.

DSI's suggestion that researchers systematically search for and include relevant omitted variables (no. 28) usefully raises the issue of confounding variables, but does not say enough about which kinds of omitted variables ought to be included and which should be excluded. The recommendation that researchers exclude irrelevant explanatory variables (no. 29) leaves the same kinds of questions unanswered: How, exactly, should analysts distinguish between relevant and irrelevant explanatory variables before making a causal inference? Likewise, the advice that analysts should avoid endogeneity (no. 31) does too little to help researchers understand the substantive and theoretical reasons that endogeneity might or might not be a problem in a particular context. The specific techniques for addressing problems of endogeneity (nos. 31a–e) are valuable in pushing analysts to seek solutions to these problems, but much more needs to be said about the rather stringent assumptions behind these techniques.

Overall, *DSI* appears to embrace the proposition that these key problems of causal inference have been largely solved in mainstream quantitative research, and that, by extension, qualitative researchers should come as close as they can to adopting these solutions. By contrast, as argued by Brady and Bartels and in chap-

[25]Gary King has played a central role in subsequent debate on this issue. See *PS: Political Science and Politics* (1995) and *APSA-CP* (1996).

ter 13 in the present volume, we are convinced that causal inference—not only in qualitative but also in quantitative research—is often problematic. Related issues of the logical foundations of inference are addressed by Ragin and McKeown.

DSI simply does not confront these difficulties squarely. The book does not give adequate recognition to problems of causal inference created by omitted variables and endogeneity. These issues are not easily resolved, even with advanced quantitative techniques. Consequently, causal inference, even with a large N, is often problematic. Hence, the applicability of *DSI*'s methodological framework for causal inference in qualitative research remains doubtful.

    b. *Important Issues Are Noted, but Seriously Neglected. DSI* mentions some key issues once or perhaps twice, yet some authors in the present volume consider them to be fundamental problems in the design of research that require far more attention. For example, *DSI* does cite Lieberson's (1985: chap. 5) incisive discussion of the need to focus empirical analysis on the range of variation relevant to the theory (no. 8); *DSI* also refers to using strong theory to address the problem of indeterminacy (no. 9b). Likewise, *DSI* notes that situating observations within a larger research program can help address the small-N problem (indeterminacy) and the problem of no-variance designs (nos. 9c, 12a–ii). Further, the book does mention the importance of knowing the context of research and of seeking validity and reliability in measurement (nos. 17, 21, 22). However, although these topics are noted briefly, they require much greater attention, given that *DSI* aims to provide a balanced set of recommendations for research design. These themes are explored below in the chapters by Brady, Rogowski, Collier, Mahoney, and Seawright, Ragin, and McKeown.

    c. *Regarding Key Advice, Practical Application May Not Be Feasible.* Many of *DSI*'s guidelines offer potentially useful methodological recommendations, yet authors in the present volume are concerned that it sometimes may not be feasible to apply this advice. For example, *DSI* usefully suggests that researchers pay close attention to the implications of measurement error for causal inference (no. 23). However, as Bartels argues, current statistical knowledge suggests that it can be difficult to know what those consequences are, even in quantitative research. Likewise, it is probably good advice to suggest that, in contexts where good causal inference is difficult, it is preferable to stick to good descriptive inference (no. 18). Yet this advice runs against the prevailing intellectual orientation within political science (and in *DSI*), where causal inference is strongly privileged over descriptive inference. As Brady and McKeown argue in the following chapters, more reflection is needed on the proper relation between descriptive and causal inference.

Returning to the topic of endogeneity (no. 31), we find it useful to raise this issue, but it is also valuable to be candid about the fact that it can be exceedingly hard to address this problem, in either qualitative or quantitative research. Finally, the priority of demonstrating that the assumptions underlying causal inference are met in a given context of research (no. 26) is obviously important—as discussed in the present volume by Munck and in chapter 13—but little attention is devoted to exploring how this is to be done. In many contexts, it is simply not possible to demonstrate that these assumptions are met.

d.   *Idea of Trade-Offs Is Mentioned, but Not Recognized as a Central Issue.* *DSI* pays insufficient attention to trade-offs, failing to recognize that they are an overarching issue in research design. Trade-offs are a central theme in the chapters below. As discussed in this volume by Brady and Bartels, and in chapters 12 and 13, the mandate to increase the number of observations—for the purpose of strengthening falsifiability, increasing leverage, and addressing indeterminacy and multicollinearity (nos. 4a, 6b, 9a, 30a)—may make it harder to achieve other important goals, such as maintaining independence of observations, measurement validity, and causal homogeneity.

Next, as emphasized by Brady and in chapter 12 of this volume, while working with concrete and observable concepts (no. 19) certainly makes measurement easier, many theories depend on abstract concepts that are well worth measuring, even if it is not easy to do so. An obvious example is the concept of causation. *DSI* (76, 79) in fact recognizes it as an abstract, theoretical concept, and much of the book is devoted to discussing how best to measure it. Many other indispensable concepts are likewise hard to measure.

Additionally, the idea of a determinate versus indeterminate research design (no. 9) raises the important issue of having a sufficient number of observations to adjudicate among rival explanations; yet, as chapter 13 in the present volume argues, this distinction creates the misleading impression that research designs based on observational, as opposed to experimental, data can really be determinate— which is not the case. Indeed, causation can generally only be inferred in observational studies if the researcher imposes several restrictive assumptions, which may be difficult to test or even to defend.

Finally, as argued by Rogowski, and by Collier, Mahoney, and Seawright, the warning against designs that lack variance on the dependent variable (no. 12a) must be weighed against the analytic gains that can derive from closely analyzing positive cases of a given phenomenon, especially if little is known about it.

Other recommendations made by *DSI* also involve trade-offs. These recommendations involve issues of inductive analysis, endogeneity, and complexity. From one point of view, the injunctions against the post hoc reformulation and testing of hypotheses (nos. 34, 35, 35a) make good sense, in that it weakens the power of statistical tests. However, as Ragin, Munck, and Tarrow argue, for qualitative researchers the refinement of theory and hypotheses through the iterated analysis of a given set of data is an essential research tool, and researchers lose other aspects of analytic leverage by not employing it.[26] Indeed, quantitative stud-

---

[26]*DSI* does discuss the interaction between theory and data, but within the framework of arguing that any further test of the theory should be undertaken with *new* data (*DSI* 21, 46).

ies regularly follow a similar path. When quantitative researchers analyze observational data, they almost never conduct one test of the initially hypothesized statistical model and then stop. Rather, they routinely carry out elaborate specification searches, involving iterated attempts to find an appropriate fit between models and data. For this reason, a major literature within econometrics has discussed procedures and tools that help quantitative researchers conduct their specification searches in a disciplined manner. This literature recognizes that the quantitative analysis of observational data routinely involves an iterated, partly inductive, mode of research.

A closely related point concerns data mining. Indiscriminate data mining is a bad idea, and the statement that selecting relevant explanatory variables requires theory is uncontroversial (no. 27). However, as just noted, all research has an inductive component, and we should not foreclose the possibility of accidental discoveries. The challenge is to be open to such discoveries that are not anticipated by our theory; yet at the same time to avoid the atheoretical, indiscriminate pursuit of new hypotheses, which may lead to findings that are not analytically meaningful.

Finally, returning to the issue of endogeneity (no. 31), selecting cases so as to avoid this problem makes sense in that it facilitates causal inference. Yet this priority absolutely should not preclude, for example, looking at processes of change over time, where endogeneity is commonly present. Given the larger intellectual movement in recent decades toward the historicization of the social sciences, scholars who study causal processes over a long time horizon must routinely treat endogeneity as a problem to be confronted, rather than avoided.

e. *Independent Contribution of Qualitative Tools Is Undervalued. DSI* pays insufficient attention to the independent contributions of qualitative tools, sometimes too quickly subordinating them to a quantitative template. *DSI* makes an interesting argument that quantitative/formal work and interpretation are *similar* in an important respect: both simplify drastically, compared to the full complexity of reality (no. 15). While this is true, for the researcher trying to learn about the distinctive strengths of alternative methodological approaches, the dissimilarity of interpretation and quantitative/formal analysis is a far more central concern, a theme that arises in chapter 13 below. *DSI*'s framing inappropriately deemphasizes the contributions of interpretive work, and of other qualitative approaches, to goals that a regression-oriented framework addresses much less successfully— including concept formation and fine-grained description.

Qualitative researchers also have distinctive perspectives on causal heterogeneity (no. 10). It is a central component within Ragin's framework, and Tarrow shows how qualitative methods provide valuable tools for explaining transitions and nonlinearity that have been discovered through quantitative analysis. With reference to separating the systematic and the random components of phenomena (no. 24), Munck suggests that qualitative researchers may approach this issue by employing insights about causal mechanisms and the larger research context. Isolating the systematic components can, in turn, provide a substitute for statistical control by eliminating the variance on the dependent variable caused by factors outside the focus of the analysis.

Finally, and most importantly, *DSI*'s arguments about strengthening causal inference through increasing the number of observations can be refined by recognizing the importance of different kinds of observations: that is, data-set observations and causal-process observations, a distinction introduced in chapter 1 above and explored at length in chapter 13 and in the appendix. Utilizing this distinction makes it easier to recognize the valuable leverage in causal inference that derives from within-case analysis—which has been a long-standing focus in discussions of qualitative methods and is an important concern in the chapters below by Rogowski, Collier, Mahoney, and Seawright, Munck, and McKeown, as well as in Tarrow's discussion of triangulation. *DSI* notes these procedures, but the book prematurely seeks to subordinate them to the standard tools of quantitative inference (*DSI* 85–87, 226–28).

To conclude, *DSI* articulates a clear summary of the mainstream quantitative framework in social science. At the same time, the book seeks to impose this framework on other kinds of research. In the process, *DSI* loses sight both of major weaknesses in the quantitative template and of many strengths that have made other tools worth developing in the first place. *DSI*'s arguments have stimulated scholars to rethink both the quantitative and qualitative traditions. Based on this rethinking, the chapters below seek to present a more balanced view of methodology and research design.

PART II

Critiques of the Quantitative Template

CHAPTER 3

Doing Good and Doing Better:
How Far Does the Quantitative Template Get Us?

Henry E. Brady

What kind of contribution is *Designing Social Inquiry* by Gary King, Robert O. Keohane, and Sidney Verba? Consider the traditional distinction between theology and homiletics.

Theology versus Homiletics

Theological seminaries distinguish between theology, or the systematic study of religious beliefs, and homiletics, the art of preaching the gospel convincingly. Theologians ask hard questions, develop new systems of theology, and often espouse opinions that would shock and horrify the practicing and devout members of the religion's congregations. Homiletics is about homilies; it is about sermons that are practical, down to earth, simple, and above all, reliable interpretations of the faith. Religions understand, as the social sciences may not, that the goal is to save souls and not simply to increase our knowledge or understanding of the world. For this reason, both theology and homiletics have pride of place in seminaries.

The social sciences have a great deal of theology, but very little homiletics. Perhaps this is why we have saved so few souls. And it may also be why we do such a bad job of training students. A little homiletics might go a long way toward improving our discipline.

Designing Social Inquiry (hereafter *DSI*) is a homily, not theology. There is art in a good homily. Like all good homiletic literature, *DSI* puts aside doubt and complexity. After all, who would want to burden the average graduate student with the tedious complexity of St. Thomas Aquinas in *Summa Theologica* or Paul Tillich in *Systematic Theology*? And who would recommend the self-doubt of St. Augustine's *Confessions* or Kierkegaard's *Fear and Trembling* or *The Sickness unto Death*? Better to give them Norman Vincent Peale's *The Power of Positive Thinking*.

DSI, however, is not just about positive thinking. It is closer to Moses Maimonides' *Guide for the Perplexed* or Luther's *A Catechism for the People, Pastor and Preacher*. It has a powerful message about the need for reform, self-sacrifice, and discipline on the part of all political scientists—especially qualitative researchers.[1] It puts forth a simple, straightforward faith. It tries very hard to treat qualitative researchers as souls worthy of salvation. And it envisions a unified social science in which there are "Two Styles of Research, One Logic of Inference" (3).[2] To practice this one logic of inference, *DSI* presents a simple, unified series of steps, a faith to live by, based upon insights from conventional quantitative methods and econometrics. In chapter 3, for example, we are told to:

- Construct falsifiable theories.
- Build theories that are internally consistent.
- Select dependent variables carefully.
- Maximize concreteness.
- State theories in as encompassing a way as possible.

---

[1]*Designing Social Inquiry*, subtitled *Scientific Inference in Qualitative Research*, begins by discussing the relationship between quantitative and qualitative research, but another dichotomy also runs through the book. Quite often the authors are more concerned with juxtaposing "small-N" versus "large-N" research than with the qualitative-quantitative distinction. These are not the same things. Small-N research is often qualitative, but it need not be, and large-N research can be qualitative. Roughly speaking, the qualitative-quantitative distinction revolves around issues of concept formation and measurement whereas the small-N versus large-N distinction brings up problems of defining the relevant populations, sampling from them, and dealing with statistical variability. I argue later in this chapter that these statistical issues are dealt with much more clearly in *DSI* than are those regarding concept formation and measurement. We return to these issues in chapter 12 below.

[2]This phrase resonates especially well with someone like myself who was brought up as a Catholic where the faithful must deal with the mystery of three manifestations of God (in the Father, Son, and Holy Spirit) in a monotheistic religion. By childhood training, I am quite receptive to a message of monomethodism, even in those circumstances where it requires a leap of faith.

In homiletic literature, exhortations such as these should be simple, and they need not always be completely consistent (witness the last two rules listed above). A good sermon should have clear points; it should avoid doubt; it should provide plenty of examples. The goal should be to convert the heathen qualitative researcher to the true faith.

This book—to its credit—does these things. It is an extraordinarily good piece of homiletic literature and it should be used in the classroom. It is very nicely written. It is generally lucid and well organized. No one can fail to hear its message.

And indeed, we should all hear the message that is preached. I, for one, have great sympathy with this enterprise, having spent far too many hours listening to talks on comparative politics in which dependent variables or independent variables (or both) did not vary, in which selection bias seemed insurmountable, in which explanations seemed more like good stories than hard-won insights gained from ruling out alternative possibilities. In my introductory statistics classes, I, too, have tried to point out to comparativists that they could do so much better if they avoided omitted variable bias, stopped selecting on the dependent variable, and so forth. I have used some of the same diagrams displayed in the text of *DSI* (e.g., figures 4.1, 5.1, and 5.2) to make didactic points about good research.

Why, then, do I find myself worried about what this book tries to do? Perhaps I am worried because, despite the authors' desire for a unified approach to social science, there may be something wrong with quantitative researchers[3]—who luxuriate in large numbers of observations and even the possibility under some circumstances of doing experiments—trying to impose a code of conduct, a morality, taken from their own experiences. Certainly the authors, three of the most distinguished and intelligent political scientists in our discipline, mean well, think well, and write well. But I worry that, in the end, they are a little like the Reverend Ike who, when asked how he reconciled living in luxury while he preached to the poor, responded that he believed that the best thing you could do for the poor was not to be one of them. The book ends, in fact, with a chapter on "Increasing the Number of Observations."[4] Is this the best thing we can do for qualitative researchers: to recommend that they not be "small-N" researchers?

Qualitative researchers may indeed profit by increasing the number of observations, and one of the great strengths of *DSI* is that it tries to indicate how the poor in observations can become richer in their understanding. At the same time, the book's unspoken presumption that qualitative researchers are inevitably handicapped by lack of quantification and small numbers of observations is bothersome.

---

[3]Keohane is not a quantitative researcher, but two of the authors, King and Verba, certainly are, and the book's approach is so rooted in quantitative research that it seems fair to make this assertion.

[4]This chapter means more and does more than just suggest that qualitative researchers get more data, although that is one of the recommendations. I make more comments about this interesting chapter later in the review.

It ignores the possibility that quantitative researchers may sometimes be handi-capped by procrustean quantification and a jumble of dissimilar cases.

Descending from the Rhetorical Heights

I have a number of specific concerns about *DSI*. Here I will focus on two: my be-lief that *DSI* is handicapped by a view of causality too closely tied to the experi-mental method, and my desire to see more discussion of measurement problems.

Before addressing these concerns, I wish to establish a fair standard for evalu-ating *DSI*. Given that I consider *DSI* to be a homily, and not a work of theology, it may be worth remarking that the value of the *Baltimore Catechism* in which I was drilled as a child should *not* be measured by its logic and argument. Rather it should be evaluated in terms of how many children it saved from perdition. In the end, I think that is how *DSI* should be judged. Does it work in a classroom? Does it make us better social scientists? By opening up a dialogue with qualitative re-searchers, the book does make us better, but in its treatment of causation and measurement, *DSI* may not help us very much.

Explanation and Causality

After a useful discussion of descriptive inference or "establishing facts" in chapter 2, *DSI* goes on in chapter 3 to discuss "Causality and Causal Inference." As far as I can tell, they equate explanation with causal thinking.[5] Yet philoso-

---

[5]It is not exactly clear how "explanation" fits into *DSI*'s categories of descriptive and causal inference, but one reasonable interpretation is that the authors consider expla-nation to be identical with causal inference. In the first three paragraphs of chapter 2, they repeatedly refer to the "dual goals of describing and explaining" (34). They also note that "description and explanation both depend upon rules of scientific inference. In this chap-ter we focus on description and descriptive inference" (34). This suggests that chapter 3, on "Causal Inference," is about explanation. Yet, things cannot be quite so simple, be-cause they go on to say that "as should be clear, we disagree with those who denigrate 'mere' description. Even if explanation—connecting causes and effects—is the ultimate goal, description has a central role in all explanation, and it is fundamentally important in and of itself." The first part of the sentence seems to define explanation as "connecting causes and effects," but the second part seems to say that description is also a form of explanation. In the sentence after this one, *DSI* retains the duality of description and ex-planation and seems to equate explanation with causal inference, but the book argues for the primacy of inference over either one: "It is not description versus explanation that distinguishes scientific research from other research; it is whether systematic inference is conducted according to valid procedures. Inference, whether descriptive or causal, quali-tative or quantitative, is the ultimate goal of all good social science" (34).

phers of science are not so sure that the only kind of explanation involves causality. Take, for example, "classification" explanations such as the observation that iron has certain properties because it appears in a certain column of the periodic table. This does not appear to be a causal explanation.[6] It could be argued that Bohr's atomic theory and its extensions in modern quantum mechanics provide a causal explanation, but this only amounts to saying that there may be causal explanations as well as classification explanations. Moreover, there was a substantial period of time when the classification explanation was all we had. Should we discard these explanations, even when they are all we have, because they do not appear to be causal? We are not so rich with explanations in the social sciences that we can afford to do this without good reason. Qualitative social scientists, in fact, seem especially fond of typologies and classification systems. Do these tools contribute to the explanatory enterprise? I do not personally have an answer to my question, so perhaps I should not fault *DSI* for failing to include a discussion of this difficult issue. But it is perplexing and thought provoking.

The approach to causality advanced in *DSI* is based upon an interesting framework developed by the statisticians Donald Rubin (1974, 1978) and Paul Holland (1986). The great strength of this approach, to my mind, is that it emphasizes that a definition of causality requires (a) the careful description of a counterfactual condition (what would have happened if the cause had been absent?) and (b) a comparison of what did happen with what would have happened had the cause been absent. These are two powerful points, and *DSI* is to be commended for bringing them to the forefront of our discussion. Researchers of all stripes should spend more time describing the counterfactual world that underlies their "becauses." What does it mean, for example, to say that "turnout is lower in that district because it has a high proportion of minorities"? What is the counterfactual world in which turnout would be higher? Is it simply one with a lower proportion of minorities? Would these nonminorities be like minorities in every other respect except race? How could this happen? What would it mean to have it happen?[7] These are not easy questions.

---

[6]For more discussion of this example and whether there are noncausal explanations, see Achinstein (1983: chap. 7). Brody and Grandy (1989) provide an excellent set of readings on these topics. Gary King has suggested (personal communication) that classification is a form of descriptive inference, but this seems to stretch *DSI's* concept of descriptive inference beyond distinguishing "the systematic component from the nonsystematic component of the phenomena we study" (56). It also adds to the confusion noted in the preceding footnote.

[7]I have deliberately chosen an example in which the putative cause is a characteristic that might be thought unchangeable. Holland, for example, argues that it is impermissible to call race or gender a cause because "for causal inference, it is critical that each unit be potentially exposable to any one of the causes. As an example, the schooling a student receives can be a cause, in our sense, of the student's performance on a test, whereas the student's race or gender cannot" (Holland 1986: 946). This point is not much in evidence

I have already argued that there might be explanation without causality. I think there might also be causal effects without (much) explanation. Suppose we find, to use *DSI*'s example, that incumbent legislators do better in elections than nonincumbent legislators. Suppose, in fact, we are as certain as we can be about this because we have done an experiment (random term limits, for example) with a large N to test it out. This finding immediately leads to other questions about what aspects of incumbency create this advantage (see, for example, Cain, Ferejohn, and Fiorina 1987). These questions amount to a desire to further specify the causal mechanism. *DSI* is not averse to specifying causal mechanisms, and the authors say that "any coherent account of causality needs to specify how the effects are exerted," but they believe that "our definition of causality is logically prior to the identification of causal mechanisms" (85–86). This claim of logical priority may or may not be true (I am not sure it is very important), but what is true is that a discussion of causality is inevitably tied up with a discussion of explanation, theories, and causal mechanisms, and *DSI* does not pay enough attention to this relationship. There is no discussion of Hempel's (1965) covering laws, of Wesley Salmon's (1984) model of statistical explanation, of Scriven's (1975) "Causation as Explanation," and many other important works on this topic. This is surprising because the philosophical literature, at least, cannot seem to separate the discussion of these issues.[8]

The statistics literature, in fact, is exceptional in defining causality without discussing explanation. Perhaps this is because statisticians want a method of inference that relies only upon the research design and the data, and not at all upon the substance of the research. Yet the net result of the Rubin-Holland papers is a definition that seems surprisingly distant from the problems of theory building and explanation as it exists in the sciences. Most importantly, this approach provides no guidance on what constitutes a "good" explanation beyond what constitutes a good causal inference. Yet an analysis of the impact of incumbency may be an excellent causal inference while being a bad explanation.[9]

---

in *DSI*, and I think the authors were wise to minimize its importance because it certainly seems possible to imagine a world in which gender or race changes, but nothing else.

[8]Brody and Grandy (1989), for example, link them in part 2 of their reader entitled "Explanation and Causality." Scriven (1975) joins the two concepts in his famous article on causation as explanation, and every philosophical writer of whom I am aware deals with explanation and causation together.

[9]If the incumbency example does not persuade, consider a doctor called upon to explain the incidence of psychedelic experiences in a remote culture. In an experiment, the doctor shows that a treated group eating a plant diet consisting of peyote, hemp, beans, carrots, and other plants has a statistically significant increase in their incidence of psychedelic experiences. Thus, eating plants causes psychedelic experiences. This is clearly an incomplete explanation. I wish *DSI* had discussed by what method I might improve it. I think a discussion of a "good explanation" that went beyond methods for finding causal impacts would have gone a long way toward solving this problem.

After defining causality, *DSI* goes on to describe a method for causal infer-ence. In this, as in its definition, *DSI* is guided by the work of Rubin and Holland. The major strength and weakness of this approach is its reliance upon the meta-phor of the controlled experiment for solving the problem of causal inference. Holland tells us that:

> because experimentation is such a powerful scientific and statistical tool and one that often introduces clarity into discussions of specific cases of causation, I un-abashedly draw on the language and framework of experiments for the model for causal inference. It is not that I believe an experiment is the only proper setting for discussing causality, but I do feel that an experiment is the simplest such set-ting. (1986: 946)

Fair enough. But it is worrisome that Holland finds it "beyond the scope of this article to apply the model for causal inference to nonrandomized studies" (949). Holland cites other literature (Rubin 1978) that essentially concludes that nonrandomized studies are exceptionally difficult to analyze. It is telling that Rubin's extension of the basic framework requires modeling "(1) the prior distri-bution of the potentially observable data, (2) the mechanism that selects experi-mental units for exposure to treatments and assigns treatments, and (3) the mecha-nism that chooses values to record for data analysis" (Rubin 1978: 35). This is a lot of modeling, and it only seems possible if we have strong theories to draw upon.

DSI provides a simplified version[10] of the Rubin and Holland framework, and in the process ignores some of its subtleties. The crucial part of *DSI*'s argument is its discussion of "Conditional Independence" (*DSI* 94–96). In the Rubin-Holland setup there are as many dependent random variables as there are variations in the treatment condition or the explanatory variable(s). In the simplest case with two levels of the treatment, this implies two random variables. One describes the val-ues on the dependent variable Y for the situation where all cases in the population[11] get one level of the treatment (call this Y^I to match *DSI*'s terminology) and the other is for the values on the dependent variable for the situation where all cases in the population get the other level of the treatment (call this Y^N and assume for simplicity that it is no treatment at all). In the real world and for any feasible de-sign, at least one of these values must be censored for each case. That is, we can-not give a case some treatment and no treatment at the same time. But Y^I and Y^N are not the censored variables; they include the unobserved (and unobservable)

---

[10]The authors do add one complexity by making a useful distinction between "real-ized causal effect" and "random causal effect," but they suppress so much notation and philosophical discussion in their presentation that many of the nuances in Holland's (1986) presentation are lost and none of the extensions in Rubin (1978) are discussed.

[11]In this exposition I ignore sampling problems by assuming observations are avail-able on all members of the population. If the entire population cannot be observed, then some assumption has to be made about random sampling.

values as well as the observed ones. A reasonable definition of the causal effect of the treatment is the average of Y^I minus the average of Y^N, but this quantity cannot be calculated because of the unobserved values in these two random variables.

In the Rubin-Holland framework, a necessary assumption for estimating a causal effect is independence between the assignment of treatments and the random variables Y^I and Y^N. This ensures, for example, that people who are high on Y^I are not more likely to get a high level of treatment than those who are low on Y^I. Consequently, we can be sure, for a large enough sample, that the size of the causal effect is the difference between (a) the average of the dependent variable for those who did get the treatment (this quantity can be calculated) and (b) the average of the dependent variable for those who did not get the treatment (another calculable quantity). One way to achieve this kind of independence is to have correctly carried out randomized experiments.

DSI's discussion of this is a bit opaque, and the authors seem to conflate the independence assumption with conditional independence.[12] Conditional independence is the assumption that the values of Y^I and Y^N conditional on "pre-exposure" or "control" variables are independent of the assignment of treatments. This is implied by independence but it is a much less stringent assumption. It is the assumption that is usually required for the analysis of quasi-experiments (Achen 1986). The conflation of these two different assumptions creates difficulties in the exposition because, whereas we have a method of random assignment to treatment for attaining independence, we have no comparable method for ensuring that the conditional independence assumption holds outside of a randomized design. The best we have is the checklist of "threats to internal validity" developed by Donald Campbell with Julian Stanley and Thomas Cook (Campbell and Stanley 1966; Cook and Campbell 1979).[13] The rest of *DSI* can be considered another approach to developing a checklist of threats to validity.

Unfortunately, *DSI* does not allow itself enough pages in this short section to make this very important transition from a discussion of causal inference for ex-

---

[12]This accounts for the confusing set of sentences at the beginning of section 3.3.2 where *DSI* first says that "conditional independence is the assumption that values are assigned to the explanatory variables independently of the values taken by the dependent variables" and then goes on to say, "that is, after taking into account the explanatory variables (or controlling for them), the process of assigning values to the explanatory variable is independent of both (or, in general two or more) dependent variables, Y_i^N and Y_i^I" (94). The first quoted sentence must refer to the independence assumption (because conditional independence does not assume that the values assigned to the explanatory or control variables are independent of the values of the dependent variables) whereas the second quoted sentence appears to be about conditional independence.

[13]I was surprised to find that none of Campbell's publications were referenced in *DSI*. Besides the books referenced in the text of the present chapter, Campbell's selected papers on *Methodology and Epistemology for Social Science* (1988) make excellent reading.

periments to causal inference with "quasi-experiments." I wish the authors had taken more time to explain the independence assumption in detail and to show how randomized experiments might provide us with an operational procedure that would make this assumption plausible. In doing this, they would no doubt have come to the conclusion presented by Cook and Campbell (and updated and expanded recently by Heckman 1992) that there are many reasons to worry about the efficacy of randomization when humans are involved. There are numerous ways in which human beings can make the treatment endogenous by changing their behaviors. There are additional problems when dropouts (and hence censoring of observations) vary by treatment. And there are the difficulties of truly randomizing units when they are people or groups. Once these problems are recognized for randomized designs, it becomes easier to understand how difficult it is to ensure conditional independence for nonrandomized designs.

This transition section might also benefit from a more careful discussion of how theories provide the fundamental basis for making a claim of conditional independence. This is an extraordinarily important step, and knowing how to do it can help researchers avoid the inferential nihilism that has crept into some statisticians' discussion of causal thinking in the social sciences (e.g., Freedman 1991). According to this line of thinking, randomized experiments are practically the only reliable way to be confident that the conditions for reasonable inferences are met. Conditional independence is considered a chimera—seldom justifiable and usually accepted by the researcher as a matter of pure faith and nothing more. Indeed, if I accepted a notion of inference as bare of theories and the logic of explanation as that proposed by Rubin and Holland, I might also be skeptical of conditional independence. But I believe it is possible to use our prior knowledge, our theories, to carry out the three modeling steps laid out by Rubin (and cited above). Hence, I am more sanguine about the possibilities for cautiously asserting conditional independence.

It might be argued that I brood unnecessarily over technical points. But the section on "Conditional Independence" is the linchpin of *DSI*. The book wants to show us that concepts from conventional quantitative methods and econometrics will improve our ability to do qualitative research. It argues that the essence of good social research is establishing causal effects. This, in turn, requires making an assumption about conditional independence. This assumption, the authors believe, can be made plausible by avoiding clear-cut violations of it described in the statistics literature. Yet at the crucial transitional moment the argument seems muddy to me. Exactly how can we rule out the violations identified by quantitative researchers? Do quantitative researchers do a good job in this regard? How sure can I be that conditional independence holds after I have followed the instructions in *DSI?*

The authors of *DSI* go on to make many useful observations about causal assessment (although, to be honest, I think that Donald Campbell and his collaborators have more useful lists of threats to validity and more trenchant comments about the problems of doing quasi-experimental research). However, in *DSI* the crucial argument about assessing causation seems to be missing.

Measurement

DSI devotes eighteen pages to measurement (151–68). About five pages cover the "nominal, ordinal, interval" distinction found in the classic papers by S. S. Stevens (1946, 1951), and the remaining thirteen are about systematic and nonsystematic measurement error. The major results on measurement error are the classic ones dating from at least Tintner (1952) on how error in the dependent variable does not bias regression results whereas error in the independent variable produces bias in regression coefficients—in fact, biases them unambiguously downward in the bivariate case. These are well-known results, often repeated in one form or another in classic primers on research design such as Kerlinger (1979), but I do not think they get at the heart of what can be learned from the extensive literature on measurement.

DSI probably gives such short shrift to measurement because the authors believe that causal inference, roughly what Cook and Campbell call "internal validity," is the central problem of doing good social science. I trace this belief to their decision to equate explanation with causal thinking, and to define causal thinking in terms of a narrow analogy to the experimental model. Through this progression, the problems of theory construction, concepts, and measurement recede into the distance. Yet it seems to me that concept formation, measurement, and measurement validity are important in almost all research and possibly of paramount importance in qualitative research. Certainly notions such as "civil society," "deterrence," "democracy," "nationalism," "material capacity," "corporatism," "groupthink," and "credibility" pose extraordinary conceptual problems just as "heat," "motion," and "matter" did for the ancients. It may be comforting for the qualitative researcher to know that the true effects of these error-laden variables are even larger in magnitude than what we would estimate using a standard regression equation, but most qualitative researchers are struggling with much more basic problems such as figuring out what it means to measure their fundamental concepts. These problems are certainly not solved by telling us to decide whether the concept is nominal, ordinal, or interval and by admonishing us to "use the measure that is most appropriate to our theoretical purposes" (*DSI* 153).

I will not pretend to have the answers to the problems of measurement validity in qualitative research, but I think that the debates on these problems would have been advanced by citing some of the more recent literature in this area. Among the notions that come to mind, let me mention three topics that might have been included. Something might have been said about the conceptualizations of measurement developed by Krantz, Luce, Suppes, and Tversky in their magisterial three-volume work on *Foundations of Measurement* (1971–1990), the related notions put forth by Georg Rasch in his quirky but very influential work on *Probabilistic Models for Some Intelligence and Attainment Tests* (1980 [1960]), and the fascinating *Notes on Social Measurement* (1984a) penned by Otis Dudley Duncan, who followed up this broadside on the limitations of social measurement with a brief for using Rasch models in the social sciences (1984b). These works show that *qualitative* comparisons are the basic building blocks of any approach to measurement, thus bridging the "quantitative-qualitative" divide by showing that the two approaches are intimately related to one another. This discussion would have easily led to a second topic: the dimensionality of concepts, the nature of similarity judgments that often underlie concept formation, and the role of taxonomies and classifications in science. Finally, there might have been a survey of how the LISREL framework (Bollen and Lennox 1991), especially when it is combined with the "multitrait-multimethod approach" of Campbell and Fiske (1959), sheds light on the practical problems of measurement.

Let me discuss each of these literatures. Duncan's observations on Stevens's scale types are probably the best starting place:

> I conclude that the Stevens theory of scale types, pruned of its terribly misleading confusion of classifications and binary variables with N scales, augmented to take more explicit account of the scales used in measuring numerousness and probability, and specified more clearly so that the examples could be properly understood and assessed, has utility in suggesting the appropriate mathematical and numerical treatment of numbers arising from different kinds of measurement. *Still, a theory of scale types is not a theory of measurement.* And I, for one, am doubtful that any amount of study devoted to either of those topics can teach you how to measure social phenomena, though it can conceivably be helpful in understanding exactly what is achieved by a proposed method of measurement or measuring instrument. (1984a: 154, italics added)

Lest anyone miss Duncan's point, his next chapter is entitled "Measurement: The Real Thing." What is "the real thing"? Krantz, Luce, Suppes, and Tversky (1971–1990) provide the fullest answer to this question, but Duncan provides a more accessible treatment. Measurement, Duncan argues, is not the same as quantification, and it must be guided by theories that emphasize the relationships of one measure to another. Take, for example, that favorite illustration of introductory methods classes, the measurement of temperature. Although the development of thermometry involves a complicated interplay between theory and invention, one of the important milestones was the discovery of the gas law for which temperature is proportional to pressure times volume. Thermometry only began to progress beyond crude ordinal distinctions such as cold, warm, or hot to true interval scales once laws like the gas law made it clear that temperature could be measured by the change in volume of some material under constant pressure.

One of the distinctive features of this way of measuring temperature is that it relies upon a simple multiplicative law, which relates temperature to two quantities that can be "extensively" measured. Extensive measurement refers to the use

of the standard millimeter, gram, second, or some other quantity that can be duplicated so that a number of them can be added together ("concatenated") and compared with some object or phenomenon whose length, weight, duration, or other
feature is unknown. There is no such standard for temperature, but it can still be
measured because it is related to two quantities that can be measured extensively
(i.e., volume as length times width times height and pressure as mass times length
per time and area squared).

A fundamental difficulty facing empirical social science is the apparent im-
possibility of developing extensive measurements of many important theoretical
quantities. Consider, for example, the notion of utility that is basic to both economics and public choice theory. Utility cannot be measured extensively, but
economists avoid this difficulty through an ingenious ploy: They throw utility out
of their empirical models by deriving demand curves from the maximization of
utility with respect to a budget constraint that consists of the sum of prices times
quantities. This produces a demand curve—an equation in prices and quantities—
both of which can be measured extensively. This ploy, unfortunately, does not
appear to be readily available to political scientists.

The contribution of Rasch (1980 [1960]; see also Andrich 1988) and of
Krantz, Luce, Suppes, and Tversky (1971–1990) in their method of "conjoint
measurement" has been to show how measurement can be carried out without an
extensive measure that can be duplicated and combined: all that is needed is the
ability to make *qualitative* distinctions about the amount of each of several variables that are thought to be multiplicatively related to one another. Rasch's
method, designed for scoring achievement tests, has the great virtue that it scores
both test-takers and the items on the test simultaneously.

All this fancy talk does not provide us with a straightforward way to measure
the basic concepts in qualitative social science, yet it does provide us with some
clues about how we might go about measuring these concepts. First, it suggests
that we have two basic strategies for measurement. We can either try to define a
concept extensively (as with length, weight, prices, or quantities) or conjointly (as
with achievement tests and subjective probability). Thus we can measure democracy extensively by the fraction of the population enfranchised or by the number
of parties, or we can measure it conjointly by using ratings from knowledgeable
observers. If we use the second method, as qualitative researchers might be inclined to do, then we might want to think about whether we should scale the raters
as well as the countries that are rated. Maybe raters differ in their willingness to
call a country a democracy; maybe they even have biases of some sort or another.

Second, this discussion suggests that theories must help to guide the measurement process. In their impressive series of papers on bias in electoral systems,
Gelman and King (1994) follow just this strategy with a simple framework for
thinking about representation. Steven Fish (1995) also does this (more implicitly
than explicitly) in his discussion of the development of civil society in Russia. One
of his indicators of civil society is the aggregation of interests by groups, which he

describes as the group's "identification of 'cleavage issues' and the formulation of specific goals and agendas [and] . . . the formation of a collective identity, which includes the identification of a membership" (53–54). Although Fish does not provide a mathematical description of his measure, it could be conceptualized as the degree to which participation or membership in a group is highly correlated with some politically relevant characteristic or cleavage. This amounts to defining this component of civil society as the product of group participation and a politically relevant characteristic—a multiplicative relationship of the sort described by measurement theorists as indicative of true measurement. Fish's approach makes sense partly because it has exactly this form. Hence, measurement theory provides a clear-cut check on when we can say that we have the framework for measuring something.[14]

This approach leads immediately into the next topic I mentioned above. There is a very rich literature on the "topology" of measurement that indicates what is required for single or multidimensional measures; what is required for dimensionality itself; what is required before something is considered the same as something else; and under what conditions objects can be better taxonomized using "trees" or Euclidian space. These methods are now widely used in biology to inform studies of evolution. I suspect that they would be quite useful for the qualitative researcher who wants to trace the evolution of the concept of democracy over time, or the similarities and differences among contemporary democracies.[15] After all, qualitative researchers often spend a great deal of time and effort developing typologies and taxonomies.

Finally, although I often worry about the wholesale use of LISREL in survey research, I think the marriage of factor analysis to simultaneous equation modeling in LISREL has made many researchers more aware of measurement problems. Kenneth Bollen (1993) presents an exemplary use of this technique in his analysis of ratings, developed by three different scholars, of political liberties and democratic rule in countries around the world. By having two concepts in mind, Bollen is able to search for "discriminant" as well as "convergent" validity as Campbell and

---

[14]Gary King (personal communication) suggests that these are points for quantitative researchers and not qualitative researchers because they deal with quantitative measures. Putting aside the fact that a discussion of measurement error or Stevens's scale types assumes the same thing (and the entirety of *DSI* is based upon the premise that quantitative methods provide lessons for qualitative researchers), it is worth noting that qualitative researchers also engage in comparisons that amount to a form of measurement. Qualitative researchers should know that quantitative research relies upon just the kinds of comparative statements that are at the core of qualitative research. In fact, a discussion of this sort would lead to a conclusion that qualitative and quantitative research are not really different at all.

[15]Those interested in these topics should peruse the pages of *Psychometrika* or the *Journal of Classification.* Krantz, Luce, Suppes, and Tversky (1971–1990) also explore many of these issues.

Fiske (1959) tell us we should do. Bollen allows for the possibility that raters may have biases, and he finds, for example, that one rater "tends to favor countries in Central America and South America, western industrial nations, and, to a lesser extent, countries in the Oceania region" while providing lower scores for sub-Saharan Africa, Eastern Europe, and Asia. One can imagine extending Bollen's work by adding other methods for rating democracy and by examining (as he does in a preliminary way) how the characteristics of the raters affect their ratings. Bollen's work suggests that qualitative researchers might improve their understanding of concepts by considering various definitions of them, by considering concepts closely related to them, and by considering concepts that are different from them. This strategy, for example, is followed by Hanna Pitkin in her classic work on representation (1967).[16]

An exploration of measurement issues along the lines sketched above would benefit both quantitative and qualitative researchers. Indeed, a discussion of these matters is worthwhile even if it only shows qualitative researchers how quantitative work must also grapple with complex measurement problems. Because its authors want to be constructive and want to instruct, *DSI* invariably tries to show how quantitative notions can improve qualitative research. This is laudable, but it leads the authors to neglect the multitude of problems that confront quantitative researchers, and it ignores the extent to which quantification is based upon qualitative judgments. Both qualitative and quantitative researchers might benefit from a less didactic approach that revealed problems as well as putative solutions. This might lead to a common effort to solve problems of concept formation and measurement that vex both quantitative and qualitative researchers.

Conclusion

DSI is an excellent sermon, without much condescension, on what qualitative researchers can learn from quantitative researchers. As a work on methodology it has some substantial defects, such as equating explanation with causal inference, proposing a narrow definition of causality, and drawing far too little sustenance from a strong literature on measurement and concept formation. But it also has substantial strengths. First and foremost, it opens a conversation between qualitative and quantitative researchers, and that is very good. Second, its presentation of causal thinking in terms of counterfactual reasoning forces researchers to consider more carefully the counterfactuals behind their putative causal models. Third, it has an interesting discussion of selection bias that should be useful to many re-

---

[16]Pitkin, of course, describes her methodology as "linguistic" analysis, and quantitative researchers might improve themselves by becoming more familiar with her methods.

searchers.[17] Fourth, the final chapter on "Increasing the Number of Observations" is one of the most important notions in the book. I wish *DSI* had given more concrete examples of how to do this, and I wish the authors had warned of the dangers of spatial and temporal autocorrelation that can thwart innovative attempts to increase observations, but the basic concept is a very important one.

Students will definitely profit from reading this book. The discipline has already benefited from the discussions it has kicked off. I look forward to seeing a generation of graduate students uplifted and improved by reciting its useful and informative homilies.

---

[17]I wish, however, that they had not used the term "selection bias" (*DSI* 126) in an example that clearly involves sampling error. The example is presented in a section entitled "The Limits of Random Selection" so the authors may have not meant to use the term "selection bias" except in a colloquial fashion, but it is disconcerting, and certainly confusing, nevertheless.

CHAPTER 4

Some Unfulfilled Promises of Quantitative Imperialism

Larry M. Bartels

King, Keohane, and Verba's *Designing Social Inquiry: Scientific Inference in Qualitative Research* (hereafter *DSI*) is an important addition to the literature on research methodology in political science and throughout the social sciences. It represents a systematic effort by three of the most eminent figures in our discipline to codify the basic precepts of quantitative inference and apply them with uncommon consistency and self-consciousness to the seemingly distinct style of qualitative research that has produced most of the science in most of the social sciences over most of their history. The book seems to me to be remarkably interesting and useful both for its successes, which are considerable, and for its failures, which are also, in my view, considerable.

Here I shall touch only briefly upon one obvious and very important contribution of the book, and upon one respect in which the authors' argument seems to me to be misguided. The rest of my discussion will be devoted to identifying some of the authors' more notable unfulfilled promises—not because they are somehow characteristic of the book as a whole, but because they are among the more important unfulfilled promises of our entire discipline. If *DSI* stimulates progress on some of these fronts, as I hope and believe it will, the book will turn out to represent a very significant contribution to qualitative methodology.

The Contribution and a Shortcoming

Anyone who thinks about social research primarily in terms of quantitative and statistical inference, as I do, has probably thought—and perhaps even said out loud—that the world would be a happier place if only qualitative researchers would learn and respect the basic rudiments of quantitative reasoning. By presenting those rudiments clearly, engagingly, and with a minimum of technical apparatus, *DSI* has helped shine the light of basic methodological knowledge into many rather dark corners of the social sciences. For that we owe its authors profound thanks.

At another level *DSI*'s argument seems to be misguided, although in a way that seems unlikely to have significant practical consequences. It is hard to doubt that "all qualitative and quantitative researchers would benefit by more explicit attention to this logic [i.e., the logic "explicated and formalized clearly in discussions of quantitative research methods"] in the course of designing research" (3). However, it simply does not seem to follow that "all good research can be understood—indeed, is best understood—to derive from the same underlying logic of inference" (4). Even if we set aside theorizing of every sort, from Arrow's (1951) theorem on the incoherence of liberal preference aggregation to Collier and Levitsky's (1997) conceptual analysis of scores of distinct types and subtypes of "democracy," it seems pointless to attempt to force "all good [empirical] research" into the procrustean bed of "scientific inference" set forth by *DSI*. Would it be fruitful—or even feasible—to recast such diverse works as Michels's *Political Parties* (1915), Polanyi's *The Great Transformation* (1944), Lane's *Political Ideology* (1962), Thompson's *The Making of the English Working Class* (1963), and Fenno's *Home Style* (1978) in the concepts and language of quantitative inference? Or are these not examples of "good research"?

The authors of *DSI* attempt to skirt the limitations of their focus by conceding that "analysts should simplify their descriptions only after they attain an understanding of the richness of history and culture. . . . [R]ich, unstructured knowledge of the historical and cultural context of the phenomena with which they want to deal in a simplified and scientific way is usually a requisite for avoiding simplifications that are simply wrong" (43). But since they provide no scientific criteria for recognizing "understanding" and "unstructured knowledge" when we have it, the system of inference they offer is either too narrow or radically incomplete. Perhaps it doesn't really matter whether we speak of the process of "attain[ing] an understanding" as a poorly understood but indispensable requirement for doing science or as a poorly understood but indispensable part of the scientific process itself. I prefer the latter formulation, but the authors' apparent insistence upon the former will not keep anyone from relying upon—or aspiring to produce—"understanding" and "unstructured knowledge."

Omissions and an Agenda for Research

Most importantly, I am struck by what *DSI* leaves out of its codification of good inferential practice. I emphasize these limitations because they seem to suggest (though apparently unintentionally) an excellent agenda for the future development of qualitative and quantitative methodology. As is often the case in scientific work, the silences and failures of the best practitioners may point the way toward a discipline's subsequent successes. Here I shall provide four examples drawn from *DSI*'s discussions of uncertainty, qualitative evidence, measurement error, and multiplying observations.

Uncertainty

One of *DSI*'s most insistent themes concerns the importance of uncertainty in scientific inference. Its authors proclaim that "inferences without uncertainty estimates are not science as we define it" (9), and implore qualitative researchers to get on the scientific bandwagon by including estimates of uncertainty in their research reports (9 and elsewhere). But how, exactly, should well-meaning qualitative researchers implement that advice? Should they simply attempt to report their own subjective uncertainty about their conclusions? How should they attempt to reason from uncertainty about various separate aspects of their research to uncertainty about the end results of that research, if not by the standard quantitative calculus of probability? What sorts of checks on subjective reports of uncertainty about qualitative inferences might be feasible, when even the systematic policing mechanism enshrined in the quantitative approach to inference is routinely abused to the point of absurdity (Leamer 1978, 1983; Freedman 1983)? Since *DSI* offers so little in the way of concrete guidance, its emphasis on uncertainty can do little more than sensitize researchers to the general limitations of inference in the qualitative mode without providing the tools to overcome those limitations. As far as I know, such tools do not presently exist; but their development should be high on the research agenda of qualitative methodologists.

Qualitative Evidence

DSI's discussion of the respective roles and merits of quantitative and qualitative evidence is equally sketchy. While its authors rightly laud Lisa Martin's (1992) *Coercive Cooperation* and Robert Putnam's (1993) *Making Democracy Work* for combining quantitative and qualitative evidence in especially fruitful ways (5), their discussion provides no clear account of *how*, exactly, Martin's or Putnam's juxtaposition of quantitative and qualitative evidence bolsters the force of their conclusions. Martin's work is rushed precipitously off the stage (as most of *DSI*'s concrete examples are), while Putnam's work only reappears—other than in an unrelated discussion of using alternative quantitative indicators of a single underlying theoretical concept (223–24)—in a discussion of qualitative immersion as a source of *hypotheses* rather than *evidence*. This in turn leads to the rather patronizing conclusion that "any definition of science that does not include room for ideas regarding the generation of hypotheses is as foolish as an interpretive account that does not care about discovering truth" (38).

There is more going on here than a simpleminded distinction between (qualitative) hypothesis generation and (quantitative) hypothesis testing, or a simpleminded faith that two kinds of evidence are better than one. Qualitative evidence does more than suggest hypotheses, and analyses combining quantitative and qualitative evidence can and sometimes do amount to more than the sum of their parts. The authors of *DSI* do little to illuminate those facts. But the larger and more important point is that nobody else does very well either. Just as the "persuasive force" of such classic works of social science as V. O. Key's (1984 [1949]) *Southern Politics in State and Nation,* Stouffer et al.'s (1949) *The American Soldier,* and Berelson et al.'s (1954) *Voting* "is not easily explained in conventional statistical theory even today" (Achen 1982: 12), neither is the persuasive force of these and other compelling works convincingly accounted for by partisans of interpretive, ethnographic, historical, or any other brand of qualitative inquiry.

With reference to both uncertainty and qualitative evidence, the limitations of *DSI*'s analysis faithfully reflect the limitations of the existing methodological literature on qualitative inference. Other gaps in *DSI*'s account are attributable to the limitations of the theory of quantitative inference it offers as a model for qualitative research. As a quantitative methodologist—and the coauthor of a rather optimistic survey of the recent literature in quantitative political methodology (Bartels and Brady 1993)—I am chagrined to notice how wobbly and incomplete are some of the inferential foundations that *DSI* claims are "explicated and formalized clearly in discussions of quantitative research methods" (3). Again, two examples will suffice to illustrate the point.

Measurement Error

The first example of the weak foundations of inferential claims is *DSI*'s treatment of measurement error, which—like much of the elementary textbook wisdom on that subject—is both incomplete and unrealistically optimistic. The authors assert that unsystematic (random) measurement error in explanatory variables "unfailingly [biases] inferences in predictable ways. Understanding the nature of these biases will help ameliorate or possibly avoid them" (155). Later, they assert more specifically that the resulting bias "takes a particular form: it results in the estimation of a weaker causal relationship than is the case" (158). At the end of their discussion the authors acknowledge that their analysis is based upon a model with a single explanatory variable. However, they assert that it "applies just the same if a researcher has many explanatory variables, but only one with substantial random measurement error," or if researchers "study the effect of each variable sequentially rather than simultaneously" (166). Their only suggestion of potential complications is a claim that "if one has multiple explanatory variables and is simultaneously analyzing their effects, and if each has different kinds of measurement error, we can only ascertain the kinds of biases likely to arise by extending the formal analysis" (166).

DSI's assertion about the case of several explanatory variables, where only one is measured with substantial error, is quite misleading in failing to note that the bias in the parameter estimate associated with the one variable measured with substantial error will be propagated in complicated ways to all of the other parameter estimates in the analysis. This will bias them upward or downward depending on the pattern of correlations among the various explanatory variables. The book's assertion about sequential rather than simultaneous analysis of several explanatory variables is also misleading, at least in the sense that the resulting omitted variable bias may mitigate, exacerbate, or reverse the bias attributable to measurement error. And the promise of "ascertain[ing] the kinds of biases likely to arise" in more complicated situations "by extending the formal analysis" (*DSI* 166) can in general be redeemed only if we have a good deal of prior information about the nature and magnitudes of the various errors—information virtually impossible to come by in all but the most well-understood and data-rich research settings (Achen 1983; Cowden and Hartley 1993). Thus, while it seems useful to have alerted qualitative researchers to the fact that measurement error in explanatory variables may lead to serious biases in parameter estimates, it seems disingenuous to suggest that quantitative tools offer reliable ways to "ameliorate or possibly avoid" (155) those biases in real qualitative research.

Multiplying Observations

The second example is *DSI*'s chapter on "Increasing the Number of Observations," which seems equally disingenuous in asserting that "almost any qualitative research design can be reformulated into one with many observations, and that this can often be done without additional costly data collection if the researcher appropriately conceptualizes the observable implications that have already been gathered" (208). While it is right to emphasize the importance of "maximizing leverage" by using the available data to test many implications of a given theory (or even better, of several competing theories), *DSI*'s discussion obscures the fact that having many *implications* is not the same thing as having many *observations*. In order for our inferences to be valid, each of our many implications must itself be verified using a research design that avoids the pitfall of "indeterminacy" inherent in having more explanatory variables than relevant observations.

Larry M. Bartels

What, then, *is* a "relevant observation"? *DSI* provides the answer in its earlier, clear, and careful discussion of causal homogeneity.[1] Relevant observations are those for which "all units with the same value of the explanatory variables have the same expected value of the dependent variable" (91). But the more we succeed in identifying diverse empirical implications of our theories, the less likely it will be that those diverse implications can simply be accumulated as homogeneous observations in a single quantitative model. Having a richly detailed case study touching upon many implications of the same theory or theories is no substitute for "seek[ing] homogenous units across time or across space" (93), as *DSI* points out in the subsequent discussion of "process tracing" (226–28).

The authors of *DSI* allow that "attaining [causal] homogeneity is often impossible," but go on to assert in the next sentence that "understanding the degree of heterogeneity in our units of analysis will help us to estimate the degree of uncertainty or likely biases to be attributed to our inferences" (93–94). How is that? Again, the authors do not explain. But once again, the more important point is that nobody else does either—a point I am compelled to acknowledge despite my own efforts in that direction (Bartels 1996). If we accept *DSI*'s assertion that the "generally untestable" assumption of causal homogeneity (or the related assumption of "constant causal effects") "lies at the base of all scientific research" (93), this is a loud and embarrassing silence.

Conclusion

In the end, *DSI*'s optimistic-sounding unification of quantitative and qualitative research seems to me to promise a good deal more than it delivers, and a good deal more than it could possibly deliver given the current state of political methodology in both its qualitative and quantitative modes. But perhaps that is the genius of the book. By presenting a bold and beguiling vision of a seamless, scientific methodology of social inquiry, *DSI* may successfully challenge all of us to make some serious progress toward implementing that vision.

---

[1] *DSI* (91) uses the label "unit homogeneity" for this assumption.

CHAPTER 5

How Inference in the Social (but Not the Physical) Sciences Neglects Theoretical Anomaly

Ronald Rogowski

Designing Social Inquiry, by King, Keohane, and Verba (hereafter *DSI*), deserves praise for many reasons. It attempts, seriously and without condescension, to bridge the gap between qualitative and quantitative political science. It reminds a new generation of students, in both traditions, of some main characteristics of good theory (testability, operationalizability, and "leverage" or deductive fertility). It clarifies, even for the profoundly mathematically challenged, some of the central strictures of quantitative inference (why one cannot have more variables than cases or select on the dependent variable, or why it biases results if measurement of the independent variable is faulty). It abounds with practical wisdom on research design, case selection, and complementary methodologies. Perhaps most importantly, it opens a dialogue between previously isolated practitioners of these two forms of analysis and provokes worthwhile discussion.

For all of these reasons and more, the book should be, will be, and—indeed even in its samizdat forms—already has been widely assigned and read. It is, quite simply, the best work of its kind now available; indeed, it is very likely the best yet to have appeared.[1] At the same time, I think, *DSI* falters in its aim of evangel-

---

[1] The only competition, long out of print and aimed more at the advanced undergraduate level, is probably Lave and March (1975).

izing qualitative social scientists; and it does so, paradoxically, because it attends insufficiently to the importance of problemation and deductive theorizing in the scientific enterprise.

Problemation and Deductive Theorizing

As natural scientists have long understood (see Hempel 1966), inference proceeds most efficiently by three complementary routes: (1) making clear the essential model, or process, that one hypothesizes to be at work; (2) teasing out the deductive implications of that model, focusing particularly on the implications that seem a priori least plausible; and (3) rigorously testing those least plausible implications against empirical reality.[2] The Nobel physicist and polymath Richard Feynman may have put it best:[3]

> experimenters search most diligently, and with the greatest effort, in exactly those places where it seems most likely that we can prove our theories wrong. In other words we are trying to prove ourselves wrong as quickly as possible, because only in that way can we find progress. (1965: 158)

The classical example is Einstein's Theory of Relativity, which: (1) uniquely provided an overarching model that could explain both the anomalies and the enduring validities of classical Newtonian mechanics, indeed could subsume it as a special case; (2) had, among its many other implications, a quite specific, rather implausible, and previously untested one about how light reflected from the planet Mercury would be deflected by the sun's gravitation; and (3) appeared at the time to be precisely accurate in this specific and implausible implication.[4] To test, however rigorously, hypotheses that challenge no deeper theory or that themselves lack deductive implications is an inefficient route of scientific inference; while theories that are precise and deductively fertile enough can often be sustained or refuted by surprisingly unelaborate tests, including ones that involve few observations or that violate normally sacrosanct principles of selection.

DSI, I contend, emphasizes the third part of scientific inquiry, the rigorous testing of hypotheses, almost to the exclusion of the first two—the elaboration of precise models and the deduction of their (ideally, many) logical implications—

---

[2] Eckstein characterized this as the strategy of the "least-likely" case (1975: 118–19). See also Hempel (1966: 37–38).

[3] I owe this citation to Mark Lichbach.

[4] To quote a famous statement on this prediction in a letter of J. E. Littlewood to Bertrand Russell, written in 1919: "Dear Russell: Einstein's theory is completely confirmed. The predicted displacement was 1".72 and the observed 1".75 ± .06. Yours, J. E. L." Quoted in Russell (1969: 149).

and thus points us to a pure, but needlessly inefficient, path of social-scientific inquiry.

Theory and Anomaly: Some Examples

I can best illustrate these points by applying *DSI*'s strictures to some landmark works in comparative politics, often cited as worthy of emulation. Each work, it seems to me, would fail *DSI*'s tests and would be dismissed as insufficiently scientific. Yet in each case, the dismissal would be incorrect: the works illustrate— indeed epitomize—valid and efficient social-scientific inquiry; and the ways in which they do so illuminate the shortcomings in *DSI*'s analysis.

Three of the classical works that I have in mind are single-observation studies; one involves three cases, but all within a single region; one selects chiefly on the independent—but also on the dependent—variable, in ways deprecated by *DSI;* and one selects on the dependent variable. I propose: (1) to sketch each briefly; (2) to argue that the conventional wisdom is right, and *DSI* is wrong, with regard to these works' worth; and (3) to reflect on the deficiencies that these works reveal in *DSI*'s analysis.

The single-observation studies are Arend Lijphart's (1968) study of the Netherlands, *The Politics of Accommodation;* William Sheridan Allen's single-city examination, *The Nazi Seizure of Power;* and Peter Alexis Gourevitch's 1978 critique of Immanuel Wallerstein's *Modern World-System.* Each involves disconfirmation of a prevailing theory, by what Eckstein called the strategy of the "most likely" case (1975: 119).

Lijphart rightly saw in the Netherlands a serious empirical challenge to David Truman's (1951) then widely accepted theory of "cross-cutting cleavages." Truman had argued, plausibly enough, that mutually reinforcing social cleavages (class coterminous with religious practice, or religion with language) impeded social agreement and made conflict more likely. Only where each deep cleavage was orthogonal to another (e.g., Switzerland, where many Catholics are German-speaking, many Francophones Protestant) was social peace likely to endure. About the Netherlands, however, two things were abundantly clear: (1) it had virtually no cross-cutting cleavages; and (2) it had about as stable and amicable a democracy as one could find. Lijphart's study was taken at the time, I believe correctly, as having refuted Truman's theory.[5]

In attempting to explain popular support for such totalitarian movements as Fascism, many social scientists had, by the 1950s, accepted a theory whose roots went back to Montesquieu and Tocqueville but whose modern version had been

---

[5]Lijphart went on to conjecture, on the basis of the Dutch case, about the precise circumstances in which non-cross-cutting cleavages were compatible with civic peace; but that is secondary to the point I am arguing here.

shaped chiefly by Lederer (1940), Arendt (1958), and—the great synthesizer of this genre—Kornhauser (1959). Again simplifying it to the point of caricature, this theory held that societies were opened to totalitarianism's Manichean zealotries by the waning (e.g., through rapid modernization) of associational life—the disappearance of those "natural" groups that afforded meaning, balance, and a sense of efficacy. Totalitarian followers were "atomized" or "mass" individuals.

Tracing the growth of the National Socialist cause in a single midsized German town where it had prospered earlier and better than the average, however, Allen (1965) found, if anything, a superabundance of associational life: singing and shooting societies, card clubs, fraternal orders, religious associations, drinking groups, and *Stammtische* of long standing, to the point that one could hardly imagine a free evening in these proto-Fascists' lives. Neither could he observe any waning of this associational activity before or during the Nazi expansion, nor were Nazis drawn disproportionately from the less active (if anything, the contrary).[6] Only *after* Hitler came to power, with the Nazi *Gleichschaltung* of all associations, did activity decline. Allen's results were read (again, I think, rightly) as having strongly impugned an otherwise plausible theory.

A central assertion of Immanuel Wallerstein's *Modern World-System*, vol. 1 (1974), was that the "core" states of the world economy, from the sixteenth century onward, had been likeliest to develop strong states (in order to guarantee capitalist property rights and to protect trade routes) and to pursue linguistic and cultural homogeneity (in order to lower administrative and transaction costs). Yet as Gourevitch and others quickly observed, it was, in fact, a central European state of what Wallerstein had called the "semiperiphery" (i.e., Prussia) that developed arguably the strongest state in the early modern world and that came earliest to mass education and the pursuit of linguistic homogeneity (1978: esp. 423–27). The case seriously undermined this aspect of Wallerstein's theory; but Gourevitch went on to speculate—and Charles Tilly (1990) has subsequently advanced considerable argument and evidence to show—that in fact, the correlation was the reverse: The economically most advanced early modern states were often the least powerful, and vice versa.

Against the record amassed by these and other single-observation studies, *DSI* contends that "[I]n general . . . the single observation is not a useful technique for testing hypotheses or theories" (211), chiefly because measurement error may yield a false negative, omitted variables may yield an unpredicted result, or social-

---

[6]To be sure, *DSI* distinguishes between *cases* and *observations*; and Allen's study could be read as a single case that encompasses many observations, given that Allen examines a variety of groups and individuals. Such a reading, in my view, would fundamentally misunderstand the underlying theory, whose central independent variable is the level of association that individuals encounter. Given the theory, the town (or, at most, the class within the town) is the relevant observation; and Allen's study is therefore a single case *and* a single observation.

scientific theories are insufficiently precise.[7] The authors would have us accept that the Lijphart, Allen, and Gourevitch studies—and even more the sweeping inferences that most comparativists drew from them—were bad science; as *DSI* states explicitly, falsification from a single observation "is not the way social science is or should be conducted" (103).

Rudolf Heberle's (1963, 1970) justly famous exploration of Nazi support in Schleswig-Holstein is exemplary in doing what *DSI* calls "making many observations from few" (217); yet Heberle's research, too, would presumably fail to meet *DSI*'s standard. Long before Barrington Moore, Jr. (1967) solidified the thesis, analysts had conjectured a close link between labor-repressive agriculture and susceptibility to Fascism. It occurred to Heberle that the north German state of Schleswig-Holstein offered an ideal test of the thesis, containing, as it did, three distinct agricultural regions, characterized respectively by: (1) plantation agriculture on the East Elbian, or the "Junker" model (the Hill district); (2) prosperous family farms like those of western and southwestern Germany (the Marsh); and (3) hardscrabble, quasi-subsistence farming (the *Geest*). The asserted link to feudalism would predict the earliest and strongest Nazi support in the first of these regions; but in fact the Fascist breakthrough occurred in the *Geest,* among the marginalized subsistence farmers; the family farmers came along only considerably later, and the feudal region resisted almost to the end. This brilliantly designed little study thus seriously undermined, even before its precise formulation, what has since come to be known as the "Moore thesis" about the origins of Fascism.

Like Atul Kohli's (1987) three-state study of poverty policy in India, Heberle's examination inventively exploits within-country—in Heberle's case, within-region—variation. Yet *DSI* dismisses precisely this aspect of Kohli's analysis, on the ground that the values of both the explanatory and the dependent variables were known in advance; "selection, in effect, is on both the explanatory and dependent variables" so that "the design . . . provides no information about his causal hypothesis" (145). Of course, Heberle, by confining his attention to a single state, partially constrained himself against biased selection; but Schleswig-Holstein itself might represent only random variation, and so (*DSI* would surely say) could not be taken as refuting the hypothesized causal link between feudalism and Fascism. Again, I think, *DSI*'s strictures, taken literally, would dismiss a brilliant study as bad (or at least inadequate) social science.

My final two examples raise the stakes considerably, for they represent, by common consent, the very best of recent work in comparative politics. Yet Peter Katzenstein's *Small States in World Markets* (1985), by *DSI*'s lights, inadmissibly restricts variation on the independent and dependent variables; and Robert Bates's

---

[7]*DSI*'s strictures on the first two points are so sweeping that they must, by implication, include theories and hypotheses in the physical sciences. Hence I take it that *DSI* would also reject the confirmation of the theory of relativity and other cases alluded to by Hempel (1966: 77), which rested on single observations.

Markets and States in Tropical Africa (1981) impermissibly selects on the dependent variable.

Katzenstein, contesting the conventional wisdom that only large states were independent enough to be worth studying, deliberately restricted his focus to the smaller European states and, within that set, to the smaller states that were "close to the apex of the international pyramid of success," thus "excluding Ireland, Finland, and some of the Mediterranean countries" (1985: 21). His reasons were straightforward: (1) the cases that he did study were *anomalous*, for small, price-taking countries were widely supposed to face particular challenges in an uncertain international environment; and (2) they were *forerunners*, in the sense that all countries were rapidly becoming as dependent on international markets as these small ones had long been. To examine why countries that theoretically should not succeed in fact did so (reminiscent of Lijphart's strategy) and to attempt to discern a possible path of adaptation of larger states, seemed, both to Katzenstein and to his generally enthusiastic readership, a sensible strategy. Yet *DSI,* at least as I read the book, must hold Katzenstein guilty of two cardinal sins that largely vitiate his analysis: (1) instead of choosing his cases to guarantee some range of variation on the independent variable, he restricts his analysis to small (and therefore quite trade-dependent) states; and (2) more seriously, taking economic success or failure as his dependent variable, he looks only at instances of success.

Bates's book is an even clearer case of selection on the dependent variable. Exactly as Michael Porter's *Competitive Advantage of Nations* (1990) examines only cases of economic success and thus draws withering fire from *DSI* (133–34), Bates focuses almost entirely on cases of economic failure or, more precisely, on the remarkably uniform *pattern* of economic failure among the states of postindependence Africa. He nonetheless develops an account that most readers have found compelling: (1) that the failures all resulted from an economic policy that heavily taxed agricultural exports to subsidize investment in heavily protected manufactures; and (2) that this self-destructive economic policy was the inevitable result of a political constellation in which urban groups were organized and powerful, rural ones scattered and weak. While Bates supports his analysis by observing that the two African cases of relative economic success (i.e., Kenya and Côte d'Ivoire) were characterized by export-friendly policy and politically more powerful farmers, this part of his discussion is brief and clearly tangential to his main argument.

Why, despite their seemingly egregious sins,[8] are all of these works believed by most comparativists—rightly, in my judgment—to have provided convincing inferences about their topics of study? Chiefly, I submit, for two reasons, which shed much light on the problems of *DSI*'s account: (1) all of them tested, relied on,

---

[8]As regards selection on the dependent variable, *DSI* takes a particularly draconian stand: "We can . . . learn nothing about a causal effect from a study which selects observations so that the dependent variable does not vary" (147).

or proposed, clear and precise *theories;* and (2) all focused on *anomalies,* either in prevailing theories or in the world—cases that contradicted received beliefs or unexpected regularities that were too pronounced to be accidental.

The theories of cross-cutting cleavages (Truman 1951), atomization (e.g., Kornhauser 1959), world-systems (Wallerstein 1974), and feudal legacy (Moore 1967) had the great advantage of being precise enough to yield implications for single, or for very few, observations. Lijphart, Allen, Gourevitch, and Heberle, respectively, took brilliant scholarly advantage of that precision: (1) to seek out anomalous cases and, usually, (2) to conjecture intelligently about a more satisfactory general theory that could avoid such anomalies.

About small states and heavy reliance on external markets there was less a prevailing theory than a prevailing prejudice—that puniness entailed constraint, insecurity, and (barring extraordinary good luck) economic trouble. By adducing seven cases of small states that had consistently prospered, Katzenstein demonstrated that insecurity and poverty were far from inevitable; by showing that their strategies, in similar circumstances, had differed, he proved that they retained considerable freedom of policy; and by analyzing their marked similarities of historical development and present-day governance, he advanced a plausible (if in this work still conjectural)[9] theory of situational requisites for highly trade-dependent states.

The African economic devastation that Bates studied was usually "explained" by a mélange of misunderstood Marxism and economic illiteracy that stressed the "dependence" of the third world on the first. By invoking standard, simple economics, Bates easily showed that local policy, and not first-world plots, must be to blame. If domestic agricultural prices were systematically suppressed, one would expect to see smuggling and rural flight; if domestic industry was protected and subsidized, one would expect cartels, uncompetitive goods, and an overvalued currency; if taxes and controls poured power and resources into the hands of bureaucrats, one would anticipate a bloated public sector and vicious competition for place and favor. In each African case, all of these in fact prevailed, and no amount of external "dependence" could so easily explain this particular concatenation of disasters.

Yet this left a riddle no less profound than the original one: why should almost all governments of the region have deliberately chosen policies so inimical to aggregate welfare and to long-term growth? Just as a psychologist might become intrigued if all but one or two of the people on a certain street began suddenly to mutilate themselves, Bates pursued a "cluster analysis" (see *DSI* 148–49) of per-

---

[9]To be sure, by looking only at successful small European states, Katzenstein had to leave open the possibilities (1) that unsuccessful small states were also governed corporatively; and (2) that small non-European states had discovered quite different recipes for success.

verse African policies and reached his highly plausible conjecture that rural weakness produced a fatal "urban bias" (see Lipton 1976) in policy.[10]

In the works of Katzenstein and Bates, then, no less than in those cited earlier, the crucial ingredient was clear, precise, powerful ("high leverage") theory with what Lave and March (1975) tellingly called a "sense of process," that is, intuitively plausible causal links. In both accounts, universally accepted economic theory underpinned the critique of received wisdom: if small, price-taking firms survived in uncertain markets, why not small, price-taking countries; if all of the symptoms of the African cases were consistent with systematic price distortions, what other diagnosis was possible? The core of Katzenstein's alternative account was a story about how democratic corporatism facilitated flexible adjustment to external markets; the core of Bates's account, a hypothesized link between power and policy. That both arguments were so clear, plausible, and precise contributed crucially to their persuasiveness.

Lessons

DSI (127), in contrast, frequently chooses as examples hypotheses that seem obvious or that lack deductive fertility. To prove, for example, that declining Communist societies were more likely to spawn mass movements of opposition the less repressive the old regime was neither contravenes received wisdom nor carries broader implications for other cases.

The aspects of larger theory and of "sense of process," consequently, seem to be sorely absent from *DSI*'s prescriptions for social inquiry. While the authors are right to fear our natural tendency to see patterns where none exist (21), they emphasize insufficiently the centrality of patterns—indeed, of "paradigms" (Kuhn 1962)—to efficient scientific inquiry. A powerful, deductive, internally consistent theory can be seriously undermined, at least in comparative politics, by even one wildly discordant observation (Lijphart's Netherlands). On the positive side, a powerful theory can, by explaining an otherwise mysterious empirical regularity (European small-state corporatism, African economic failure), gain provisional acceptance at least as a highly plausible conjecture worthy of further research. As most discussions of spurious correlation make clear, we gain confidence in a proposed explanation to the extent that it *both* (1) fits the data *and* (2) "makes sense" in terms of its consistency with other observations and its own deductive implications. *DSI*, it seems to me, emphasizes the former at the expense of the latter. In consequence, its advice to area specialists focuses almost entirely on "increasing

---

[10]It is worth noting that Bates has pursued this conjecture *not* through any large-N study, but by close analysis of an apparently anomalous case: Colombia, where dispersed coffee farmers of modest means prevailed politically not only against city dwellers but over concentrated plantation owners of considerable wealth.

the number of observations" (chap. 6). Many comparativists, I think, would instead counsel: "Choose better theory, which can make better use of few or single observations."[11]

Valuable as *DSI*'s strictures are, I fear that devout attention to them may paralyze, rather than stimulate, scientific inquiry in comparative politics. The authors write eloquently and insightfully about the trade-offs between close observation of a few cases and more cursory measurement of many (chap. 2, esp. 66–68); I wish they had as perceptively discussed how better theory permits inference from fewer cases, allows restriction on the independent variable, and may even profit from judicious selection on the dependent variable.

In short, I suspect *DSI* does not mean quite as stern a message as it sends; or perhaps the authors view the studies I have discussed here in a different and more redeeming light. However, the book would have spoken more clearly to comparativists if it had specifically addressed the major literature of the less quantitative tradition.

---

[11]As I note at the outset, *DSI* does discuss—at some length and quite sensibly—some major characteristics of good theory (section 3.5). The authors seem, however, to despair that social-scientific theories can ever be precise enough to permit valid inference from few cases (210–11); and they explicitly reject parsimony as an inherently desirable property of social-scientific theory (20, 104–5). On neither point, I suspect, will most comparativists find their arguments persuasive; and they seem to me to be refuted by the examples I adduce here.

CHAPTER 6

Claiming Too Much:
Warnings about Selection Bias

David Collier, James Mahoney, and Jason Seawright

How well do the tools and insights of mainstream quantitative methods[1] serve as a template for qualitative analysis? The present chapter addresses this question by evaluating forceful warnings about selection bias that have been offered, from a quantitative perspective, to qualitative researchers. Specifically, we discuss warnings about bias in studies that deliberately focus on cases with extreme values on the dependent variable. Assessing these warnings provides an opportunity to examine the leverage gained, as well as the pitfalls encountered, in applying insights about quantitative methods to qualitative investigation.

Within the quantitative tradition, selection bias is recognized as a challenging problem of inference. James Heckman's (1976, 1979) widely known research on this topic, and his Nobel Prize in economics for this work, underscore the impor-

---

Mark I. Lichbach provided insightful suggestions about the version of this material earlier published in the *American Political Science Review*.

[1]Mainstream quantitative methods are understood here as strongly oriented toward regression analysis, econometric refinements on regression, and the search for alternatives to regression models in contexts where specific regression assumptions are not met.

tance of selection bias.[2] In light of the effort that has gone into exploring this problem, it is perhaps not surprising that selection bias is a complex issue, the nature of which is not intuitively obvious for many scholars.[3]

This chapter first briefly reviews these warnings about selection bias, as well as counterarguments to these warnings that have been presented by various researchers. We then turn to an extended discussion of the role of selection bias in qualitative research. We provide an overview of how selection bias works in regression analysis, and then draw on these insights to discuss its role in qualitative investigation. We find that selection bias does pose a problem in qualitative *cross-case* analysis, but that *within-case* analysis need not be subject to this form of bias. We then consider the implications for different types of comparisons, including no-variance designs. Overall, we are convinced that the warnings about selection bias have inappropriately called into question the legitimacy of case-study research.

Do the Warnings Claim Too Much?

Qualitative analysts in political science have received stern warnings that the validity of their findings may be undermined by selection bias. King, Keohane, and Verba's *Designing Social Inquiry* (hereafter *DSI*) identifies this form of bias as posing important "dangers" for qualitative research (116). In extreme instances, its effect is "devastating" (130). Further, "the cases of extreme selection bias—where there is by design no variation on the dependent variable—are easy to deal with: avoid them! We will not learn about causal effects from them" (*DSI* 130). The book's recommendations echo advice offered by Achen and Snidal, who view such bias in comparative case studies as posing the risk of "inferential felonies" that, again, have "devastating implications" (1989: 160, 161). Similarly, Geddes explores the consequences of "violating [the] taboo" against selecting on the dependent variable, which is understood to be a central issue in selection bias, and she sees such bias as a problem with which various subfields are "bedeviled" (1991: 131; see also Geddes 2003).

Among the circumstances under which selection bias may arise in qualitative research, these critics focus on the role of deliberate case selection by the investigator. In particular, the critics are concerned about decisions by some researchers to restrict attention to extreme outcomes, for example, revolutions, the onset of

---

[2]The focus in this chapter is selection bias in causal inference, as this problem has been discussed in the econometrics literature. Achen's (1986) carefully crafted book played a key role in introducing these ideas into political science. Selection bias deriving from survey nonresponse is also a long-standing issue in research on public opinion and political behavior.

[3]In addition to Heckman (1976, 1979, and 1990b), work in this tradition includes Maddala (1983), Achen (1986), and Manski (1995), as well as standard reference book and textbook treatments such as Heckman (1990a) and Greene (2000: chap. 20).

war, and the breakdown of democratic regimes. This focus on extreme cases is a well-established tradition in case-study research; the justification for this focus is that it provides a better opportunity to gain detailed knowledge of the phenomenon under investigation. This same justification applies to a closely related case-selection strategy: concentrating on a narrow range of variation, involving cases that all come close to experiencing the outcome of interest. For example, scholars may focus on serious crises of deterrence as well as episodes of all-out war, but excluding more peaceful relationships.

However, this case-selection strategy that makes sense from the perspective of many qualitative researchers poses a major problem from the standpoint of scholars concerned with selection bias. According to these critics, if researchers thus "truncate" on the dependent variable by focusing only on extreme values, it leaves them vulnerable to error that is systematic and potentially devastating. The impressive tradition of work on regression analysis and related techniques lends considerable weight to this strong claim. This advice may also seem compelling because a straightforward solution suggests itself: simply focusing on a full range of cases. Hence, qualitative researchers may be tempted to conclude that these warnings about selection bias constitute valuable methodological advice.

Notwithstanding the legitimacy of the methodological tradition that stands behind these warnings about selection bias, several scholars argue that these critiques have serious limitations. We briefly note such counterarguments before turning to the main focus of this chapter—that is, the implications of selection bias for qualitative research. At a broad level, Brady (55–56, 59–62 this volume) and Bartels (71–73 this volume) express concern that *DSI* at times exaggerates the capacity of quantitative researchers to address methodological problems within their own tradition of research, that *DSI* makes important mistakes in applying quantitative ideas, and that the book needs to be considerably more cautious in applying, to qualitative analysis, advice from a quantitative perspective. For example, Brady (67 n. 17 this volume) and Collier (1995a: 463) note that at a key point, *DSI* (126) confounds selection bias with conventional sampling error. The arguments of Stolzenberg and Relles suggest that these insights from Brady and Bartels very much apply to warnings about selection bias. Writing about quantitative sociology, Stolzenberg and Relles (1990) argue that selection bias is not as serious a problem as some have claimed; that some statistical corrections for selection bias create more problems than they solve; and that, among the many problems of quantitative analysis, selection bias does not merit special attention.

A related argument, presented by Rogowski (77–83 this volume), suggests that constraining research design according to the norms suggested by critics concerned with selection bias may distract from a major, alternative priority: that is, zeroing in on theoretically crucial cases, which can provide decisive tests of theories. Though Rogowski's arguments are debated (King, Keohane, and Verba, 188–91 this volume; see also 198 this volume), it is clear that warnings about selection bias raise complex issues about contending analytic goals.

Finally, concern has been expressed about procedures for detecting and overcoming selection bias. Writing on this form of bias is sometimes based on the assumption that a given set of cases is analyzed with the goal of providing insight into a well-defined larger population. Yet the nature of this larger population may be ambiguous or in dispute, and addressing the question of selection bias before establishing an appropriate population puts the cart before the horse. Hence, if scholars claim that inferences from a given data set suffer from selection bias on the basis of comparison with findings derived from a broader set of cases, the relevance and plausibility of this claim is dependent on the appropriateness of the broader comparison. Moving to this broader set of cases can under some conditions help evaluate and address selection bias—but sometimes at the cost of introducing causal heterogeneity, which is also a major problem for causal inference (Collier and Mahoney 1996: 66–69). Apart from the question of causal homogeneity, a long-standing tradition of research underscores the contextual specificity of measurement (Verba 1971; Adcock and Collier 2001). If the measures employed are not appropriate across the broader comparison, different findings in the sample and population might be due to problems of descriptive inference, again yielding at best an ambiguous evaluation of selection bias.

These warnings and skeptical responses suggest that selection bias is indeed a complex topic and that each aspect of this methodological problem must be analyzed with great care. In that spirit, we now seek to explore the implications of selection bias for qualitative research. To do so, we first review key points in the argument about why selection bias occurs in regression analysis.

Selecting Extreme Values on the Dependent Variable: Why Is It an Issue?

In regression analysis, selecting cases that have extreme values on the dependent variable—that is, truncation—does indeed lead to biased estimates of causal effects. This problem is one aspect of the general issue of selection bias, which is systematic error in causal inference that derives from the selection processes through which the data are generated, and/or through which the researcher's access to the data may be filtered.[4] The assertion that the error is systematic means that the expected value of the error in estimating causal effects is not zero. The bias, which can be dramatic, is not just a coincidence, nor does it result from peculiarities in a particular data set. It might not always occur, but it is expected to occur. We now illustrate the problem of deliberate truncation on the dependent vari-

---

[4]For a further discussion of these alternative selection and filtering processes, see 209–13 this volume.

able.[5] For the purpose of this example, the discussion focuses on the bivariate case, with only one independent variable.[6]

An Example

Let us assume that a group of scholars is engaged in extending the ideas in Putnam's (1993) *Making Democracy Work*, seeking to pursue Putnam's argument that civicness[7] is a key cause of good performance by regional governments at the subnational level. These scholars base their analysis on a comparison of hundreds of regional governments located in different European countries. With the goal of gaining deeper insight into high-performance governments, they decide to focus only on high-performance cases, thereby truncating their sample. At the same time, these scholars believe that measurement validity and causal homogeneity hold for their entire sample. Hence, the full set of cases is treated here as a benchmark for evaluating inferences from the truncated sample.

Figure 6.1, which is based on simulated data,[8] shows how truncation can change a bivariate relationship. The figure displays the full range of cases, with the government performance score ranging from zero to two hundred. Within this set of cases, the (unstandardized) slope[9] of .73 would commonly be interpreted as reflecting a strong relationship between civicness and government performance. This slope corresponds to the solid regression line in the figure.

---

[5]*DSI* (130–32) centers its discussion of selection bias on a parallel example.

[6]With more than one independent variable, the effects of selection bias are essentially identical to the effects in the bivariate case. All slopes associated with the independent variables will, on average, be flattened (Greene 2000: 902). In *DSI*'s (130) terms, regression results that are subject to selection bias thus form a "lower bound" for the true effects. The uniform effect of selection bias on all independent variables in multivariate analysis contrasts, for example, with the impact of measurement error. If one independent variable is measured with error in a multivariate regression, the consequences for other independent variables are complex and may involve an increase or a decrease in the corresponding slopes, or even a reversal of their signs. See Bartels (72–73 this volume).

[7]Putnam (1993: chaps. 3–4, esp. 85, 98–99). His term is actually "civic-ness" (99).

[8]Monte Carlo data are used here to produce a figure that would make the patterns under discussion as clear as possible. The same basic result occurs with real-world data, for example, in standard regressions of democracy on level of economic development. The data in figure 6.1 were generated randomly, with a slope of .73 and a normally distributed error term with a variance of 27.

[9]In this chapter, when we refer to the "slope" we mean the unstandardized slope. Achen (1977: 807; 1982: 68–71) played a key role in pushing political scientists to focus on the unstandardized slope, as opposed to the correlation or the standardized slope, as a basis for causal inference. The unstandardized slope is not affected by truncation on the independent variable.

A striking contrast emerges here. If we narrow the focus to the high-performance governments located in the upper part of the figure with scores between 120 and 200—that is, if we truncate on the dependent variable—the slope is flattened dramatically, from .73 to .28 (see the dashed regression line in the figure). This drop in the slope is not due to idiosyncratic features of the data set. With an exclusive focus on cases with high scores on government performance, a drop in the slope is expected to occur. Consequently, if the flatter slope for the upper part of the figure is used to estimate the slope for the full distribution of cases, that inference will suffer from selection bias. This reduced slope also provides a misleading estimate for the importance of civicness even among the high-performance cases. Given the dramatic change in the slope that results from truncation in regression analysis, it is easy to understand why this topic has commanded considerable methodological attention.

Selecting cases toward the lower end of the dependent variable also creates bias. By contrast, with truncation on an explanatory variable, as long as one is dealing with a linear relationship, the slope on average does not change. In light of these considerations, methodologists have focused their critiques on designs that restrict the range of the dependent variable.

Understanding Why Selection Bias Results from Truncation

Why does truncation in figure 6.1 bias causal inference? Among cases included in this truncated sample, in relation to particular values of the explanatory variable X, the dependent variable Y is not free to assume any value. Rather, toward the left side of the figure,[10] where the values of X are smaller, the truncated sample favors cases above the original regression line. As X becomes larger and passes approximately 130, cases below the original regression line start to be included, and the proportion of cases well above the regression line declines. On the right side, the truncated sample comes to resemble the original sample.

A closer examination of figure 6.1 will further clarify this pattern. Consider the cases with a civicness score of between zero and fifty. Among this large number of cases, only two are included in the truncated sample. Both cases are far above the original regression line, more so than any other case in the entire data set. As civicness increases, the average distance above the original regression line decreases among cases in the truncated sample. Among the cases with civicness

---

[10]In the following pages, we refer periodically to the left and right sides of the figure. This discussion presumes that the slope of the original regression line is positive, and that the analyst has truncated to include only cases with high values on the dependent variable. If the original regression line instead has a negative slope, or if cases with low values on the dependent variable have been chosen, the observations about the left and right sides would be reversed. But the basic argument would remain unchanged.

Figure 6.1. Illustration of Selection Bias Resulting from Truncation

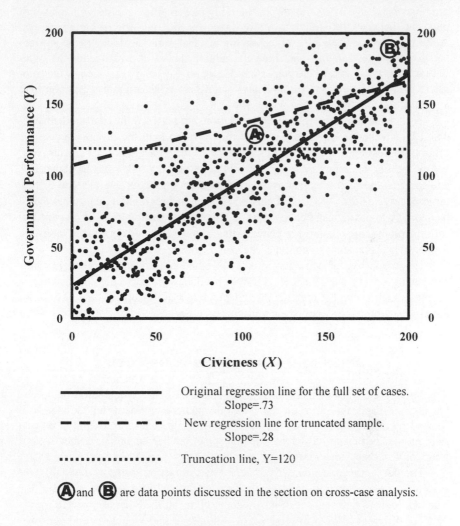

Original regression line for the full set of cases.
Slope=.73

New regression line for truncated sample.
Slope=.28

Truncation line, Y=120

Ⓐ and Ⓑ are data points discussed in the section on cross-case analysis.

Based on simulated data prepared by the authors.

scores of between fifty and one hundred, a dozen cases are included in the truncated sample. While all these cases are above the original regression line, and most are fairly far above it, several are considerably closer. Among cases with a level of civicness between 100 and 150, a few dozen make it into the truncated sample. Although some of these are well above the original regression line, many are reasonably close to that line, and three are actually below it. Finally, for the cases with scores on civicness between 150 and 200, all but 16 are included in the truncated sample. These cases are both above and below the original regression line, and some are relatively far below that line.

Truncation thus creates a negative relationship between the independent variable (X) and the error term. By error term, we mean here the distance above the original regression line for the cases included in the truncated sample (with cases below the line counting as negative errors). A "negative relationship between X and the error term" means that to the extent values on X are low, we tend to find large positive errors. A crucial limitation of standard regression analysis is that it has no way to distinguish between this negative relationship, which is due to truncation, and the true relationship between the independent and dependent variables. Rather, regression analysis conflates the two, resulting in a reduced slope.

To summarize, selection bias results from the interplay among three elements. Truncating on (1) the dependent variable produces selection bias by creating a negative relationship between (2) the independent variable and (3) the error term, thereby flattening the slope for the truncated sample.[11]

Selection Bias in Qualitative Research

What is the relevance of these ideas about selection bias for qualitative research? On the one hand, this form of bias may be a generic problem that extends well beyond regression analysis. On the other hand, qualitative research might be carried out in a sufficiently different way that selection bias becomes another kind of issue, or is perhaps not an issue at all.

To address this question, we consider two contrasting forms of qualitative research: cross-case analysis and within-case analysis. In cross-case analysis, the research focuses on instances of the outcome being studied that are located in two or more different cases. A diverse set of examples could include paired comparisons, as in Dreze and Sen's (1989) effort to explain contrasts between China and India in the achievement of human welfare; the comparison of a dozen cases, as in Haggard and Kaufman's (1995) comparative-historical analysis focused on the political and economic consequences of transitions to democracy under different economic conditions; and a medium-N study, as in Wickham-Crowley's (1992:

---

[11]In those rare instances where there is no scatter around the regression line—that is, where there is no error term—the cases in the truncated sample should have the same slope as the overall sample, and selection bias simply does not arise.

302–26) study of revolutionary movements in twenty-six Latin American countries, in which revolutionary movements are the outcome to be explained. Although these studies do look at "internal" evidence (from within the cases), they have a strong focus on cross-case evidence, involving one observation for each case on the main dependent variable, as well as on various independent variables. This form of data may be called data-set observations.[12]

By contrast, within-case analysis is concerned with diverse forms of internal evidence about causation that are brought to bear on explaining a single, overall outcome within that case. This approach is identified with a methodological tradition in the social sciences that dates back at least to the 1940s. Lazarsfeld, in an early statement on tools for qualitative analysis, uses the label "discerning," and he specifically emphasizes that, within the framework of a larger comparative study, discerning seeks to "isolate the causes of a single event" (1940: preface). Subsequent labels have included Barton and Lazarsfeld's (1969 [1955]: 184–87) "process analysis," Smelser's (1968: 72–73; 1976: 217–18) "intra-unit" or "within-unit comparison," Campbell's (1975: 181–82) "pattern matching," George's (1979b: 113–14) "process tracing," Dessler's (1991: 342–46) "causal theory," Sewell's (1996: 261) "causal narrative," Bates, Greif, Levi, Rosenthal, and Weingast's (1998) "analytic narratives," and Hall's (2003: 391–95) "systematic process analysis."

In contemporary qualitative research, such internal evidence is routinely used to evaluate hypotheses about the overall outcome in the case or cases under study. This could, for instance, involve using multiple sources of internal evidence to test explanations concerning the decline of a labor union, the successful reform initiatives of a government agency, or the fragmentation of a political party. Examples discussed in the literature on selection bias include in-depth studies of large-scale events such as wars, revolutions, and national economic competitiveness (Collier and Mahoney 1996). As just noted, Dreze and Sen, Haggard and Kaufman, and Wickham-Crowley combine cross-case analysis with internal evidence in assessing explanations of the national-level outcomes they are studying. When they use within-case analysis, these scholars maintain their focus on the original dependent variable: the outcome to be explained is, for example, a lower level of national welfare, strong authoritarian influence in a democratic transition, or revolution. Diverse forms of evidence may be introduced through within-case analysis, but the focus is still on explaining a single outcome. The evidence employed here may be characterized as "causal-process observations."[13]

---

[12]See 12 and 252–64 in the present volume (chaps. 1 and 13).

[13]See again 12 and 252–64 in the present volume (chaps. 1 and 13). An illustration of causal-process observations, which demonstrates their contribution to resolving an important controversy about the 2000 presidential election in the United States, is presented in the appendix.

This mode of within-case analysis should not be confused with an alternative approach, in which the researcher looks at multiple instances of the dependent variable and the independent variables in different subunits (spatial or temporal) of the original case. Time-series regression analysis is an example of this type of within-case analysis, which in effect becomes cross-case analysis. By contrast, in the present chapter, when we refer to "within-case analysis," we mean analysis based on causal-process observations.

Cross-Case Analysis and Selection Bias

Qualitative, cross-case analysis shares important similarities with basic ideas of regression. Obviously, qualitative studies do not generally employ numerical coefficients and quantitative tests. Yet qualitative researchers carrying out cross-case analysis can, in some respects, be seen as doing "intuitive regression," and correspondingly, the issue of selection bias arises. Let us explain.

Consider, in relation to figure 6.1, the situation in which qualitative researchers engaged in cross-case analysis are carrying out paired comparisons. For example, if they focus on Governments A and B in the figure, they may note that the substantial difference in government performance between the two cases corresponds to a notable difference in civicness. Reasoning in terms of such differences or magnitudes is an important part of the practice of qualitative research—as in George and McKeown's (1985: 29–34) "congruence" procedure for case-study analysis, which places a single case in comparative perspective and depends on judgments about the magnitude of differences among cases. Such reasoning is employed in many small-N comparisons.[14]

If researchers examine cross-case differences, focusing on Governments A and B, they may reasonably conclude that civicness is an important causal factor. Indeed, if they have the actual scores for the two cases, they might even place these cases in a diagram like figure 6.1 and draw a line through them to summarize the relationship. Such a line would be parallel to the original regression line, suggesting that the strong relationship in the overall data set is reflected in the comparison of this particular pair of cases.

Using this idea of paired comparisons, we now illustrate the impact of truncation in qualitative, cross-case analysis. Consider the comparisons among all pairs of cases in the upper part of the figure, that is, located above the dotted truncation line. Although the relative position of the two cases within any particular pair varies greatly, on average a given increment in civicness is associated with a rela-

---

[14]For example, see again Dreze and Sen (1989), Haggard and Kaufman (1995), and Wickham-Crowley (1992). For a discussion of how reasoning at higher levels of measurement involving magnitudes (e.g., interval or ratio scales) may play a role in qualitative research, see 245, 249 this volume.

tively small increment in government performance. Hence, these paired comparisons generally suggest a misleadingly weak relationship between civicness and government performance. If these increments on the independent and dependent variable are summarized in terms of lines drawn through pairs of points, the slope of these lines, on average, corresponds to the flatter slope of the regression line for the truncated sample. This pattern points to a strong analogy between regression analysis and qualitative cross-case comparison, suggesting that such qualitative work may therefore be subject to selection bias.

The contrast between the finding derived from comparing A and B, as opposed to the full set of paired comparisons in the upper part of the figure, reflects a basic point about bias: it is error that may not always occur, but that is expected to occur. Correspondingly, for the paired comparisons among all the cases with scores on civicness of 120 and above, we find the basic pattern we would expect to find with selection bias: they will generally underestimate the relationship, even though the line drawn through some pairs may estimate it correctly. Thus, paired comparisons within the truncated sample are, on average, subject to selection bias. Further, by extension, this analogy to regression analysis is relevant not only to paired comparisons, but also to cross-case qualitative analysis that employs an N of more than two.

In sum, qualitative research can be subject to selection bias if it is based on cross-case analysis, considers multiple outcomes on the dependent variable for these cases, and focuses on a sample that is truncated vis-à-vis a larger comparison that is considered substantively meaningful.

Within-Case Analysis and Selection Bias

Is within-case analysis likewise subject to selection bias? Two insights about selection bias in regression analysis, presented above, will help answer this question. The first insight concerns the finding that the regression slope for the truncated sample underestimates the main relationship between civicness and government performance. We ask whether this problem of underestimating the main relationship likewise arises for within-case analysis. Our answer is that selection bias is not a problem—because within-case analysis does not involve intuitive regression. Instead, it employs different tools of inference. The second insight is that truncated samples overrepresent a particular type of case—that is, cases located well above the original regression line in figure 6.1. Note, for example, that in the left half of figure 6.1, the fourteen cases in the truncated sample are all above the original regression line, and most are well above it. A scholar focused on these cases would be likely to emphasize the causal role of idiosyncratic factors. This concern leads to the following question: Does within-case analysis produce faulty inferences when it focuses specifically on these overrepresented cases? More broadly, does knowledge about the position of a given case toward the left or right side of the figure help the analyst address this potential problem?[15] We focus on the analogy with regression analysis to demonstrate that within-case analysis involving causal-process observations in fact raises different issues.

Evaluating the Causal Relationship

Does within-case analysis based on a truncated sample underestimate the importance of civicness as an explanatory factor? We observed above that this occurs with regression analysis because it cannot distinguish the negative relationship between the independent variable and the error term from the true relationship between the independent and dependent variables. Standard regression analysis lacks tools for exploring causal effects other than examining relationships among variables across cases within the sample. Does this same problem arise for within-case analysis?

In fact, within-case analysis can sort out these relationships because it makes use of tools for causal inference—that is, causal-process observations—that do not depend on examining relationships among variables across cases. Consider the right side of the figure, where we find cases with high levels of civicness. The original regression line tells us that for these cases, civicness does have a major impact on government performance. Yet using regression analysis with the truncated sample, we will not arrive at this finding. However, if qualitative researchers can find evidence of the causal processes through which civicness operates, then in principle they can infer that civicness has a substantial causal effect.

How is this accomplished? Within-case analysis proceeds by evaluating evidence about the causal processes and mechanisms that link the independent variable to the dependent variable, looking for the specific ways that civicness alters the goals and decision-making constraints of political, social, and economic actors. For instance, it might be argued that civicness reduces the likelihood of violence (Putnam 1993: 112–13), which in turn creates greater incentives for productive public and private investment. If this argument is correct, then government decision makers in contexts of high civicness should view the level of violence as a decisive factor in decisions to invest in schools, roads, and other productive public services. In turn, a qualitative analyst using within-case analysis should be able to use interviews with decision makers and minutes of meetings to demonstrate the role of civicness in contributing to government performance. This would be true even if other variables, or some form of randomness, also have an important effect. Hence, these findings should not be subject to selection bias.

We may also ask what happens with cases that have lower levels of civicness but high levels of government performance, and are therefore located well above

---

[15]Whereas there are certainly cases well above the original regression line on the right side of the figure, on the left side all cases in the truncated sample are not only above the original regression line, but are far above it. Again, these conclusions about the left and right sides presume upper truncation and a positive slope.

the original regression line. These cases are the principal culprits in creating a negative relationship between the error term and the independent variable.

In fact, researchers should be able to conclude correctly that civicness is relatively unimportant in accounting for the outcome in these cases. The reason is that decision makers could report that the lack of civicness affected their goals and constraints, but that something else compensated for this. In the example discussed above, government leaders might state in interviews that concerns about violence had been a major argument against public investment—but that this argument was overcome by some other factor.

In sum, within-case analysis can consider evidence that, in effect, distinguishes between the causal effect of the independent variable and the error term. It does so by looking for evidence of the causal processes through which the independent variable has an impact. Hence, for cases with low levels of the independent variable that are located well above the original regression line, this kind of analysis can correctly conclude that the independent variable has little to do with the outcome.

Further, if researchers compare the results of the two hypothetical within-case analyses just discussed, they could conclude that civicness plays a major role in one case and little role in the other. These researchers could therefore make an appropriate inference about the overall relevance of civicness across the larger range of this independent variable. Because the inferences can distinguish between the effect of the independent variable and the error within each case, comparisons of effects across cases are not confounded with those errors. Thus, the basic problem of selection bias in regression analysis is avoided.

The point here is straightforward. When there is scatter around a regression line, truncation will tend to discriminate in favor of observations with particularly large errors, especially when the value of the independent variable is low. Regression does not distinguish between this pattern of discrimination and the actual causal relationship, so selection bias results. By contrast, in qualitative, within-case analysis, if the researcher does a careful job of sifting evidence, these features simply need not be operative. Hence, selection bias need not arise in this form of qualitative investigation.

Atypical Cases and Overgeneralization

The second concern in assessing whether within-case analysis is subject to selection bias is with problems that may arise in analyzing cases that are substantially above the original regression line. Let us explore how this might work in the Putnam example.

Consider the left side of figure 6.1. These cases may well have unusually high levels of government performance for idiosyncratic reasons.[16] Hence, scholars

---

[16]These high values of government performance might also be due to substantively important variables other than civicness. However, if omitted variables are statistically

carrying out a nuanced causal assessment based on within-case analysis might well uncover the role of idiosyncratic factors in one or a few such cases. The capacity to generate this finding reflects a distinctive strength of within-case analysis. However, these qualitative analysts might also make the mistake of concluding that these idiosyncratic factors play a major role in producing high performance in local governments more broadly, thereby overgeneralizing a finding based on a quite atypical sample. This kind of overgeneralization from case studies drawn from a truncated sample is a mistake in inference that Collier and Mahoney have called "complexification based on extreme cases" (1996: 71–72). Of course, generalization from one or a few cases is often problematic, due to conventional sampling error. But the risk may be intensified here because of the higher proportion of atypical cases in the truncated sample, a problem that is clearly related to selection bias.

By contrast, toward the right side of the figure, especially where civicness scores are above 150, nearly all cases from the original sample are included. In other words, cases that achieved high scores on government performance because of idiosyncratic factors are no longer overrepresented. While small-N inferences from the right side of the figure are still subject to sampling error, they are less prone to the mistake of erroneous overgeneralization and complexification of idiosyncratic findings. Hence, researchers can avoid the extra risk of overgeneralizing highly atypical findings associated with truncation if they choose cases with higher values of the independent variable.[17]

This section suggests two conclusions. First, within-case analysis focused on a truncated sample need not be subject to the bias that arises in regression analysis of underestimating the causal relationship. In other words, to reiterate, within-case, causal-process analysis is not intuitive regression. Second, truncation does overrepresent certain kinds of cases, and qualitative researchers must be particularly careful to avoid overestimating the general causal importance of context-specific factors on the basis of these cases.

---

related to civicness, the analysis suffers from omitted variable bias, in addition to potentially having problems of selection bias—which would make the example far more ambiguous. Because claims of statistical independence among macrolevel variables are generally unpersuasive, the example will emphasize idiosyncratic alternative explanations.

[17]Cases with high values on the independent variable can, of course, also have large errors vis-à-vis the original regression line, which may signal a substantial role for idiosyncratic patterns of causation. However, among cases with high levels of civicness in the truncated sample, large errors are essentially no more common than they are in the overall population. Therefore, while errors related to sampling may still occur, the extra risk of complexification discussed in the text is avoided. To address these issues, qualitative researchers must obviously be able to determine where a particular case falls on the civicness scale relative to the full distribution of cases.

Stern Warnings about No-Variance Designs

Let us now return to the warnings about no-variance designs discussed in the introduction. The arguments concerning cross-case and within-case analysis just presented are helpful in evaluating these strong warnings about designs that lack variance on the dependent variable. We will discuss the limitations of regression analysis in analyzing such designs and the fact that many scholars instead employ within-case analysis in making causal inferences based on this same constellation of cases.[18]

DSI (130) argues quite emphatically, as noted at the beginning of this chapter, that no-variance designs are subject to extreme selection bias and provide no leverage for causal inference. The book states that avoiding such designs is "a basic and obvious rule. . . . This point seems so obvious that we would think it hardly needs to be mentioned." Thus, "nothing whatsoever can be learned about the causes of the dependent variable without taking into account other instances when the dependent variable takes on other values" (129); this design "makes it impossible to evaluate any individual causal effect" (134).

It should be noted that *DSI* briefly recognizes alternative views of no-variance designs, in part in a footnote on one of the pages just cited. Thus, *DSI* does point out that a broader comparison can be created by placing a no-variance design within the framework of a larger literature (129 n. 6; 147–49), and that a no-variance "cluster" approach, which is essentially Mill's (1974b [1843]) method of agreement, can be valuable for pointing to potential explanations. These explanations should then be tested on the basis of more appropriate methods (148–49). Yet these observations assign these designs a subordinate status of generating, rather than testing, hypotheses. The main point is to condemn such designs.

Our position is that *DSI*'s strongly worded advice about no-variance designs is correct for regression analysis, but it is unhelpful for qualitative research based on within-case analysis. Regression analyses of no-variance designs are certainly subject to extreme selection bias. In regression analysis, no-variance designs guarantee a perfect correlation between the independent variable and the error term within the truncated sample. For this reason, regression analysis estimates all causal effects as zero and is completely uninformative.

Yet a striking paradox emerges here: qualitative analysts frequently make nonzero causal claims on the basis of no-variance designs. This occurs because, in the hands of qualitative researchers, these essentially become a different kind of design. Whereas from the perspective of regression analysis these may be no-variance designs, from the perspective of qualitative researchers the cases selected

---

[18]Scholars testing necessary and/or sufficient causes also use no-variance designs. See the discussion by Munck (114) and Ragin (128–30), and also chapter 12 (213–20) in the present volume.

may well provide excellent opportunities for within-case analysis. *DSI*'s condemnation of this pattern of case selection fails to consider this alternative approach.

This insight places in perspective *DSI*'s claim that no-variance designs "make it impossible to evaluate any individual causal effect." While *DSI*'s argument applies to regression analysis, it may not be true for other techniques, and it certainly is not true for within-case, causal-process analysis. The argument should therefore be seen as an overextension of a narrowly regression-based framework.

Further Observations about Cross-Case and Within-Case Comparison

Given that the analogy to regression analysis is in many ways not helpful, what can we conclude about the inferential leverage actually provided by small-N studies using either cross-case analysis, or within-case, causal-process analysis? With a small N, cross-case design that (a) encompasses a substantial range of variance on the dependent variable, and (b) is based, let us say, on three, five, or eight cases, it is simply unrealistic to imagine that comparisons across these cases provides a strong basis for causal inference. The N is too small. Rather, it is productive to think of these cross-case comparisons as helping to frame the analytic problem and to suggest causal ideas that are also explored and evaluated through within-case analysis. This observation certainly applies to the studies of Dreze and Sen, and also Haggard and Kaufman, discussed above, as well as works of comparative-historical analysis such as Luebbert (1991) and R. Collier and D. Collier (1991).

A basic point emerges here regarding no-variance designs. If one takes a realistic view of the genuine sources of leverage in causal inference, qualitative no-variance designs employing cross-case comparison and a small N are, in a fundamental respect, *similar* to small-N designs with variance on the dependent variable. Both rely on examining causal ideas in great depth through the internal analysis of individual cases. Studies that at one level of analysis (for example, macrocomparative research) are small-N designs with variance on the dependent variable can definitely supplement this within-case leverage through cross-case comparison, and additional leverage is always welcome. Yet it is simply incorrect to assert that comparison across a small number of cases with variance on the dependent variable provides much greater leverage in causal inference than a no-variance design. In both approaches, when causal effects are evaluated, it is centrally through within-case analysis.

Further, in studies of this type, cross-case comparisons encompassing the full range of variance on the dependent variable yield a greater capacity to refine conceptualization and measurement, which is in turn a foundation for good causal inference. Gaining a sense of major contrasts among cases may sensitize the researcher to issues in the application of concepts and decisions about measurement that might be overlooked in examining only extreme cases. For example, these broader comparisons may stimulate the creation of typologies, which in turn help to frame within-case analysis. To take a specific instance, efforts to conceptualize and measure democracy are routinely framed in relation to scholarly understandings of authoritarianism. Thus, the contribution of small-N, full-variance designs may be as much to descriptive inference as to causal inference.

In sum, adopting a broader view of the goals of research and of available sources of analytic leverage, one could argue that full-variance comparisons may serve to refine conceptualization and measurement, as well as to suggest explanations and provide exploratory tests. But crucial leverage in testing explanations comes from within-case analysis, and this leverage is valuable irrespective of whether these cases are embedded in a full-variance design or a no-variance design. These observations essentially turn *DSI*'s argument about no-variance designs on its head.

This is not to say that scholars should avoid full-variance designs. In fact, researchers face a real trade-off between alternative designs. On the one hand, if little is known about a given outcome, then the close analysis of a few cases of that outcome may be more productive than a broader study in which the researcher never becomes sufficiently familiar with the phenomenon to gain the descriptive information necessary for good choices about conceptualization and measurement, as well as for within-case analysis that provides important leverage in causal inference. On the other hand, by not utilizing the comparative perspective provided by the examination of negative cases, the researcher gives up important leverage in descriptive inference, as well as supplementary leverage in causal inference.

Conclusion

Warnings about the devastating errors presumed to result from selection bias have raised a potentially important idea: if qualitative scholars pay attention to this problem, they can dramatically improve their research. However, this idea derives from the mistaken conviction that quantitative and qualitative research employ the same sources of inferential leverage. In fact, they often employ different sources of leverage, and consequently selection bias is not always a problem in qualitative research. Correspondingly, much of the damage to the credibility of qualitative research that has resulted from forceful warnings about selection bias in case studies is in fact undeserved.

Scholars should be careful in applying the idea of selection bias to qualitative research. In contrast to the authors who have offered strong warnings about selection bias in qualitative analysis, we have focused on the specific causes and consequences of the correlation that arises, in selection bias based on truncation, between the independent variable and the error term. This focus provides clearer insight into how this form of bias may or may not distort the findings of qualitative investigation. We have explored the contrasting relevance of selection bias for cross-case analysis and for within-case, causal-process analysis. We have also considered the implications of these two research strategies for the question of no-variance designs

This discussion also offers new insights into potential pitfalls of qualitative research focused on extreme cases. In research that involves truncation, for example, within-case analysis can sometimes lead researchers to over generalize idiosyncratic findings derived from cases that have a high score on the dependent variable but a low score on the main independent variable. Qualitative researchers who have been sensitized to issues of selection bias can do a better job of evaluating the impact of the main causal variable being studied by devoting more attention to cases with high scores on both the independent and dependent variables. Thus, we hope that our discussion can provide qualitative researchers with a framework that will help guide the choices they make in working with cases that have extreme values on the dependent variable.

Productive methodological insights can indeed emerge from a dialogue between qualitative and quantitative methods. However, achieving such insights requires that we pay attention both to the fine details behind methodological problems such as selection bias, as well as to the actual sources of leverage utilized in qualitative inference.

PART III

Qualitative Tools

CHAPTER 7

Tools for Qualitative Research

Gerardo L. Munck

The late 1960s to mid-1970s was a major period of innovative writing on qualitative methodology and small-N research. Following an abatement of discussion, scholars again began to actively debate these aspects of methodology in the 1990s.[1] This new work has focused on a diverse set of issues, including case selec-

I would like to acknowledge the excellent and careful feedback I received from David Collier, Diana Kapiszewski, Sally Roever, and Jason Seawright, who generously commented on this article more than once. I am also grateful for the useful comments offered by Robert Adcock, Chad Atkinson, Ruth Berins Collier, Andrew Gould, Gary King, Alexander Kozhemiakin, James Kuklinski, James Mahoney, Sebastián Mazzuca, Richard Snyder, Jarolav Tir, and Jay Verkuilen. Any errors that remain, of course, are my responsibility.

[1]Some key works from the 1970s include: Smelser (1973; 1976; and see also 1968), Przeworski and Teune (1970), Sartori (1970), Lijphart (1971; 1975), and Eckstein (1975). Obviously, publication on comparative methodology did not cease during the late 1970s and the 1980s. See, for example, Skocpol and Somers (1980), Skocpol (1984), Sartori (1984), and Tilly (1984). This period, nonetheless, saw nothing similar to the current explosion of publications. Some of the most significant contributions to this methodological revival include: Ragin (1987; 1994; 2000), Ragin and Becker (1992), Sartori (1991), Geddes (1991), Collier and Mahon (1993), Collier and Mahoney (1996), Collier and Levitsky (1997), King, Keohane, and Verba (1994), Janoski and Hicks (1994),

tion, conceptual stretching, process tracing, the role of historical narratives in causal inference, and multiple conjunctural causation. Indeed, this new literature has addressed most issues that affect the conduct of research.[2]

While the contributions of a wide range of scholars are undeniable, it is equally true that the publication of one single book—Gary King, Robert O. Keohane, and Sidney Verba's *Designing Social Inquiry: Scientific Inference in Qualitative Research* (hereafter *DSI*)—has been a landmark event with an enormous impact on qualitative methods and research. *DSI*'s central message is that qualitative and quantitative research share a common logic of inference. Therefore, methodological lessons derived from one tradition can be applied fruitfully to the challenges faced by researchers in the other tradition. Unfortunately, *DSI* largely confines itself to applying tools of quantitative research to the problems of qualitative research, and undervalues the methodological insights and procedures that qualitative researchers bring to the table.

In fact, qualitative analysts have their own well-developed tools for addressing many tasks discussed by *DSI*. These tools certainly do not solve all of the problems faced by researchers, any more than quantitative tools do. Yet these qualitative tools deserve a central place within the standard repertoire of methodological practices. To balance the discussion, this chapter therefore considers some of the tools that qualitative researchers use in their efforts to produce valid social scientific inference. I consider specifically tools that qualitative researchers employ in five distinct steps in the research process.

The discussion below first shows how qualitative researchers seek to define the universe of cases to which their theories are deemed to apply, using contextually grounded analysis, typologies, and process tracing. Second, concerning case selection, I explore how qualitative researchers address the "many variables, small-N" problem. Qualitative analysts are often cautious about seeking to enhance inferential leverage by increasing the number of observations, recognizing that this practice may lead to problems of conceptual stretching and of causal heterogeneity. I discuss the approach of within-case analysis, and I stress that even though standard discussions of selection bias are clearly applicable to qualitative research, "no-variance" designs in qualitative research make an important contribution under some circumstances. I also show that qualitative researchers have long been concerned with the analytic leverage produced by different types of intentional case selection.

Tetlock and Belkin (1996), McDonald (1996), Mjøset, Engelstad, Brochmann, Kalleberg, and Leira (1997), Van Evera (1997), Bates, Greif, Levi, Rosenthal, and Weingast (1998), Peters (1998), J. S. Valenzuela (1998), Mahoney (1999; 2000a), Collier and Adcock (1999), Goldthorpe (2001), Abbott (2001), Mahoney and Rueschemeyer (2003), and George and Bennett (forthcoming).
[2]For an early effort at synthesis of this growing body of literature, see Collier (1993). See also Ragin, Berg-Schlosser, and de Meur (1996).

Third, regarding measurement and data collection, I discuss how qualitative researchers' concern with measurement validity may lead them to employ system-specific indicators and/or contextualized comparisons. I also explore the role of qualitative field research techniques such as in-depth interviews and participant observation. Fourth, I discuss qualitative procedures for causal assessment, with an emphasis on techniques for causal inference based on causal models other than the linear, additive model underlying most forms of regression analysis. I also consider the tools qualitative researchers use to distinguish systematic causal effects from causal effects produced by factors outside of the central hypothesis of concern, and I suggest why these tools are valuable.

In the fifth section, I go beyond *DSI*'s view of methodology as a set of tools primarily intended for addressing research questions that have already been formulated, and I consider the ongoing interaction among theory, hypotheses, and a given data set. Hypothesis testing is best seen as an iterative process that interacts with the development of theory, rather than as a process in which theory is more nearly treated as static. Table 7.1 provides an overview of research tools relevant to these several steps in the research process.[3]

Qualitative Methods: A Survey of Tools

Defining the Universe of Cases: Context, Typologies, and Process Tracing

A fundamental task in any research project is defining the universe of cases.[4] Ideally, there is a close interaction between the investigator's understanding of this universe and choices about the theory that guides the study, the specific hypotheses to be investigated, the approach to measurement that is adopted, and the selection of cases for analysis. As investigators establish the fit between their hypotheses/models and the universe of cases, a standard concern is that, across the set of cases, the criteria of causal homogeneity[5] and conditional independence should be met. Qualitative researchers have various tools for addressing these two issues.

To evaluate the assumption of causal homogeneity, in relation to a given set of cases and a particular explanatory model, qualitative researchers may turn this assumption into an initial hypothesis to be investigated in the course of research

---

[3]Many of these tools are, of course, not unique to qualitative investigation. The point, rather, is that they are carefully and explicitly discussed in standard works on qualitative methodology.

[4]"Universe of cases" is a standard term in methodology; however, at certain points in the discussion below, it appears more natural to refer to this as the "domain of cases."

[5]This is sometimes called unit homogeneity.

Table 7.1. Tools for Qualitative Research [a]

Research Step	Task	Tool
DEFINING UNIVERSE OF CASES	Establish Causal Homogeneity	*Knowledge of context.* Helps in assessing homogeneity of causal processes. *Ragin's QCA and critical juncture/path dependency frameworks.* Qualitative Comparative Analysis and these other frameworks point to additional variables that explain and potentially overcome causal heterogeneity. *Within-case analysis.* Evaluates causal processes within cases. *Scope restrictions.* Specify appropriate domains of comparison. *Typologies.* Serve to identify multiple domains of causal homogeneity.
	Establish Conditional Independence	*Within-case analysis, process tracing.* Help identify reciprocal causation. These tools, especially when focused on a sequence of causal steps, serve to test for reciprocal causation as part of the theory.
	Add Observations without Overextending the Analysis	*Reconceptualization.* Addresses conceptual stretching through mutual fine-tuning of concepts and case selection. *Addressing causal homogeneity and conditional independence.* Help in dealing with problems of overextension.
CASE SELECTION	Select Cases Nonrandomly	*No-variance designs.* Facilitate close examination of causal mechanisms and yield descriptive insight into novel political phenomena. *Matching cases on independent variables.* Serves the same purpose as statistical control. *Selecting sharply contrasting cases.* May permit stronger tests of hypotheses through focus on diverse contexts. High variability specifically on rival explanations may yield more leverage in test of theory.

Research Step	Task	Tool
MEASUREMENT AND DATA COLLECTION	Increase Measurement Validity	*System-specific indicators.* Use of distinct indicators in different settings.
		Contextualized comparison. Achieves analytic equivalence across contexts by focusing on phenomena that, in concrete terms, appear distinct.
	Collect Data	*In-depth interviews, participant observation, qualitative content analysis.* Yield data of greater depth compared with quantitative data sets.
	Assess Deterministic Causation	*Crucial experiments, crucial case studies.* Focus on cases that provide strong tests of a deterministic hypothesis.
		Testing deterministic hypotheses against probabilistic alternatives. Serves to bridge these alternative causal models.
		Boolean algebra. Evaluates deterministic causes.
CAUSAL ASSESSMENT	Assess Historical Causation	*Critical juncture and path dependence frameworks.* Offer a systematized approach to assessing historical causation.
	Separate Systematic vs. Random Components	*Within-case control.* Serves to isolate analytically relevant components of phenomena and provides a substitute for statistical control, based on within-case analysis and process tracing.
ITERATED REFINEMENT OF HYPOTHESES AND THEORY	Inductive Learning from Data	*Hypothesis testing and refinement of concepts.* Reframe and sharpen the analysis throughout the research cycle.
	Identify New or Alternative Explanatory Factors	*Case studies.* Different types of case studies—heuristic, hypothesis-generating, disciplined-configurative, and deviant case studies—as well as no-variance designs, serve to generate new explanations.

[a]Many of these tools are, of course, not unique to qualitative investigation. The point, rather, is that they are carefully and explicitly discussed in standard works on qualitative methodology

(Ragin, Berg-Schlosser and de Meur 1996: 752–53; see also Ragin 125–28 this volume). Although qualitative analysts have many procedures for assessing causal homogeneity, three deserve special attention here. First, researchers often use close knowledge of the cultural, historical, and political context to evaluate whether the causal processes identified in the hypothesis have the same form and significance across the various cases. Within the comparative-historical research community, this process corresponds to the effort to find the boundaries of causal arguments that is a central concern of what Skocpol and Somers (1980: 178–81) call the "contrast of contexts" approach to historical comparison.

Second, qualitative researchers may seek to *achieve* causal homogeneity by considering the various factors that could produce heterogeneity and conceptualizing them as additional variables to be included in the analysis. If, in the course of the analysis, these variables prove unimportant, they are discarded; otherwise they ultimately form part of the substantive explanation produced by the study. This process is perhaps most widely known in the formalized, Boolean-algebraic version created by Ragin (1987), which he calls Qualitative Comparative Analysis (QCA). However, qualitative researchers commonly apply informal versions of the same approach. For example, analyses that employ the frameworks of critical junctures (Collier and Collier 1991: chap. 1) or path dependency (Pierson 2000) follow this technique. These approaches typically identify variables that place countries (or other cases) on different paths or trajectories of change. Such trajectories often involve causal processes that work themselves out in contrasting ways within different groups of cases. The critical juncture can thus be understood as an event that explains subsequent causal heterogeneity. In this specific sense, the causal heterogeneity is explained and thereby effectively overcome.

Third, qualitative researchers assess causal homogeneity by applying different forms of within-case analysis. They examine detailed evidence about the causal process that produced the outcome of concern. For example, if the focus is on institutional decision making, qualitative researchers may analyze records of the conversations and thought processes involved in that decision making, using what Alexander George and Timothy McKeown (1985: 34–41) describe as process tracing. More generally, analysts search for evidence about the causal mechanisms that would give plausibility to the hypotheses they are testing. If this evidence suggests that a similar mechanism produced or prevented the outcome in each case, this constitutes evidence for causal homogeneity.

These procedures help scholars make carefully calibrated statements about the appropriate universe of cases, involving "scope restrictions" (Walker and Cohen 1985) that delimit the domain to which the argument applies. For example, Theda Skocpol (1979: 40–42, 287–92; 1994: 4–7) argues that it would be a mistake to apply her original theory of revolution directly to twentieth-century revolutions. This is because a central feature of the cases she studied, the presence of agrarian-bureaucratic monarchies that had not experienced colonial domination, is simply not present in most twentieth-century revolutions. Although recognition that theories are bounded in this manner is also found in quantitative research, qualitative researchers have generally been more sensitive to this issue.

An alternative approach to assessing causal homogeneity is to identify multiple domains, within each of which the analyst finds causal homogeneity and between which there is causal heterogeneity. Researchers routinely present such findings in the form of *typologies*. This use of typologies merits particular emphasis here, given that *DSI* dismisses them as a research tool of limited value (48). Yet, as George and McKeown (1985: 28–29, 45) argue, typologies can play a valuable role in defining the universe of cases that can productively be compared (see also Stinchcombe 1968: 43–47; Ragin 1987: 20, 149).

For instance, establishing typologies of political regimes has been very useful in helping scholars delimit domains of cases. Perhaps the most influential set of typologies of regimes is that associated with Juan Linz (1964; 1975). Linz and others working within his general framework distinguish, for example, among democratic, authoritarian, totalitarian, post-totalitarian, military, one-party, and sultanistic regimes. This family of typologies has played a key role in helping analysts of regime change identify universes of cases within which causal processes are seen as working in similar ways. For example, Linz and Stepan (1996: 55–64) theorize that regime type, defined according to the categories noted above, affects the probability and nature of regime change. Transitions from a given type of regime may tend to have dynamics and explanations that are similar to one another, but different in comparison to transitions from other regime types. Geddes (1999) argues that the type of regime that existed prior to the transition—one-party, military, or personalistic/sultanistic—defines domains of cases within which the causal story of transition involves different independent variables. She thereby specifies domains of causal homogeneity. Thus, typologies can play a central role in developing statements about the scope of theories.[6]

Qualitative researchers also address the criterion of conditional independence, which includes the challenges of avoiding endogeneity (i.e., a situation in which the values of the explanatory variables are caused by the dependent variables) and of including all-important explanatory variables. Within-case analysis is again valuable here, in that it encourages researchers to identify and analyze the temporal sequence through which hypothesized explanatory variables affect outcomes.

---

[6]On efforts to ensure causal homogeneity, see also the discussion of "frames of comparison" and "contrast space" in Collier and Mahoney (1996: 66–69) and of positive and negative cases in Ragin (128–33 this volume). These various suggestions are still in need of refinement. Nonetheless, they are certainly worth pursuing, especially given Bartels's (74 this volume; see also 1996) argument that quantitative methodologists have still not dealt with this problem adequately, even though it may be possible to address causal heterogeneity with a complex regression model.

Within-case analysis privileges evidence about causal mechanisms, pushing researchers to ask whether change in the independent variables in fact preceded change in the dependent variable and, more significantly, by what process change in the independent variables produced the outcome. This process of studying sequences of change may also alert qualitative researchers to important missing variables, thereby addressing another aspect of the conditional independence assumption. A focus on sequences and changes over time is by no means unique to qualitative research; quantitative researchers obviously analyze time-series data. The point here is simply that qualitative researchers likewise have tools for this type of analysis.

Of course, in many studies endogeneity is impossible to avoid. In these situations, qualitative researchers may seek to focus explicitly on the reciprocal interactions among relevant variables and make inferences about the several causal links involved. This focus is found, for example, in studies that analyze "virtuous" or "vicious" cycles of political and economic events and of policy change,[7] as well as in studies of the dynamic interaction among leaders or other political actors.[8]

Case Selection: Dilemmas of Increasing the Number of Observations

A recurring piece of advice regarding case selection is to increase inferential leverage by adding new observations beyond those previously studied. This procedure is recommended repeatedly by *DSI*,[9] and it is extensively discussed in standard treatments of qualitative methodology (Lijphart 1971: 686; Smelser 1976: 198–202). *DSI*'s advice that qualitative researchers increase the number of observations drawn from within the cases already being analyzed (24, 47, 120, 217–28) corresponds to a standard practice among qualitative researchers.[10]

However, three concerns must be raised about increasing the number of observations. First, it may be "neither feasible nor necessarily desirable" (Ragin, Berg-Schlosser, and de Meur 1996: 752), and in many ways this advice amounts to little more than saying that "qualitative researchers are inevitably handicapped" and that they should "not be 'small-N' researchers" after all (Brady 55 this volume; see also McKeown 145–46 this volume).[11]

---

[7]See, for example, Kahler (1985: 477–78); Doner (1992: 410); Kapstein (1992: 271); Pierson (1993: passim); and Costigliola (1995: 108–9).

[8]See, for example, Stepan (1978), Higley and Gunther (1992), or Linz and Stepan (1996: 87–115).

[9]*DSI* 52, 67, 99, 116–20, 178–79, 213–17, 228.

[10]Smelser (1973: 77–80; 1976: 217–18), Campbell (1975), George and McKeown (1985), Collier and Mahoney (1996: 70).

[11]Like Lijphart (1971: 685), the authors of *DSI* operate with the assumption that we would always be better off using quantitative methods, and that small-N research and the

Second, if a qualitative researcher does choose to study more observations, *DSI*'s advice fails to recognize the problem of conceptual stretching that can arise when new cases are studied or when the use of within-case analysis brings about a shift in the unit of analysis (Ragin 125–28 this volume).[12] Conceptual stretching is the problem of taking concepts that validly apply to a given set of cases and extending them to a domain where they do not fit. While some might see this problem as an insurmountable obstacle that would simply make comparative analysis untenable, the pioneering work on conceptual stretching by Sartori (1970; 1984; 1991), recently reworked and refined by Collier and collaborators,[13] has sought to spell out procedures to guide the reconceptualization that may be needed to avoid conceptual stretching. Thus, insights developed by qualitative methodologists go considerably further than *DSI* in offering practical suggestions for dealing with this fundamental methodological challenge.

Third, efforts to increase inferential leverage by adding new cases may raise problems of causal heterogeneity. As discussed above, qualitative researchers are often hesitant to assume that causal homogeneity holds across a given range of cases, and they devote considerable attention to testing for heterogeneity. Extending an analysis beyond the domain for which causal homogeneity has been established requires researchers to choose between: (a) simply assuming that causal homogeneity holds among the new cases; or, (b) intensively testing each new case for causal homogeneity and including only those cases that pass the test, a process that may demand resources that could be better devoted to intensive analysis of the original set of cases.

DSI (116, 126–32, 135) gives considerable attention to the problem of selection bias.[14] The authors present the standard argument that selecting on the dependent variable can yield cases that are skewed to the high or low end of the distribution on that variable, with the likely consequence of biasing estimates of causal effects. Qualitative researchers are advised, as a first solution, to select their cases on the independent variable. This approach eliminates a significant source of selection bias, although *DSI* (129, 141, 147–49) emphasizes that in selecting on the independent variable, scholars should seek sufficient variation. Alternatively,

---

comparative method should only be used as a backup option, when quantitative methods cannot be used.

[12]However, this problem generally does not emerge in within-case analysis that generates the causal-process observations discussed in detail below (chap. 11), as opposed to data-set observations.

[13]Collier and Mahon (1993) and, since the publication of *DSI,* Collier (1995b), and Collier and Levitsky (1997).

[14]This issue has been among the most debated aspects of *DSI.* See Collier, Mahoney, and Seawright (chap. 6, this volume), the exchange between Rogowski (77–82 this volume) and King, Keohane, and Verba (188–91 this volume), and Dion (1998).

scholars can select on the dependent variable, but here again it is essential to ensure an appropriate range of variation.

Yet *DSI*'s advice concerning selection bias rests on the premise that causal inference requires the analysis of covariation between independent and dependent variables, a premise that can often be problematic (Lieberson 1985: 90–91; Ragin 1994: 107, 145–48). Because qualitative work often assesses causal effects through an analysis of covariation,[15] *DSI*'s insistence that studies include variation on both the explanatory and the dependent variable is, of course, relevant to qualitative researchers. However, many qualitative researchers make causal inferences by focusing attention centrally on processes and decisions *within* cases. While such analysis is certainly framed by at least implicit comparison with other cases, it is a different research strategy from that of explicit and systematic comparison. If this close analysis of processes and decisions focuses only on cases where the overall outcome being explained (e.g., war or revolution) has occurred, then it may be called a *no-variance design*. Qualitative researchers see such studies as making a key contribution in the research process, helping to generate the kind of insights into causal mechanisms without which the analysis of covariation is incomplete. This kind of design can be valuable for gaining descriptive insight into a political phenomenon about which researchers have little prior knowledge.

A great deal of methodological attention has been paid to research designs in which the analyst intentionally selects cases that do not vary on the dependent variable. However, these research designs should be situated in relation to the broad range of intentional case selection strategies that qualitative researchers routinely employ. Cases matched on independent variables may be selected, for example, to control for the effects of these explanatory factors. Sharply contrasting cases may be selected to explore the hypothesis that a given cause produces an outcome across various domains. These designs correspond to the standard procedures for analyzing matching and contrasting cases discussed by J. S. Mill (1974b [1843]) and by Przeworksi and Teune (1970: 32–39). Cases that exhibit substantial variability on important rival explanations may be selected to provide a difficult test for a theory (Eckstein 1975: 113–32). These three approaches to intentional case selection provide qualitative researchers with valuable leverage in testing their hypotheses.

---

[15]It bears emphasizing, as Collier and Mahoney (1996: 75–80) argue, that many studies that are seen to lack variance on the dependent variable actually do exhibit variance. Part of the reason for this misperception is the fact that analysts fail to see how the study of cases over time naturally introduces variance on the dependent variable. *DSI* (129) does not appear to appreciate the significance of the longitudinal dimension of much comparative research, as the discussion of Skocpol's work on revolution demonstrates.

Measurement and Data Collection

With regard to measurement, *DSI*'s lack of attention to standard methodological-cal texts on—and the established practices of—qualitative research is again appar-ent in its overly brief discussion of measurement validity. *DSI* (25, 153) is on solid ground in calling for qualitative researchers to maximize the validity of their measurements. However, the book does little to incorporate prior work by com-parativists who have grappled with the problem of validity,[16] or to acknowledge the difficulty of developing equivalent indicators across different cases. For quali-tative researchers, a key aspect of the problem is, simply, that just as words can take on different meanings when used in different contexts, indicators can also measure different things in different contexts. To take a traditional example, while the magnitude of economic activity can be measured quite accurately in monetary terms in western societies, money is an incomplete indicator in less developed societies that are not fully monetized (Smelser 1973: 69). More recently, concerns with this indicator arise due to the magnitude of the extralegal or underground economy in many developed countries. Thus, a researcher cannot assume that the same indicator will be a valid measure of a concept across different cases and time periods.

Qualitative researchers, for the most part, have not been self-conscious about ensuring measurement validity. Nonetheless, as Collier (1998a: 5) suggests, the close familiarity that qualitative researchers tend to have with their cases has al-lowed them to implicitly follow the long-standing advice of Przeworski and Teune (1970: chap. 6) to construct "system-specific indicators" as opposed to "common indicators" (see also Verba 1971; Zelditch 1971). More recent recommendations for tackling this problem have been offered by Locke and Thelen (1995), who urge scholars to carry out "contextualized comparison."[17] Thus, *DSI*'s discussion can be criticized on two grounds. First, it ignores key earlier literature, merely making the general argument that researchers should ensure the validity of their measurements (25, 153) and draw upon their knowledge of context (43), but fail-ing to focus on specific procedures for accomplishing this in comparative research. Second, *DSI* fails to note that the sensitivity to context that researchers bring to small-N studies gives them an alternative form of leverage in dealing with issues

---

[16]Early discussions of measurement equivalence that draw on both the quantitative and qualitative traditions include: Przeworski and Teune (1970), Zelditch (1971), and Warwick and Osherson (1973: 14–28). See also Smelser (1976: 174–93).

[17]Considering the study of labor politics and economic restructuring, Locke and Thelen (1995) argue that a researcher should not simply focus, for example, on disputes over wages. Instead, a researcher should search for those points where conflicts emerge, which might vary from case to case. Thus, to ensure the equivalence of measurements one might have to focus on conflicts over wages in one case, over employment in an-other, and over working hours in yet another.

of validity, compared to large-N researchers. An important reason for choosing a small N is thus simply ignored.

With regard to data collection, qualitative researchers employ intensive methods that produce richer, more multifaceted information than is contained in most quantitative data sets. In-depth interviews provide qualitative researchers with a great deal of valuable evidence. In such interviews, informants not only answer the specific, prepared questions that the researcher poses, but often offer their own more nuanced responses and unprompted insights. For these reasons, such interviews do not constitute a single "data point" in any normal sense; rather, they are a complex array of data, different parts of which can be used to support or undermine a theory. Other common qualitative practices such as participant observation and content analysis produce data that has similar "depth."

Causal Assessment in Cross-Case and Within-Case Designs

Much of quantitative researchers' treatment of causal assessment is essentially based on a standard regression model. This model tends to assume, as a default position, that causal effects are uniform across cases and operate in a probabilistic fashion (Abbott 1988; Abbott 1992: 432–34). Qualitative researchers, by contrast, have frequently employed different models of causation, and they utilize a variety of tools appropriate to these models.

First, qualitative researchers sometimes use a deterministic, as opposed to a probabilistic, model of causation (Ragin and Zaret 1983: 743–44; Ragin 1987: 15–16, 39–40, 52; Ragin 135–38 this volume), and have designed procedures for assessing this model. A deterministic understanding of causation, which allows the analyst to reject a potential explanatory factor on the basis of a single deviation from an overall pattern (Dion 1998: 128), is implicit in arguments that even single case studies can be used to test theories. Well-known examples include Lijphart's (1971: 692) "crucial experiments" and Eckstein's (1975: 113–32) "crucial case studies" (see also Rogowski 77–82 this volume). More recent discussions have creatively focused on the problem of testing the hypothesis of deterministic causation against the alternative hypothesis of probabilistic causation (Dion 1998; Ragin 2000; Braumoeller and Goertz 2000; Seawright 2002a,b).

Second, additional tools employed by qualitative researchers for testing alternative models of causation include Ragin's (1987, 2000) Qualitative Comparative Analysis (see above), which is used to test multiple, conjunctural causes; the use of Mill's methods jointly with process tracing to test what Stinchcombe (1968: 101–29) designates as "historical" as opposed to "constant" causes; and the closely related analytic procedures offered by the growing literature on critical junctures and path dependence.[18] Once again, quantitative researchers likewise have procedures for assessing these specific models of causation;[19] I would merely stress that qualitative researchers have a long history of working with such models.

Third, as Seawright and Mazzuca argue, through the procedure they call "within-case control," qualitative researchers have a distinctive means of addressing an aspect of descriptive inference that *DSI* (56–61) emphasizes strongly: distinguishing between outcomes that are systematic with respect to a given theory and outcomes that are random with respect to that theory, or that are better treated as the result of different processes.[20] The idea of separating the systematic component of a phenomenon from the random component, summarized in chapter 2 of the present volume, is one of the three basic components in *DSI*'s account of descriptive inference.

Though the reason for making this distinction may be unclear to some researchers, it is in fact valuable in qualitative analysis for two closely linked reasons. First, in qualitative research it is difficult to introduce control variables. Hence, disaggregating the dependent variable by removing variation that is caused by factors other than those central to the explanatory model is a way of meeting the "other things being equal" criterion necessary for causal inference, and thereby achieving within-case control. Second, some causal factors are genuinely outside of the researcher's explanatory framework, and removing variance that results from these factors permits better inference about the aspects of social phenomena that are of greatest theoretical interest. For example, it may be interesting for a social movements scholar to learn that the intensity of some urban riots in the United States during the summer of 1968 was increased by hot weather, but this

---

[18]For valuable discussions of methodological issues that arise in developing critical juncture/path-dependent models, see Collier and Collier (1991: chap. 1), Jackson (1996: 722–26, 730–45), Pierson (2000), and Mahoney (2000b). For discussions of critical juncture models in research on party systems, regime change, and economic transformations, see Lipset and Rokkan (1967), Collier and Collier (1991), Stark (1992), and Ekiert (1996).

[19]Beyond the distinctive issues raised by deterministic, multiple, conjunctural, and historical causes, a significant challenge concerns the assessment of models of asymmetrical (Lieberson 1985: chap. 4) and cumulative causation (Stinchcombe 1978: 61–70). See also Zuckerman (1997). I would stress that the need to assess this range of causal models is not a point that divides quantitative and qualitative researchers. Thus, it is noteworthy that quantitative methodologists have also sought to devise tools to assess necessary and sufficient causes (Braumoeller and Goertz 2000), models of multiple causal paths (Braumoeller 1999), and path dependent causes (Jackson 1996: 730–45), and, more generally, have sought to fashion quantitative methods more suited to historically oriented analysis (Griffin and van der Linden 1999).

[20] Jason Seawright and Sebastián Mazzuca, personal communication.

scholar might well want to remove this aspect of the variance in the outcome, to permit a more direct test of social and political hypotheses.

Qualitative researchers can achieve within-case control by closely examining the causal process and separating out distinct components of the variance being explained. Within-case analysis helps researchers assess to what degree the mechanism hypothesized by a theory was present among all the cases under study. Researchers can thus make inferences not only about the extent to which the hypothesized cause was found across cases, but also about the extent to which that cause produced the outcome for each case. For deviant cases, that is, cases that do not follow the causal pattern predicted by the theory, within-case analysis gives qualitative researchers an opportunity to discover the processes that caused the case to diverge from the hypothesized outcome. These processes may involve variables quite unrelated to the main hypothesis, and therefore may be seen as random with respect to that hypothesis. However, in qualitative research the variance associated with these processes is not automatically separated out, as it is in regression analysis. Rather, the researcher must carefully consider evidence about the nature of each "random" process in order to eliminate from the dependent variable the variance associated with that process.

The value of separating the systematic and the random component through within-case control may be illustrated by an example. Thomas Ertman's (1997) analysis of early-modern state building hypothesizes that the interaction of (a) the type of local government during the first period of state-building, with (b) the timing of increases in geopolitical competition, strongly influences the kind of regime and state that emerge. He tests this hypothesis against the historical experience of Europe and finds that most countries fit his predictions. Denmark, however, is a major exception. In Denmark, sustained geopolitical competition began relatively late and local government at the beginning of the state-building period was generally participatory (305–6), which should have led the country to develop "patrimonial constitutionalism." But in fact, it developed "bureaucratic absolutism." Ertman carefully explores the process through which Denmark came to have a bureaucratic absolutist state and finds that Denmark had the early marks of a patrimonial constitutionalist state. However, the country was pushed off this developmental path by the influence of German knights, who entered Denmark and brought with them German institutions of local government (307). Ertman then traces the causal process through which these imported institutions pushed Denmark to develop bureaucratic absolutism (307–11), concluding that this development was caused by a factor well outside his explanatory framework. Ertman makes a parallel argument for Sweden (311–14), and summarizes his overall interpretation of these cases by stating that:

> In both Sweden and Denmark, the two factors highlighted throughout this book also operated, broadly speaking, in the manner expected. . . . Yet in both cases contingent historical circumstances intervened to shunt these states off the path

leading to noble dominance and patrimonial constitutionalism and onto rather different roads. (Ertman 1997: 316)

This conclusion could be misunderstood as an inappropriate attempt to discard information that runs counter to the main hypothesis. A better way of thinking about this, as we have emphasized, is to see it as analogous to the initiative in quantitative research of introducing a control variable. Adding a control variable in effect poses the question: other things being equal, does the main hypothesis in fact explain part of the outcome? Through within-case control, qualitative researchers have a means of addressing this question.

Beyond Strict Hypothesis Testing: Theory Generation, Reformulation, and the Iterated Assessment of Hypotheses

Quantitative methodologists often take a relatively strict view of hypothesis testing, issuing warnings against data mining and against testing a given hypothesis with the data used to generate it. Qualitative methodologists, on the other hand, point to opportunities for moving beyond strict hypothesis testing by engaging in the ongoing refinement of concepts, the iterated fine-tuning of hypotheses, and the use of specially targeted case studies that appear likely to suggest new hypotheses and theoretical ideas.

DSI undervalues the contribution to theory development and reformulation that is made by ongoing interaction with the data. *DSI*'s cautionary remarks about reformulating the theory after analyzing the data (21–22) and about data mining (174) are unduly restrictive. Theory reformulation that occurs after looking at the data is critical because it allows social scientists to learn from their research. Indeed, it would be an important constraint on the accumulation of knowledge if analysts did not routinely revise their explanations of a set of cases and then test the new explanation—if need be, with the same set of data. The concerns with contextual specificity discussed above may convince the researcher that moving beyond this initial set of cases is not analytically productive. Of course, careless revisions of theory should be considered suspect, yet it is vital to recognize the legitimacy of efforts to inductively reformulate theory by carefully incorporating insights drawn from research findings.

With regard to refining concepts, Ragin (125–28, 130–33 this volume) suggests that an ongoing process of concept formation should be intimately interconnected with the analysis of positive and negative cases that exemplify the variation of interest. This does not occur merely at the onset of a study, but is a process that continues throughout the study. More generally, scholars frequently refine their variables, often through disaggregation, in order to more adequately capture the ideas involved in the hypotheses they are testing.[21]

Qualitative researchers routinely build on their in-depth knowledge of cases to gain further insights about causal processes (Collier 1999), which among other things can improve causal inference by suggesting important missing variables. To do this, qualitative researchers rely on a spectrum of case-oriented research designs, such as Lijphart's (1971: 691–93) "hypothesis-generating" case study, which corresponds to what Eckstein (1975) calls a "heuristic" case study; Eckstein's "disciplined-configurative" case study; and the "no-variance" small-N designs discussed above. Lijphart's "deviant" case-study design, like these other approaches, can play a central and creative role in suggesting further hypotheses.

The core point, as Ragin (125–28, 135–38 this volume) states, is that researchers should not treat tests of causal hypotheses as the endpoint of a study, but rather as an ongoing activity that should be closely intertwined with these other components of the research process.

Conclusion

This chapter argues that just as quantitative researchers can draw upon a relatively standardized set of methodological procedures, so qualitative scholars also have well-developed procedures—which in fact address every step in the research process. The problem is not that qualitative researchers lack tools to conduct their research, but rather that these tools have not been adequately systematized. The goal of this chapter has been to formulate them more systematically (see again table 7.1).

Although qualitative researchers can take considerable satisfaction in this set of tools, the contributions of qualitative methodology should not be overstated. As Bartels (74 this volume) suggests, part of the problem with *DSI* is that its authors "promise a good deal more than . . . [they] could possibly deliver given the current state of political methodology" (see also Brady 55–56 this volume; Jackson 1996: 742–45). Correspondingly, even though *DSI* persistently undervalues the contributions of qualitative methodologists (McKeown 145–46 this volume), qualitative researchers should not try to correct this imbalance by overselling their own ap-

---

[21]Skocpol's (1979) research on social revolution exemplifies this approach. She disaggregates her dependent variable into two parts—state breakdown and peasant uprising—a decision that allows her to build her argument around two distinct, though interrelated outcomes. This allows her to focus more clearly on the mechanisms that generate these distinct outcomes. In addition, she is able to avoid potential confusion by showing how certain variables (e.g., international pressures) are used to explain state breakdown and not (at least not directly) peasant uprising. Finally, this approach allows Skocpol (1994) to integrate her findings as well as those of other researchers in the context of a general framework.

proach. Substantively oriented research will be advanced most effectively to the extent that a more meaningful dialogue between quantitative and qualitative researchers is established, and the strengths of alternative methods are brought to bear on interesting questions of political analysis.

CHAPTER 8

Turning the Tables:
How Case-Oriented Research Challenges
Variable-Oriented Research

Charles C. Ragin

In this chapter, I respond to recent commentaries on the practice of what I call "case-oriented" qualitative research (Ragin 1987: chap. 3) that have been offered from the standpoint of quantitative, "variable-oriented" methodology. Whereas most of these commentaries are basically critiques of the case-oriented tradition (e.g., Goldthorpe 1991, 1997; Lieberson 1991, 1994, 1997), *Designing Social Inquiry* by King, Keohane, and Verba (hereafter *DSI*) is more ecumenical in spirit. *DSI* presents a broad programmatic statement offering detailed suggestions for improving case-oriented research using principles derived from the variable-oriented approach. This ambitious work attempts to show, contrary to the claims of many, that the case-oriented approach has a great deal in common with the variable-oriented approach and thus can be improved using insights and techniques gleaned from the variable-oriented tradition.

While some of the advice offered in these commentaries, especially in *DSI,* is very good and completely on target, much of it misses the mark. In what follows, I

I thank Bruce Carruthers, David Collier, and Larry Griffin for their many useful comments.

turn the tables and argue that case-oriented inquiry poses important obstacles to the use of variable-oriented methods. Indeed, key aspects of the analytic strategies at the core of case-oriented inquiry are completely outside the scope of the variable-oriented approach. I demonstrate these incompatibilities by translating some of the central concerns of case-oriented research to variable-oriented research and showing the difficult methodological problems these concerns pose for the variable-oriented approach.[1] My central goal in this discussion is to show that case-oriented research is not a primitive form of variable-oriented research that can be improved through stricter adherence to variable-oriented standards. Rather, the case-oriented approach is better understood as a different mode of inquiry with different operating assumptions.

This chapter does *not* repeat familiar statements about uniqueness, holism, experience, meaning, narrative integrity, or cultural significance—the concerns most often voiced by qualitative, case-oriented researchers in defense of their methods. Nor do I waste time repeating the claim that the goals of qualitative research differ diametrically from those of quantitative research. After all, there is no necessary wedge separating the goal of inference—a key concern of quantitative approaches—from the goal of making sense of cases, a common concern of qualitative approaches (Ragin 1994: 47–52). Instead, I elucidate practical concerns that are at the core of case-oriented strategies. These practical concerns pose important challenges to the variable-oriented approach. I do not claim that these difficulties throw insurmountable obstacles in the path of variable-oriented methods. Rather, my concern is that these practical issues are usually obscured in the process of variable-oriented research or neutralized through assumptions.

By *practical concerns,* I refer to the deceptively simple mechanics of constructing useful social scientific summaries of empirical evidence, a task common to virtually all forms of social research. The features of case-oriented research I discuss here constitute only a subset of the features that pose practical difficulties for variable-oriented approaches. The features I address are centered in five overlapping domains: (1) the constitution of cases, (2) the study of uniform outcomes, (3) the definition of negative cases, (4) the analysis of multiple and conjunctural causes, and (5) the treatment of nonconforming cases. These practical concerns, or

---

[1]To maximize the exchange between these two approaches, I impose a restriction: I limit the discussion to case-oriented approaches that are explicitly concerned with patterns across multiple cases, not with the examination of a single case (see Miles and Huberman 1994). The extreme in this regard is the country specialist who might spend an entire career coming to grips with a "single case" like the fall of the Berlin Wall or the outcome of the Korean War. This researcher has "only one case" but may consider thousands of factors and conditions in his or her effort to explain the case—to "get it right." In research of this type, the goal is to piece together a whole, a single case, from the elements that constitute the case. Obviously, this research strategy cannot be made commensurable, at least not in any simple or straightforward manner, with the concern of quantitative methodologists regarding an abundance of observations relative to the number of explanatory variables.

tasks, as well as the tools employed in addressing them, are summarized in table 8.1.

I offer this discussion of practical concerns in the spirit of enriching the dialogue between case-oriented and variable-oriented research. After all, it is much better for the two sets of practitioners to share ideas about compatibilities and incompatibilities than it is to ignore or dismiss each other altogether.

Constitution of Cases

Case-oriented researchers see cases as meaningful but complex configurations of events and structures. They treat cases as singular, whole entities purposefully selected, not as homogeneous observations drawn at random from a pool of equally plausible selections. Most case-oriented studies start with the seemingly simple idea that social phenomena in like settings (such as organizations, neighborhoods, cities, countries, regions, cultures, and so on) may parallel each other sufficiently to permit comparing and contrasting them. The clause, "may parallel each other sufficiently," is a very important part of this formulation. The qualitative researcher's specification of relevant cases at the start of an investigation is really nothing more than a working hypothesis that the cases initially selected are in fact alike enough to permit comparisons. In the course of the research, the investigator may decide otherwise and drop some cases, or even whole categories of cases, because they do not appear to belong with what seem to be the core cases. Sometimes, this process of sifting through the cases leads to an enlargement of the set of relevant cases and a commensurate broadening of the scope of the guiding concepts. For example, a researcher might surmise in the course of studying "military coups" that the relevant category could be enlarged to include all "irregular transfers of executive power."

Usually, this sifting of the cases is carried out in conjunction with concept formation and elaboration. Concepts are revised and refined as the boundary of the set of relevant cases is shifted and clarified. Important theoretical distinctions often emerge from this dialogue of ideas and evidence. Imagine, for example, that Theda Skocpol (1979) had originally included Mexico along with France, Russia, and China at the outset of her study of social revolutions. The search for commonalities across these four cases might prove too daunting. By eliminating Mexico as a case of *social* revolution in the course of the research, however, it might prove possible to increase the homogeneity within the empirical category and, at the same time, to sharpen the definition of the concept of social revolution.

This interplay of categorization and conceptualization is a key feature of qualitative research (Ragin 1994: chap. 4). In their treatise on the design of qualitative research, however, the authors of *DSI* strongly discourage this practice,

Table 8.1. Tasks and Tools in Case-Oriented Research

Task	Tool
Defining the Population of Cases	Analyze cases to clarify scope of empirical categories, in conjunction with refinement of concepts.
Focusing on Positive Cases	Select cases where the outcome occurs, then identify causal conditions shared by these cases.
Defining Relevant Negative Cases	Use theory and knowledge of positive cases to establish the relevant negative cases.
Analyzing Multiple and Conjunctural Causes	Explore causal factors that produce the outcome. This often involves identifying different combinations of factors that produce the same outcome.
Addressing Nonconforming Cases	Identify cases that do not conform to common causal patterns and identify the factors at work in these cases, even if these factors are outside the study's theoretical framework.

arguing that it is not appropriate to "add a restrictive condition and then proceed as if our theory, with that qualification, has been shown to be correct" (21). They offer the following example of their concern:

> If our original theory was that modern democracies do not fight wars with one another due to their constitutional systems, it would be less permissible, having found exceptions to our "rule," to restrict the proposition to democracies with advanced social welfare systems *once it has been ascertained by inspection of the data that such a qualification would appear to make our proposition correct.* (21, italics in original)

The authors of *DSI* state subsequently "*we should not make it* [i.e., our theory] *more restrictive without collecting new data to test the new version of the theory*" (22, italics in original). Unfortunately, this well-reasoned advice puts an end to most case-oriented research as it is practiced today. The reciprocal clarification of empirical categories and theoretical concepts is one of the central concerns of qualitative research (Ragin 1994: chap. 4). When the number of relevant cases is limited by the historical record to a mere handful, or even to several handfuls, it is simply not possible to collect a "new sample" to "test" each new theoretical clarification.

Both *DSI* and Goldthorpe (1997) recommend switching to a different unit of analysis, for example, subnational units or time periods, to enlarge the number of "cases" relevant to an argument formulated for larger units.[2] However, most case-oriented comparative social scientists do not find this practice satisfactory. They study the cases they do because these cases are historically, politically, or culturally significant in some way. Typically, the shift to smaller units (i.e., to subnational units or to different time periods) entails an unavoidable reformulation of the research question, which, in turn, severely undermines the substantive value of the study. (Lieberson 1985: chap. 5 concurs with this position.) Researchers end up asking questions dictated by methods or by data availability, not by their theoretical, substantive, or historical interests. One common reformulation, for example, is to transform questions about qualitative change (i.e., historically emergent phenomena) to questions about variation in cross-sectional levels (i.e., static phenomena).

In fairness to both *DSI* and Goldthorpe it is important to note that the primary concern is theory testing, not concept formation, elaboration, and refinement. Neither would object to the common practice of using knowledge of the empirical world—however it may have been gained—to build better concepts and thus, ultimately, stronger theories. Still, it is worth pointing out that from their perspective, theory testing is the primary, perhaps sole, objective of social science, and researchers should organize their research efforts around this important task. It is as though *DSI* and other critics start with the assumption that social scientists already possess well-developed, well-articulated, testable theories. Nothing could be further from the truth. In case-oriented research, the bulk of the research effort is often directed toward constituting "the cases" in the investigation and sharpening the concepts appropriate for the cases selected (Ragin and Becker 1992).

The first practical concern can now be summarized in succinct terms: In case-oriented research, cases usually are not predetermined, nor are they "given" at the outset of an investigation. Instead, they often coalesce in the course of the research through a systematic dialogue of ideas and evidence (see McMichael 1990, especially his discussion of Polanyi). In many qualitatively oriented studies, the conclusion of this process of "casing" (Ragin 1992) may be the primary and most important finding of the investigation (see, e.g., Wieviorka 1993). Consider the serious practical problem this poses for conventional quantitative analysis: The boundary around the "sample of observations" must be relatively malleable throughout the investigation, and this boundary may not be completely fixed until the research is finished. Thus, any quantitative result (for example, the correlation between two variables across cases) is open to fundamental revision up until the very conclusion of the research because the cases that comprise the sample may be revised continually before that point. By contrast, quantitative analysis of the rela-

---

[2]There is great slippage in what is meant by the term "case" (Ragin and Becker 1992). Usually, *DSI* and other defenders of quantitative methods in macrosocial research switch terms and speak only of "observations" and thus skirt the issue of identifying what, exactly, the case is.

tionships among variables presupposes a fixed set of relevant observations. Indeed, having a reasonably well-delimited population is a precondition for the
quantitative analysis of cross-case patterns. Once constituted by the researcher, a
population is treated as an analytic space containing "like objects"—comparable,
substitutable, independent instances of "the same thing." Consequently, in quantitative analysis, a crucial process of ongoing learning about the cases is cut short.

Study of Uniform Outcomes

Because the constitution and selection of cases is central to qualitative inquiry,
case-oriented researchers may intentionally select cases that differ relatively little
from each other with respect to the outcome under investigation. For example, a
researcher might attempt to constitute the category "anti-neocolonial revolutions,"
both empirically and conceptually, through the reciprocal process just described.
At the end of this process his or her set of cases might exclude both lesser upris-
ings (e.g., mere anti-neocolonial "rebellions") and mass insurrections of varying
severity that were successfully repressed. In the eyes of the variable-oriented researcher, however, this investigator has committed a great folly—selecting cases
that vary only slightly, if at all, on the outcome, or dependent variable.

The first and most obvious problem with this common practice—in the eyes
of the variable-oriented scholar—is thus the simple fact that the dependent variable in this example, anti-neocolonial revolution, does not vary substantially
across the cases selected for study. All cases selected display, more or less, the
same outcome—anti-neocolonial revolutions. Variable-oriented researchers tend
to equate "explanation" with "explaining variation." If there is no variation in the
outcome, they reason, then there is nothing to explain. From the perspective of
quantitative analysis, therefore, the case-oriented investigation of anti-neocolonial
revolutions just described may seem to lack even the possibility of analysis or
research design. It appears to be an analytic dead end.

The second problem with this common case-oriented practice is known to
quantitative researchers as "selecting on the dependent variable."[3] Assume (1) that
the category "anti-neocolonial revolutions" encompasses cases with the highest
scores (say, 90 through 100 on a 100-point scale) on the more general variable
"level of mass insurrection," and (2) that this dependent variable has a strong positive correlation with measures of foreign capital penetration, for example, the proportion of fixed capital that is owned by transnational corporations. No doubt, the
cases of "anti-neocolonial revolt" identified by the qualitative researcher would all

---

[3] A parallel and more detailed illustration is offered in *DSI* (130–32). Unfortunately,
the authors' example does not resonate well with the substantive concerns of comparative
social science. Thus, they follow the lead of Lieberson (1991), who used automobile
accidents to illustrate his arguments, thus presenting examples that simply do not ring
true to the concerns of comparative social science.

have high levels of foreign capital penetration. However, within the relatively narrow range of mass insurrection that encompasses "anti-neocolonial revolution" (i.e., countries with scores over 90), there may be no apparent relationship between level of foreign capital penetration and the level of mass insurrection. Instead, the relationship between these two variables might be visible only across the entire range of variation in the dependent variable, level of mass insurrection, with scores ranging from near zero to 100. For this reason all researchers are advised, based on sound quantitative arguments, to examine the entire range of variation in broadly defined dependent variables and thereby avoid this analytic sin.

From the perspective of variable-oriented analysis, therefore, not only is there little to explain when qualitative investigators "select on the dependent variable," as in the example just described, but investigators are likely as well to be misled about the impact of underlying factors—those that account for the "entire range" of variation in an outcome.

These criticisms drawn from the quantitative perspective are well reasoned. However, they are based on a very serious misunderstanding of case-oriented research. The first response to these criticisms concerns the theoretical status of the categories elaborated through case-oriented research. The fact that anti-neocolonial revolutions all have very high scores on the variable "level of mass insurrection" does not alter the possibility that anti-neocolonial revolutions are fundamentally (i.e., qualitatively) different from other forms of insurrection and therefore warrant separate analytic attention. Social scientists study the phenomena they study because these phenomena are often culturally or historically significant. The fact that some phenomena (e.g., anti-neocolonial revolutions) can be reconstrued as scores on more general variables (e.g., mass insurrection) does not negate their distinctive features or their substantive importance.

The second response to these criticisms is the simple observation that most case-oriented investigators would not be blind to the fact (in the hypothetical example) that countries with anti-neocolonial revolutions have unusually high levels of foreign capital penetration. Indeed, the very first step in the qualitative analysis of anti-neocolonial revolutions, after constituting the category and specifying the relevant cases, would be to identify the possible causal conditions they share— their commonalities. Their high levels of foreign capital penetration no doubt would be one of the very first commonalities identified. It is not a causal factor that would be overlooked because of its lack of apparent correlation with the intensity of anti-neocolonial revolutions within the relatively narrow range of outcomes selected for study.

The second practical issue, therefore, concerns the function and importance of what quantitative methodologists call constants in case-oriented analysis. Often the outcome (i.e., the "dependent variable") and many of the explanatory factors in a case-oriented analysis are constants—all cases have more or less the same values. In the example just presented, anti-neocolonial revolutions (the uniform outcome) occur in countries with uniformly high scores on one causal variable (foreign capital penetration) and probably with relatively uniform values on other causal variables as well (for elaboration of these ideas about constants see Griffin et al. 1997). While using constants to account for constants (i.e., the search for commonalities shared by similar instances) is common in case-oriented, qualitative work (and in everyday life), it is foreign to quantitative techniques that focus exclusively on relationships among variables—that is, on causal conditions and outcomes that must vary across cases.

Definition of Negative Cases

The discussion so far has brought us to a debate recognizable to many as the controversy surrounding the method of analytic induction, a technique that follows John Stuart Mill's (1974b [1843]: chap. 8) method of agreement. The method of agreement looks only at positive cases (that is, cases displaying an effect) and assesses whether or not these positive cases all agree in displaying one or more causes. The usual objection to this practice from the standpoint of quantitative methods is that only two cells of a two-by-two cross-tabulation (presence/absence of a cause by presence/absence of an effect) are studied and that, therefore, causal inference is impossible. After all, what if many of the negative cases (that is, cases not displaying the effect) display the same causal factors (e.g., in the example just elaborated, a high level of foreign capital penetration)?

This criticism appears sound. However, it is very important to recognize that this criticism *assumes* a preexisting population of relevant observations, embracing both positive and negative cases, and thus ignores a central practical concern of qualitative analysis—the constitution of cases, as described above.[4] From the perspective of case-oriented qualitative analysis, the cross-tabulation of causes and effects is entirely reasonable as long as these analyses are conducted *within an appropriately constituted set of cases.* For example, it would be entirely reasonable to assess whether or not the emergence of "multiple sovereignty" in anti-neocolonial revolutions is linked to the prior existence of democratic institutions. However, this analysis would be conducted only within the duly constituted category of anti-neocolonial revolutions. The quantitative critique of analytic induction and the method of agreement ignores this essential precondition for conventional variable-oriented analysis, namely, that relevant cases must be properly constituted through a careful dialogue of ideas and evidence involving the reciprocal clarification of empirical categories and theoretical concepts.

From the perspective of case-oriented analysis, to cross-tabulate the presence/absence of causes of anti-neocolonial revolution with the presence/absence of anti-neocolonial revolution, it first would be necessary to constitute the category

---

[4]Consider, for example, the category "not instances of anti-neocolonial revolutions." This category is as infinite as it is vague.

of relevant negative cases (for example, the category "countries with a strong possibility of anti-neocolonial revolution"). Before doing this, of course, it would be necessary to examine actual anti-neocolonial revolutions closely and identify their common causes, using theory, substantive knowledge, and interests as guides. In other words, the investigator would have to constitute the empirical category "anti-neocolonial revolutions" and identify common causal factors (using the method of agreement or some other method appropriate for the study of uniform outcomes) before attempting to constitute the category "countries with a strong possibility of anti-neocolonial revolutions" and then proceed with conventional variable-oriented analysis of the differences between positive and negative cases (see also Griffin et al. 1997).

For an illustration of the complex task of establishing populations in case-oriented research, consider the following: A researcher studying an elementary school in St. Louis concludes that racial consciousness is highly developed among its students because of the strong link between race and class boundaries in this school. The African American children mostly come from lower- and working-class homes. The European-American children mostly come from middle- and upper-middle-class homes. The researcher's implied causal argument is that the greater the correlation between race and class, the stronger the racial consciousness. Note that the researcher in this hypothetical study did not actually observe variation in the degree of race/class correlation or in the strength of racial consciousness. Rather, he observed that both were strong in a single case. Thus, the researcher's selection of the race/class correlation as the primary causal connection rests on the strength of corroborating ethnographic evidence, not on an observed pattern of covariation.

If asked, "What is this case a case of?" most case-oriented researchers would say that it is a case of strong racial consciousness among children. That is, they would emphasize the outcome. This understanding of the population locates this case in the set of instances of strong racial consciousness, which in turn might include not only schools, but also public settings, neighborhoods, and other places where people from different racial groups interact on a routine basis. Looking at the case study from this point of view, the implicit argument is that wherever children display a high degree of racial consciousness, a careful observer is likely to find that it is fueled and perhaps engendered by the strong link between race and class in the setting. If an accumulation of case studies of instances of strong racial consciousness among children confirmed this link, then one could argue that a strong link between race and class is a condition for strong racial consciousness, perhaps even one of several *necessary* conditions.

Relevant populations also may be constituted from causal conditions, not just from outcomes. Before addressing this issue, it is important to examine the hypothetical case study just described more closely, especially with respect to its causally relevant features. While it would be seductive to frame the study's argument monocausally (the greater the race/class coincidence, the stronger the racial consciousness), it would be simplistic to do so. In fact, there are several features of this case that could be considered causally relevant to its high level of racial consciousness, including aspects of its setting:

1. It is an elementary school (a prime location for acquiring racial consciousness in the United States).
2. It is located in a racially heterogeneous urban area.
3. It has a substantial proportion of both African American and European American students.
4. There is a substantial link between race and class among the students in the school.

At the most basic level, the researcher in this example would argue simply that settings that are *similar* to the one studied—with respect to relevant causal conditions—should exhibit strong racial consciousness. In essence, the argument would be that the conditions identified by the researcher are sufficient for racial consciousness. Notice, though, that in the extreme, the definition of *similarity* could be very strict, so much so that very few instances would qualify. For example, it could be argued that a strong correlation between race and class yields a high level of racial consciousness only when an elementary school in a racially heterogeneous urban area has 60 percent European American students and 40 percent African American students—the same as the racial composition of the school studied.

1. elementary schools;
2. elementary schools in racially heterogeneous urban areas; or
3. elementary schools in racially heterogeneous urban areas that also enroll a substantial proportion of both European American and African American students.

The first set is the broadest and most inclusive; the third is the least inclusive. Of course, this set of concentric circles could be extended in both a more inclusive or a less inclusive direction.

Note that there is an interplay between population definition and causal analysis in case-oriented research. Any causally relevant feature of a case can be interpreted either as a condition for the operation of a cause or as a cause. If the feature is treated as a condition, it may become part of the definition of the population—the larger set of cases thought to be comparable to the case under investigation. If it is treated as a cause, then it becomes a central part of the investigator's argument and a key component of any hypothesis the researcher might draw from his or her case study. For example, it might be reasonable to see racial consciousness as a function of not only the correlation between race and class, but also as a function of racial composition. Perhaps the closer a school approximates a racial balance, the greater the racial consciousness. In this formulation there are two features treated as causal factors (race/class correlation and racial composition) and two that can be used to define the relevant population (elementary schools in racially heterogeneous urban areas).

Of course, there is no way to know from a single case which features are key causal factors and which should be used to define relevant populations. The investigator's theory and substantive knowledge must provide the necessary guidance. The central point is that case-oriented researchers may construct a variety of different populations as they decide how to frame the results of their research. Further, there is an array of possible populations, ranging from less inclusive ones, those that resemble the case under investigation in many respects, to very broad, inclusive populations, resembling the studied case in perhaps only one way. The entire process of case-oriented research—learning more about a case to see what lessons it has to offer—can be seen, in part, as an effort to specify the population or populations that are relevant to the case. When a case-oriented researcher completes a study and draws conclusions, these populations may be invoked explicitly or they may be implicated in various summary statements about the case. In short, there is a close link in case-oriented research between the constitution of populations and statements about the generality of its findings. Statements about generality, in turn, may be based on the outcome (and thus implicitly invoke arguments about necessary conditions) or about causes (and thus implicitly invoke arguments about sufficient conditions).

The fact that conventional variable-oriented analysis makes neither of these arguments explicit means that it *assumes* the very thing that case-oriented analysis typically considers most problematic—the relevant population of cases, including both positive and negative instances. The many simpleminded critiques of the method of agreement (and analytic induction) fall apart as soon as it is recognized that the constitution of populations is a theory-laden, concept-intensive process. Further, as I have argued, the constitution of relevant "negative cases" typically rests on the careful prior constitution of "positive cases." Thus, the third practical concern of case-oriented researchers is the difficulty of defining negative cases (and thus the population of candidates for an outcome) in the absence of a well-grounded understanding and definition of positive cases. Even once both positive and negative cases have been identified, the boundaries of the relevant population of cases may be adjusted still further in the course of case-oriented research. That is, they should remain flexible.

Examination of Multiple and Conjunctural Causes

After constituting and selecting relevant instances of an outcome like "antineocolonial revolutions" and, if possible, defining relevant negative cases as well, the case-oriented investigator's task is to address the causal forces behind the outcome, with special attention to similarities and differences across cases. Each case is examined in detail—using theoretical concepts, substantive knowledge, and interests as guides—in order to answer the question of "how" the outcome came about in each positive case and why it did not in the negative cases—assuming they can be confidently identified. While it is standard practice for case-oriented researchers to search for constants (e.g., high levels of foreign capital penetration) across positive cases in their attempts to identify the causal forces behind an outcome (e.g., anti-neocolonial revolutions), the typical case-oriented inquiry does not assume or even anticipate causal uniformity across positive cases. On the contrary, the usual expectation is that *different* combinations of causes may produce the same outcome. That is, case-oriented researchers often pay special attention to the diverse ways a common outcome may be reached.

When examining similarities and differences across cases, case-oriented researchers usually expect evidence to be causally "lumpy." That is, they anticipate finding several major causal pathways in a given body of cross-case evidence. A typical finding is that different causes combine in different and sometimes contradictory ways to produce roughly similar outcomes in different settings. The effect of any particular causal condition depends on the presence and absence of other conditions, and several different conditions may satisfy a general causal requirement—that is, two or more different causes may be equivalent at a more abstract level. Thus, causal explanations in case-oriented research often have the form: "When conditions *A*, *B*, and *C* are present, *X* causes *Y*; however, if any one of these conditions (*A*, *B*, or *C*) is absent, and *X* is also absent, then *Z* causes *Y*." This argument is multiple and conjunctural in form because it cites alternate combinations of causal conditions. The hypothetical causal argument just presented essentially states that there are four combinations of conditions that result in the outcome *Y*. It can be formulated using Boolean algebra (see Ragin 1987) as follows:

$$Y = ABCX + ABcxZ + AbCxZ + aBCxZ$$

(Upper-case letters indicate the presence of a condition; lower-case letters indicate its absence; multiplication indicates causal conjunctures; addition indicates alternative causal pathways.)

The search for patterns of multiple conjunctural causation, a common concern of case-oriented researchers, poses serious practical problems for variable-oriented research. To investigate this type of causation with quantitative techniques, one must examine high-level interactions (e.g., four-way interactions in the causal argument just described). However, these sophisticated techniques are very rarely used by variable-oriented researchers. When they are, they require at least two essential ingredients: (1) a very large number of diverse cases, and (2) an investigator willing to contend with a difficult mass of multicollinearity. These techniques are simply not feasible in investigations with small or even moderate Ns, the usual situation in comparative social science. When Ns are small to moderate, causal complexity is more apparent, more salient, and easier to identify and interpret; yet it is also much less amenable to quantitative analysis.

Goldthorpe (1997) laments the inability of case-oriented methods to reveal the relative strengths of different effects or combinations of effects. However, multiple conjunctural causation, as sketched here, challenges the very idea of "relative strengths." It is not possible to assess a variable's "unique" or separate contribution to the explanation of variation in some outcome unless the model in question is a simple additive model. To isolate a single causal factor and attempt to assess its separate or "independent" impact across all cases, a common concern in multivariate quantitative analysis, is difficult in research that pays close attention to causal conjunctures. When the focus is on causal conjunctures, the magnitude of any single cause's impact depends on the presence or absence of other causal conditions. The impact of X on Y in the causal statement just presented, for example, requires the copresence of conditions A, B, and C. Of course, it *is* possible in the case-oriented approach to assess which cases (or what proportion of cases) included in a study follow which causal path. Indeed, linking cases to causal pathways and assessing the relative importance of different paths should be an essential part of case-oriented comparative research.

In variable-oriented research, assessing the relative importance of alternative paths requires a focus on all cases. It involves computing partial relationships, which, in turn, are constructed from bivariate relationships. (To compute a multiple regression, for example, only a matrix of bivariate correlations, along with the means and standard deviations of all the variables, is required.) However, bivariate relationships can give false leads, even when controls are introduced. Note, for example, that condition X in the Boolean equation just described must be present in some contexts and absent in others for Y to occur. A conventional quantitative analysis of the bivariate relationship between X and Y might show no relationship (i.e., a Pearson's r of 0).

Simply stated, the fourth practical concern of case-oriented researchers is causal heterogeneity. Because they conduct in-depth investigations of individual cases, case-oriented researchers are able to identify complex patterns of conjunctural causation. While researchers interested only in testing general theories might find this level of detail uninteresting, in-depth study offers important insight into the diversity and complexity of social life, which, in turn, offers rich material for theoretical development and refinement.

Treatment of Nonconforming Cases and "Determinism"

Because Ns tend to be relatively small in case-oriented research, it is possible to become familiar with every case. Each case selected for examination may be historically or culturally significant in some way and thus worthy of separate attention. For these reasons, case-oriented researchers often account for every case included in a study, no matter how poorly each may conform to common causal patterns. Thus, researchers hope to find causal lumps (i.e., an interpretable pattern of multiple conjunctural causation), but they also anticipate finding causal specks—cases that do not conform to any of the common causal pathways. Causal specks are usually not discarded, even though they may be inconvenient. Suppose, for example, that Iran offers the only instance of anti-neocolonial revolution with a strong religious slant. Do we simply ignore this important case? Relegate it to the error vector? Call it a fluke?

The variable-oriented critics of case-oriented work argue that accounting for every case is equivalent to trying to do the impossible—explaining "all the variation"—and that this trap should be avoided. They argue that researchers instead should stick to well-known and well-understood probabilistic models of social phenomena. This criticism of case-oriented research has two important bases. The first is that explanations that "account for every case" are deterministic, and there is simply too much randomness in human affairs to permit deterministic explanations. The implication here is that case-oriented researchers forsake true science when they attempt to account for each case. The second part of the criticism is that the effort to "explain all the variation" may lead to the inclusion of theoretically trivial causal variables or, even worse, to the embrace of theoretically incorrect causal models, understandings that take advantage of the peculiar features of a particular "sample" of cases.

These arguments can be addressed with a simple example. As is well known, the typical case-oriented study has a paucity of cases relative to the number of variables. This feature, in fact, could be considered one of the key defining characteristics of case-oriented research. Consider the typical contrast: A quantitative study of voting with 3,000 voters and fifteen main variables has a statistically "healthy" ratio of two hundred observations per variable (200:1). A comparative study of third world countries with violent mass protest against the International Monetary Fund (IMF), by contrast, might have about twenty cases and thirty independent variables, an "unhealthy" ratio of 2:3. Anyone who has attempted sophisticated quantitative analysis of small Ns knows that with twenty cases and thirty independent variables, it is possible to construct many different prediction equations that account for 100 percent of the variation in a dependent variable (say, the longevity of the mass protest against the IMF). No special effort is required to "explain all the variation" in this hypothetical variable-oriented analysis. The researcher would not have to "take advantage" of the "sample" or of any of its "peculiar" (i.e., historically or culturally specific) features. The high level of explained variation in this hypothetical variable-oriented study is a simple artifact of the ratio of cases to explanatory factors—just as it would be in a case-oriented study of the same evidence.

No one would describe a quantitative model derived in this manner as *deterministic* simply because of the level of explained variance achieved (100 percent). A truly deterministic argument should involve explicit theorizing and explicit statements about the nature of the determinism involved. I know of no case-oriented or variable-oriented researcher who has proposed such an argument, even though it is always possible for researchers using either research strategy to explain "all the variation" in some outcome.

The more important issue here is the fact that *many different models* will perform equally well, not that it is possible to "explain all the variation." For example, suppose that with twenty cases and thirty independent variables, it is possible to derive eleven different prediction equations, each with only five predictors, that account for 80 percent of the variation in the dependent variable. Which one should the investigator choose? The key question, of course, is the *plausibility* of the explanations implied by the different equations. Faced with the possibility of achieving a very high level of explained variation with many different prediction models, the variable-oriented researcher is usually stymied. The issue of plausibility cannot be resolved by running more and more equations or by plumbing the depths of probability theory. Instead, it is usually necessary to assess the relative plausibility of equivalent prediction models by going back to the cases included in the study and trying to determine *at the case level* which model makes the most sense. In other words, having a surplus of explanatory variables—the usual situation in comparative social science—often *necessitates* case-oriented analysis.

Thus, when there are more independent variables than cases, the problem is not one of "determinism," where determinism is equated with 100 percent explained variation. This so-called determinism is a simple artifact of the ratio of independent variables to cases and has nothing to do with the researcher's arguments. On the contrary, the problem here is one of extreme *indeterminism*—the fact that there may be many different models that do equally well. The best antidote for a multiplicity of equally predictive models (indeterminism) is more knowledge of cases. All researchers should be wary of models, especially simple models, that "explain every case." They should check each case to see if the model in question offers a plausible picture of the case.

Most case-oriented investigators do not explain all their cases with a single model (even when the model incorporates multiple conjunctural causation). More typically, they confront nonconforming cases and account for them by citing factors that are outside their explanatory frameworks (a procedure endorsed by Goldthorpe 1997). The specifics of each case are not irrelevant to social science, even when knowledge of specifics has only limited relevance to theory. Consider an example from *DSI* (55–57): Weather fluctuations or a flu epidemic might affect turnout among lower income groups on election day. The Labour Party thus suffers a poor turnout and loses an election it should have won. This example is a wonderful demonstration of both randomness and of our potential for identifying the play of such forces in producing nonconforming outcomes. For those interested in what happened or in winning elections, this bit of knowledge might be very important. For those interested in studying shifts in the link between class and party support, it may simply be an annoyance (i.e., error).

The practical issue here is that "error" is usually conceived very differently in case-oriented and variable-oriented research. The fifth practical concern of case-oriented research can be stated very simply: Prediction error should be explained, rather than simply acknowledged. Case-oriented investigators try to account for every case in their attempt to uncover patterned diversity. Cases often deviate from common patterns, but these deviations are identified and addressed. Investigators make every effort to identify the factors at work in nonconforming cases, even when these factors are outside the frameworks they bring to the research. In variable-oriented research, by contrast, the "error" that remains at the end of an investigation may embrace much more than it does in qualitative research. It includes randomness, omitted variables, poor measurement, model misspecification, and other factors, including ignorance of the cases studied.

Conclusion

Case-oriented and variable-oriented researchers are joined by their common objective of constructing social scientific portraits of social phenomena from empirical evidence. They are joined as well by their use of common concepts and analytic frames to facilitate this fundamental objective. In practice, however, case-oriented qualitative research, especially the variety common in the comparative study of social and political phenomena, adopts a very different approach to the work of analyzing and summarizing evidence. The practical concerns sketched in this chapter present a bare outline of several distinctive features of the process of case-oriented research, from the constitution of cases to the examination of uniform causes and outcomes, and from the analysis of multiple conjunctural causes to the explanation of nonconforming cases.

The case-oriented approach poses important challenges to variable-oriented research, challenges that, if answered, would make variable-oriented research more rigorous. For example, in most variable-oriented research, the sample of relevant observations is established at the outset of a study and is not open to reformulation or redefinition. In most variable-oriented research, the operation of causal conditions that are constant across cases is obscured. In most variable-oriented research, it is difficult to examine multiple conjunctural causation because researchers lack in-depth knowledge of cases and because their most common analytic tools cannot cope with complex causal patterns. Finally, in most variable-oriented research, ignorance of cases may find its way into the error vector of probabilistic models. Of course, the practical concerns of case-oriented research are difficult to address in the variable-oriented approach. It is still reasonable to hope, at a minimum, for greater appreciation of the special strengths of different ways of constructing social scientific portraits of social life.

CHAPTER 9

Case Studies and the Limits of the Quantitative Worldview

Timothy J. McKeown

Is there a single logic common to all empirical social scientific research? Is that logic a quantitative one? Gary King, Robert Keohane, and Sidney Verba's *Designing Social Inquiry* (hereafter *DSI*) answers "yes" to both questions. Although their book seems to be oriented primarily to the practical problems of research design in domains that have traditionally been the province of quantitative analysis, its sub-

Special thanks to Janice Stein and Alexander George for encouraging me to return to this subject. I received helpful comments on earlier versions of this article at two seminars hosted by the Center for International Security and Arms Control, Stanford University, in 1996, and at a presentation to Robert Keohane's graduate seminar at Duke University in 1997. My thanks to Lynn Eden and Alexander George for inviting me to CISAC and providing an extraordinary opportunity to discuss the issues in this article in great detail, and to Robert Keohane for being so magnanimous and helpful. Thanks also to seminar participants for their probing questions and comments. I received helpful comments, in many cases at great length, from Hayward Alker, Aaron Belkin, Andrew Bennett, David Collier, David Dessler, George Downs, James Fearon, Ronald Jepperson, William Keech, Catherine Lutz, Michael Munger, Thomas Oatley, Robert Powell, John Stephens, Sidney Tarrow, Isaac Unah, Peter Van Doren, the editors of *International Organization,* and an anonymous reviewer. I assume full responsibility for whatever errors remain.

title—*Scientific Inference in Qualitative Research*—reveals a much larger agenda. *DSI* assumes at the outset that qualitative research faces the same problems of causal inference as quantitative research; that assumption, in turn, forms the basis for analyzing causal inference problems in qualitative research as if they were problems of parameter estimation and significance testing. The solutions to the problems of qualitative research are therefore deemed to be highly similar to those in quantitative research. Although this is not an entirely new position—Paul Lazarsfeld and Morris Rosenberg (1955: 387–91) outlined a similar view more than forty years ago—its exposition in *DSI* is more extensive and theoretically self-conscious.

I discuss the nature and implications of that assumption. I argue that it is problematic in ways that are not discussed by *DSI* and that it is an error to attempt to squeeze all empirical practice in the social sciences into a quantitative mold. Because the quantitative worldview embodied in *DSI* is usually not the worldview that animates case studies, *DSI*'s approach leads to a series of misconceptions about the objectives and accomplishments of case studies. These misconceptions are constructive, however, in the sense that exposing them leads to a clearer notion not only of the underlying logic behind case studies, but also of the important role played by other kinds of reasoning and research activity in all domains of investigation—even those dominated by quantitative data analysis. The discussion below first focuses on issues of philosophy of science and the logic of inquiry, and it then explores research practices that exemplify the alternative approaches I have in mind. Table 9.1 provides a summary of specific research tools that are employed in these alternative approaches.

Philosophy of Science and the Logic of Research

DSI's Philosophy of Science

Although the book disclaims any interest in the philosophy of science, *DSI* (4) adopts essentially Popperian positions on many important questions. In particular, *DSI*'s emphasis on a clear distinction between forming or stating hypotheses and testing them, an accompanying reluctance to treat hypothesis formation as anything other than an art form (14), the book's stress on the need for simplicity in theories, and its insistence on subsuming each case within a class of cases are all highly consistent with logical positivism or Karl Popper's (1959) reworking of it. The *DSI* project—to delineate a theory of confirmation that specifies a priori rules for using observations to evaluate the truthfulness of hypotheses, regardless of the field of inquiry or the specifics of the hypotheses—is a project not only of Popper but of logical positivism more broadly understood (Miller 1987: 162).

Table 9.1. Tools for Comparative Case-Study Research

Tool	Comments
Detailed Contextual Knowledge	Helps assess the appropriateness of the empirical methods employed in hypotheses testing, and provides the practical understanding that is the basis for theorizing.
Bayesian Inference	Evaluates new data in light of prior empirical and theoretical knowledge.
Analysis of Crucial Cases	Selects cases that offer valuable tests because they are strongly expected to confirm or disconfirm prior hypotheses.
Counterfactual Analysis	Allows the researcher, on the basis of relevant theories and historical facts, to trace forward the empirical implications of rival hypotheses. Provides an alternative means of evaluating the hypotheses being tested and of situating the research in relevant theoretical debates. May be especially useful in areas where theory is weak.
Process Tracing	Identifies causal mechanisms and evaluates hypotheses through tracing causal processes.
Iterated Dialogue among Theory, Data, and Research Design	Contributes to greater learning from the data. Ex post model-fitting is a legitimate aspect of a research cycle, which should include the ongoing evaluation and (re)formulation of theory. New explanations may be suggested by analyzing outliers. Learning from a case may also lead to a change in research design.

Like Popper, *DSI* accepts two departures from strict positivism. First, the book treats observations as theory-laden, so the separation of theory and data is more a matter of degree and emphasis than of kind. Second, the book argues that parsimony as an end is not very important and can often be abandoned as an objective. However, neither concession has much practical impact on the advice *DSI* offers, and the authors do not face squarely the inconsistencies that arise between their practical advice and their philosophical position.

Does it make any difference that *DSI*'s approach is Popperian? How one answers that depends on what one believes should be the evaluation criteria for the book's argument. If the design and execution of research are best understood as a pragmatic activity heavily informed by the substantive requirements of a particular field, then its philosophical underpinnings might seem unimportant. Research methods could be evaluated in terms of the quality of the research produced when the advice is followed. The evaluation of quality, in turn, could be based on pragmatic, field-specific grounds. However, this viewpoint creates two problems for *DSI*. One is that the only justification the authors could then offer for their approach is that "it works." If it could also be shown that another approach "works" or that theirs does not always do so, there would be no basis for privileging *DSI*'s prescriptions, unless somehow we could demarcate a domain in which these prescriptions have a comparative advantage over others. The second problem is that the philosophical side of the argument would be reduced to a ceremonial role. Perhaps that is why, when the pragmatic requirements of doing research conflict with Hempelian notions, the authors are not averse to leaving Hempel behind. That this pragmatic viewpoint is itself the embodiment of a philosophy that is distinctly non-Hempelian does not concern them.

Although it is tempting to adopt such a task-oriented view of proper research methodology in order to move quickly to concrete issues, there are two reasons to resist doing so. First, an argument for a particular way of pursuing research would be more convincing if it could be shown that it were constructed on a firmer philosophical foundation. Second, to the extent that the foundation guides thinking about research methods, and to the extent that the foundation is deficient, the concrete conclusions might also be deficient.

DSI and the Popperian View of Theory

The authors of *DSI* are partisans of causal analysis. This is a departure from Popper, who was very skeptical of the idea that the mere identification of causal processes is sufficient to warrant the term *theory*. (His views on evolutionary theory, for example, were decidedly negative. See Popper 1959.) Popper, in common with positivists more generally, wished to dispense with references to causation and restrict discussion to regularities and entailments (Popper 1968: 59–62; Miller 1987: 235). He wished, in other words, to make the relation between theory and observation one of *logic*. *DSI* takes for granted that causal laws are readily accommodated within the "covering law" approach of positivism.[1] This approach to explanation introduces one or more general if-then propositions ("laws") relating outcomes to antecedents in a given situation and then establishes that a given ob-

---

[1]*DSI*'s examination of this issue was apparently confined to consulting Daniel Little (1991: 18), who approvingly cites Hempel's (1965: 300–301) claim that causal explanations can be subsumed within such a framework.

servation is an instance of an event or situation specified in (that is, "covered" by) the general laws. However, the claim that causal analysis can be so accommodated is widely doubted, particularly by those who are partisans of causal analysis. Richard Miller (1987), for example, contends that the positivist project of establishing general logical relationships between observations and theories is essentially unworkable and that a causal conception of explanation avoids the problems said to plague the former perspective.

Although Miller's full argument is lengthy and complex, a sense of his criticisms can be gleaned from the following excerpt:

> Causal explanation is not analyzed by the covering-law model. Here, counterexamples really are sufficient. A derivation fitting one of the two basic patterns often fails to explain. When a barometer falls, a change for the worse in the weather is very likely to follow. The high probability is dictated by laws of meteorology. But the weather does not change because the barometer falls. In conjunction with basic and utterly general laws of physics and chemistry, the shift toward the red of spectral lines in spectra from more distant stars entails that the observed universe is expanding. [However, t]he red shift does not explain why the universe is expanding. . . . Because these examples fit the covering-law model so well . . . and because the failure to explain is so obvious, they are overwhelming. (Miller 1987: 34)

For those who are aware of such criticisms, the simultaneous commitments of *DSI* to the notion of a general logic of inquiry founded on a covering law approach and to an account of explanation that stresses the role of causal mechanisms thus creates a strong tension that is never confronted, let alone resolved.

A Single Logic of Research

Ironically, a powerful argument that there is *not* more than one logic is provided by a prominent critic of positivist methodological dicta. In discussing the research techniques of those who work within a hermeneutic mode of analysis, Paul Diesing corroborates the claim of *DSI* that a unified logic of inference exists, at least at the most basic level:

> The hermeneutic maxim here is: no knowledge without foreknowledge. That is, we form an expectation about the unknown from what we "know." Our foreknowledge may be mistaken, or partial and misleading, or inapplicable to this text; but in that case the interpretation will run into trouble. . . . Our foreknowledge directs our attention. . . . The passages that answer these questions point in turn to other passages. . . .
>
> We form hypotheses about the meanings of a text based on our prior theory of the text, which in turn has emerged from our own experience. If our hypotheses are disconfirmed, then our prior theory is called into question.

In finding an analogue to external validity in hermeneutic approaches, Diesing sounds remarkably like *DSI* as he discusses how to pursue a qualitative research program:

> We can call our foreknowledge into question if it sometimes produces an expected interpretation that cannot make a coherent message out of the text, in context. To question our own foreknowledge, we must first focus on it and become aware of what we are assuming; then we must devise a different assumption, perhaps one suggested by this case, and see whether it produces better hypotheses. This process does not produce absolute truth, but a validity that can be improved within limits. (Diesing 1991: 108–10)

Nothing in Diesing's account is inconsistent with the advice that *DSI* offers on how to do research aimed at uncovering and testing propositions about cause-and-effect relationships. Indeed, the authors' most likely response would probably be "we told you so."[2] Since we might suppose that the epistemological "distance" between hermeneutics and the quantitative analyses of survey research responses is large, we have powerful support for an important part of *DSI*'s analysis in a place where we might least expect to find it: that is, from an author who is notably unsympathetic to *DSI*'s project. Diesing (1991: 143) himself is not averse to these conclusions, suggesting that hermeneutic approaches are compatible with Popper's "conjectures and refutations" description of scientific activity. Inspecting what we know about the world in order to draw some tentative conclusions about the processes that govern that world and then examining how well those conclusions account for existing or newly acquired knowledge are fundamental to empirical research. What is less clear is whether this activity is always governed by the quantitative logic proposed by *DSI*.

Is Inference Fundamentally Quantitative?

The best description of how *DSI* views qualitative research is that it is "prequantitative" (my term): most of the time, it is undertaken because of the infeasibility of quantitative methods, and it is governed by the same objectives as quantitative research, uses procedures that are shadows of quantitative procedures, and is evaluated by procedures that are shadows of those used to evaluate quantitative research. *DSI* mentions one situation where a case study is superior to quantitative research: When accurate measurement is too costly to be conducted repeatedly, an "intensive research design" (my term)—in which a great deal of effort is expended on a single case—is preferable to relying on measurements of doubtful validity collected in an extensive design for purposes of quantitative analysis (67). Then

---

[2]*DSI* (37) comes close to Diesing's position when it notes that both science and interpretation rely on "formulating falsifiable hypotheses on the basis of more general theories, and collecting the evidence needed to evaluate these hypotheses."

one must either rely on the case study alone or else use the information gleaned from the case study to adjust one's measurements in a larger sample that is then subsequently subjected to quantitative assessment (68–69). However, except for this single situation, qualitative research is viewed as a second-best research strategy, undertaken because quantitative strategies are infeasible. Correspondingly, conclusions about causal processes in qualitative research are possible, but are said to be "relatively uncertain" (6).

DSI's argument is founded on applying quantitative logic to causal inference. *Every* concept the authors apply to empirical social science is borrowed from the quantitative approach:

1. At its most basic, empirical activity is viewed as the making of discrete "observations," which are represented as values assigned to variables.
2. Its model of the representation of observations is a data point (e.g., 130–31, 164–65).
3. The three criteria that it applies to judging methods of making inferences are "unbiasedness, efficiency, and consistency" (63)—terms familiar to anyone who has ever studied quantitative methods. The brief formalizations of important concepts—bias, efficiency, measurement error, endogeneity—are also familiar quantitative territory.

DSI does not consistently apply any nonquantitative criteria. The authors explicitly mention construct validity[3] once in a discussion of precision versus accuracy (151), and they also seem to be discussing this subject in the guise of the "bias-efficiency trade-off" (69), but they do not devote any sustained attention to this or any other matters connected with the movement between the language and propositions of a theory and those of an empirical investigation. Thus, the question of assessing the adequacy of operationalizations—the defining of the empirical referents to theoretical concepts—seems to fall outside the scope of their inquiry.

In spite of their sympathy for Eckstein's idea that different hypothesis tests might possess different levels of stringency (*DSI* 209), the authors of *DSI* are skeptical of the overall thrust of his brief for "crucial cases" (Eckstein 1975), contending that:

> (1) very few explanations depend upon only one causal variable; to evaluate the impact of more than one explanatory variable, the investigator needs more than one implication observed; (2) measurement is difficult and not perfectly reliable; and (3) social reality is not reasonably treated as being produced by deterministic processes, so random error would appear even if measurement were perfect. (*DSI* 210)

Missing here is any sense that in some contexts the reliability of the observations is known to be high, and is therefore not an important consideration. Further,

---

[3]As defined by Cronbach and Meehl (1955), construct validity refers to whether an empirical test can be shown to be an adequate measure of some theoretical term.

DSI does not address the implicit Bayesianism of Eckstein's call to focus on crucial cases. The authors' position seems to leave them with very little leeway for arguing that one case is superior to another one as a subject of research. Although they seem to accept Eckstein's notion that some tests are more demanding than others, they provide no basis for making such an assessment.

What has happened in *DSI*'s argument is that the problem of making inferences about the correctness of a theoretical account of causal processes has been redefined without comment as the problem of making quantitative inferences about the properties of a sample or of the universe that underlies that sample. Although at the outset the inferences the authors profess to consider are of the former type (7–8), by the time they discuss the barriers to drawing correct inferences about a theory from the properties of the data (63ff.), they treat the entire problem as one of quantitative analysis. Later qualifications to the effect that negative empirical results need not entail the automatic rejection of a theory (104), though useful practical advice, are not grounded in this discussion and certainly do not follow as a matter of "logic" from any preceding argument in the book.

Although *DSI* would have us believe that model acceptance or rejection rests on the results of significance tests or equivalent procedures, that does not seem to be what happens in several well-known domains. To claim that inferences are drawn and tested is not to claim that they are tested using a process that mimics standard quantitative methods or relies only on the results of significance tests.

Making Inferences from One or a Few Cases

Stephen Toulmin (1972) has suggested that legal proceedings be taken as an exemplar of how a community arrives at judgments about the truthfulness of various statements. In such proceedings judges or juries are asked to make judgments about causation and intent based quite literally on a single case. Although quantitative evidence is sometimes used in court, the only way that judicial judgments are quantitative in any more general sense is if the term is meant to apply to the implicitly probabilistic conception of guilt that underlies an evidentiary standard such as "beyond a reasonable doubt." Likewise, if one considers the standard set of successful scientific research programs that are commonly used as exemplars in discussions of the philosophy of science, one searches in vain among these cases from early modern chemistry, astronomy, or physics, from the germ theory of disease or the theory of evolution, for any instance where explicit quantitative inference played a noticeable role in the development of these research programs.[4] If *DSI* is correct, how could any judge or jury ever convict anyone (unless perhaps the defendant were being tried for multiple crimes)? If there is a quantitative logic to all scientific inference, what are we to make of situations in the physical or bio-

---

[4]Genetics and psychometrics are exceptions to this generalization (Glymour et al. 1987: chap. 9).

logical sciences where a few observations (or even a single one for Einstein's theory of relativity and the bending of light by gravity) in nonexperimental situations were widely perceived to have large theoretical implications?

DSI seeks to accommodate the drawing of valid conclusions about causes in such situations by means of two claims. The first, noted earlier, is that causal inference is possible in such situations, though with a relatively lower degree of confidence. The second is its repeated acknowledgments that case studies often contain many observations, not just one (47, 52, 212, 221). The claims taken together may appear to offer a way to reconcile the drawing of causal conclusions in such situations with the overall thrust of its argument. However, this is so only if one finesses the issue of degree of confidence and ignores the implications of the fact that many observations within cases are generally made on many variables. If a case contains too few observations per variable to warrant quantitative analysis, it is difficult to see how its observations could persuade any quantitatively inclined jury beyond a reasonable doubt. Although all sorts of criticisms are leveled against judicial systems, I am aware of no one who claims that judges and juries are literally incapable of coming to defensible judgments about guilt or innocence on the basis of a single case. Likewise, nobody seems to criticize the empirical work of premodern scientists for their seeming lack of concern about the need to repeat their observations often enough to attain meaningful sample sizes for quantitative analysis.

How then can we make sense of what happens in trials or in fields like astronomy or biology—or in case studies? One way to speak in quantitative terms about some domains such as astronomy is to declare that they possess zero or near-zero sample variability—the members of the population are so similar on the dimensions of interest that the informational value of additional observations approaches zero. To the uninitiated, an a priori assumption of zero sample variability is no more and no less plausible than an assumption of some arbitrarily large sample variability. If observations are costly and sample variability is believed to be quite low, the case for more observations is hardly self-evident. However, it is probably not wise to proceed very far in political science on the assumption that sample variability can be neglected.

A more fundamental difficulty lies in *DSI*'s contention that how one reacts to quantitative results is a matter of logic. The problem with this claim is revealed once we consider how researchers might respond to quantitative results that are unexpectedly inconclusive or even disconfirming. When are poor quantitative results to be viewed as (1) "bad luck"—that is, sampling from a tail of a distribution; (2) arising from problems of faulty observation or measurement (reflecting a faulty operationalization of key concepts); (3) suggesting the impact of previously ignored variables; (4) the result of a misspecification of the relationships among variables already included in the model; (5) due to overoptimistic assumptions about the degree of homogeneity of the cases under observation; or (6) evidence that the entire explanatory strategy is misconceived and ought to be abandoned?

DSI (p. 6) views *quantitative* inference as but the most clear-cut form of *scientific* inference, which is perfectly consistent with its notion that decisions about which model to accept are a matter of "logic." But if it were a matter of logic, what is the logic of the modeler's decision in this situation? Although some of these questions yield to the application of various quantitative diagnostics or to repeated analysis with different samples or specifications, even then researchers' conceptions of what is a "reasonable" way to remeasure the data or to respecify the model are heavily dependent on their substantive understandings of the problem being investigated.

If there is a "logic" of how to do this, *DSI* does not supply it. Perhaps the authors' practical experience as researchers has convinced them that this sort of decision cannot be guided by abstract, general rules and must be based on a context-sensitive understanding of the adequacy of empirical methods, the theory in question, the plausibility of rival theories, and the level of confidence in the myriad "auxiliary hypotheses" that provide the mostly unspoken set of assumptions underlying the research task. That perspective is one that is both widely shared and possessed of articulate and persuasive defenders, but it is not consistent with *DSI*'s claim to present a general "logic" governing all social scientific research or the Hempelian approach that they believe to be the foundation for their inquiry.

Here, what guides research is not logic but craftsmanship, and the craft in question is implicitly far more substantively rich than that of "social scientist without portfolio." The latter's lack of context-specific knowledge means that the researcher cannot call on information from outside the sample being analyzed to supplement the information gleaned from quantitative analyses. Just how qualitative information from outside a sample is weighted and combined with quantitative information to produce a considered judgment on the accuracy of a theory is not well understood, but if the qualitative information is accurate, the resulting judgment ought to merit more confidence. For someone equipped with adequate contextual knowledge, a given quantitative (or quasi-quantitative) analysis still affects the evaluation of the accuracy of a theory, but it is only one consideration among several, and its preeminence at an early point in the research project is far from obvious.

If scientific inference is treated as essentially quantitative, it is no wonder that *DSI* views case studies as chronically beset by what I term a "degree-of-freedom problem" or what *DSI* terms "indeterminate" research designs (119–20): the number of "observations" is taken to be far fewer than the number of "variables."[5] This situation precludes the identification of models within a quantitative framework—hence *DSI*'s use of the "indeterminate" label.

James Fearon counters this contention in his discussion of what he terms "counterfactual" explanations:

---

[5]Here again, the qualifiers about case studies containing many observations are set aside.

Support for a causal hypothesis in the counterfactual strategy comes from *arguments* about what would have happened. These arguments are made credible (1) by invoking general principles, theories, laws, or regularities distinct from the hypothesis being tested; and (2) by drawing on knowledge of historical facts relevant to a counterfactual scenario. (Fearon 1991: 176, emphasis in original)

What Fearon offers is a strategy for constructing a nonquantitative basis for causal inferences. However, if one can support causal inferences by means of arguments of the sort that Fearon mentions, there is no need for counterfactual speculation. One can just move directly from the arguments to the conclusions about causal processes operating in the case, without any need to construct counterfactuals. Fearon's strategy is always available, whether or not one is interested in constructing counterfactuals. However, as discussed later, case-study researchers might have good reasons to be interested in counterfactuals.

As applied to a setting such as a trial or a case study, two types of arguments can be mustered in support of causal conclusions. The first are causal claims that are so uncontroversial that they operate essentially as primitive terms. If the jury views an undoctored videotape in which a suspect is seen pointing a gun at the victim and pulling the trigger, and the victim is then seen collapsing with a gaping hole in his forehead, it reaches conclusions about the cause of the victim's death and the intent of the suspect to shoot the victim that are highly certain. Barring the sort of exotic circumstances that a philosopher or a mystery writer might invoke (for example, the victim died of a brain aneurysm just before the bullet struck, or the gun was loaded with blank cartridges and the fatal shot was fired by someone else), the assessment of causation is unproblematic. Even if exotic circumstances are present, a sufficiently diligent search has a good chance of uncovering them, as any reader of detective fiction knows.

A second type of causal claim is weaker: It is the "circumstantial evidence" so often used by writers of murder mysteries. An observation may be consistent with several different hypotheses about the identity of the killer and rule out few suspects. No one observation establishes the identity of the killer, but the detective's background knowledge, in conjunction with a series of observations, provides the basis for judgments that generate or eliminate suspects. As the story progresses, we are usually presented with several instances in which "leads" (that is, hypotheses) turn out to be "dead ends" (that is, are falsified by new observations). Sometimes an old lead is revived when still more new observations suggest that previous observations were interpreted incorrectly, measures or estimates were mistaken, or low-probability events (coincidences) occurred. Typically, the detective constructs a chronology of the actions of the relevant actors in which the timing of events and the assessment of who possessed what information at what time are the central tasks. This tracing of the causal process leads to the archetypical final scene: All the characters and the evidence are brought together and the brilliant detective not only supplies the results of the final observation that eliminates all but one suspect, but proceeds to explain how the observations fit together into a consistent and accurate causal explanation of events. Rival theories are assessed and disposed of, generally by showing that they are not successful in accounting for all the observations. The suspect may attempt to argue that it is all a coincidence, but the detective knows that someone has to be the killer and that the evidence against the suspect is so much stronger than the evidence against anybody else that one can conclude beyond a reasonable doubt that the suspect should be arrested.

It may be objected that in this situation all that is happening is that the quantitative basis for conclusions has merely been shifted back from the immediate case at hand to the formation of the prior beliefs. The hypothetical juror then deduces the correct verdict on the basis of those prior beliefs, which are themselves based on quantitative inference. Although there is no reason why this is impossible, it is a less than satisfactory defense of the attempt to ground all conclusions on a foundation of quantitative inference. First, it is merely an epistemological "IOU"—it does not resolve the issue, it merely displaces it back to the question of how the prior beliefs were formed. Moreover, it uses the idea of "quantitative inference" metaphorically, as a catchall descriptor for the process of making sense of experience. As such, it attempts to finesse the need to use judgment. However, judgments cannot be avoided—for example, in the earlier discussion of how to respond to negative results from quantitative analysis, or in the question of deciding what rules or laws are relevant to a single case, or of classifying a single case as a member of one set and not another.

Although Johannes von Kries argued more than a hundred years ago that conclusions about causal linkages in singular cases such as legal proceedings can be treated as resting on probabilistic "nomological knowledge" of links between events, each of a certain type (Ringer 1997: 64), formulations such as his fail to deal with the question of how events are to be sorted into types in the first place. Such an activity is one of judgment, not just quantitative testing. The standard quantitative view of prior knowledge provides no way of making sense of operations that are nondeductive—it cannot, for example, make sense of its very own use of the "juror as statistician" metaphor, because creating or invoking metaphors is not a mathematical operation. Finally, it offers no defense of the Humean reliance on deduction from prior knowledge and current observations to a conclusion. "Beyond a reasonable doubt" and the "reasonable person" standard are not equivalent to certainty. Although they might sometimes be interpreted as the verbal equivalent of significance levels with a very small "p" value, they are also terms that apply to operations of judgment and classification. If certainty is a better standard to use, the case for it ought to be made. Such a case would have to explain how certainty could ever be reached on questions of judgment and classification and what is to be done if it cannot.

The detective's reconstruction of the case is what Wesley Salmon terms an "ontic" explanation. Although it rests on a foundation of observed regularities, the regularities themselves are only the basis for an explanation—they are not the explanation itself. The explanation provides an answer to a "why" or "how" question in terms of mechanisms of (probabilistic) cause and effect:

> Mere fitting of events into regular patterns has little, if any, explanatory force. . . . [Although] some regularities have explanatory power, . . . others constitute precisely the kinds of natural phenomena that demand explanation. . . .
>
> To provide an explanation of a particular event is to identify the cause and, in many cases at least, to exhibit the causal relation between this cause and the event-to-be-explained. (Salmon 1984: 121–22)[6]

The ontic conception is a more demanding standard than the following common strategy in quantitative work in political science: (1) Positing a series of bivariate functional relationships between a dependent variable and various independent variables, rooted perhaps in intuition or in expectations formed from prior research; (2) demonstrating quantitative regularities in a set of observations; and (3) claiming to have a satisfactory explanation of variation in the dependent variable because there is an adequate quantitative accounting of covariation. From the ontic perspective, we do not have an adequate explanation of the phenomenon under study until we can say why the model works.[7] Moreover, if we can do this, we are much less likely to succumb to what Andrew Abbott (1988) has called "general linear reality"—the casual acceptance of the behavioral assumptions implicit in general linear quantitative models in situations where they are not appropriate.

Equipped with this understanding of explanation, we can now make sense of Ronald Rogowski's (77–79 this volume) point that one case sometimes seems to have an impact on theorizing that is far out of proportion to its status as nonquantitative, low-N "observation." He cites Arend Lijphart's study of political cleavages in the Netherlands as an example of such a case study. Though it analyzed only one political system, its publication led to major changes in the way that political cleavages were theorized. A similar example from the study of international relations is Graham Allison's (1971) study of the Cuban missile crisis, which had a large impact on the extant practice of theorizing the state as if it were a unitary, rational actor. Understanding such situations from the standpoint of *DSI*'s analysis is difficult.

Does the reassessment of a theory require the replication of any anomalous finding first obtained in a case study? *DSI* (120ff.) seems usually to answer "yes," as when the authors extol the value of various strategies to increase the number of

---

[6]For a very similar account in explaining why Darwin's work was critical to the development of biology, see Rescher 1970: 14–16.

[7]Aronson, Harré, and Way (1994) contend that the deductive-nomological framework drastically underestimates the importance of models for doing science and argue that the provision of adequate models rather than the writing of general laws is the primary activity of science.

observations. However, King, Keohane, and Verba (186–87 this volume) seem to answer "no" in the process of discussing the relation of Lijphart's (1975) findings in his case study of the Netherlands to the literature on pluralism that preceded it. Although one could justify a "no" answer in terms of case-based explanations of the sort mentioned by Fearon, that is not the path that the authors choose. Like Fearon, they seem to believe that case studies are beset by a degree-of-freedom problem; unlike him, they cannot offer any alternative to quantitative evidence but the mimicking of quantitative analyses in verbal, nonquantitative form. How then can a single case study alter our confidence in the truth or falsity of any theory?

One way is that when the existence of a phenomenon is in question, only one case is needed to establish it. Since Lijphart and Allison do just that, it is important, because it suggests that a phenomenon that previous theory had argued could not exist does in fact occur. However, if it occurs only once, is that enough to pass a significance test? King, Keohane, and Verba (186 this volume) describe Lijphart's study as "the case study that broke the pluralist camel's back." For that to be so, the quantitative camel must already have been under a great deal of strain due to the accumulation of previous anomalous findings. But no other anomalous findings are mentioned. The authors note that there had been many previous studies of the relation between cleavages and democracy. If so, the mystery of why this one study should have such an impact only deepens. Unless one believes that this prediction failure is especially threatening to the previous pluralist theory, the presence of many previous studies that found the predicted association between cleavage structure and democracy would provide even more reason to write off Lijphart's case study as an outlier. No quantitative model is rejected because it fails to predict only one case, and the influence of any one case on judgments (or computations) about the true underlying distribution is a decreasing function of sample size—so more previous case studies would imply that Lijphart's study would matter *less*. Unless the sample is quite small, adding just one "observation" (assuming for the moment that a case study is just an observation) is going to make very little difference. And, from a conventional quantitative standpoint, small samples are simply unreliable bases for inferences—whether or not one adds one additional case.

If one accepts that the Lijphart and Allison studies had a pronounced impact on theorizing in comparative and international politics, and if one views this impact as legitimate and proper, there is no way to rationalize this through quantitative thinking. Rogowski's original suggestion for how to understand this situation—as an example of a clear theory being confronted with a clear outlier—is a step in the right direction. But if that were all that were happening, one would simply be presented with an unusually strong anomalous finding, to which one could respond in a large variety of ways.

If a case study can succeed in explaining why a case is an outlier by identifying causal mechanisms that were previously overlooked, it will have a much more pronounced impact. It is not the fact that the old theory is strongly disconfirmed that makes the Lijphart or Allison studies so important; rather, it is their provision of such mechanisms—connecting cleavage structure to democracy, or the state's organizational structure to observed outcomes—in empirical accounts that fit the data at least once. In the provision of alternative accounts of causation, perhaps relying on different concepts than formerly employed, one finds the primary reason for the impact of the single case (Laitin 1995; Caporaso 1995). John Walton assesses a set of "classic" cases in sociology similarly—their importance lies in their provision of "models capable of instructive transferability to other settings" (Walton 1992: 126). In the same vein, Nicholas Rescher (1970: 15) speaks of Darwin as providing a "keystone" for the development of modern biology; the keystone was not a missing piece of data, but a missing step in a causal argument. That missing step was developed from a combination of intense observation and theoretical arbitrage (his borrowing from Malthus).

Cases are often more important for their value in clarifying previously obscure theoretical relationships than for providing an additional observation to be added to a sample. In the words of one ethnographer, a good case is not necessarily a "typical" case, but rather a "telling" case, in which "the particular circumstances surrounding a case serve to make previously obscure theoretical relationships sufficiently apparent" (Mitchell 1984: 239). Max Weber seems to have had a similar conception of ideal types—he saw them as deliberately "one-sided" constructs intended to capture essential elements of causation and meaning in a particular setting, without regard to whether they adequately represented all relevant situations (Burger 1976: 127–28; Hekman 1983: 25).

John Walton (1992: 129) and Arthur Stinchcombe (1978: 21–22) offer an even stronger claim—that the process of constructing a case study is superior to other methods for the task of theory construction. This is supposedly so because completing a case study requires the researcher to decide exactly what something is a case of and exactly how causation works. Although case studies do not seem to be unique in this regard (at the very least, the same could be said about two other research strategies discussed later), it seems plausible that the activity of searching for and identifying sources of variation in outcomes is likely to lead to richer models than a research strategy that can easily use quantitative controls to build a firewall separating a larger causal mechanism from a small number of variables of immediate interest.

The issue of whether a causal mechanism must be provided in order for an argument to be considered a scientific theory is precisely the point at which *DSI*'s inattentiveness to the conflicts between Hempel's deductive-nomological conception of theory and more recent philosophical accounts leads to confusion about what case studies are capable of accomplishing. It is not merely that a case provides an explanation for a particular set of events. Rather, the source of its potentially large impact is its capacity to incite us to reformulate our explanations of previously studied events.

Toward a Methodology of Intensive Research:
An Alternative Logic for Case Studies

DSI's choice of a quantitative framework for thinking about all studies, and its attempt to distinguish descriptive from explanatory constructs and to privilege the latter, leaves unclear the status of several standard research techniques (*DSI* chap. 2). What is the status of such projects as the construction of decision or game trees, or computer language, or ordinary language representations of a decision-making process? These are possible end products of a "process tracing" research strategy. Are they just "descriptions"? Or are these "theories" in any sense that *DSI* would recognize as legitimate? If a verbal description can be a "model," are these other constructs also models? Are they explanations? More broadly, how (if at all) can we make sense of such activities from the standpoint of *DSI*'s explication of good research design? Diesing explicitly argues that these research activities cannot be subsumed within the quantitative framework; is he right?

Claims that nonquantitative tests of explanations are possible matter little if they cannot be substantiated with examples of how such tests can be constructed and evaluated. The earlier examples of courts, hermeneutic readings, and theory building in the physical and biological sciences do substantiate the contention that such research is an important alternative to conventional quantitative approaches. Yet the philosophical and practical issues involved in such research have received far less attention within political science than they have in quasi-experimental research.

Although a complete explication of the philosophical and operational issues involved in intensive research could easily be as long as a book, we can identify some issues that such a methodology must address, as well as some ways of addressing them.

Understanding Existing Research

A substantial body of literature within the field of international relations is much more easily understood from within Salmon's ontic conception of explanation than the modified Hempelian framework preferred by *DSI*. Examining two well-known research programs in terms of the language and concepts of *DSI* is helpful in revealing exactly how far one can extend the kind of framework the book offers without encountering research practices that are not readily accommodated within its account. In each case, the discussion parallels that of *DSI*: First, the elementary empirical "atom" is defined; second, how the "atoms" are assembled is described; third, how these assemblies are evaluated is addressed. I then note some problems in attempting to carry through *DSI*'s conception of research in these domains.

Cognitive Mapping

An important research program in the study of foreign policy decision making builds on Richard Snyder, H. W. Bruck, and Burton Sapin's (1954) suggestion to construct a theory that captures the decision makers' "definition of the situation" and the decision-making process they use. If our project is to construct ordinary language or machine language representations of decision-making processes along the lines of "cognitive maps" in Robert Axelrod's (1976) sense or expert systems in Charles Taber's (1992) or Hayward Alker's (1996) sense, the basic "atom" of empirical work would be the sentence (in ordinary language) or the statement (in machine language) rather than the value (typically, though not necessarily, numerical) of a variable. There does not seem to be nor does there have to be any kind of representation of the atomic units in reduced form (something equivalent to the moments of a distribution in the quantitative example). However, we can speak of the ensemble of empirical atoms as a "protocol" (in ordinary language) or a "program" (in machine language). There is little point in speaking of the output of a program as being "caused" by one line of computer code apart from the other lines of code; thus, the objective of apportioning causal weights to the various components of the model, an important part of the quantitative project, has no counterpart in an artificial intelligence or a cognitive mapping context. (If translating such a model into a quantitative framework is necessary, it would be akin to a quantitative model in which each of the explanatory variables has no main effect, but rather enters the model only interactively.) After being appropriately initialized with assumptions deemed to capture essential aspects of a historical situation, the model is fitted to historical data, and this fitting exercise can be assessed quantitatively (Cyert and March 1963: 320). However, an assessment method such as comparing root mean squared errors can be undertaken without reference to a defined universe, samples, or significance and in this sense is not quantitative at all. Anders Ericsson and Herbert Simon have articulated the research strategy used in cognitive mapping in terms that are highly similar to the ontic conception outlined earlier:

> A single verbal protocol is not an island to itself, but a link in a whole chain of evidence, stretching far into the past and the future, that gradually develops, molds, and modifies our scientific theories. It needs to be processed with full attention to these linkages. (Ericsson and Simon 1984: 280)

For Ericsson and Simon, theories suggest data to acquire, while data suggest theories to investigate—one is not logically prior to or dependent on the other. Unlike Popper's world, where research is typified in terms of a single movement from the logic of discovery to the logic of falsification, the research process here cycles between theory (re)formulation and theory evaluation. Hypotheses and theory formulation are treated as activities amenable to normative guidance, rather than a completely subjective realm.

Game Theory Applied to Empirical Situations

The story is much the same from a rational choice standpoint. Here a formal representation of the decision-making process involving strategic interaction is constructed, based on a relatively slender and simple set of postulates. The empirical accuracy of this game is then assessed by comparing its predictions with actual outcomes in a situation thought to be relevant to assessing the performance of the formal model. Bruce Bueno de Mesquita and David Lalman (1992) provide a good example of this approach. (In many game-theoretic accounts the fit to empirical situations is addressed more cursorily, because the analyst's primary intention is to elucidate the consequences of a given set of initial assumptions, rather than to provide a good empirical fit per se.)[8] In a game-theoretic representation, there is not one kind of atom, but five: players, nodes (representing outcomes), branches (representing alternatives), utilities, and probabilities. The ensemble of atoms forms a tree, or a game in extensive form. The ensemble as a whole governs choice, and, again, framing queries about the relative causal weight of one atomic unit versus another one is pointless. Goodness of fit can be assessed as in the cognitive-artificial intelligence situation, or (more commonly) a quantitative model is constructed based on the tree and auxiliary hypotheses ("operationalizations") (Signorino 1998). In this latter situation one can, if one wishes, assess the weight or influence of individual factors. Although the quantitative evaluation of the performance of such models is an activity that raises no difficulties from *DSI*'s point of view, the question of how one settles on a given cognitive map or tree for evaluation is not answerable from within the confines of its perspective.

Although games can be infinitely long, a game tree often is finite; it does not attempt to trace causation back beyond a starting point chosen by the analyst; nor does it attempt to discover causation at a more differentiated level than human intentionality. Thus, *DSI*'s (86) objection that attempting to describe completely the causal mechanisms in a concrete situation leads to explanations that are in principle infinitely large is irrelevant, since explanations do not aim at being complete, but merely at answering the question that the researcher asks (Levi 1984: 51). Human decision making is inherently limited in the number of factors that impinge on the awareness of the decision maker, thus allowing the construction of trees that are reasonably complete representations of the decision-making situations facing historical actors, as those actors see them. As George and McKeown (1985: 36) argued, "Because the limitations on the perceptual and information-processing capabilities of humans are well known and pronounced, the process-tracing technique has a chance of constructing a reasonably complete account of the stimuli to which an actor attends." Constructing such a tree is thus feasible, though in any given historical situation the limitations of the available evidence may create a situation where we are not confident that our tree representation of

---

[8]I am grateful to Robert Powell (personal communication) for emphasizing this distinction.

the decision-making situation is accurate and complete. An additional limitation to this approach is that once we leave the world of binary interaction and attempt to model three or more independent agents, the capacity of formal theories of optimizing behavior to provide solutions that are relevant to empirically encountered situations diminishes sharply unless we adopt many seemingly arbitrary restrictions (Ekeland 1988: esp. chap. 1).

The strategy of constructing a tree based on historical information can in principle also address two other problems that *DSI* rightly discusses as common failings of qualitative research: inattentiveness to selection bias and a failure to specify counterfactual claims with enough precision or accuracy to permit their intelligent use in an assessment of which factors really matter in shaping behavior in any given situation. *DSI* and its critics discuss selection bias as if it amounts to a problem of quantitative analysis (that is, an error in sample construction), which is certainly one way to think of it. However, another way to view it is to say that it amounts to being unaware of the fact that the game that one has just analyzed is merely a subgame of a larger game. The difference in conceptualizations is important, because how one views selection bias determines how one evaluates work plagued by it. From the standpoint of conventional quantitative research design, an improperly drawn sample will likely result in findings that are useless for making inferences about an underlying population—particularly when the nature of the bias is not known. However, from a game-theoretic standpoint the analysis of a subgame, if conducted correctly, still provides a valid and useful result. If an analyst does not realize that the outcomes of interest can be reached from branches of the tree that occur prior to the node at which the analysis begins to investigate the decision-making process—as happens in the studies of deterrence mentioned in *DSI* (134–35)—then the analyst will likely be mistaken in judgments about which factors are most important in reaching an outcome. Once the analyst has realized that the relevant tree for analyzing the outcome of interest is larger than initially recognized, the results are still useful as part of a larger tree. What before were (mistakenly) viewed as unconditional probabilities are now seen as conditional ones. Although this change may destroy the case for policy prescriptions based on the old, incorrect view, the tree of the subgame survives intact and is now nested within a larger tree and a more complete explanation.

Another advantage of thinking in terms of trees is that they explicitly represent counterfactual situations. By doing so, they delineate which counterfactual situations among the infinite number available for consideration are the most theoretically relevant. Assuming we know the preferences attached by actors to these counterfactual outcomes, we can address the question of how changes in the payoffs—either of the outcome that occurred or of the outcomes that did not—affect the choices made in the given decision situation.[9]

---

[9]Brady (56–62 this volume) seems to suggest a similar treatment in discussing the implications of *DSI*'s approach to causal analysis and counterfactuals.

It has been objected that trees or other decision-theoretic representations are just as mechanistic a method as relying on quantitative inference for the development of theories of cause and effect (Almond and Genco 1977: 509). Both methods are seen to be fundamentally in error because they treat political phenomena as "clocklike," when in reality there are aspects of political life that make the clock metaphor ultimately inappropriate—in particular (imperfect) memory and learning. Such an argument fails to grasp that even with the use of some clocklike representation of decision making, the resulting explanation of behavior will still be incomplete. Although the problem of modeling preference change was addressed nearly forty years ago, very little progress has been made.[10] The "rules of the game" must generally be analyzed the same way, since our current capacities to understand institutions as the outcome of strategic interaction are still quite limited. The use of trees, computer simulations, and so on should be understood as an attempt not to model political systems as if each were a single clocklike mechanism, but to extract the clocklike aspects from a social situation in which we possess "structural" knowledge—in Jon Elster's (1983) sense—only of some features.

Although they are not typically described in this fashion, both the cognitive-artificial intelligence and choice-theoretic approaches can also be understood as implementations of Weber's venerable concept of "ideal types." This family resemblance is seldom discussed in treatments of Weber's methodology, but it becomes a good deal more understandable once one learns that his work on ideal types was in part a response to economic theory and that he persistently cited that theory to illustrate the uses of "ideal-typical" construction (Burger 1976: 140–53; Ringer 1997: 110). Cognitive-artificial intelligence and choice-theoretic approaches amount to a way of fusing a conception of each actor's definition of the situation with a conception of a social structure within which social action occurs. Although they part company with Weber on the question of whether a model can be empirically accurate (with Weber seemingly arguing that empirical accuracy is not a property usefully attached to an ideal type—see Burger 1976: 152–53), they share with Weber an interest in fusing the "subjective" and "objective" aspects of a social situation in a single model.

A "Folk Bayesian" Approach

We can make use of the notion that humans (particularly social scientists) are intuitive statisticians and view them as folk Bayesians, as Hillary Putnam does (1981: 190–92). This is a different metaphor than was applied by *DSI*, which utilizes the conventional quantitative perspective and does not cover Bayesian approaches. Supplanting or replacing *DSI*'s conventional quantitative approach with

---

[10]Cohen and Axelrod (1984) provide what is apparently the only model of this process developed by political scientists.

a Bayesian framework would improve its account in two ways. First, it would enable us to make sense of several previously inexplicable research activities, some of which *DSI* acknowledges and approves, some of which it does not. Second, it would extend and enrich the normative directives they provide by giving researchers guidance on how to think and act systematically about likelihoods and loss functions, rather than continuing to rely solely on their intuitions to guide them.

A Bayesian approach to the problem of explanation is not a panacea: There are important difficulties on both an operational (Leamer 1994) and a philosophical (Miller 1987) level. Moreover, to say of researchers that they are folk Bayesians implies that their application of Bayesian principles is largely intuitive—it has usually been more a matter of making research decisions in the spirit of Bayes than of consciously applying Bayesian techniques. It is therefore more useful in this context to view Bayesian statistical theory as a metaphor than as an algorithm.

The Bayesian metaphor comes to mind when one considers that researchers in the social sciences, even in the branches that rely heavily on standard quantitative methods, are "interactive processors." They move back and forth between theory and data, rather than taking a single pass through the data (Gooding 1992). As Edward Leamer (1994: introduction, p. x) notes, one can hardly make sense of such activity within the confines of a conventional quantitative approach. A theory of probability that treats this activity as a process involving the revision of prior beliefs is much more consistent with actual practice than one that views the information in a given data set as the only relevant information for assessing the truth of a hypothesis.

If we treat researchers as folk Bayesians, several research practices seen as anomalous by *DSI* become much easier to understand. I have already suggested that Eckstein's ideas on crucial cases seem to emanate from a folk Bayesian perspective: The selection of cases for investigation is guided by the researcher's beliefs regarding the prior probability of a given explanation being correct in a certain kind of setting, coupled with that researcher's assessment of the costs of being wrong in that assessment. A "hard case" for a theory—for example, Stephen Van Evera's (1997: 31–32) "smoking gun" case—then would be one where the prior probability of a theory being a correct explanation is low, but the degree of confidence in that prior assessment is also low. A "crucial case" would be one where the prior probability is an intermediate value, such that either a confirmation or a disconfirmation will produce a relatively large difference between the prior and posterior probabilities. One might also select a case in which the expected cost of being wrong was low and then proceed to more demanding tests only if the initial results are encouraging. This would make good sense if investment in a large research project entailed substantial costs.

A Bayesian perspective can also make sense of *DSI*'s (105 n. 15) "file drawer problem" in which negative research findings are relegated to researchers' private files, and only positive findings are submitted for publication. From this perspective, *DSI*'s contention that a negative result is as useful as a positive one is only true if one originally thought that both results were equally likely. If one conjectured that a positive result was highly likely, then getting such a result would be minimally informative. Thus, a journal devoted to electoral behavior would probably not publish the "positive result" that white American evangelical Protestants in 1994 were more likely to vote for the Republicans than the Democrats, simply because nobody would view that as news. Conversely, the negative result that a sector-specific model of coalitions in U.S. trade politics does not account for the coalitional pattern surrounding NAFTA is news indeed, simply because the prior model had become so well accepted (Magee 1980; Commins 1992).

A Bayesian perspective likewise yields a different normative judgment about the preconceptions of researchers than that offered by *DSI*. Whereas in *DSI*'s view having a preconception makes one "slightly biased" (71), from a Bayesian perspective having a preconception, derived from theory and contextual knowledge, is *necessary* in order to make sense of one's research results. One cannot do Bayesian analysis without establishing an intelligible prior probability for the outcomes in question.[11] *DSI*'s position on preconceptions is not unreasonable—succumbing to motivated perceptual bias is always a danger, and it is well that it should be flagged. However, thinking that a researcher has no preconceptions is unrealistic, and ignoring the useful role that preconceptions can play is not at all "conservative."

If a Bayesian begins a case study with a prior estimate of some variable that is close to zero, but with a prior estimate of the variance of that estimate that is relatively large—because the number of prior observations has been zero or very small—the observation of the first anomalous result is going to raise the posterior estimate of the anomalous finding a very considerable distance above zero. Thus, the change in the subjective assessment on the basis of just a single case would be quite large, but it would be understood as a simple application of Bayesian statistical theory, rather than as a finding that poses any unusual challenge to a conventional quantitative understanding of cases.

The Bayesian perspective is also implicit in *DSI*'s (19) own advice to begin with theories that are "consistent with prior evidence about a research question." This seemingly amounts to de facto acceptance of the prior evidence (that is, assigning it a relatively high prior probability of being based on a correct theory of observation), and this too is far from innocuous. A concrete example illustrates what is at stake. In studying U.S. foreign policy decision making, one confronts a raft of studies by diplomatic historians and political scientists that purport to explain foreign policy decision making by what amounts to a "realist" model—one in which the geostrategic environment drives decisions, and other factors intrude at most in a secondary way. These studies take as their evidence a mountain of declassified government documents that offer geostrategic justifications for vari-

---

[11] The difficulty in forming such priors in some cases is an important criticism of the indiscriminate use of Bayesian analysis (Miller 1987: 269).

ous foreign policy decisions. However, the decision of these researchers about where to search for evidence about the motivations of U.S. central decision makers is itself driven by their theoretical conception of what motivates decision makers and how they decide. The resulting studies are vulnerable to criticism because (1) they generally fail to consider whether policy options that were not chosen also have plausible geostrategic justifications, (2) they generally offer no method for distinguishing between plausible post hoc rationalizations for policy and the reasons why a policy is adopted, and (3) they inadequately address rival hypotheses or theories. As a result, the research program is liable to criticism that it creates a circular argument (Gibbs 1994). Whether this argument is always true is less important than the broader and more general implication that "prior evidence" is unproblematic only to the extent that one accepts the theoretical preconceptions that generated it. If one disagrees with those preconceptions, it makes no sense to assign the evidence generated on the basis of those preconceptions a high prior probability of being correct. In such situations it would not be surprising or improper if those who propose a new theory respond to an inconsistency between their theory and existing data by criticizing the "form of these data" (Tanner and Swets 1954: 40).

The sharpest difference between folk Bayesians and *DSI* is in the differing assessments of ex post model fitting. *DSI*'s (21) view is that ex post model revisions to improve the fit of the model to the data "demonstrate nothing" about the veracity of the theory. Some disagree. For example, Ericcson and Simon (1984: 282–83) argue that the time when a hypothesis was generated is not, strictly speaking, relevant to assessing the posterior probability of it being true. However, they concede that having the data before the hypothesis should probably incline us to place less credence in it.

Similarly, Richard Miller contends that

> When a hypothesis is developed to explain certain data, this can be grounds for a charge that its explanatory fit is due to the ingenuity of the developer in tailoring hypotheses to data, as against the basic truth of the hypothesis. If an otherwise adequate rival exists, this charge might direct us to a case for its superiority. But such a rival does not always exist, and the advantages of having first been developed, then tested against the data are not always compelling. As usual, positivism takes a limited rule of thumb for making a fair argument of causal comparison, and treats it as a universal, determinate rule, functioning on its own. . . .

> While confirmation often does exist in such cases, it is usually weaker than it would be on a basis of discovery. . . . A theory of confirmation that makes . . . questions of timing invisible neglects phenomena that are clearly relevant to the comparison of hypotheses—and that ought to be if confirmation is fair causal comparison. (Miller 1987: 308–09)

These viewpoints are sensitive to *DSI*'s concern about "fiddling" with models solely to improve the goodness of fit, but they do not view that concern as dispositive because they value having a fragile model much more highly than having no model. From a Bayesian standpoint, any attempt to retrofit a model onto data, using a model that is not plausible on other grounds, will likely begin with the assignment to that model of a low prior probability of being correct. If the objective is to find a model that has a high posterior probability of being correct, in light of the fact that it fits the data, it is far better to begin with a model that has a high prior probability. In that sense the Bayesian perspective incorporates a safeguard against the sort of abuse that *DSI* fears, without being categorical in its rejection of ex post fitting.

In contemporary American political science a Bayesian conception of probability has only recently begun to receive attention (Western and Jackman 1994; Jackman and Marks 1994; van Deth 1995; and Bartels 1996, 1997). In the discussion of case-study methodology it has received no attention at all (except for a fleeting mention in George and McKeown 1985: 38). Given its capacity for linking preobservation to postobservation beliefs about the world, and its explicit consideration of the costs of being wrong, greater attention to Bayesian approaches seems sensible, both for case-study researchers and for practitioners of conventional quantitative analysis.

Heuristics for Theory Construction

An unfortunate practical consequence of the Popperian perspective and positivism more generally is that they fixate on testing theory at the expense of constructing it. If the extent of one's knowledge about political science were the tables of contents of most research methods books, one would conclude that the fundamental intellectual problem facing the discipline must be a huge backlog of attractive, highly developed theories that stand in need of testing. That the opposite is more nearly the case in the study of international relations is brought home to me every time I am forced to read yet another attempt to "test" realism against liberalism. If only for this reason, a philosophy of science that took seriously the task of prescribing wise practices for constructing theories would be quite refreshing and genuinely helpful.

Such a prescriptive body of theory has been produced piecemeal by researchers who are in contact with the problems that arise in the performance of intensive research. However, to the extent that its existence is even acknowledged, the nature of that theory is often misconstrued. Rather than constituting a set of surefire methods, guaranteed to work because they harness deductive logic to the task of theory construction, these prescriptions are a series of highly useful heuristics. Intended for the boundedly rational inhabitants of a messy world, they provide guidance on how to generate theories or frame problems and where to search for evidence that is relevant to assessing extant theories.

Case Selection Heuristics

Case studies are often undertaken because the researcher expects that the clarification of causal mechanisms in one case will have implications for understanding causal mechanisms in other cases. Indeed, it is precisely for that reason that heuristics for case selection—from Mill's methods of difference and agreement, to Eckstein's discussion of crucial cases, to George and McKeown's discussion of typological sampling—have been proposed. *DSI* (134) points out that such heuristics do not guarantee statistical control and that the generalization of case-study findings is problematic. This conclusion is correct, but unimportant in this context. Whether a causal account that fits one historical circumstance will fit others is an open question. What matters here is that a causal mechanism has been identified, and the researcher has some framework within which to begin to investigate the validity of the causal claims. Such a framework permits initial judgments about which cases are theoretically "near" the case in question and whether similarities and dissimilarities in causal patterns in different cases are in line with or diverge from initial understandings of how similar the cases are.

Thought Experiments and Counterfactuals

Some social scientists and philosophers (Tetlock and Belkin 1996; Gooding 1992) have argued that developing and exploring counterfactuals is an important part of the research process. The assertion of counterfactuals is typically associated with attempts to find a causal pattern or to explore the implications of a causal pattern that one believes to be present in the situation being analyzed. In the latter case, an explicit and complete theory (such as the earlier-mentioned completed game tree) generates conclusions about counterfactual circumstances while accounting for the outcomes that did occur. Although such counterfactual conclusions, if valid, may be an important and valuable guide to action, the counterfactual statements themselves merely help the analyst to see the implications of a previously developed theory. In situations where theory is ill formed and immature, thought experiments reveal latent contradictions and gaps in theories and direct the analyst's search toward nodes in the social interaction process where action might plausibly have diverged from the path that it did follow (Tetlock and Belkin 1996: chap. 1). Although in principle there is no reason to associate counterfactual analysis with case studies any more than with other empirical methods, the frequent concern of case-study researchers with theories that are relatively immature means that they probably use counterfactuals as a heuristic guiding the search for causal patterns more than those who work with highly developed theories where causality is better understood.

Exploiting Feedback from Observation to Design

In a general way all research relies on feedback from empirical work to modify theory and to redirect subsequent inquiry. Yet in case-study designs the feedback loop often operates within the case as well. As *DSI* (46) has noted, such modification of theory within a single case study is quite difficult to reconcile with a conventional conception of quantitative inference. Indeed, such a conception is not well suited to a research environment in which the costs of an inappropriate research design are quite high and relying on the next study to correct the mistakes of the current one is impractical. Both circumstances often pertain in fieldwork. In a common fieldwork situation the researcher arrives at the site and quickly learns that certain key assumptions of the research design were based on a mistaken understanding of the case. Perhaps the envisioned data-gathering technique is not feasible. Or the ministry thought to be central to decision making concerning the issue of interest turns out to be a rubber stamp for another less visible set of interests. This leads to a redesign of the fieldwork, which, as was noted, consumes degrees of freedom. However, the weeks or months of fieldwork that follow this redesign are not rendered worthless simply because they capitalized on information learned early in the research process.

Identifying Causal Processes Rather than Testing

If the investigator is searching empirical evidence to identify causal processes, terming this activity "identification" seems preferable. We can then reserve the term *test* for those situations where more than one substantive model[12] has been developed and brought to bear, and there is a comparative assessment of the success of the models in explaining the outcomes of interest. The advantage of speaking in this fashion is that it allows us to discuss model identification as an activity that is conceptually distinct from hypothesis formation and testing, and then to address in a systematic way the process involved in doing this well rather than poorly. This saves identification from being thrown in with hypothesis formation, where it would succumb to the Popperian prejudice against the possibility of saying anything helpful about any other part of the research enterprise than testing. The issue of the generalizability of the model can thus be separated from the question of whether the model is an accurate explanation of cause and effect in the situation in which it has been putatively identified.

Superficially, this may seem to concede an advantage to the quantitative view, because a quantitative model is always "tested" when its performance is compared to a null model. However, this is an advantage of little importance if one accepts, as *DSI* seems to, the goal of finding the model of a causal mechanism that best

---

[12]The null model is not considered here to be a substantive model.

accounts for the observations. Given a choice between a null (that is, random) model of planetary motion and one developed by Ptolemy, we would choose the Ptolemaic model every time, because it would perform significantly better than the null model. As long as the relevant statistical tests justified it, we would keep adding epicycles to the model ("variables") to improve our R^2. Hypothetically it is possible that a latter-day Copernicus would write an entirely different specification that would succeed in producing a significantly better goodness of fit. Yet given the paltry theoretical weaponry of most empirical investigations (typically, lists of bivariate relations between a dependent variable and other variables that specify the signs of the coefficients, with little or no theoretical guidance on interactions among independent variables, or the precise nature of feedback from the dependent variable to the independent variables), this cannot be relied on.

Clark Glymour, Richard Scheines, Peter Spirtes, and Kevin Kelly (1987: 7) provide a telling example of the difficulties involved in hitting on the correct representation of an underlying causal mechanism in their brief but sobering analysis of the combinatorics of a six-variable system. Assume that there are four different relations applicable to each pair of variables x and y (x affects y but is not affected by it, y affects x but is not affected by it, they each affect the other, neither affects the other). Given that six variables create fifteen possible variable pairs, there are 415 possible path diagrams one may draw and hence 415 different models to test in order to identify the one that fits the data best. Showing that a model performs significantly better than a null model does little to settle the question of whether it is the best model of the observations that can be written. Accepting "significantly better than null" as the criterion for a successful explanation leads to a perverse, tacit stopping rule for quantitative empirical research: search the universe of plausible model specifications bounded by prior theoretical restrictions until you find one that yields results better than null, then publish. If there are something like 415 specifications from which to select, it would not be at all surprising to find that published models are inferior in terms of goodness of fit to hitherto undiscovered models (which is precisely what Glymour and his colleagues repeatedly show). Thus, the fact that a model can be identified in a statistical sense—and that a computer program embodying the model will indeed run (*DSI* 118)—is no guarantee that the model is the best account of causal processes that can be written.

How then does model identification proceed? Glymour and his colleagues (1987) propose the systematic application of explicit search heuristics to the task of finding models. Gerg Gigerenzer (1991) claims that researchers often work in just this fashion. He argues that between the alternatives of treating discovery of models either as a matter of logic or as entirely idiosyncratic, there are intermediate possibilities in which research may be guided by one or more heuristics. One possibility that Gigerenzer finds to have been repeatedly applied in research in cognitive psychology is what he terms the "tools-to-theories heuristic"—enlisting methods of justifying claims about models to the cause of organizing the exploration of empirical events. Thus, quantitative analysis becomes not merely a method for evaluating hypotheses, but an organizing concept that affected how psychologists came to think about human thought: The heuristic of decision maker as intuitive statistician has become a central perspective in work on human cognition.

Conclusion

The authors of *DSI* are experienced and skilled researchers, and the most successful and original parts of their book are their discussions and recommendations based on their practical experience. The more theoretically self-conscious aspects of their argument—using conventional quantitative methods as an exemplar for all questions of research design, and their rather perfunctory attempt to ground such an argument in a philosophical framework of Popper and Hempel—are problematic when they are employed to provide a basis for assessing research practices that rely on intensive investigation of a small number of cases rather than extensive investigation of as many cases as sampling theory suggests are needed. Simply stated, the disparities between case-study research and conventional quantitative hypothesis testing are too great to treat the latter as an ideal-typical reconstruction of the former. Rather than treating that disparity as a reason for abandoning case studies or regarding them as pointlike observations, it is just as reasonable to treat it as a reason for rethinking the usefulness of methodological advice founded on such bases as quantitative methods and a Hempel-Popper view of epistemology.

What would be an alternative basis for methodological advice? In contrast to *DSI*'s (9) definition of science as "primarily [its] rules and methods"—and not its subject matter—Paul Diesing (1991: 108) quotes approvingly the hermeneutic maxim "no knowledge without foreknowledge," suggesting that what researchers already know has a decisive impact on how they conduct research. Indeed, the relationship between a researcher's knowledge of the system being studied, and the choice of research method and the interpretation of research findings, is a central issue in a variety of contexts. This relationship is important in the choice of subjects to be investigated, in the choice of the case-study method rather than a quantitative method, in the selection among alternative models to be applied to the data and in the interpretation of findings, in the choice of counterfactuals to be assessed, and in the interpretation of the findings of a single case. Although thinking of researchers as folk Bayesians in their approach to these topics is helpful in making sense of some practices that otherwise appear puzzling or just mistaken, there is little to be gained and much to be lost by interpreting everything that a researcher does or thinks from a purely statistical or quantitative standpoint, Bayesian or otherwise.

A more general point is that researchers almost never begin from the starting point envisioned by Descartes or Hume—their thought experiments involving radical doubt radically misstate the research challenge. Typically, the task is not how to move from a position of ignorance to one of certainty regarding the truth of a single proposition. Rather, it is how to learn something new about a world that one already knows to some degree. Framed in this fashion, the basic tasks of research are then (1) to devise ways of leveraging existing understanding in order to extend our knowledge, and (2) to decide what are sensible revisions of prior understandings in light of the knowledge just acquired. Bayesian statistics, case selection heuristics, counterfactual speculation, and "interactive processing"—moving back and forth between theory formulation and empirical investigation—are all strategies that take into account the mutual dependence of understanding and observation. They are all consistent with a pattern model of explanation, in which the research task is viewed as akin to extending a web or network, while being prepared to modify the prior web in order to accommodate new findings (George and McKeown 1985: 35–36). Seen in this light, the test of a hypothesis—the central theoretical activity from the standpoint of conventional quantitative research—is but one phase in a long, involved process of making sense of new phenomena.

Recent developments in the history and philosophy of science, artificial intelligence, and cognitive psychology provide a more useful foundation for thinking about the problems of knowledge inherent in performing and evaluating case studies than can be found in Hempel or Popper. Unfortunately, interest in these developments among case-study researchers or their quantitatively inclined critics has been minimal. The result has been a discourse dominated by the conventional quantitative metaphor, which is often adopted even by those who wish to defend the value of case studies. What is needed if the theory and practice of case-study research are to move forward is to explicate case studies from a foundation that is more capable than logical positivism of dealing with the judgments involved in actual research programs. Such a method will not discard or devalue the genuine advances that more positivistic research methodologies have brought to the study of clocks, but will supplement them with better advice about how to cope with the clouds.

PART IV

Linking the Quantitative and
Qualitative Traditions

CHAPTER 10

Bridging the Quantitative-Qualitative Divide

Sidney Tarrow

In *Designing Social Inquiry* (hereafter *DSI*), Gary King, Robert O. Keohane, and Sidney Verba have performed a real service to qualitative researchers. I, for one, will not complain if I never again have to look into the uncomprehending eyes of first-year graduate students when I enjoin them—in deference to Przeworski and Teune—to "turn proper names into variables." The book is brief and lucidly argued and avoids the weighty, muscle-bound pronouncements that are often studded onto the pages of methodological manuals.

But following *DSI*'s injunction that "a slightly more complicated theory will explain vastly more of the world" (105), I will praise the book no more, but focus on an important weakness in the book: *DSI*'s central argument is that the same logic that is "explicated and formalized clearly in discussions of quantitative research methods" underlies—or should—the best qualitative research (3). If this is so, then the authors really ought to have paid more attention to the *relations* between quantitative and qualitative approaches and what a rigorous use of the latter can offer quantifiers. While they offer a good deal of generous (if at times patronizing) advice to qualitatively oriented scholars, they say very little about how

I wish to thank Henry E. Brady, David Collier, Miriam Golden, Peter Katzenstein, David D. Laitin, Peter Lange, Doug McAdam, Walter Mebane, Robert Putnam, Shibley Telhami, and Charles Tilly for their comments on drafts of this review.

qualitative approaches can be combined with quantitative research. Especially with the growth of choice-theoretic approaches, whose practitioners often illustrate their theories with narrative, there is a need for a set of ground rules on how to make intelligent use of qualitative data.

DSI does not address this issue. Rather, it uses the model of quantitative research to advise qualitative researchers on how best to approximate good models of descriptive and causal inference. (Increasing the number of observations is its cardinal operational rule.) But in today's social science world, how many social scientists can simply be labeled "qualitative" or "quantitative"? How often, for example, do we find support for sophisticated game-theoretic models resting on the use of anecdotal reports or on secondary evidence lifted from one or two qualitative sources? More and more frequently in today's social science practice, quantitative and qualitative data are interlarded within the same study. In what follows, I will discuss some of the problems of combining qualitative and quantitative data, as well as some solutions to these problems.

Challenges of Combining Qualitative and Quantitative Data

A recent work that *DSI* warmly praises illustrates both that its distinction between quantitative and qualitative researchers is too schematic and that we need to think more seriously about the interaction of the two kinds of data. In Robert Putnam's (1993) analysis of Italy's creation of a regional layer of government, *Making Democracy Work,* countless elite and mass surveys and ingenious quantitative measures of regional performance are arrayed for a twenty-year period of regional development. On top of this, he conducted detailed case studies of the politics of six Italian regions, gaining, in the process, what *DSI* (quoting Putnam) recommends as "an intimate knowledge of the internal political maneuvering and personalities that have animated regional politics over the last two decades" (5) and what Putnam calls "marinating yourself in the data" (*DSI:* 5; Putnam 1993: 190). *DSI* (38) uses *Making Democracy Work* to praise the virtues of "soaking and poking," in the best Fenno (1977: 884) tradition.

But Putnam's debt to qualitative approaches is much deeper and more problematic than this; after spending two decades administering surveys to elites and citizens in the best Michigan mode, he was left with the task of explaining the sources of the vast differences he had found between Italy's northcentral and southern regions. In his effort to find them, his quantitative evidence offered only indirect help, and he turned to history, repairing to the halls of Oxford, where he delved deep into the Italian past to fashion a provocative interpretation of the superior performance of northern Italian regional governments vis-à-vis southern ones. This he based on the civic traditions of the (northern) Renaissance city-states, which, according to him, provided "social capital" that is lacking in the traditions of the South (chap. 5). A turn to qualitative history—probably not even in Putnam's mind when he designed the project—was used to interpret cross-sectional, contemporary quantitative findings.

Putnam's procedure in *Making Democracy Work* pinpoints a question in melding quantitative and qualitative approaches that *DSI*'s canons of good scientific practice do not help to resolve. In delving into the qualitative data of history to explain our quantitative findings, by what rules can we choose the *period* of history that is most relevant to our problem? What *kind* of history are we to use; the traditional history of kings and communes or the history of the everyday culture of the little people? And how can the effect of a particular historical period be separated from that of the periods that precede or follow it? In the case of *Making Democracy Work,* for example, it would have been interesting to know by what rules of inference Putnam chose the Renaissance as determining the Italian North's late twentieth-century civic superiority. Why not look to its sixteenth-century collapse faced by more robust monarchies, its nineteenth-century military conquest of the South, or its 1919–21 generation of Fascism (not to mention its 1980s corruption-fed pattern of economic growth)? None of these are exactly "civic" phenomena; by what rules of evidence are they less relevant in "explaining" the northern regions' civic superiority over the South than the period of the Renaissance city-states? Putnam doesn't tell us; nor does *DSI.*

To generalize from the problem of Putnam's book, qualitative researchers have much to learn from the model of quantitative research. But quantitative cousins who wish to profit from conjoining their findings with qualitative sources need, for the selection of qualitative data and the intersection of the two types, rules just as demanding as the rules put forward by *DSI* for qualitative research on its own. I shall sketch some useful tools for bridging the quantitative-qualitative divide from recent examples of comparative and international research (see table 10.1).

Tools for Bridging the Divide

Tracing Processes to Interpret Decisions

One such tool that *DSI* cites favorably is the practice of *process tracing* in which "the researcher looks closely at 'the decision process by which various initial conditions are translated into outcomes'" (226; quoting George and McKeown 1985: 35). The authors of *DSI* interpret the advantages of process tracing narrowly, assimilating it to their favorite goal of increasing the number of theoretically relevant observations (227). As George and McKeown actually conceived it, the goal of process tracing was not to increase the number of discrete decision stages and aggregate them into a larger number of data points but to *connect* the phases of the policy process and enable the investigator to identify the reasons for the emergence of a particular decision through the dynamic of events (George

Table 10.1. Tools for Bridging the Qualitative-Quantitative Divide

Tool	Contribution to Bridging the Divide
Process Tracing	Qualitative analysis focused on processes of change within cases may uncover the causal mechanisms that underlie quantitative findings.
Focus on Tipping Points	Qualitative analysis can explain turning points in quantitative time series and changes over time in causal patterns established with quantitative data.
Typicality of Qualitative Inferences Established by Quantitative Comparison	Close qualitative analysis of a given set of cases provides leverage for causal inference, and quantitative analysis then serves to establish the representativeness of these cases.
Quantitative Data as Point of Departure for Qualitative Research	A quantitative data set serves as the starting point for framing a study that is primarily qualitative.
Sequencing of Qualitative and Quantitative Studies	Across multiple research projects in a given literature, researchers move between qualitative and quantitative analysis, retesting and expanding on previous findings.
Triangulation	Within a single research project, the combination of qualitative and quantitative data increase inferential leverage.

and McKeown 1985: 34–41). Process tracing is different *in kind* from observation accumulation and is best employed in conjunction with it—as was the case, for example, in the study of cooperation on economic sanctions by Lisa Martin (1992) that *DSI* cites so favorably.

Systematic and Nonsystematic Variable Discrimination

DSI gives us a second example of the uses of qualitative data but, once again, underestimates its particularity. The authors argue that the variance between different phenomena "can be conceptualized as arising from two separate elements: *systematic* and *nonsystematic* differences," the former more relevant to fashioning generalizations than the latter (56). For example, in the case of Conservative voting in Britain, systematic differences include such factors as the properties of the district, while unsystematic differences could include the weather or a flu epidemic at the time of the election. "Had the 1979 British elections occurred during a flu epidemic that swept through working-class houses but tended to spare the rich," the authors conclude, "our observations might be rather poor measures of underlying Conservative strength" (56–57).

Right they are, but this piece of folk wisdom hardly exhausts the importance of nonsystematic variables in the interpretation of quantitative data. A good example comes from how the meaning and extension of the strike changed as systems of institutionalized industrial relations developed in the nineteenth century. At its origins, the strike was spontaneous, uninstitutionalized and often accompanied by whole-community "turnouts." As unions developed and governments recognized workers' rights, the strike broadened to whole sectors of industry, became an institutional accompaniment to industrial relations, and lost its link to community collective action. The systematic result of this change was permanently to affect the patterns of strike activity. Quantitative researchers like Michelle Perrot (1986) documented this change. But had she regarded it only as a case of "nonsystematic variance" and discarded it from her model, as *DSI* proposes, Perrot might well have misinterpreted the changes in the form and incidence of the strike rate. Because she was as good a historian as she was a social scientist, she retained it as a crucial change that transformed the relations between strike incidence and industrial relations.

To put this point more abstractly, distinct historical events often serve as the tipping points that explain the shifts in an interrupted time-series, permanently affecting the relations between the variables (Griffin 1992). Qualitative research that turns up "nonsystematic variables" is often the best way to uncover such tipping points. Quantitative research can then be reorganized around the shifts in variable interaction that such tipping points signal. In other words, the function of qualitative research is not only, as *DSI* seems to argue, to peel away layers of unsystematic fluff from the hard core of systematic variables; but also to assist researchers in understanding shifts in the values of the systematic variables.

Framing Qualitative Research within Quantitative Profiles

The uses of qualitative data described in the two previous sections pertain largely to aiding quantitative research. But this is not the only way in which social scientists can combine quantitative and qualitative approaches. Another is to focus on the qualitative data, using a systematic quantitative database as a frame within which the qualitative analysis is carried out. Case studies have been validly criticized as often being based on dramatic but frequently unrepresentative cases. Studies of successful social revolutions often focus on characteristics that may also be present in unsuccessful revolutions, rebellions, riots, and ordinary cycles of protest (Tilly 1993: 12–14). In the absence of an adequate sample of revolutionary episodes, no one can ascribe particular characteristics to a particular class of collective action.

The representativeness of qualitative research can never be wholly assured until the cases become so numerous that the analysis comes to resemble quantitative research (at which point the qualitative research risks losing its particular properties of depth, richness, and process tracing). But framing it within a quantitative database makes it possible to avoid generalizing on the occasional "great event" and points to less dramatic—but cumulative—historical trends.

Scholars working in the "collective action event history" tradition have used this double strategy with success. For example, in his 1993 study of over 700 revolutionary events in over 500 years of European history, Charles Tilly assembled data that could have allowed him to engage in a large-N study of the correlates and causes of revolution. Tilly knows how to handle large time-series data sets as well as anybody. However, he did not believe the concept of *revolution* had the monolithic quality that other social scientists had assigned to it (1993: chap. 1). Therefore, he resisted the temptation for quantification, using his database, instead, to frame a series of regional time-series narratives that depended as much on his knowledge of European history as on the data themselves. When a problem cried out for systematic quantitative analysis (e.g., when it came to periodizing nationalism), Tilly (1994) was happy to exploit the quantitative potential of the data. But the quantitative data served mainly as a frame for qualitative analysis of representative regional and temporal revolutionary episodes and series of episodes.

Putting Qualitative Flesh on Quantitative Bones

An American sociologist, Doug McAdam, has shown how social science can be enriched by carrying out a sustained qualitative analysis of what is initially a quantitative database. McAdam's 1988 study of Mississippi Freedom Summer participants was based on a treasure-trove of quantifiable data—the original questionnaires of the prospective Freedom Summer volunteers. While some of these young people eventually stayed home, others went south to register voters, teach in "freedom schools," and risk the dangers of Ku Klux Klan violence. Two decades later, both the volunteers and the no-shows could be interviewed by a researcher with the energy and the imagination to go beyond the use of canned data banks.

McAdam's main analytic strategy was to carry out a paired comparison between the questionnaires of the participants and the stay-at-homes and to interview a sample of the former in their current lives. This systematic comparison formed the analytical spine of the study and of a series of technical papers. Except for a table or two in each chapter, the texture of *Freedom Summer* is overwhelmingly qualitative. McAdam draws on his interviews with former participants, as well as on secondary analysis of other people's work, to get inside the Freedom Summer experience and to highlight the effects that participation had on their careers and ideologies and their lives since 1964. With this combination of quantitative and qualitative approaches, he was able to tease a convincing picture of the effects of Freedom Summer activism from his data.

As I write this, I imagine the authors of *DSI* exclaiming, "But this is *precisely* the direction we would like to see qualitative research moving—toward expanding the number of observations and re-specifying hypotheses to allow them to be tested on different units!" (see chap. 6). But would they argue, as I do, that it is the *combination* of quantitative and qualitative methods trained on the same problem (not a move toward the logic of quantitative analysis alone) that is desirable? Two more ways of combining these two logics illustrate my intent.

Sequencing Quantitative and Qualitative Research

The growth industry of qualitative case studies that followed the 1980–81 Solidarity movement in Poland largely took as given the idea that Polish intellectuals had the most important responsibility for the birth and ideology of this popular movement. There was scattered evidence for this propulsive role of the intellectuals; but since most of the books that appeared after the events were written by them or by their foreign friends, an observer bias might have been operating to inflate their importance in the movement vis-à-vis the workers who were at the heart of collective action in 1980–81 and whose voice was less articulate.

Solid quantitative evidence came to the rescue. In a sharp attack on the "intellectualist" interpretation and backed by quantitative evidence from the strike demands of the workers themselves, Roman Laba demonstrated that their demands were overwhelmingly oriented toward trade union issues, and showed little or no effect of the proselytizing that Polish intellectuals had supposedly been doing among the workers of the Baltic coast since 1970 (1991: chap. 8). This finding dovetailed with Laba's own qualitative analysis of the development of the workers' movement in the 1970s and downplayed the role of the Warsaw intellectuals, which had been emphasized in a series of books by their foreign friends.

The response of those who had formulated the intellectualist interpretation of Solidarity was predictably indignant. But there were also more measured responses that shed new light on the issue. For example, prodded by Laba's empirical evidence of worker self-socialization, Jan Kubik returned to the issue with both a sharper analytical focus and better qualitative evidence than the earlier intellectualist theorists had employed, criticizing Laba's conceptualization of class and reinterpreting the creation of Solidarity as "a multistranded and complicated social entity . . . created by the contributions of various people" whose role and importance he proceeded to demonstrate (1994: 230–38). Moral: a sequence of contributions using different kinds of evidence led to a clearer and more nuanced understanding of the role of different social formations in the world's first successful confrontation with state socialism.

Triangulation

I have left for last the research strategy that I think best embodies the strategy of combining quantitative and qualitative methods—the *triangulation* of different methods on the same problem. Triangulation is particularly appropriate in cases in which quantitative data are partial and qualitative investigation is obstructed by political conditions. For example, Valerie Bunce used both case methodology and quantitative analysis to examine the policy effects of leadership rotation in western and socialist systems. In her *Do New Leaders Make a Difference?* she wrote: "I decided against selecting one of these approaches to the neglect of the other [the better] to test the impact of succession on public policy by employing *both* methodologies" (1981: 39).

Triangulation is also appropriate in specifying hypotheses in different ways. Consider the classical Tocquevillian insight that regimes are most susceptible to a political opportunity structure that is partially open. The hypothesis takes shape in two complementary ways: (1) that liberalizing regimes are more susceptible to opposition than either illiberal or liberal ones; and (2) that within the same constellation of political units, opposition is greatest at intermediate levels of political opportunity. Since there is no particular advantage in testing one version of the hypothesis over the other, testing both is optimal (as can be seen in the recent social movement study, Kriesi et al. 1995).

My final example of triangulation comes, with apologies, from my own research on collective action and social movements in Italy. In the course of a qualitative reconstruction of a left-wing Catholic "base community" that was active in a popular district of Florence in 1968, I found evidence that linked this movement discursively to the larger cycle of student and worker protest going on in Italy at the same time (Tarrow 1988). Between 1965 and 1968, its members had been politically passive, focusing mainly on neighborhood and educational issues. However, as the worker and student mobilization exploded around it in 1968, their actions became more confrontational, organized around the themes of autonomy and internal democracy that were animating the larger worker and student movements around them.

Researchers convinced of their ability to understand political behavior by interpreting "discourse" might have been satisfied with these observations; but I was not. If nothing else, Florence was only one case among potential thousands. And in today's global society, finding thematic similarity among different movements is no proof of direct diffusion, since many movements around the world select from the same stock of images and frames without the least connection among them (Tarrow 1994: chap. 11).

As it happened, quantitative analysis came to the rescue by triangulating on the same problem. For a larger study, I had gathered a large sample of national collective action events for a period that bridged the 1968 Florentine episode. And as it also happened, two Italian researchers had collected reliable data on the total number of religious "base communities" like that in Florence throughout the country (Sciubba and Pace 1976). By reoperationalizing the hypothesis cross-sectionally, I was able to show a reasonably high positive correlation (.426) between the presence of Catholic base communities in various cities and the magnitude of general collective action in each city (Tarrow 1989: 200). Triangulation demonstrated that the findings of my longitudinal, local, and qualitative case study coincided with the results of cross-sectional, national, and quantitative correlations. My inductive hunch that Italy in the 1960s underwent an integrated cycle of protest became a more strongly supported hypothesis.

DSI does not take the position that quantification is the answer to all the problems of social science research. But the book's single-minded focus on the logic of quantitative research (and of a certain *kind* of quantitative research) leaves underspecified the particular contributions that qualitative approaches make to scientific research, especially when combined with quantitative research. As quantitatively trained researchers shift to choice-theoretic models backed up by illustrative examples (often containing variables with different implicit metrics) the role of qualitative research grows more important. We are no longer at the stage when public choice theorists can get away with demonstrating a theorem with an imaginary aphorism. We need to develop rules for a more systematic use of qualitative evidence in scientific research. Merely wishing that it would behave as a slightly less crisp version of quantitative research will not solve the problem.

This is no plea for the veneration of historical uniqueness and no argument for the precedence of "interpretation" over inference. (For an excellent analysis of the first problem, see *DSI* 42–43; and of the second, see *DSI* 36–41.) My argument, rather, is that a single-minded adherence to *either* quantitative or qualitative approaches straightjackets scientific progress. Whenever possible, we should use qualitative data to interpret quantitative findings, to get inside the processes underlying decision outcomes, and to investigate the reasons for the tipping points in historical time-series. We should also try to use different kinds of evidence together and in sequence and look for ways of triangulating different measures on the same research problem.

Conclusion

DSI gives us a spirited, lucid, and well-balanced primer for training our students in the essential unity of social science work. Faced by the clouds of philosophical relativism and empirical nominalism that have recently blown onto the field of social science, we should be grateful to its authors. But the book's theoretical effort is marred by the narrowness of its empirical specification of qualitative research and by its lack of attention to the qualitative needs of quantitative social scientists. I am convinced that had a final chapter on combining quantitative and qualitative approaches been written by these authors, its spirit would not have been wildly at variance with what I argue here.

CHAPTER 11

The Importance of Research Design

Gary King, Robert O. Keohane, and Sidney Verba

Receiving five serious reviews in this symposium[1] is gratifying and confirms our belief that research design should be a priority for our discipline. We are pleased that our five distinguished reviewers appear to agree with our unified approach to the logic of inference in the social sciences, and with our fundamental point: that good quantitative and good qualitative research designs are based fundamentally on the same logic of inference. The reviewers raise virtually no objections to the main practical contribution of our book—our many specific procedures for avoiding bias, getting the most out of qualitative data, and making reliable inferences.

---

[1]Editors' note: This chapter is reprinted from the 1995 symposium on *Designing Social Inquiry*, published in the *American Political Science Review*. In this chapter, the authors respond to arguments developed in three additional articles in the *APSR* symposium that are reprinted in the present volume: those by Rogowski, Tarrow, and (reprinted in part) Collier. King, Keohane, and Verba likewise respond here to the two other articles in the symposium—by Laitin (1995) and Caporaso (1995)—to which reference is made in the present volume, but which are not included here. The full original citation for this chapter is Gary King, Robert O. Keohane, and Sidney Verba (1995) "The Importance of Research Design in Political Science." *American Political Science Review* 89, no. 2 (June): 475–81. The table of contents, preface, and chapter 1 of *Designing Social Inquiry* are available at pup.princeton.edu/titles/5458.html.

However, the reviews make clear that although our book may be the latest word on research design in political science, it is surely not the last. We are taxed for failing to include important issues in our analysis and for dealing inadequately with some of what we included. Before responding to the reviewers' most direct criticisms, let us explain what we emphasize in *Designing Social Inquiry* and how it relates to some of the points raised by the reviewers.

What We Tried to Do

Designing Social Inquiry grew out of our discussions while coteaching a graduate seminar on research design, reflecting on job talks in our department, and reading the professional literature in our respective subfields. Although many of the students, job candidates, and authors were highly sophisticated qualitative and quantitative data collectors, interviewers, soakers and pokers, theorists, philosophers, formal modelers, and advanced statistical analysts, many nevertheless had trouble defining a research question and designing the empirical research to answer it. The students proposed impossible fieldwork to answer unanswerable questions. Even many active scholars had difficulty with the basic questions: What do you want to find out? How are you going to find it out? and, above all, How would you know if you were right or wrong?

We found conventional statistical training to be only marginally relevant to those with qualitative data. We even found it inadequate for students with projects amenable to quantitative analysis, since social science statistics texts do not frequently focus on research *design* in observational settings. With a few important exceptions, the scholarly literatures in quantitative political methodology and other social science statistics fields treat existing data and their problems as given. As a result, these literatures largely ignore research design and, instead, focus on making valid inferences through statistical corrections to data problems. This approach has led to some dramatic progress; but it slights the advantage of improving research design to produce better data in the first place, which almost always improves inferences more than the necessarily after-the-fact statistical solutions.

This lack of focus on research design in social science statistics is as surprising as it is disappointing, since some of the most historically important works in the more general field of statistics are devoted to problems of research design (see, e.g., Fisher 1935, *The Design of Experiments*). Experiments in the social sciences are relatively uncommon, but we can still have an enormous effect on the value of our qualitative or quantitative information, even without statistical corrections, by improving the design of our research. We hope our book will help move these fields toward studying innovations in research design.

We culled much useful information from the social science statistics literatures and qualitative methods fields. But for our goal of explicating and unifying the logic of inference, both literatures had problems. Social science statistics focuses too little on research design, and its language seems arcane if not impenetrable. The numerous languages used to describe methods in qualitative research are diverse, inconsistent in jargon and methodological advice, and not always helpful to researchers. We agree with David Collier that aspects of our advice can be rephrased into some of the languages used in the qualitative methods literature or that used by quantitative researchers. We hope our unified logic and, as David Laitin puts it, our "common vocabulary" will help foster communication about these important issues among all social scientists. But we believe that any coherent language could be used to convey the same ideas.

We demonstrated that "the differences between the quantitative and qualitative traditions are only stylistic and are methodologically and substantively unimportant" (*DSI* 4). Indeed, much of the best social science research can combine quantitative and qualitative data, precisely because there is no contradiction between the fundamental processes of inference involved in each. Sidney Tarrow asks whether we agree that "it is the *combination* of quantitative and qualitative" approaches that we desire (177 this volume). We do. But to combine both types of data sources productively, researchers need to understand the fundamental logic of inference and the more specific rules and procedures that follow from an explication of this logic.

Social science, both quantitative and qualitative, seeks to develop and evaluate theories. Our concern is less with the development of theory than *theory evaluation*—how to use the hard facts of empirical reality to form scientific opinions about the theories and generalizations that are the hoped-for outcome of our efforts. Our social scientist uses theory to generate *observable implications*, then systematically applies publicly known procedures to infer from evidence whether what the theory implied is correct. Some theories emerge from detailed observation, but they should be evaluated with new observations, preferably ones that had not been gathered when the theories were being formulated. Our logic of theory evaluation stresses maximizing leverage—explaining as much as possible with as little as possible. It also stresses minimizing bias. Lastly, though it cannot eliminate uncertainty, it encourages researchers to report estimates of the uncertainty of their conclusions.

Theory and empirical work, from this perspective, cannot productively exist in isolation. We believe that it should become standard practice to demand clear implications of theory and observations checking those implications derived through a method that minimizes bias. We hope that *Designing Social Inquiry* helps to "discipline political science" in this way, as David Laitin recommends; and we hope, along with James Caporaso, that "improvements in measurement accuracy, theoretical specification, and research should yield a smaller range of allowable outcomes consistent with the predictions made" (1995: 459).

Our book also contains much specific advice, some of it new and some at least freshly stated. We explain how to distinguish systematic from nonsystematic components of phenomena under study and focus explicitly on trade-offs that may exist between the goals of unbiasedness and efficiency (*DSI* chap. 2). We discuss causality in relation to counterfactual analysis and what Paul Holland (1986) calls the "fundamental problem of causal inference" and consider possible complications introduced by thinking about causal mechanisms and multiple causality (*DSI* chap. 3). Our discussion of counterfactual reasoning is, we believe, consistent with Donald Campbell's "quasi-experimental" emphasis (Campbell and Stanley 1966); and we thank James Caporaso for clarifying this.[2]

We pay special attention in chapter 4 to issues of what to observe: how to avoid confusion about what constitutes a "case" and, especially, how to avoid or limit selection bias. We show that selection on values of explanatory variables does not introduce bias but that selection on values of dependent variables does so; and we offer advice to researchers who cannot avoid selecting on dependent variables.

We go on in chapter 5 to show that while random measurement error in dependent variables does not bias causal inferences (although it does reduce efficiency), measurement error in explanatory variables biases results in predictable ways. We also develop procedures for correcting these biases even when measurement error is unavoidable. In that same chapter, we undertake a sustained analysis of endogeneity (i.e., when a designated "dependent variable" turns out to be causing what you thought was your "explanatory variable") and omitted variable bias, as well as how to control research situations so as to mitigate these problems. In the final chapter, we specify ways to increase the information in qualitative studies that can be used to evaluate theories; we show how this can be accomplished without returning to the field for additional data collection. Throughout the book, we illustrate our propositions not only with hypothetical examples but with reference to some of the best contemporary research in political science.

This statement of our purposes and fundamental arguments should put some of the reviewers' complaints about omissions into context. Our book is about doing empirical research designed to evaluate theories and learn about the world—to

---

[2]To clarify further, we note that the definition of an "experiment" is investigator control over the assignment of values of explanatory variables to subjects. Caporaso emphasizes also the value of random assignment, which is desirable in some situations (but not in others, see *DSI* 124–28) and sometimes achievable in experiments. (Random selection and a large number of units are also desirable and also necessary for relatively automatic unbiased inferences, but experimenters are rarely able to accomplish either.) A "quasi-experiment" is an observational study with an exogenous explanatory variable that the investigator does not control. Thus, it is not an experiment. Campbell's choice of the word "quasi-experiment" reflected his insight that observational studies follow the same logic of inference as experiments. Thus, we obviously agree with Campbell's and Caporaso's emphases and ideas and only pointed out that the word "quasi-experiment" adds another word to our lexicon with no *additional* content. It is a fine idea, much of which we have adopted; but it is an unnecessary category.

make inferences—not about generating theories to evaluate. We believe that researchers who understand how to evaluate a theory will generate better theories—
theories that are not only more internally consistent but that also have more observable implications (are more at risk of being wrong) and are more consistent
with prior evidence. If, as Laitin suggests, our single-mindedness in driving home
this argument led us implicitly to downgrade the importance of such matters as
concept formation and theory creation in political science, this was not our intention.

Designing Social Inquiry repeatedly emphasizes the attributes of good theory.
How else to avoid omitted variable bias, choose causal effects to estimate, or derive observable implications? We did not offer much advice about what is often
called the "irrational nature of discovery," and we leave it to individual researchers
to decide what theories they feel are worth evaluating. We do set forth some criteria for choosing theories to evaluate—in terms of their importance to social science and to the real world—but our methodological advice about research design
applies to any type of theory. We come neither to praise nor to bury rational-
choice theory, nor to make an argument in favor of deductive over inductive theory. All we ask is that whatever theory is chosen be evaluated by the same standards of inference. Ronald Rogowski's favorite physicist, Richard Feynman, explains clearly how to evaluate a theory (which he refers to as a "guess"): "If it
disagrees with [the empirical evidence], it is wrong. In that simple statement is the
key to science. It does not make any difference how beautiful your guess is. It does
not make any difference how smart you are, who made the guess, or what his
name is—if it disagrees with [the empirical evidence] it is wrong. That is all there
is to it" (1965: 156).[3]

One last point about our goal: we want to set a high standard for research but
not an impossible one. All interesting qualitative and quantitative research yields
uncertain conclusions. We think that this fact ought not to be dispiriting to researchers but should rather caution us to be aware of this uncertainty, remind us to
make the best use of data possible, and energize us to continue the struggle to improve our stock of valid inferences about the political world. We show that uncertain inferences are every bit as scientific as more certain ones so long as they are
accompanied by honest statements of the degree of uncertainty entailed in each
conclusion.

---

[3]Telling researchers to "choose better theories" is not much different than telling
them to choose the right answer: it is correct but not helpful. Many believe that deriving
rules for theory creation is impossible (e.g., Popper, Feynman), but we see no compelling
justification for this absolutist claim. As David Laitin correctly emphasizes, "the development of formal criteria for such an endeavor is consistent with the authors' goals."

Our Alleged Errors of Omission

The major theme of what may seem to be the most serious criticism offered above is stated forcefully by Ronald Rogowski. He fears that "devout attention" to our criteria would "paralyze, rather than stimulate, scientific inquiry." One of Rogowski's arguments, echoed by Laitin, is that we are too obsessed with increasing the amount of information we can bring to bear on a theory and therefore fail to understand the value of case studies. The other major argument, made by both Rogowski and Collier, is that we are too critical of the practice of selecting observations according to values of the dependent variable and that we would thereby denigrate major work that engages in this practice. We consider these arguments in turn.

Science as a Collective Enterprise

Rogowski argues that we would reject several classic case studies in comparative politics. We think he misunderstands these studies and misses our distinction between a "single case" and a collection of observations. Consider two works that he mentions, *The Politics of Accommodation*, by Arend Lijphart (1968), and *The Nazi Seizure of Power*, by William Sheridan Allen (1965). Good research designs are rarely executed by individual scholars isolated from prior researchers. As we say in our book, "A single observation can be useful for evaluating causal explanations if it is part of a research program. If there are other observations, perhaps gathered by other researchers, against which it can be compared, it is no longer a single observation" (*DSI* 211; see also sections 1.2.1, 4.4.4, the latter devoted entirely to this point). Rogowski may have overlooked these passages. If we did not emphasize the point sufficiently, we are grateful for the opportunity to stress it here.

Lijphart: The Case Study That Broke the Pluralist Camel's Back
What was once called *pluralist theory* by David Truman and others holds that divisions along religious and class lines make polities less able to resolve political arguments via peaceful means through democratic institutions. The specific causal hypothesis is that the existence of many cross-cutting cleavages increases the level of social peace and, thus, of stable, legitimate democratic government.

In *The Politics of Accommodation*, Arend Lijphart (1968) sought to estimate this causal effect.[4] In addition to prior literature, he had evidence from only one

---

[4]Lijphart also went to great lengths to clarify the precise theory he was investigating, because it was widely recognized that the concept of pluralism was often used in conflicting ways, none clear or concrete enough to be called a theory. Ronald Rogowski's de-

case, the Netherlands. He first found numerous observable implications of his descriptive hypothesis that the Netherlands had deep class and religious cleavages, relatively few of which were cross-cutting. Then—surprisingly from the perspective of pluralist theory—he found considerable evidence from many levels of analysis that the Netherlands was an especially stable and peaceful democratic nation. These descriptive inferences were valuable contributions to social science and important in and of themselves, but Lijphart also wished to study the broader causal question.

In isolation, a single study of the Netherlands, conducted only at the level of the nation at one point in time, cannot produce a valid estimate of the causal effect of cross-cutting cleavages on the degree of social peace in a nation. But Lijphart was *not* working in isolation. As part of a community of scholars, he had the benefit of Truman and others having collected many prior observations. By using this prior work, Lijphart could and did make a valid inference. Prior researchers had either focused only on countries with the same value of the explanatory variable (many cross-cutting cleavages) or on the basis of values of the dependent variable (high social conflict). Previous researchers therefore made invalid inferences. Lijphart measured social peace for the other value of the explanatory variable (few cross-cutting cleavages) and, by using his data in combination with that which came before, made a valid inference.

Lijphart's classic study is consistent with our model of good research design. As he stressed repeatedly in his book, Lijphart was contributing to a large scholarly literature. As such, he was not trying to estimate a causal effect from a single observation; nor was he selecting on his dependent variable. Harvesting relevant information from others' data, although often overlooked, may often be the best way to obtain relevant information.

By ignoring the place of Lijphart's book in the literature to which it was contributing, Rogowski is unable to recognize the nature of its contribution. Rogowski's alternative explanation for the importance of this book and the others he mentions—that "(1) all of them tested, relied on, or proposed, clear and precise *theories*; and (2) all focused on *anomalies*" (80–81 this volume)—suggests one of many possible strategies for choosing topics to research; but it is of almost no help with practical issues of research design or ascertaining whether a theory is right or wrong. Indeed, the only way to determine whether something is an anomaly in the first place is to follow a clear logic of scientific inference and theory evaluation, such as that provided in *Designing Social Inquiry*.

Allen: Distinguishing History from Social Science

The Nazi Seizure of Power is an account of life in an ordinary German community. Allen is not a social scientist: In his book, he proposes no generalization,

---

scription of pluralism as a "powerful, deductive, internally consistent theory" (82 this volume) is surely the first time it has received such accolades.

evaluates no theory, and does not refer to the scholarly literatures on Nazi Germany; rather, he zeroes in on the story of what happened in one small place at a crucial moment in history, and he does so brilliantly. In our terms, he is describing historical detail and occasionally also conducting very limited descriptive inference. We emphasize the importance of such work: "Particular events such as the French Revolution or the Democratic Senate primary in Texas may be of intrinsic interest: they pique our curiosity, and if they were preconditions for subsequent events (such as the Napoleonic Wars or Johnson's presidency) we may need to know about them to understand those later events" (*DSI* 36).

In our view, social science must go further than Allen. The social scientist must make descriptive or causal inferences, thus seeking explanation and generalization. Indeed, we think even Rogowski would not accept Allen's classic work of history as a dissertation in political science. Allen's work is, however, not irrelevant to the task of explanation and generalization that is of interest to us. In the hands of a good social scientist, who could place Allen's work within an intellectual tradition, it becomes a single case study in the framework of many others. This, of course, suggests one traditional and important way in which social scientists can increase the amount of information they can bring to bear on a problem: read the descriptive case-study literature.

The Perils of Avoiding Selection Bias

We agree with David Collier's observation that, if our arguments concerning selection bias are sustained, then "a small improvement in methodological self-awareness can yield a large improvement in scholarship" (1995a: 461). Indeed, because qualitative researchers generally have more control over the selection of their observations than over most other features of their research designs, selection is an especially important concern (a topic to which we devote most of our chapter 4).[5]

Rogowski believes that we would criticize Peter Katzenstein's (1985) *Small States in World Markets* or Robert Bates's (1981) *Markets and States in Tropical Africa* as inadmissibly selecting on the dependent variable. We address each book in turn.

---

[5]Selection problems are easily misunderstood. For example, Caporaso claims that "if selection biases operate independently of one's hypothesized causal variable, it is a threat to internal validity; if these same selection factors interact with the causal variable, it is a threat to external validity" (1995: 460). To see that this claim is false, note, as Collier reemphasizes, that Caporaso's "selection factors" can also be seen as an omitted variable. But omitted variables cannot cause bias if they are independent of your key causal variable. Thus, although the distinction between internal and external validity is often useful, it is not relevant to selection bias in the way Caporaso describes.

Katzenstein: Distinguishing Descriptive Inference from Causal Inference

Peter Katzenstein's (1985) *Small States in World Markets* makes some important descriptive inferences. For example, Katzenstein shows that small European states responded flexibly and effectively to the economic challenges that they faced during the forty years after World War II; and he distinguishes between what he calls "liberal and social corporatism" as two patterns of response. But many of Katzenstein's arguments also imply causal claims—that in Western Europe "small size has facilitated economic openness and democratic corporatism" (1985: 80), and that in the small European states, weak landed aristocracies, relatively strong urban sectors, and strong links between country and city led to cross-class compromise in the 1930s, creating the basis for postwar corporatism (1985: chap. 4).

Katzenstein seeks to test the first of these causal claims by comparing economic openness in small and large states (1985: 86, table 1). To evaluate the second hypothesis, he compares cross-class compromise in six small European states characterized by weak landed aristocracies and strong urban sectors, with the relative absence of such compromise in five large industrialized countries and Austria, which had different values on these explanatory variables. Much of his analysis follows the rules of scientific inference we discuss—selecting cases to vary the value of the explanatory variables, specifying the observable implications of theories, and seeking to determine whether the facts meet theoretical expectations.

But Katzenstein fudges the issue of causal inference by disavowing claims to causal validity: "Analyses like this one cannot meet the exacting standards of a social science test that asks for a distinction between necessary and sufficient conditions, a weighting of the relative importance of variables, and, if possible, a proof of causality" (1985: 138). However, estimating causal inferences does not require a "distinction between necessary and sufficient conditions, a weighting of the relative importance of variables," or an absolute "proof" of anything. Katzenstein thus unnecessarily avoids causal language and explicit attention to the logic of inference which results. As we explain in our book, "Avoiding causal language when causality is the real subject of investigation either renders the research irrelevant or permits it to remain undisciplined by the rules of scientific inference" (*DSI* 76).

Remaining inexplicit about causal inference makes some of Katzenstein's claims ambiguous or unsupported. For example, his conclusion seems to argue that small states' corporatist strategies are responsible for their postwar economic success. But because of the selection bias induced by his decision to study only successful cases, Katzenstein cannot rule out an important alternative causal hypothesis—that any of a variety of other factors accounts for this uniform pattern. For instance, the postwar international political economy may have been benign for small, developed countries in Europe. If so, corporatist strategies may have been unrelated to the degree of success experienced by small European states.

In the absence of variation in the strategies of his states, valid causal inferences about their effects remain elusive. Had Katzenstein been more attentive to the problems of causal inference that we discuss, he would have been able to claim causal validity in some limited instances, such as when he had variation in his explanatory and dependent variables (as in the 1930s analysis). More importantly, he would also have been able to improve his research design so that valid casual inferences were also possible in many other areas.

Rogowski is not correct in inferring that we would dismiss the significance of *Small States in World Markets.* Its descriptions are rich and fascinating, it elaborates insightful concepts such as liberal and social corporatism, and it provides some evidence for a few causal inferences. It is a fine book, but we believe that more explicit attention to the logic of inference could have made it even better.

Bates: How to Identify a Dependent Variable

Rogowski claims that Robert Bates's purpose in *Markets and States* was to explain economic failure in tropical African states, and that by choosing only states with failed economies and low agricultural production, Bates biased his inferences. If agricultural production were Bates's dependent variable, Rogowski would be correct, since (as we argue in *Designing Social Inquiry;* see also Collier 1995) using—but not correcting for—this type of case selection does bias inferences. However, low agricultural production was, in fact, not Bates's dependent variable.

Bates's book makes plain his two dependent variables: (1) the variations in *public policies* promulgated by African states and (2) differences in the *group relations* between the farmer and the state in each country. Both variables vary considerably across his cases. Bates also proposed several explanatory variables, which he derived from his preliminary descriptive inferences. These include (1) whether state marketing boards were founded by the producers or by alliances between government and trading interests, (2) whether urban or rural interests dominated the first postcolonial government, (3) the degree of governmental commitment to spending programs, (4) the availability of nonagricultural sources for governmental funds, and (5) whether the crops produced were for food or export. These explanatory variables do vary, and they helped account for the variations in public policy and state-farmer relations that Bates observed.

As such, Bates did not select his observations so they had a constant value for his dependent variable. Moreover, he did not stop at the national level of analysis, for which he had a small number of cases and relatively little information. Instead, he offered numerous observable implications of the effects of these explanatory variables at other levels of analysis within each country. As with many qualitative studies, Bates had a small number of cases but an immense amount of information. We believe one of the reasons Bates's study is—and should be—so highly regarded is that it is an excellent example of a qualitative study that conforms to the rules of scientific inference. In sum, Rogowski says that Bates wrote an excellent book that we would reject. If the book were as Rogowski describes it, we very well might reject it. Since it is not—and indeed is a good example of our logic of research design—we join Rogowski in applauding it.[6]

Triangular Conclusions

We conclude by emphasizing a point that is emphasized both in *Designing Social Inquiry* and in the reviews. We often suggest procedures that qualitative researchers can use to increase the amount of information they bring to bear on evaluating a theory. This is sometimes referred to as "increasing the number of observations." As all our reviewers recognize, we do not expect researchers to increase the number of full-blown case studies to conduct a large-N statistical analysis: our point is not to make quantitative researchers out of qualitative researchers. In fact, most qualitative studies already contain a vast amount of information. Our point is that appropriately marshaling all the thick description and rich contextualization in a typical qualitative study to evaluate a specific theory or hypothesis can produce a very powerful research design. Our book demonstrates how to design research in order to collect the most useful qualitative data and how to restructure it even after data collection is finished, to turn qualitative information into ways of evaluating a specific theory. We explain how researchers can do this by collecting more observations on their dependent variable, by observing the same variable in another context, or by observing another dependent variable that is an implication of the same theory. We also show how one can design theories to produce more observable implications that then put the theory at risk of being wrong more often and easily.

This brings us to Sidney Tarrow's suggestions for using the comparative advantages of both qualitative and quantitative researchers. Tarrow is interested specifically in how unsystematic and systematic variables and patterns interact, and seems to think that principles could be derived to determine what unsystematic events to examine. We think that this is an interesting question for any historically sensitive work. Many unsystematic, nonrepeated events occur, a few of which may alter the path of history in significant ways; and it would be useful to have criteria to determine how these events interact with systematic patterns. We expect that our discussions of scientific inference could help in identifying which apparently random, but critical, events to study in specific instances, and we are confident that our logic of inference will help determine whether these inferences are

---

[6]Subsequently, Bates pursued the same research program. For example, in *Essays on the Political Economy of Rural Africa* he evaluated his thesis for two additional areas— colonial Ghana and Kenya (1983: chap. 3). So Bates did exactly what we recommend: having developed his theory in one domain, he extracted its observable implications and moved to other domains to see whether he observes what the theory would lead him to expect.

correct; but Tarrow or others may be able to use the insights from qualitative researchers to specify them more clearly. We would look forward to a book or article that presented such criteria.

Another major point made by Tarrow is that all appropriate methods to study a question should be employed. We agree: a major theme of our book is that there is a single unified logic of inference. Hence it is possible effectively to combine different methods. However, the issue of triangulation that Tarrow so effectively raises is not the use of different logics or methods, as he argues, but the triangulation of diverse *data sources* trained on the same problem. Triangulation involves data collected at different places, sources, times, levels of analysis, or perspectives, data that might be quantitative, or might involve intensive interviews or thick historical description. The best method should be chosen for each data source. But more data are better. Triangulation, then, refers to the practice of increasing the amount of information brought to bear on a theory or hypothesis, and that is what our book is about.

PART V

Diverse Tools, Shared Standards

CHAPTER 12

Critiques, Responses, and Trade-Offs:
Drawing Together the Debate

David Collier, Henry E. Brady, and Jason Seawright

The past two decades have seen the emergence of an impressive spectrum of new techniques for quantitative analysis, as well as the strong resurgence of interest in developing and refining the tools of qualitative research. The intellectual vitality of these two traditions, along with the apparent divergences between them, has sharply posed the challenge of evaluating their respective strengths and weaknesses, producing a major new methodological dialogue. The present volume seeks to extend and refine this dialogue.

A basic point of reference in this discussion has been King, Keohane, and Verba's *Designing Social Inquiry* (*DSI*), which has broken new ground in the ongoing effort to develop a shared framework for both quantitative and qualitative analysis. Compared to *DSI*, the present volume places far greater emphasis on the limitations of quantitative tools and on the contributions of qualitative methods to addressing these limitations.

The chapters in the present volume present diverse perspectives on this debate. Chapters 3 and 4 by Brady and Bartels, respectively, draw in part on insights from what we have referred to as statistical theory. They argue that the perspective of mainstream quantitative methods advocated by *DSI* is an inadequate foundation for a general methodological framework. Chapters 5 to 10 by Rogowski, Collier,

Mahoney, and Seawright, Munck, Ragin, McKeown, and Tarrow offer insights more centrally drawn from the qualitative tradition. These chapters systematically review methodological tools employed by qualitative researchers and maintain that our understanding and evaluation of these tools cannot simply be subordinated to the framework of mainstream quantitative methods, as they argue *DSI* proposes. In chapter 11, King, Keohane, and Verba's interim response (reprinted from an earlier review symposium) focuses on key issues in this discussion of quantitative versus qualitative methods, questioning arguments made in other chapters regarding theory, concepts, selection bias, no-variance designs, and the evaluation of evidence from case studies. Their chapter, like several others, underscores the importance of linking quantitative and qualitative methods in the framework of careful attention to research design.

We now synthesize and push further this discussion. We first revisit four critiques of *DSI*, concerning the challenge of doing research that is "important," conceptualization and measurement, selection bias, and probabilistic versus deterministic models of causation. Given our concern with finding new ways to bridge alternative methodological traditions, we consider statistical responses that might be made to each critique and the overall conclusions that may be drawn. In the final part of the chapter, given that these critiques and responses often hinge on contending goals of research, we explore the basic theme that methodology involves fundamental trade-offs. A major concern of research design should be with managing these trade-offs. Chapter 13 then further develops our conclusions to the book by focusing on alternative sources of leverage in causal inference.

Critiques and Statistical Responses

In addressing broad issues of methodology, *DSI* relies centrally on the framework of mainstream quantitative methods. The book has attracted wide attention in part because this framework provides a standardized perspective and vocabulary for addressing many methodological questions. Given that the quest for shared standards of methodology and research design is an abiding concern in the social sciences, *DSI*'s framework appropriately commands great attention. For example, David Laitin (1995: 454), in his review essay on *DSI*, underscores the book's potential role in "disciplining political science."

In light of the positive reception accorded to *DSI*, how are we to evaluate the diverse critiques that have been offered in the present volume—critiques that incorporate both a qualitative perspective and statistical arguments? One option is to ask: can we gain additional leverage by stepping back and further exploring these critiques of *DSI* from the standpoint of statistical theory? The following sections adopt this approach to reviewing four significant critiques. For each of these four topics, we first present a brief synopsis of *DSI*'s position, occasionally adding examples or points of clarification. We then summarize the critiques of *DSI* presented in the chapters above, which combine the broader statistical perspective offered by Brady and Bartels and the qualitative perspective that is central to the other chapters. Occasionally, we supplement this discussion by reference to additional writings of our authors, or closely related critiques made by other scholars. Finally, we explore further responses to the critique that could be made from the viewpoint of statistical theory.

For two of the topics addressed—the challenges of doing research that is "important" and of evaluating deterministic models of causation—we find that the statistical response calls into question some aspects of the qualitative critique of *DSI*, and we seek to reconcile these alternatives. By contrast, for two other topics—conceptualization and measurement and selection bias—we find arguments from a statistical perspective that reinforce the critiques.

Within the larger framework of this book, the discussion of these critiques shows how perspectives drawn from statistical theory can potentially offer shared standards for accommodating the claims advanced by both quantitative and qualitative methodologists.

Doing Research That Is Important

DSI briefly argues (see chapter 2) that scholars should study topics that are important, both in the real world and in relation to a given scholarly literature. But *DSI* does not provide guidance for how to choose important topics; nor does the book address the concern that the methodological norms it advocates might make it *harder* to do research that is important, which would of course represent a major trade-off in research design. This section reviews these concerns, takes a close look at the statistical rationale for *DSI*'s deliberately limited attention to theory, and considers the most appropriate balance between these alternative views.

Establishing that research is substantively "important"—or theoretically "innovative" or "creative"—is a complex matter. For the purpose of this discussion, studies that address questions evaluated as being of great normative significance would be considered important—as in Bates's (1981) study, discussed below, which seeks to explain a pervasive pattern of failed economic growth and human misery across an entire continent. Likewise, studies that help advance theory in a way that gives scholars new leverage in conceptualizing and explaining significant outcomes would also be considered important. For example, recent advances in Downsian spatial modeling provide valuable new tools for analyzing dramatic change in party systems (e.g., Kitschelt 1994; Greene 2002). By contrast, some critiques of *DSI* raise the concern that, in adopting the book's framework, scholars may sharply narrow their substantive research questions, thus producing studies that are less important.

Critique

A recurring theme in the critiques of *DSI* is that the book provides little guidance in how to achieve major advances in our substantive and theoretical understanding of politics and society. Rogowski argues that *DSI*'s approach is, in general, insufficiently theory driven. He draws on ideas about the philosophy and practice of science to develop his thesis. Rogowski suggests that *DSI*'s framework fails to account for the achievements of many well-known studies that have greatly advanced theory, even though they do not follow *DSI*'s guidelines. His examples include such influential works as William Sheridan Allen's (1965) *The Nazi Seizure of Power* and Arend Lijphart's (1975) *The Politics of Accommodation*, as well as Bates's study noted above.[1] Rogowski points out that these studies do not meet the methodological standards proposed by *DSI*, in that they lack variance on the dependent variable, which should, in turn, undermine causal inference. King, Keohane, and Verba (188–91 this volume) disagree with Rogowski's interpretation of some of these studies, arguing, for example, that Bates did have variance on some dependent variables.[2] Notwithstanding these specific disagreements, Rogowski's overall argument stands: We sometimes do face a conflict between (a) the methodological goals of improving descriptive and causal inference on the basis of empirical data, and (b) the objective of studying humanly important outcomes and developing theory that helps us to conceptualize and explain them.

McKeown raises the concern that *DSI* provides no heuristics for theory construction (162–63 this volume). Ragin suggests that *DSI*'s warning against the use of "no-variance" research designs would preclude a valuable method for gaining new theoretical understanding. Analysts may observe telling commonalities within a set of cases that all share the relevant outcome, and subsequent efforts to explain

---

[1] In addition to Rogowski's summary of these books, see the discussion by King, Keohane, and Verba (186–91 this volume).

[2] We wish to comment here on alternative interpretations of Bates's study. Rogowski's (80 this volume) position is that Bates lacks variance on his main dependent variable, in that he focuses on "cases of economic failure, or, more precisely, on the remarkably uniform *pattern* of economic failure among the states of post-independence Africa." By contrast, King, Keohane, and Verba (190–91 this volume) argue that a number of key factors in Bates's study do vary, including the two factors they identify as his dependent variables. In our view, Bates develops a complex, multistep causal argument, and some of the variables in that argument certainly do vary across his cases. For example, Bates finds that in Ghana, a small group of wealthy farmers receives a disproportionate amount of government aid compared to the many poor farmers (Bates 1981: 54–61). However, other dependent variables of the study, such as "the apparent shortfalls in agricultural production in Africa" (Bates 1981: 2), are treated as constant across the cases. Our overall conclusion is that although Bates essentially treats his principal dependent variable as not varying, there is variance on additional dependent variables included in his argument. Thus, Rogowski, as well as King, Keohane, and Verba, focusing on different parts of Bates's argument, both have a point.

these commonalities can generate new theoretical insights (128–30 this volume). Ragin (2000: 88–104), for example, has presented a method for theoretically generalizing this kind of insight. Munck (114 this volume), and also Collier, Mahoney, and Seawright (99–101 this volume), likewise argue that no-variance research designs can be a valuable source of insight if the scholar employs within-case analysis.

Statistical Response

In formulating a statistical response, we first underscore *DSI*'s emphasis on the goals of descriptive and causal inference, as well as the book's statements about what it is not trying to accomplish. *DSI* is quite explicit about the fact that it is not attempting to provide guidelines for theoretical innovation, quoting Popper's statement that "there is no such thing as a logical method of having new ideas. . . . Discovery contains 'an irrational element,' or a 'creative intuition'" (*DSI* 14). Although *DSI* (38) allows that any definition of science must have "room for ideas regarding the generation of hypotheses," the book maintains a strict separation between this process and the procedures of "valid scientific inference," which are its main focus. For example, when *DSI* (130) rejects no-variance designs, the book does so on grounds wholly unrelated to the goals of generating hypotheses and learning about unfamiliar phenomena. Instead, it rejects no-variance designs because they provide a weak basis for causal inference. In their response to commentators, King, Keohane, and Verba (184–85 this volume) reiterate their goal: to improve inference, not to provide guidelines for generating theory. As these authors formulate it in *DSI* (16), "[t]his book offers no advice on becoming brilliant."

From a statistical perspective, *DSI*'s advice need not be understood as identifying the only types of studies that can lead to productive findings. Indeed, any given piece of research may yield correct inferences or incorrect inferences, regardless of the procedures used in conducting that research. What statistical reasoning seeks to provide are guidelines that *increase the probability* of generating a correct inference, as well as tools for estimating that probability. Therefore, very crucially, an appropriate way to judge *DSI*'s procedures is not to compare them with those employed in producing the most innovative works in political science. Rather, it is to inquire whether following their advice will, on average, produce superior inferences.

A closely related statistical rationale for *DSI*'s approach is that the book's framework for descriptive and causal inference provides a standard by which other scholars can evaluate a given study. Thus, scholars may evaluate an inference by judging whether it was made using appropriate methodological tools. *DSI*'s (7–9) definition of scientific research emphasizes public scrutiny of research procedures, and the book's tools for inference represent a valuable step toward a framework that may help scholars meet this standard.

Finally, we wish to insist that any conflict between achieving inferential goals and carrying out theoretically productive research is not just a dilemma in *DSI*. Rather, it poses a dilemma for all researchers. Further, this is not merely a dilemma that arises in conjunction with specific issues such as selection bias, but rather is a much more general methodological problem. For example, in our discussion in the next chapter of determinate versus indeterminate research designs, we argue that *DSI*'s legitimate objectives of avoiding multicollinearity and increasing the number of observations may pull scholars away from the most direct possible test of their theoretical ideas. This points to the issue of trade-offs: we may face a basic trade-off between attention to certain standards of good inference and the broader priorities of pursuing interesting theoretical ideas.

The Challenge of Promoting Creativity

If we can establish standards for improving and evaluating inference, can we also establish procedures that promote theoretical creativity and lead to important research? On the one hand, the view that we lack systematic procedures for generating novel insights into political phenomena is widely held. As noted above, *DSI* explicitly states that it does not intend to provide advice on how to be brilliant. Making a parallel argument, a leading advocate of the systematization of case studies, Harry Eckstein, similarly writes that "the Tocquevilles or Bagehots might have been successful in spawning plausible theories without writing case studies, since their imagination and incisiveness clearly matter more than the vehicles chosen for putting them to work" (1975: 146). A researcher may be inspired to think of a new variable that helps explain the outcome of interest by reading Aristotle, Borges, Conan Doyle, or even John Grisham—in addition to gaining insight through carrying out counterfactual thought experiments, or by employing no-variance research designs. The research community should hardly expect hard-and-fast guidelines about how to be creative.

On the other hand, there is good reason to believe that some research practices are more likely to produce theoretical insights than others. Formal, deductive theory can make valuable contributions, although a significant component of the insight associated with such theory depends on substantive insights derived from sources other than the deductive procedures (Powell 1999: chap. 1; Munck 2001: 193–94). Inductive tools for gaining new insights are also well established. Older approaches include Lazarsfeld's elaboration model (Lazarsfeld 1955; Babbie 2004: chap. 15), grounded theory methodology (Glaser and Strauss 1967; Strauss and Corbin 1994), and the procedure of "replacing proper names" of political systems with relevant analytic variables (Przeworski and Teune 1970: 26–30). A more recent formulation of inductive procedures is found in Ragin's (chap. 8 this volume; also 1987, 2000) methods of "Qualitative Comparative Analysis," including the use of no-variance research designs.

Moreover, specific research activities can be especially useful stimuli for theoretical innovation, even if such activities by no means guarantee inspiration.

For example, field research has produced many fundamental insights. Prominent scholars such as Campbell (1975: 182–85) and Piore (1979: 560–61) have underscored the role of fieldwork in overturning established understandings and generating new ideas. Collier's (1999) discussion of the research practice of "extracting new ideas at close range" likewise suggests how field research can generate novel findings. A careful exploration of the specific ways in which field research produces theoretical insights would represent a genuine contribution to social science methodology.

Some of the chapters in the present volume suggest valuable starting points for a broader exploration of techniques that contribute to theoretical innovation. For example, Rogowski (77–82 this volume) emphasizes the value of studying anomalous cases. He discusses famous single-case studies that focus on "most-likely" cases—that is, cases that *should* fit the predictions of an established theory. Such studies can be especially fruitful for gaining insight if these cases turn out *not* to fit, thereby pointing to analytically revealing exceptions to the theory. In a similar vein, Munck (119–20 this volume) discusses several approaches to how case-study research can help analysts generate new theories and hypotheses.

Overall, although no one has an exact formula for being creative, we can certainly identify specific research practices that contribute to creativity.

Innovative Research, Trade-Offs, and DSI*'s Framework*

Scholars can identify research practices that contribute either to improving inference or to promoting theoretical innovation, but not necessarily to both. Hence, we may often face a trade-off in pursuing these alternative goals. *DSI*'s framework for improving causal inference can distract researchers from expanding the range of substantive questions that social science seeks to address. Given that, as McKeown (162 this volume) observes, modern social science does not possess "a huge backlog of attractive, highly developed theories that stand in need of testing," this trade-off between theory building and testing is well worth pondering.

This trade-off is made more complex by the fact that theory is routinely seen as a prerequisite for good empirical inference, in that theory generally plays a central role in specifying the models that are tested. For example, theory plays a central role in dealing with the problems of inference highlighted by conditional independence and related assumptions (chap. 2, guideline 26, and Brady 61 this volume). Adequately addressing these assumptions requires, for example, heavily theory-dependent choices about including and excluding variables. Consequently, procedures for improving causal inference that hinder the development of theory may, in turn, impede causal inference.

These potential tensions and complementarities between achieving good inference and developing strong theory also raise issues for how we define "science." As noted in chapter 2 above, *DSI* does not merely discuss inference, but also raises a much larger set of issues involved in carrying out "scientific research." *DSI*'s carefully formulated definition of scientific research includes the stipulations that "[t]he goal is inference" and "[t]he content is the method" (7, 9). The book could equally well have stated that both the goal and the content of science is theory. The theories employed in different domains of science are certainly heterogeneous, but so also are the methods. There is no reason to think that method, any more than theory, is the essence of science. Both are fundamental, and scholars must recognize the value of both goals.

Conceptualization and Measurement

DSI devotes chapter 2 to descriptive inference, and both there and in many other parts of the book the authors make a number of recommendations about conceptualization and measurement. These recommendations include brief, general advice about the validity and reliability of measurement, the effects of measurement error on causal inference, the kinds of concepts that should be studied, and typologies (see guidelines 19–23 in chap. 2 above). Thus, *DSI* (25, italics omitted) states that scholars should "maximize the validity of . . . measurements," and they should use reliable data-collection procedures that, if applied again, would yield the same data. The book (157–68) discusses the impact of measurement error on descriptive and causal inference, pointing, for example, to the relatively familiar claim that whereas error in measuring the dependent variable does not bias causal estimates, error in the independent variable biases causal estimates toward zero.

Regarding the selection of concepts, *DSI* urges researchers to "choose observable, rather than unobservable, concepts wherever possible" (109). Specifically, "[a]ttempting to find empirical evidence of abstract, unmeasurable, and unobservable concepts will necessarily prove more difficult and less successful than for many imperfectly conceived specific and concrete concepts" (110). *DSI* also expresses strong skepticism about the use of typologies: "in general, we encourage researchers *not* to organize their data in this way" (48). Further, the book claims that "it is easiest to maximize validity by adhering to the data and not allowing unobserved or unmeasurable concepts [to] get in the way" (25).

DSI provides brief but useful comments on trade-offs in conceptualization and measurement. Regarding the issue of generality versus concreteness in concepts and theory, the book comments on the tension between the effort to "maximize the concreteness" of our theories (109–12) and the priority that theories should be stated in the most encompassing way feasible (113–14). *DSI* likewise notes the trade-off, in the use of nominal categories as opposed to higher levels of measurement, between "descriptive richness and facilitation of comparison" (154), as well as the familiar trade-off between measurement validity, on the one hand, and reliability and precision on the other (152).

In the present section, we focus on general issues of conceptualization and measurement. The question of trade-offs is explored later in this chapter.

Critique

The authors in the present volume have several concerns about *DSI*'s approach to conceptualization and measurement. First, in a book of *DSI*'s scope, such topics require extensive attention, rather than brief commentary. Conceptualization and measurement are, after all, basic to the way scholars frame topics and establish procedures for making observations. Furthermore, the validity of causal inference often depends just as much on conceptualization and measurement as it does on *DSI*'s central concerns with having adequate variance, sufficient degrees of freedom, and well-specified models.

Yet Brady observes that, notwithstanding the importance of conceptualization and measurement, in *DSI*'s framework "the problems of theory construction, concept formation, and measurement recede into the distance" (62 this volume). Bartels likewise suggests that *DSI*'s methodological framework neglects research aimed at refining concepts (70 this volume), and Laitin's (1995: 455–56) review essay similarly underscores *DSI*'s inattention to conceptual issues. Overall, commentators believe that research focused on concepts makes just as big a contribution to advancing knowledge as empirical research that seeks to make descriptive or causal inferences.

Second, regarding *DSI*'s advice to employ concepts that readily lend themselves to operationalization, Brady (62 this volume) underscores the central methodological challenge of coming to grips with difficult concepts such as civil society, deterrence, democracy, nationalism, material capacity, corporatism, groupthink, and credibility. Successful measurement always depends on having a well-developed understanding of the concept we want to measure, and efforts at conceptualization and measurement routinely need to tackle theoretical concepts such as these. Laitin (1995: 455–56), in his commentary on *DSI*, likewise calls attention to the complex concepts with which scholars routinely work: charisma, hegemony, political culture, social mobilization, and division of labor, as well as exit, voice, and loyalty. Serious attention to the methodological challenges inherent in conceptualizing and measuring complex concepts is imperative if they are to be useful in political research.

Third, *DSI*'s skeptical advice about typologies is seen as striking at the heart of the qualitative enterprise, in much the same way that *DSI*'s recommendations about increasing the number of observations are seen as a mandate for qualitative, small-N researchers to give up the kind of research they do.[3] Munck emphasizes the importance of typologies as a fundamental tool in political analysis. Typologies play a central role not only in areas in which their use is familiar—for example, delineating types of national political regimes and types of international systems—but also in other domains: for example, Sundquist's (1973: chap. 2) typology of electoral realignment, Collier and Collier's (1991: 7–8, 15–18, 162–68) typology of labor incorporation, and Boix's (1998: chap. 1) typology of eco-

---

[3]This concern about *DSI*'s advice regarding the number of observations is expressed by Brady (55–56 this volume) and Munck (112–14 this volume).

nomic growth strategies. Further, Brady emphasizes the importance of typological thinking as an explanatory tool (57 this volume).

Fourth, other concerns focus on the treatment of measurement. Bartels (72–73 this volume) finds *DSI*'s discussion of measurement error "incomplete and unrealistically optimistic." He suggests that the book's observations concerning the effect of random measurement error in the independent variable pertain only in the bivariate case. In the multivariate case, error in the estimate for any one variable can produce complex forms of error in the estimates for other variables, even if these other variables are measured without error (see also Bollen 1989: 154–67). Brady likewise discusses the broader literature on measurement and measurement theory, arguing that *DSI*'s framework inappropriately neglects basic ideas and research tools in this literature. He suggests that the leverage methodologists can bring to reasoning about the differences between quantitative and qualitative research would be greatly strengthened by close attention to these ideas and tools (62–66 this volume).

DSI pays almost no attention to contextual specificity of conceptualization and measurement. This key issue arises not only in broad cross-national comparisons, but also in disaggregated comparisons of subunits and in comparisons of change over time. This lack of concern with contextual specificity leads to strong misgivings about several of *DSI*'s recommendations, especially the recurring advice to increase the number of observations. Increasing the N has a downside—specifically, it may take the analysis outside of the domain where given concepts are appropriate and measurements remain valid. This may occur either when the analyst moves to a new spatial or temporal domain of cases, or when researchers focus on subunits within an established domain. These subunits may in effect involve a different context, due to heterogeneity within units.

Ragin and Munck devote considerable attention to this question of contextual specificity. One issue they discuss is conceptual stretching, which occurs when, in a new empirical context, the phenomena to which the component attributes of the concept refer are sufficiently different that an established operationalization no longer yields valid measurement. Two well-known means of avoiding conceptual stretching and establishing analytic equivalence are to restrict the domain of cases and, alternatively, to adapt the concept to fit a wider range of cases. Munck (115–16 this volume) points to another option: establishing equivalence by employing system-specific or context-specific indicators, that is, indicators that tap the underlying concept by measuring it in different ways in different contexts. This approach, which remains a basic tool of comparative analysis, has recently been extended by Adcock and Collier (2001: 534–36).

Statistical Response

In light of these critiques, it is productive to consider the response that might be advanced from the standpoint of statistical and psychometric reasoning about these issues. Ideas will also be drawn from the perspective of mathematical measurement theory—including the work of Carl Hempel, whose writings encompass early efforts to formalize basic ideas about measurement.[4]

The very existence of a substantial literature on psychometrics and measurement theory is a useful reminder that conceptualization and measurement are fundamental methodological topics in the social sciences. The perspective that emerges from these literatures generally supports the critiques just discussed, reinforcing arguments about the need for close attention to concept formation, measurement validity, and the contextual specificity of measurement.

With regard to concept formation, the psychometrics literature underscores the importance of careful formulation of concepts as a prerequisite for measurement. Shepard (1993: 417) suggests that careful work with concepts should include the specification of both the internal dimensions of a concept and its relationship to other, closely connected concepts. Bollen's (1989: vi, 185–86, 194) analysis, which bridges structural equation modeling and the tradition of content validation,[5] emphasizes the need for careful analysis focused on the meaning of concepts. He stresses that sophisticated quantitative forms of validity assessment—such as covariance structure models, which he labels structural equation models with latent variables[6]—stand on weak foundations unless basic conceptual questions are resolved. These models provide tools for making choices about what are potentially numerous alternative indicators of a given concept. Bollen argues that, "[j]ust as a nonrepresentative sample of people can lead to mistaken inferences to the population, a nonrepresentative sample of measures can distort our understanding of a concept" (1989: 186). Bollen therefore calls for careful examination of theory and concepts, along with detailed substantive knowledge, to ensure that the set of indicators analyzed is appropriate to the concept. This in turn is essential to achieving valid measurement.

Mathematical measurement theory likewise offers valuable lessons for understanding the relationship between quantitative and qualitative approaches to measurement. These lessons suggest a different perspective about this relationship than that proposed by *DSI*, which is centrally focused on applying quantitative tools to qualitative research. By contrast, measurement theory comes closer to emphasizing a perspective that might be adopted by qualitative researchers. A fundamental theme in measurement theory is that all quantitative research, in its logical foundations, is ultimately based on qualitative, pairwise comparisons. Measurement theory rests on the appraisal of different logical relations—for example, coincidence, precedence, additivity, reflexivity, symmetry, and transitivity—to establish

---

[4]The following discussion incorporates some ideas from Collier and Adcock (1999) and Adcock and Collier (2001).

[5]Content validation focuses on whether the indicators used to measure a concept are judged to correspond to the substantive "content" of the concept.

[6]Other standard labels for these techniques are MIMC (multiple-indicator multiple-cause) models and LISREL-type models.

whether they validly characterize similarities and contrasts within pairs of observations. Reasoning about larger numbers of observations and about higher levels of measurement logically depends on establishing the validity of claims about simple paired comparisons and then aggregating these claims. For example, if the complex requirements of ordinal measurement are not met for two cases, then they certainly are not met for one thousand cases. A major statement of this fundamental idea in measurement theory is found in Krantz, Luce, Suppes, and Tversky (1971: 1–6).[7]

Brady and Ansolabehere (1989) provide a substantive illustration of how ideas about ordinal relationships drawn from measurement theory can be used to evaluate the ordinality assumptions behind the concept of preference, which is central to many lines of inquiry, including, for example, rational choice theory. Their analysis focuses on complex differences in the kinds of ordinality that emerge in respondents' preference orderings regarding candidates in U.S. presidential primaries—involving what are called linear, weak, semi-, interval, partial, and sub-orderings. Distinctions of this kind are standard in the field of psychometrics (Michell 1990: 165–75).

We are convinced that quantitative social scientists should, in general, pay more attention to the foundations of measurement. Further, the procedures through which some qualitative researchers build up their concepts and comparisons on the basis of careful analysis of a few cases is, in many respects, closer to fundamental ideas in measurement theory. An example, drawn from comparative research on democracy, is provided by discussions of how qualitative researchers develop "diminished" subtypes that designate specific forms of "partial" democracy—for example, illiberal democracy or one-party democracy. These subtypes may capture gradations vis-à-vis the concept of democracy more validly than do multistep ordinal scales, which sometimes make the mistake of aggregating nonequivalent gradations of democracy.[8]

Another basic argument in the psychometric tradition is that theory and measurement validity are mutually dependent.[9] Measurement validity is not an inherent property of a particular indicator. Rather, validity entails a specific understanding of that indicator in relation to a given conceptual and theoretical framework. The reconceptualization of validity by psychometricians in recent years thus embraces a more "theory-based view" that measurement validation must be strongly linked to the analyst's theoretical concerns (Shultz, Riggs, and Kottke 1998: 270; see also Moss 1995: 6; Shepard 1993: 406). Thus, a measure of "democracy" that is appropriate for a scholar seeking to conceptualize, observe, and explain transitions from

---

[7] Useful overviews of these issues are found in Coombs, Dawes, and Tversky (1970); Roberts (1976); and Michell (1990: 165–75).

[8] Collier and Adcock (1999: 560–61); Collier and Levitsky (1997).

[9] *DSI* does recognize one aspect of the way in which descriptive inference is theory dependent (e.g., 55–63), but this topic could have received a more thorough treatment.

authoritarian to democratic rule could be quite different from that employed by a scholar focused on conceptualizing, observing, and explaining contrasts in "democracy" in advanced industrial countries.

Further, *DSI*'s warnings about avoiding unobserved and unmeasurable variables would seem to be at odds with the three-decades-long tradition of research identified with what are now called covariance-structure models, as well as the hundred-year-long tradition of work on factor analysis. Both factor analysis and covariance-structure models are based on the recognition that scholars often work with concepts that cannot be directly measured.[10] In these traditions of research, which make an effort to merge insights drawn from psychometrics and econometrics, unmeasured concepts, that is, latent variables, are the point of departure for both descriptive and causal inference. This represents a different perspective from that embodied in *DSI*'s suggestion, noted above, that validity can be maximized by sticking to the data and avoiding unobservable or unmeasured concepts.

Notwithstanding *DSI*'s advice to avoid difficult-to-operationalize concepts, the book (chap. 3) does in fact follow the approach laid out by statistical theorists (e.g., Neyman 1990 [1923]; Rubin 1974, 1978; Pratt and Schlaifer 1984; Rosenbaum 1984; Holland 1986; and Stone 1993) by putting in the painstaking work required to arrive at a plausible systematization of one of the hardest concepts of all—the concept of causation. Thus, the majority of *DSI*'s advice focuses on how to conceptualize and measure causation. Some scholars in fact believe it is simply too hard, and hence an unproductive enterprise, to conceptualize causation or to measure it in the sense of making adequate causal inferences. However, that is not *DSI*'s position, and it is certainly not ours. Conceptualizing and measuring causation unquestionably deserves the sustained attention it receives both in *DSI* and in the present volume. Our point is simply that many other difficult concepts similarly require such sustained attention.

Regarding the argument that *DSI* is excessively optimistic about addressing issues of measurement error, we would note that Bartels's critique (72–73 this volume), discussed above, builds directly on standard statistical treatments of this topic. Evaluating the consequences of measurement error for any particular study is difficult, not only in qualitative research, but also in quantitative research. Quantitative researchers do of course have tools for addressing such error. These include reliability indices, regression using instrumental variables, factor analysis, and, more broadly, covariance structure models, which subsume many other approaches. Such tools are relatively easy to apply, and having some tools available is definitely better than having none. Yet in practice, these tools necessarily pro-

---

[10]For a historical overview, see Bollen's (1989: 1–9) discussion regarding the development of covariance-structure models. Obviously, making inferences with these techniques requires a great many assumptions, and these assumptions should be treated with the same caution that we advocate in addressing, for example, the specification assumption in regression analysis.

vide imperfect estimates, given that they depend on complex and often unverifiable assumptions about the underlying causal structure of the data (Kim and Mueller 1978: 43–46; Bollen 1989: 40–80, 179–223; Greene 2000: 375–86).

If these tools for addressing measurement error are subject to major limitations in quantitative analysis, attempts to apply them would seem to pose even greater problems for qualitative researchers, in that they rely on quantitative procedures that are often inapplicable in this latter tradition. However, this gap may not be as great as it appears. Whereas qualitative researchers may not think of themselves as working with the multiple indicators that are essential to these techniques, in making choices about measurement these researchers do often consider alternative indicators. Indeed, these choices can be made in a self-conscious way that at least implicitly utilizes some of the underlying ideas about validation employed by quantitative researchers (Adcock and Collier 2001: 536–43).

DSI's skepticism about typologies likewise seems surprising from the standpoint of the broader statistical tradition discussed here. Relevant statements range from Hempel's (1965: chaps. 6 and 7) discussion of the role played by taxonomy and typological methods in the natural and social sciences, to Bailey's (1994) book *Typologies and Taxonomies*, which provides an overview of statistical procedures for developing classifications. Furthermore, a wide range of common quantitative tools, such as regression with dummy variables and multinomial logit analyses, have been developed for the specific purpose of causal inference with categorical/typological independent and dependent variables.

With regard to the qualitative critics' concern with the contextual specificity of measurement, this idea is also central to measurement theory and psychometrics. Measurement theory treats the notion of a specified domain of applicability as essential to reasoning about conceptualization and measurement, and specifically as a requirement for working with the logical relations that underlie measurement, as discussed above. Hempel's classic *Fundamentals of Concept Formation* designates this domain as "D," and he treats it as the starting point for constructing arguments about different levels of measurement (1970 [1952]: 703–20, 723). As Roberts puts it, "a relation is not properly defined without giving its underlying set" (1976: 476; see also Coombs, Dawes, and Tversky 1970: 13; Michell 1990: 165–66). Thus, the claim that arguments about measurement must be developed in relation to specific contexts or domains is not solely a preoccupation of qualitative researchers who undertake comparisons across diverse cultures and political systems.

Psychometricians likewise argue that the validity of a given indicator must always be treated as context-specific, in that it pertains to a particular domain of cases. The late Samuel Messick, a leading specialist in psychological and educational testing, argues that the validity of a measure should be understood in relation to the specific domain of cases analyzed in the process of validation. The measure should not be generalized to other contexts until the researcher has evidence of its validity in those contexts (Messick 1989: 14–15; 1975: 956; see also Moss 1992: 236–38). For example, a measure of deference to authority that has been exhaustively validated among American college undergraduates is not necessarily valid for Liverpool dockworkers or Brazilian politicians.

To summarize, writing linked to the traditions of psychometrics, mathematical measurement theory, and statistics supports the critics of *DSI* with respect to conceptualization and measurement validity. Careful decisions about conceptualization and measurement are crucial for empirical research, and these decisions must be a central concern in discussions of methodology and research design.

Finally, we should note that King, Keohane, and Verba (184–85 this volume) respond to concerns about the role of concepts in *DSI* by suggesting that tools for "concept formation and theory creation," while valuable, are not emphasized because of the book's central focus on "empirical research designed to evaluate theories . . . ," that is, on descriptive and causal inference. On the one hand, this is a plausible justification. Concept formation is, in part, an element of theory building. As discussed in the section above on doing research that is important, *DSI* deliberately chooses not to emphasize theory building, so inattention to concept formation might seem justified and reasonable. On the other hand, as just discussed, concept formation is also a step in the process of operationalization and is therefore central to descriptive inference—and, by extension, causal inference. In this sense, the additional perspectives on conceptualization and measurement offered in the present section are essential in moving beyond *DSI*'s excessively limited treatment of these topics.

Selection Bias

DSI presents strong and detailed advice about selection bias, framing it as a central problem in causal inference (128–39). Selection bias arises either when cases are selected according to an unrepresentative sampling rule, or when some unknown, nonrandom process assigns causes to cases. This bias can result from selection procedures employed by the investigator, from self-selection of individuals or other units of analysis into the sample, or from self-selection of the cases under study into the categories of a major independent variable.[11] Under any of these conditions, tests of explanatory hypotheses can suffer from systematic error.

DSI specifically focuses on the problem of investigator-induced selection bias. The book argues that using any truncated sample will yield causal inferences that, on average, underestimate the importance of the independent variable or variables being evaluated (130). Further, *DSI* suggests that research designs in which all cases included in the analysis exhibit just one outcome on the dependent variable—for example, a revolution or a severe international crisis—suffer from "ex-

---

[11]Of these three sources of bias, the problem of the deliberate selection of cases on the dependent variable by the investigator is of particular concern in the present volume. Another principal source of bias, which involves the self-selection of cases specifically into the categories of an independent variable, is explained below.

treme selection bias," and hence "[w]e will not learn about causal effects from them" (130). At the same time, *DSI* (e.g., 141–42) provides advice about appropriate ways to select on the dependent variable, arguing that researchers should select cases across the entire range of that variable.[12]

Critique

A recurring concern of the present volume is that, in making recommendations for qualitative researchers, *DSI* overextends rules and norms identified with conventional quantitative research. Perhaps in part because "selection bias" sounds like an especially grave error in research design, it has become a catchphrase that lends itself to emphatic advice that further encourages this overextension.

These issues are explored in the chapters by Rogowski, and by Collier, Mahoney, and Seawright. Several arguments will be reviewed here. First, concern with selection bias should often be considered in light of trade-offs vis-à-vis other methodological and theoretical priorities, as emphasized by Rogowski (83 this volume; see also 201–2 in this chapter).

Second, Collier, Mahoney, and Seawright ask whether qualitative research based on cross-case analysis and within-case analysis is subject to selection bias. Qualitative researchers must recognize that such bias can be an issue for cross-case analysis. However, when within-case analysis is based on causal-process observations, selection bias need not arise. Hence, with regard to selection bias, the analogy between regression analysis and these qualitative tools is flawed.

Third, *DSI*'s treatment of no-variance research designs (i.e., designs focused only on cases with positive scores on the dependent variable) as an extreme case of selection bias is correct for regression analysis, but it provides an inadequate perspective on the application of other analytic tools to such designs. Within-cases analysis based on causal-process observations can be fruitfully employed in what from a regression perspective are no-variance designs (Collier, Mahoney, and Seawright 99–101; Munck 113–14; Ragin 128–30, all this volume).

Fourth, the very definition of selection bias depends on how the universe of cases is defined. The idea that a researcher is working with a truncated sample only makes sense in relation to a well-defined universe, in relation to which the sample is nonrandom and unrepresentative. Yet defining the universe can be highly problematic, depending as it does on the researcher's assumptions about causal homogeneity and measurement validity, and relatedly on the substantive research question. These issues are of great concern to many qualitative researchers, as emphasized especially in Munck's and Ragin's chapters. It may not be meaningful to raise questions of selection bias until such issues are resolved.

Compared to *DSI*, commentators in the present volume thus offer a different view of studies focused on extreme cases: They argue that the concern with selecting extreme values on the dependent variable has been oversold, and qualitative

---

[12]King, Keohane, and Verba (184 this volume) again call attention to the idea of criteria for selecting on the dependent variable.

researchers have distinctive tools for making valid causal inferences, even if they are dealing with a truncated sample.

Statistical Response

Statistical arguments offer support for *DSI*'s basic claims about selection bias in regression analysis. At the same time, a statistical perspective likewise provides an underpinning for the critiques focused on the application of *DSI*'s ideas to qualitative research.

Statistical theory endorses *DSI*'s argument that regression analysis is useless for the analysis of no-variance designs. When researchers select only cases with one fixed value (which we will call *C*, for constant) on the dependent variable, they force the error term for each case to be equal to the difference between the causal effect of the independent variable and *C*. If the causal relationship is positive, this creates a negative relationship between the error term and the independent variable that is exactly equal in magnitude to the positive relationship between the independent variable and the dependent variable. Regression confounds these two relationships, so the overall estimate of the causal effect is zero. This argument generalizes to multivariate regression.[13]

This argument suggests that *DSI*'s claim that designs with no variance in the dependent variable make it impossible to evaluate any causal effect is therefore imprecise. With a no-variance design on the *independent* variable, it is indeed impossible to carry out a regression analysis at all because the matrix containing the independent variable will be impossible to invert. By contrast, no such mathematical disaster occurs when there is no variance on the dependent variable. Instead, the causal estimates go to zero due to selection bias. Thus, the regression produces an estimate of the causal effects—but that estimate is wrong. DSI is right to state that regression cannot produce useful estimates of any causal effect with a no-variance design—although the book is technically incorrect in saying that regression-based inferences are impossible with such a design.

Statistical ideas likewise support several arguments about selection bias advanced by qualitative researchers. Discussions of selection bias presuppose a stable, precise definition of the universe of cases. Freedman, Pisani, and Purves (1998: 353) argue that many issues of bias cannot be addressed without having a clear prior understanding of the relevant population, and Stolzenberg and Relles (1990: 408), writing from the standpoint of quantitative sociology, observe that our conception of selection bias depends entirely on our conception of the population to which we wish to make inferences.

---

[13] In the context of a regression model where $\mathbf{Y} = \mathbf{Xb} + \mathbf{e}$, choosing only cases where $\mathbf{Y}$ is equal to the fixed value, *C*, completely determines the value of the error term. Stated another way, $\mathbf{e} = C - \mathbf{Xb}$. Therefore, the regression normal equations, $\mathbf{Y} = \mathbf{Xb} + \mathbf{e}$, are equivalent to $\mathbf{X'Y} = \mathbf{X'Xb} + \mathbf{X'}C - \mathbf{X'Xb} = \mathbf{X'}C + \mathbf{X'X}(0)$. As a result, regression will estimate the slopes associated with each independent variable as zero.

Finally, there is a sound statistical basis[14] for the claim that conventional quantitative discussions of selection bias do not directly consider the potential contribution of qualitative no-variance designs to the broader goals of theoretical and substantive learning. Specifically, these goals are hard to quantify, so they are not included in the equations behind claims about selection bias. In other words, quantitative analysis can produce specific figures that represent the magnitude of bias associated with a given research design, but such analysis cannot describe the amount of new theoretical and substantive knowledge the design will produce. Hence, qualitative judgment is required if we are to consider these broader goals.

Drawing together these arguments, we conclude that ideas drawn from statistical theory support several of the critiques. Issues of investigator-induced selection bias sometimes arise in quantitative research and in qualitative cross-case analysis—although not for within case analysis. However, other issues need to be addressed before conclusions can be drawn about this kind of selection bias in any particular study.

In concluding this discussion, a broader concern should be raised: for a discipline such as political science, prominent warnings about investigator-induced selection bias may have been something of a red herring. While truncation is in theory a major problem for many statistical tools, it is in practice relatively uncommon for quantitative researchers in the social sciences to deliberately use truncated samples. Likewise, as discussed in chapter 6, it appears that for qualitative research, concerns about selection bias due to truncation have been seriously overstated. Hence, warnings about this source of selection bias may have distracted scholarly attention from other forms of selection bias which, overall, may be far more prevalent. Specifically, from the standpoint of broader statistical thinking, selection bias that arises either from political and social processes, or through a mismatch between the analytic models employed by the researcher and empirical reality, is almost certainly a more serious and prevalent concern in the social sciences than selection bias due to deliberate truncation.

The problem of self-selection of individuals into the categories of included (independent) variables routinely arises in observational studies in the social sciences. For example, Heckman (1990) has explored this challenge in efforts to assess the impact of unionism on wage differentials, given that workers' decisions about taking unionized jobs generally involve a component of self-selection. The problem of self-selection can also arise at the level of macrocomparative analysis whenever cases are selected into different categories of the included variables through social and political processes that are, inevitably, beyond the investigator's control. For example, Przeworski et al.[15] suggest that democracies may be more likely than authoritarian regimes to break down in the face of poor economic performance. If this is true, then some countries will be "selected in" to the catego-

---

[14]We view the following as a statistical argument because it reflects the basic idea that a statistical equation cannot capture the relevance of a variable that is not included in that equation.

[15]See Przeworski (1995); and Przeworski, Alvarez, Cheibub, and Limongi (2000: 9).

ries of the explanatory variable (regime type) due to their scores on the outcome variable (economic performance). The expected result is an incorrect causal attribution, due to selection bias, concerning the relation of regime type and economic growth.

Selection bias may likewise occur when individuals or other units are selected into or out of the sample through a nonrandom process. Manski (1995: 21) discusses the obvious example of survey research, given that large numbers of potential respondents routinely choose not to participate in surveys. This problem has become particularly severe in telephone surveys. Manski (1995: 21–22) points to other examples as well, including the partially related problem that arises in longitudinal panel surveys, as well as in research on how schooling influences wages, how welfare programs influence labor supply, and how sentencing influences the commission of crimes. In all these areas, the self-selection of some individuals out of the sample forces researchers to make causal inferences through extrapolating from the data about those who participated in the study to those who did not. If, as is likely, these two groups of people are different in substantively relevant ways, adequate extrapolation from one group to the other may be difficult.

In summary, although poor decisions about case selection can sometimes induce selection bias in both quantitative research and qualitative cross-case analysis, selection bias produced by social and political processes is probably a more important problem. In observational studies, when researchers cannot control the processes through which cases are selected into categories on the independent variables (i.e., in observational studies), such bias can severely distort causal inferences because some unmeasured variables may affect both the dependent variable, on the one hand, and the process of assignment to categories of the independent variable, on the other. In essence, this is the problem of the specification assumption—which we discuss in the next chapter—viewed from the standpoint of selection issues.

Probabilistic versus Deterministic Models of Causation

DSI adopts an exclusively probabilistic model of causation, arguing that "the world, at least as we know it, is probabilistic rather than deterministic" (89 n. 11). This focus leads the book (87–89, 204–5, 209–12) to reject techniques for causal assessment that use a "deterministic" perspective.

Before we discuss these issues, a point of terminology must be clarified. In statistics, "deterministic causation" sometimes designates the broad set of models in which the error variance is specified to be zero—that is, models that have no random component. In the vocabulary of qualitative methodologists, by contrast, "deterministic causation" often refers to models of necessary and/or sufficient causation, which represent a subset of the causal models that are deterministic according to the statistical definition. In this section, we follow traditional qualita-

tive usage and treat deterministic causation as referring to necessary and/or sufficient causation.[16]

Critique
  Some authors are convinced that *DSI* is limited by its inattention to deterministic models of causation. Munck (116 this volume) expresses concern about approaches like *DSI*'s, which rely on standard regression models and assume a probabilistic approach. *DSI*'s approach fails to recognize the importance in qualitative
research both of hypotheses about deterministic causation, and of the effort to develop tools that directly test such hypotheses. McKeown (145–46 this volume)
also expresses misgivings about *DSI*'s strictly probabilistic perspective, and Ragin
(135–38 this volume) maintains that deterministic causation requires scholarly
attention (see also Ragin 1987: 39–44, 54–55, 113–18; 2000: 95–96).
  Further, critics argue that *DSI*'s recommendation to seek variance on the independent and dependent variable may impede efforts to test deterministic causal
models (Ragin 130–33 this volume; see also Ragin 2000: 96–99). If the independent and the dependent variables are dichotomous, these authors suggest that the
cases providing the main test of necessary causation are those in which the outcome occurs (see cells A and B in figure 12.1), based on what may be called a
"positive on outcome" design; further, the cases providing the main test for sufficient causation are those in which the hypothesized cause occurs (cells A and C in
the figure), based on what may be called a "positive on cause" design. This approach is a major challenge to *DSI*'s contention that variance on both the independent and dependent variables is essential to causal assessment. More specifically, the argument of these critics challenges *DSI*'s (130) warning that designs
lacking variance on the dependent variable (i.e., include only observations in cells
A and B, and not in C and D) always constitute an extreme case of selection bias
and should be avoided.
  Before we turn to the statistical response, it is useful to provide a brief further
introduction to deterministic causation, given that this topic may be relatively unfamiliar to some readers. Examples of familiar research procedures that presume
deterministic causation include Harry Eckstein's crucial case studies, John Stuart
Mill's methods of difference and agreement, and Ragin's method of qualitative
comparative analysis. The application of these procedures depends in part on the
idea that, in a given bivariate analysis,[17] if a single case deviates from a hypothesized causal pattern, this finding casts serious doubt on the hypothesis. Thus,

---

  [16]We emphasize the distinction between deterministic and probabilistic causal models. Some scholars instead emphasize the contrast between linear models of causation, as
opposed to models of necessary and/or sufficient causation. The main idea in this section
is that necessary and/or sufficient causation is both deterministic and nonlinear.
  [17]Of course, the scholar may be concerned with multiple explanatory variables. The
point is that the hypothesis of deterministic causation posits a decisive relationship between *each* explanatory variable and the outcome variable. Hence, within this framework,
each bivariate relationship can productively be evaluated in isolation.

Figure 12.1. Evaluating Necessary and/or Sufficient Causes

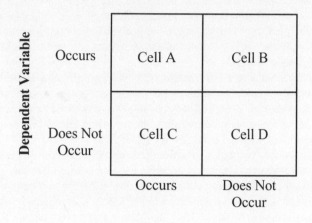

Independent Variable

Research Designs for Testing Necessary and Sufficient Causes

    1. Positive on Outcome Design, for Assessing a Necessary Cause: A design with no variance on the *dependent* variable, focusing on cells A and B. Hypothesis is supported by observations in cell A and rejected if observations are found in cell B.

    2. Positive on Cause Design, for Assessing a Sufficient Cause: A design with no variance on the *independent* variable, focusing on cells A and C. Hypothesis is supported by observations in cell A and rejected if observations are found in cell C.

    3. All Cases Design, for Assessing Necessary or Sufficient Causes: A design in which all cases in the relevant universe (i.e., cells A, B, C, and D) can be included. If cases are found in cell B, necessary causation is ruled out. If cases are found in cell C, sufficient causation is ruled out. All cases that do not rule out a particular causal hypothesis are treated as evidence in favor of that hypothesis.

Note: Adapted from Seawright 2002a: 180.

within a deterministic causal framework, a single variable on its own is hypothesized to have a distinctive causal impact. The variable's presence inevitably causes an outcome if it is a sufficient cause, and its absence definitively prevents an outcome if it is a necessary cause, regardless of the values of other variables. By contrast, a researcher employing a standard probabilistic, multivariate model may be more strongly inclined to treat a deviant case as the result of excluded variables, or as a random outlier.

The other background point that should be underscored is that deterministic causes are increasingly viewed as substantively important in the social sciences. Scholars who have addressed deterministic causation from both Bayesian and non-Bayesian statistical perspectives maintain that deterministic causes play a significant role in political and social theory. Dion (1998: 141) and Seawright (2002a: 180–81) present numerous examples of influential hypotheses about necessary or sufficient causes, and Goertz (2003) has compiled a remarkable inventory of 150 examples of claims about necessary causes, many drawn from prominent authors. A frequently cited example is Wickham-Crowley's (1992: 9) comparative study of modern revolutions in Latin America. He finds that specific weaknesses of "patrimonial praetorian regimes" are a necessary (and nontautological) requisite for revolution. This study (1992: 312, 316–18) further hypothesizes that a withdrawal of U.S. support for the existing regime is a necessary cause of social revolution in the region (i.e., cell B in figure 12.1 is empty). In another example, Migdal (1988: 269–71) hypothesizes that, over a long time horizon, weak societal networks are a sufficient cause of state-building (i.e., cell C is empty). It is against this background that Munck and Ragin, in their contributions to the present volume, argue that deterministic causation is neglected in *DSI*.

Statistical Response

A statistical response to the debate about *DSI*'s position on necessary and sufficient causes provides some support for *DSI*'s critics, but also some support for *DSI*'s perspective. We will present the response in three steps, focusing on the problems that arise if probabilistic tests are employed in assessing what in fact prove to be deterministic causes; the issue of selection bias; and the challenge of finding the most efficient test for assessing necessary and/or sufficient causation.

Probabilistic Tests of Deterministic Causes. Statistical arguments support the position of *DSI*'s critics by showing that, if a deterministic cause is indeed present, then a researcher who only considers a probabilistic model may make invalid inferences. Braumoeller and Goertz (2000: 846–47) provide a statistical demonstration of this point. Unless the hypothesis of necessary causation is explicitly modeled, which would depart from the probabilistic approach of mainstream quantitative methods, then quantitative tools are biased toward inferring that there is some likelihood of the outcome in the absence of the necessary cause. Yet in fact, that probability is zero (i.e., cell B is empty). Such inferential errors occur because some variables that are correlated with the outcome will usually be present to at least some degree, even when the necessary cause is absent. Adopting a conventional quantitative approach based on multivariate linear regression and probabilistic causation invites such errors.

It is therefore essential to use tests that explicitly consider necessary and/or sufficient causation. Dion (1998), Ragin (2000), Braumoeller and Goertz (2000), and Seawright (2002a), drawing in part on Bayesian analysis, suggest that this challenge can be addressed by a variety of research designs and statistical tools. For example, Braumoeller and Goertz (2000) offer a specific procedure for assessing the probability that a given independent variable is a necessary, rather than a probabilistic, cause of the dependent variable. This procedure, which takes the important step of directly testing the hypothesis that the outcome is impossible without the cause, starts with assumptions about the underlying sampling distribution and then estimates the level of measurement error. When confronted with a case that appears to disconfirm the hypothesis of necessary causation (i.e., a case in cell B of figure 12.1), Braumoeller and Goertz's approach provides criteria for deciding whether the evidence is consistent with necessary causation, given potential problems of sampling error and measurement error; or, alternatively, whether the evidence should count against the hypothesis of necessary causation.

Necessary and/or Sufficient Causes and Selection Bias. Several of the research designs just discussed involve testing a deterministic causal model with no-variance research designs, thereby violating some of *DSI*'s basic precepts. Thus, a test for a necessary cause that focuses solely on cells A and B (figure 12.1), that is, the positive on outcome design, lacks variance on the dependent variable. Likewise, a test for a sufficient cause that focuses only on cells A and C, that is, the positive on cause design, lacks variance on the independent variable.

These designs would therefore appear to pose a major dilemma. *DSI* argues that research designs which allow no variance on the dependent variable suffer from extreme selection bias (129–30). Yet Ragin, Dion, and Braumoeller and Goertz are correct in ignoring the issue of selection bias in this instance. As discussed above (90–92 this volume), selection bias from truncation arises when the mechanism of selection generates a correlation between the error term in the causal model and the independent variable. However, this problem is irrelevant in research based on a deterministic model, because the variance of the error term in such a model is zero—that is, there is no error term. Hence, no matter how cases are selected, there cannot be a correlation between the independent variable and the error term.

To put this point more intuitively, selection bias distorts inferences in regression analysis by overrepresenting atypical cases. However, with a deterministic model, it is irrelevant whether atypical cases are overrepresented or not, since deterministic causal models require even atypical cases to follow the overall pattern. Hence, the unusual pattern of cases generated by truncated sampling does not distort the conclusions that can be drawn about deterministic causation.

Identifying the Most Efficient Test.[18] Apart from the issue of selection bias, the question remains of whether, in general, no-variance designs are the most productive way to assess deterministic causation. This issue is currently the subject of an interesting debate, which points to the possibility that *DSI*'s original advice to seek variance on the dependent and independent variable is effectively correct, though for different reasons than the book suggests.

We address this question using the example of necessary causation—although a parallel argument can be made for sufficient causation. Ragin (2000: 96–99), Dion (1998: 128–29), and Braumoeller and Goertz (2000: 846, 852–56) argue, following the positive on outcome design, that only cases actually manifesting the outcome being explained (cells A and B) are relevant to assessing a necessary cause. The hypothesis of necessary causation asserts that only cases experiencing the cause (cells A and C) can possibly experience the outcome. Hence, an appropriate test of this hypothesis consists of examining all cases that experience the outcome and verifying that they all experience the cause. Thus, all cases should be in cell A, cell B should be empty, and cells C and D are irrelevant to the assessment.

Is this type of no-variance design the only way to assess necessary causation? In fact, it is not. Seawright (2002a) uses a simple Bayesian analysis to demonstrate that research designs based on sampling from all available cases (including cells C and D) are also a statistically appropriate test of necessary causation. Further, he argues that, on the basis of the standard of statistical efficiency,[19] this "all-cases" design may sometimes be preferable (see figure 12.1). This is particularly true in the study of relatively rare phenomena, for example, the three revolutions studied by Skocpol. She argues that these are the only social revolutions that have occurred in the large domain of historical cases that she identifies as proto-bureaucratic autocracies, located in agrarian societies that have not experienced colonial domination (1979: 40–41). Analysts who study such phenomena may quickly run out of cases that experienced the outcome, yet, using an all-cases design, they can potentially draw on a large pool of analytically equivalent cases where the outcome did not occur. The point here is that any one of these cases might have fallen in cell B, but did not. Other things being equal (for example, the appropriateness of the cases to the analytic question), considering these additional cases therefore yields a stronger inference.

Given that drawing the sample from the entire universe of cases can produce a more efficient causal inference, the central issue is whether or not all cases are in fact relevant as tests of the hypothesis that the causal process is deterministic. As noted above, Dion, Ragin, and Braumoeller and Goertz argue that, for necessary causation, the most appropriate test focuses on cases that experience the outcome (cells A and B), while another possible test focuses on cases that do not experience

---

[18]This section draws heavily on Seawright (2002a, 2002b).

[19]Efficiency is the extent to which a given analytic procedure fully utilizes available evidence to maximize inferential leverage.

the cause (cells B and D). Cases that experience the cause but not the outcome (cell C) are irrelevant to both types of tests. These researchers start by conditioning on, or treating as fixed in advance, either the value of the dependent variable or the value of the independent variable, and then considering whether or not the values of the *other* variable confirm or negate the hypothesis of necessary causation. On the basis of this reasoning, cases that experience the cause but not the outcome (cell C) are not relevant for falsifying the hypothesis and hence do not constitute tests (e.g., Ragin 2000: 96; Braumoeller and Goertz 2002).

However, Seawright (2002a: 187–89; 2002b: 205–6) argues that it is inappropriate, in working with observational data, to claim that the value of either variable must be treated as fixed in advance. Thus, it is not mandatory that the researcher condition on either the independent or the dependent variable. In observational studies, the scores on the independent and dependent variables are not assigned by the researcher; thus, it is not logically necessary to take either as fixed. Rather, all cases assume their values on the independent and dependent variables through the unfolding of the political and social processes, and all cases are free to assume any combination of values on these variables. Hence, any of the cases could, a priori, have falsified the hypothesis, and the examination of any of the cases (cell C, as well as A, B, and D) constitutes a test of the hypothesis. A parallel argument can be made for sufficient causation.

Additional advantages of the all-cases design should be noted. If analysts find evidence against the hypothesis of deterministic causation, they can use the data already collected to estimate the strength of the probabilistic association between the two variables. By contrast, with a positive on outcome or positive on cause design, they cannot. Relatedly, the all-cases design is also more productive if it turns out that: (1) A necessary or sufficient cause ultimately turns out to fit the hypotheses of both necessary and sufficient causation; (2) what was initially hypothesized to be a necessary cause proves to instead be sufficient; or (3) what was initially thought to be a sufficient cause proves instead to be necessary. In any of these situations, if the researcher limits case selection to a positive on outcome or positive on cause design, it is impossible to do further hypothesis testing without collecting additional data. These are important drawbacks of no-variance designs.

This discussion demonstrates a number of statistical tools are available for empirically testing hypotheses of deterministic causation against probabilistic alternatives.[20] Moreover, researchers are working to refine the statistical foundations of these tools (e.g., Clarke 2002; Braumoeller and Goertz 2002; and Goertz and Starr 2003). As just discussed, recent work suggests that the strongest tests of deterministic hypotheses may in fact include variance on both the independent and the dependent variables. In this respect, the more traditional advice of mainstream quantitative methods remains relevant to the study of these distinctive forms of

---

[20]The tests discussed in this section are incapable of distinguishing among probabilism due to unobserved variables, measurement error, or a genuinely probabilistic causal process. However, they do distinguish between these three forms of probabilism, on the one hand, and deterministic hypotheses on the other.

causation, although conventional regression analysis does not provide an appropriate test. Rather, analysts should use statistical techniques, such as those discussed above, that directly evaluate hypotheses about necessary and/or sufficient causation.

The Statistical Responses

One of our goals, both in this section and in this book overall, is to explore a range of methodological issues from three different perspectives: mainstream quantitative methods, qualitative methods, and statistical theory. *DSI* presents a synthesis of mainstream quantitative methods. The four critiques just discussed draw heavily on the perspective of qualitative methodologists, although they include commentaries by Brady and Bartels that, to a significant degree, employ the broader perspective of statistical theory. In response to each critique, we introduce additional arguments from statistical theory in order to gain new leverage for addressing each concern.

For two of the topics addressed in this chapter—that is, doing research that is important and probabilistic versus deterministic views of causation—we find that statistical responses in some respects support *DSI*. For the question of doing research that is important, the statistical perspective calls attention to the potential trade-off between striving for importance, as opposed to valid inference. With regard to testing hypotheses about deterministic causation, the no-variance designs employed for this purpose have been criticized as being subject to extreme selection bias. On the one hand, the discussion above shows that *DSI*'s rejection of no-variance designs is based on a regression perspective that is not appropriate for evaluating necessary and sufficient causes. On the other hand, all-cases designs, with variance on the independent and dependent variables, can in fact be more efficient than no-variance designs, a conclusion that more nearly supports *DSI*'s priorities in research design, though for different reasons than those offered by *DSI*.

For the other two topics—conceptualization and measurement and selection bias—the responses drawn from statistical theory either directly reinforce the critiques advanced by qualitative researchers, or make parallel arguments that push the discussion in the same direction. This is particularly the case with regard to conceptualization and measurement. With regard to selection bias, we point to statistical arguments, beyond the mainstream quantitative arguments advanced by *DSI*, that can provide valuable guidance to qualitative researchers. Scholars who use statistical tools, based on detailed and precise arguments about evidence and inference, thus reach the same conclusions about these issues as the qualitative critics. This points to a convergence between qualitative and statistical perspectives on research design, yet a convergence quite distinct from the imposition of quantitative norms on qualitative research proposed by *DSI*.

In sum, perspectives drawn from statistical theory sometimes reinforce the views of qualitative methodologists and sometimes those of mainstream quantitative methodologists. Statistical theory can thus provide an independent standard for adjudicating these methodological debates.

Trade-Offs in Research Design

The critiques and statistical responses concerning these four major topics point to the fact that, in social science methodology, all good things do not necessarily go together. Indeed, research involves fundamental trade-offs. An unusually effective introduction to the idea of trade-offs is found in John Gerring's (2001) *Social Science Methodology: A Criterial Framework.* Gerring explores the complex trade-offs entailed in working with concepts, in developing propositions, and in the design of research. With regard to choices about refining concepts, he explores, for example, trade-offs among differentiation, operationalizability, familiarity, parsimony, resonance, and theoretical utility.[21] Our goal in this section is to situate trade-offs within the more balanced view of methodology we advocate in this volume.

Trade-Offs, Goals, and Tools

Trade-offs may involve conflicts among the *goals* pursued by researchers. Trade-offs also arise with respect to the *tools* employed in pursuing these goals. It is likewise productive to contrast *overarching* and *intermediate* goals, as we explain below. These distinctions will also help us in developing a further theme of this book: the idea that working with diverse tools does not preclude establishing shared standards for evaluating research.

In the methodological framework of the present volume, one overarching goal is to seek valid descriptive and causal inferences about important phenomena in the political and social world. This goal is clearly shared with *DSI*. The pursuit of this goal can be advanced through a second overarching goal: refining theory, in order both to gain leverage in establishing what is important, and to strengthen

---

[21]For an overview, see Gerring (2001: 22–26 and 234–39). Other valuable statements about trade-offs are found in Sartori's (1970: 1040–46) discussion of a trade-off between the *intension* (i.e., the meaning) and *extension* (i.e., the range of corresponding observations) of concepts; Ragin's (1987: chaps. 3 and 4) account of case-oriented versus variable-oriented research; and Coppedge's (1999) distinction between concepts and theories that are thick and thin. Sil (2000) discusses a fundamental trade-off between analytic alternatives that broadly parallel those of Ragin. See also the discussion of trade-offs by Przeworski and Teune, Cohen, and Blalock cited in the text below.

these descriptive and causal inferences.[22] Some scholars may use a different vocabulary in discussing these two overarching goals, but we are convinced that these goals are widely shared in contemporary social science.

Of course, scholars make different choices about how they pursue these overarching goals, and these choices are usefully understood at the level of intermediate goals, which involve more specific research objectives. We noted above David Laitin's priority of "disciplining political science," and we believe that a promising source of such discipline is to be found in the careful discussion of how these intermediate goals can serve the overarching goals.

With regard to intermediate goals related to descriptive inference, according to Cohen (1989: 31–36) scholars may alternatively seek precise communication, empirical import, or fertility in the application of concepts; and, according to Blalock (1982: 27–31), generalizability, simplicity, and precision in conceptualization and measurement. In causal assessment, scholars may strive for generality, parsimony, accuracy, and/or causality[23] (Przeworski and Teune 1970: 20–23). The potential diversity of intermediate goals might be an obstacle to the coherence of scholarship. Yet this obstacle may be overcome: Studies that pursue divergent intermediate goals can make complementary contributions to achieving the overarching goals.

Tools, on the other hand, are specific research practices and procedures aimed at achieving intermediate goals, and through them the overarching goals. Some tools are highly systematized and have elaborate statistical and mathematical underpinnings. Other tools, more commonly found in qualitative research, involve practices and procedures that were not developed with explicit statistical or mathematical justifications—although, as we suggest at various points in this book, statistical justifications can serve to illuminate the leverage provided by these tools. Methodology is concerned both with developing tools and with reasoning about how particular tools succeed or fail in achieving research goals. For example, Rogowski argues that an emphasis on narrow methodological criteria for case selection may distract scholars from a larger focus on theoretical innovation and generating valuable substantive insights into politics and society.

Rogowski's concern is one of many demonstrations that goals and tools involve trade-offs. At the level of intermediate goals, for example, the pursuit of one particular objective may make it harder to achieve another. In promoting the idea of shared standards that is a basic theme in the present volume, our purpose is to encourage recognition that different choices at the level of intermediate goals may constitute legitimate, alternative means of pursuing the overarching goals. In the examples noted above, in the application of concepts we may encounter a trade-off among precise communication, empirical import, and fertility. Likewise, Przeworski and Teune's formulation constitutes a major example of a trade-off among

---

[22]*DSI* has been criticized for neglecting theory. Yet as can be seen in the guidelines in chapter 2, the book does consider the links between the methodological issues they discuss and questions of theory.

[23]By causality they mean a fully specified causal model.

intermediate goals. They argue, for example, that more general theories are often less accurate and parsimonious. These trade-offs are often quite real, and scholars must recognize that different combinations of generality, parsimony, and accuracy, or of precision and fertility, can be productive in pursuing the overarching goals of causal and descriptive inference.

At the level of tools, trade-offs are also fundamental. For example, in a regression analysis, a no-variance or "low-variance" research design may be a poor choice from the standpoint of concern with selection bias. Yet it can be a good choice in a research domain where basic descriptive information is lacking, and a scholar is using within-case analysis to unearth new information. *DSI* discusses the strength of nominal categories in terms of "descriptive richness," yet also calls attention to their relative weakness in the "facilitation of comparison" (154). Similarly, cross-national regression analysis based on cross-sectional data has the virtue of providing a concise summary of the relationships among a set of variables across many contexts and of testing the "comparative statics" of theories, that is, contrasts among cases at a given point in time. Yet large-N, cross-national studies too often give insufficient attention to causal mechanisms and to hypotheses about the development of phenomena over time, and such studies may also depend heavily on untested assumptions. In the face of these trade-offs, the idea of shared standards becomes relevant. Thus, it is necessary not merely to criticize given tools in light of their weaknesses, but also to carefully weigh their strengths against these weaknesses in light of what the investigator is trying to accomplish.

In developing what we view as a more balanced approach to the relation between quantitative and qualitative methodology, we are centrally concerned with maintaining this distinction between overarching goals, intermediate goals, and tools, and with focusing on the trade-offs that arise among them. Seeking shared standards for research is much easier if scholars recognize the distinctions among these levels—and if they acknowledge the overarching goals that they share.

A central focus on trade-offs is indispensable, given the tensions among alternative intermediate methodological goals. If we pretend that trade-offs do not exist, it is impossible to have an informed discussion of the objectives being pursued in a given study. Further, the exploration of trade-offs is not a formula for methodological anarchy. Rather, it is a step toward avoiding anarchic situations where scholars are simply talking past one another. The notion of trade-offs rests on the idea that we do have standards; and we need to be explicit about goals, as well as strengths and weaknesses of alternative means for pursuing these goals. As Gerring emphasizes (2001: 26), the number of criteria relevant to evaluating research is relatively limited. Raising the issue of trade-offs challenges us to specify the criteria we are emphasizing, and to justify our choices.

Trade-Offs in *DSI*

We see a striking contrast between this focus on trade-offs and the position of *DSI*. In most research, some methodological goals are simply incompatible. By contrast, *DSI*'s central argument is that scholars should adopt a set of tools that is presumed to meet almost all major methodological priorities; only secondarily does the book mention trade-offs among those priorities.

In fact, scattered throughout the book, *DSI* does briefly discuss five basic trade-offs. With regard to descriptive inference, *DSI* briefly comments on the trade-off (just noted above) between measurement validity and precision (152). The trade-off between "descriptive richness" in the use of nominal categories, and "facilitation of comparison" in higher levels of measurement, is mentioned (154). The authors note the tension between the advice to "maximize the concreteness" of theories (109–12) and the suggestion to make them as encompassing as is feasible (113–14). Concerning issues that arise in both descriptive and causal inference, *DSI* comments, for example, on the trade-off between maximizing observable implications and studying cases that are sufficiently independent of one another to add new information to the analysis (222–23). The book also discusses the trade-off that sometimes arises between minimizing the variance of estimators and achieving unbiasedness in both descriptive and causal inference (66–71, 97).[24] However, these are in every case isolated observations. The reader finds no suggestion that a central challenge in methodology is to address choices among potentially incompatible goals, or to evaluate these trade-offs in light of alternative goals.

Placing Trade-Offs at the Center of Attention

We are convinced that making choices among potentially incompatible goals is, in fact, the essence of research design. A major challenge for methodologists is to do a better job of recognizing and explicating the trade-offs they inevitably encounter.

The first section of this chapter focused on the complex trade-off between theoretical innovation and rigorous testing. Additional trade-offs include the five to which *DSI* refers, as well as the many trade-offs identified by Przeworski and Teune, Blalock, Cohen, and Gerring (see above). We would draw attention to three further trade-offs that are central to this debate: between the precision and generality offered by quantitative tools and the reliance on the often untested assumptions required by these tools; between seeking to avoid bias by including all relevant independent variables in an analysis and seeking to maintain inferential leverage by limiting the number of independent variables; and between the repre-

---

[24]King, Keohane, and Verba (183–84 this volume) again underscore the importance of this particular trade-off.

sentativeness and interpretability of quantitative tests associated with random sampling, versus the close focus on theoretically relevant comparisons (involving both similarities and contrasts) afforded by careful, nonrandom case selection.

However, for several critics, the most fundamental trade-off raised by *DSI*'s recommendations is between increasing the number of observations and other significant goals. As Brady (55–56 this volume) and Munck (112–14 this volume) observe, this recommendation appears to suggest that qualitative, small-N researchers should solve their basic research problems by ceasing to be small-N researchers. In discussing these trade-offs, we first emphasize that within *DSI*'s framework, increasing the N does serve several legitimate purposes. As noted in chapter 2 above, *DSI* argues that increasing the N can help in strengthening falsifiability, enhancing explanatory leverage, and addressing indeterminacy and multicollinearity (guidelines no. 4a, 6b, 9a, 30a). Thus, *DSI* proposes increasing the number of observations in pursuit of legitimate goals.

Yet increasing the number of observations may have serious disadvantages. First, it may take the analysis to a domain that is not appropriate to the research question. In making the case in favor of sticking to observations that are theoretically relevant and appropriate to the research question, *DSI* does usefully quote Lieberson's (1984: chap. 5) incisive statement regarding this priority. The book fails, however, to mention that Lieberson's argument is a critique of a study in which a researcher sought to greatly increase the N by switching the level of analysis to subunits that Lieberson saw as inappropriate to the research question. Further, *DSI* does not really follow Lieberson's advice. For example, *DSI* (24–25) at one point advocates an enormous shift in the domain of analysis in order to add observations to the test of a given hypothesis. Specifically, *DSI* suggests that scholars might study topics in economics such as pricing strategies and entry into markets as a means of testing the theory of deterrence in international politics. Comparing these different domains might be useful as a source of hypotheses, but there is no reason to believe that the same causal processes will operate in each of these domains. These comparative "leaps" can involve a major trade-off: they may move scholars too far away from the original research question.

A closely related disadvantage of increasing the number of observations concerns concepts, measurement validity, and causal homogeneity. Overextending concepts to domains in which they are inappropriate is a recurring methodological problem. Measurement validity is context specific, and extending the research domain to increase the number of observations can impose a high cost in terms of validity and reliability. Extending the research domain can likewise make it more difficult to maintain causal homogeneity. The quest to increase the N can too easily lead a researcher to introduce cases with different causal structures from those that are central to the research question. The resulting loss in validity of causal inference may more than offset any gain in leverage from having a larger N.

Increasing the N also makes it more difficult to maintain knowledge of the context. In chapter 2 under guideline no.17, we quoted *DSI*'s (43) forceful statement on the importance of deep knowledge of the research context. Yet this priority receives little attention in the book. Rich background knowledge can be diffi-

226   *David Collier, Henry E. Brady, and Jason Seawright*

cult and time-consuming to acquire. Thus, a key question concerns the number of cases for which it can in fact be acquired. Further, scholars face a trade-off between obtaining rich, unstructured knowledge of the context and treating either geographic or temporal subunits of cases as the unit of analysis. After all, cultures and the relevant aspects of history change in complex ways within a society over time, and they may vary in equally intricate ways within each subunit of a society. Obtaining detailed background knowledge of observations at other levels of analysis adds to the cost of research in terms of time and other resources, as does adding new cases. Therefore, seeking to increase the number of observations and also achieve deep knowledge involves a fundamental trade-off.

Finally, as *DSI* (222–23) does note, multiplying observations can pose a trade-off in relation to the independence of observations. A focus on temporal or spatial subunits can add observations that are not independent either from the initial set of observations, or from one another. Hence, adding observations that are not independent creates a misleading appearance of a bigger N, leading, for example, to incorrect estimates of statistical significance.

The trade-offs discussed in the previous paragraphs involve several major intermediate goals that become more difficult to achieve when scholars increase the number of observations. Seeking to increase leverage by moving to a larger N may come at a high price. Scholars should be very clear about this trade-off when designing research.

The existence of such trade-offs means that no one set of methodological guidelines can ensure that researchers will do good work. Diverse methodological tools will always be relevant to any substantive problem. The best approach to trade-offs is to recognize them explicitly, to acknowledge that there is usually no single "correct" resolution, and to identify the strengths and weaknesses of different combinations of goals and tools.

Conclusion

Given the pervasive role of trade-offs, we argue that several methodological issues are far more complex than they appear in *DSI*. We have placed particular emphasis on dilemmas related to the book's most frequently repeated piece of advice: increase the number of observations. The five corresponding trade-offs summarize part of the reason why choices about the N are complex. More broadly, the pervasive importance of trade-offs in research design means that methodological advice must be presented more cautiously than it is in *DSI*.

We have likewise argued that descriptive inference entails hard decisions about concepts, typologies, measurement relations, and domains of measurement validity. Decisions such as these are largely neglected by *DSI*. Finally, in our discussions of deterministic causation and selection bias, we have emphasized that advice about causal inference that is valuable in some situations may be counterproductive in others. Methodologists should be careful to tailor their advice to the actual inferential situation of the researcher, a norm that *DSI* largely disregards.

The goal of the final chapter in this volume, which follows, is to further refine both the statistical and the qualitative perspective on these dilemmas. We offer a new conceptualization of the different kinds of observations employed in causal inference and in research design more broadly. A central goal is to illustrate how diverse tools can be evaluated in terms of shared standards and overarching goals. Specifically, we show how an emphasis on the goal of valid causal inference can lead to fundamental critiques of mainstream quantitative methods, and to a renewed focus on alternative tools that grow out of the qualitative tradition.

CHAPTER 13

Sources of Leverage in Causal Inference:
Toward an Alternative View of Methodology

David Collier, Henry E. Brady, and Jason Seawright

The challenge of identifying, assessing, and eliminating rival explanations is a fundamental concern in social research.[1] The goal of this final chapter is to synthesize the view of methodology offered in the present volume by considering further the contribution of alternative quantitative and qualitative tools in evaluating rival explanations.

We seek to clarify several methodological distinctions that are essential to understanding causal inference. We also propose a new distinction: between dataset observations and causal-process observations. Our discussion considers the contrasting, yet complementary, forms of inferential leverage provided by each type of observation. In the final section of the chapter, we offer some observations about balancing methodological priorities in the face of the ongoing technification of method and theory in many branches of the social sciences.

---

[1]Snyder (1984/85: 91–92), in contrast to *DSI* (7–9), explicitly makes the elimination of rival explanations one of his criteria for the scientific method.

Revisiting Some Key Distinctions

Understanding the leverage for causal inference provided by different styles of research requires close attention to several basic distinctions. If these are not treated carefully, conclusions about alternative sources of leverage may be misleading.

Two broad contrasts are indispensable to the argument we seek to develop: between experiments and observational studies, and between mainstream quantitative methods and perspectives drawn from statistical theory. We then consider three other distinctions, involving more specific statistical issues: determinate versus indeterminate research designs, data mining vis-à-vis specification searches, and the assumptions of conditional independence versus the specification assumption. Readers may refer to the glossary for a compilation of the definitions we employ.

Experiments, Quasi-Experiments, Observational Studies, and Inferential Monsters

As is well known, in experiments analysts randomly assign cases to different treatments, that is, to different values of the key independent variable. In observational studies, by contrast, analysts observe the values that the independent variables acquire through the unfolding of political and social processes. For the purpose of evaluating rival explanations, the most fundamental divide in methodology is neither between qualitative and quantitative approaches, nor between small-N and large-N research. Rather, it is between experimental and observational data. All researchers know this, but they often do not give adequate attention to the severe inferential problems that arise with observational data. In addition to differing on the explanatory variables of interest, such real-world cases may also differ in many other ways that the researcher cannot measure and control for, and that can distort causal inference.[2]

Concern with these severe inferential problems has led the econometrician Edward Leamer to underscore "the truly sharp distinction between inference from experimental and inference from non-experimental data. . . ." He points out that with the latter, "there is no formal way to know what inferential monsters lurk beyond our immediate field of vision" (Leamer 1983: 39).

Given this apparently sharp dichotomy between experimental and observational data, what are we to make of the intermediate, or hybrid category, the

---

[2]Important problems of causal inference also arise in experiments. External validity is a recurring issue, and obstacles to internal validity can arise as well. Nonetheless, problems of causal inference are far more severe in observational studies.

"quasi-experiment," popularized by Campbell and Stanley (1966: 34–64)?[3] A quasi-experimental design is typically based on time-series data, involving a sequence of observations focused on the outcome being explained. At some point within this time series, an event, policy innovation, or other change occurs, and the analyst examines prior and subsequent values of the dependent variable in an effort to infer the impact of this event. This design is sometimes called an "interrupted time-series." A stunning exemplar is Campbell and Ross's (1968) study of the crackdown on speeding in the State of Connecticut. They explore the surprising difficulties of causal inference encountered in assessing the impact of this crackdown on death rates in automobile accidents. Many of the obstacles to good causal inference they consider are parallel to those confronted in experiments, which reinforces the idea that this design is in many ways like an experiment— hence, quasi-experimental.

Although the idea of quasi-experiments is strongly identified with Campbell, he subsequently had misgivings about this hybrid category. He recognized that the studies he had included in this category were actually observational studies, and that it had been misleading to suggest that there is an intermediate type between observational and experimental research. With characteristic humor and irony, Campbell suggests that:

> It may be that Campbell and Stanley (1966) should feel guilty for having contributed to giving quasi-experimental designs a good name. There are program evaluations in which the authors say proudly, "We used a *quasi*-experimental design." If responsible, Campbell and Stanley should do penance, because in most social settings, there are many equally or more plausible rival hypotheses. . . . (Campbell and Boruch 1975: 202)

The central legacy of Campbell's work on these issues, as both Brady (60 this volume) and Caporaso (1995: 459) emphasize, is Campbell's insightful inventory of threats to validity in observational studies (Campbell and Stanley 1966: 5–6; Cook and Campbell 1979: 51–55). This inventory points to the surprisingly large number of things that can go wrong in making causal inferences from what may initially appear to be relatively straightforward observational data.

These words of caution from both Leamer and Campbell are crucial in assessing *DSI*'s methodological framework. *DSI* provides recommendations for researchers engaged in observational studies, yet the book's discussion of causation

---

[3]A second legacy of Campbell's work has been the emergence, under the broad heading of quasi-experiments, of a renewed emphasis on "natural experiments," in which the mechanisms through which cases receive a value on the main explanatory variable are demonstrably unrelated to the error term. Hence, some of Campbell's threats to validity (see below) are at least partially averted. Unfortunately, it is often hard to find research contexts in which this criterion is met.

takes as a point of departure an experimental model. *DSI* employs the counterfactual definition of causation, grounded in the model of experiments introduced by Neyman (1990 [1923]), Rubin (1974, 1978), and Holland (1986). We think that this definition is indeed valuable in helping scholars to reason about causation as an abstract concept. However, Neyman, Rubin, and Holland intended their definition primarily for application to experimental research. They express skepticism about causal inference based on observational data (Rubin 1978; Holland 1986: 949), and their initial discussions of causation were only secondarily concerned with the challenges faced by researchers who use such data.[4] An account of causal inference in the social sciences must explicitly consider obstacles to causal inference in observational studies and address their practical implications for research. Yet Brady (59–61 this volume) is concerned that *DSI* does not adequately address these issues.

As Brady observes, *DSI* could have been more careful about distinguishing between the methodological strengths of experiments and those of quantitative observational studies. In fact, *DSI* sometimes seems to confound the tools relevant to experiments and those relevant to conventional quantitative research. For example, *DSI* is not clear enough in distinguishing between the independence assumption and conditional independence (Brady 60–61 this volume; see also the discussion later in this chapter), the former being relevant to experiments, and the latter applying primarily to observational studies.

Relatedly, *DSI* offers a somewhat confusing statement about the relationship between randomization and the quantitative/large-N versus qualitative/small-N distinction.[5] The book argues that:

> Randomness in selection of units and in assigning values to explanatory variables is a common procedure used by some quantitative researchers working with large numbers of observations to ensure that the conditional independence assumption is met. . . . Unfortunately, random selection and assignment have serious limitations in small-*n* research. (*DSI* 115; see also 94)

In this statement, *DSI* overstates the role of random assignment in conventional quantitative research and in effect lumps together random selection and random assignment, thereby merging the characteristic strengths of experimental de-

---

[4]Rubin (1980) developed the "stable-unit-treatment-value assumption" (SUTVA) as a formalization of one situation in which observational studies can be analyzed as if they were experiments. This initial move in the direction of discussing causal inference in observational studies is perhaps especially valuable as a statement of the difficulties involved in such inference.

[5]In this sentence, we refer to quantitative/large-N versus qualitative/small-N to accommodate the combined usage in the following quotation from *DSI*. For further discussion of these distinctions, see 245–49 in this chapter.

sign and of quantitative analysis. The book thus comes too close to making it appear as if the main divide is between these two approaches, on the one hand, and small-N, qualitative studies, on the other.

Caporaso's (1995: 459) commentary on *DSI*, by contrast, emphasizes the importance of sharply separating these two types of randomization: the random *assignment* carried out in most experiments, versus the random *sampling* that is often used in quantitative observational studies. Caporaso emphasizes that, while random assignment does indeed eliminate several challenges to causal inference, "[r]andom sampling does not solve the problems of drawing inferences when numerous causal factors are associated with outcomes" (1995: 459). Thus, large-N quantitative studies—which rarely employ random assignment—are still left with the basic inferential problem faced by small-N studies.

In sum, experimental and observational studies are profoundly different. The traditions of scholarship discussed in the present volume are based on observational data; quantitative and qualitative researchers therefore face the same fundamental problems of inference. *DSI*'s effort to address the major inferential challenges of small-N, qualitative research—based on the norms and practices of large-N, quantitative research—thus faces a major obstacle: Large-N, quantitative methods confront many of the same inferential challenges as qualitative observational studies. In important respects, quantitative researchers do not have strong tools for solving these dilemmas, as Bartels (71–74 this volume) emphasizes above.

Mainstream Quantitative Methods versus Statistical Theory

Given that our basic concern is with challenges to causal inference that arise in analyzing observational data, where can we turn for help in identifying and dealing with these inferential monsters discussed by Leamer? This question points to the need to distinguish two alternative views of how effective quantitative analysis can be in achieving valid inference: first, the perspective of mainstream quantitative methods in political science, which is at times insufficiently attentive to the difficulty of using quantitative tools; and second, perspectives drawn from statistical theory, which sometimes express serious warnings about these tools.

Mainstream quantitative methods are a subset of applied statistics. In the years before the publication of *DSI*, a central focus in political science methodology was the refinement and application of regression analysis and related econometric techniques. This body of work has been influential across several social science disciplines, and it is a major source of *DSI*'s methodological advice. When commentators argue that *DSI* adopts a quantitative perspective, they should be understood as referring to mainstream quantitative methods in this sense. Chapter 2 above (e.g., table 2.1) seeks to provide a summary of *DSI*'s quantitative tools.

The main point, for present purposes, is that mainstream quantitative methods and important currents of thinking in statistical theory have adopted quite different perspectives on the feasibility of effectively eliminating rival hypotheses in observational studies through regression-based tools. Within political science, mainstream quantitative methods have been associated with the advocacy of quantitative approaches—treating them as a set of research tools that provide superior leverage in both descriptive and causal inference. We view *DSI* as a clear expression of such advocacy, a form of advocacy that is also strongly reflected in the standards for "good research" applied by many political science departments and disciplinary journals.

By contrast, according to arguments that can be made from the standpoint of statistical theory, the superiority of quantitative methods is less clear. Such statistical arguments place far greater emphasis on the many assumptions and preconditions required to justify the use of specific quantitative tools, suggesting that these tools may often be inapplicable in observational research.[6] As emphasized above, more skeptical norms about inference are also fundamental to the work of Campbell.[7]

Statistical ideas quite distinct from those presented in *DSI* are also found in psychometrics and mathematical measurement theory (8, 204–9 this volume). These fields offer valuable insights into concepts, the foundations of measurement, the complex assumptions required in justifying higher levels of measurement, and the contextual specificity of measurement claims—insights that present a different picture than that offered by mainstream quantitative methodology.

Bayesian statistical analysis is likewise a relevant branch of statistical theory largely neglected by *DSI*,[8] as McKeown (158–62 this volume) emphasizes. Ideas drawn from Bayesian analysis, which have recently come to be more widely used in political science methodology, provide tools for estimating uncertainty that are relevant for several problems of research design that *DSI* discusses.

For example, *DSI* argues that qualitative researchers are often better off not working with random samples. Yet many of the book's statements in favor of estimating uncertainty would seem to rely on procedures for testing statistical significance originally designed for use with inferences from a random sample to a universe of cases. Unfortunately, extending significance tests to situations where

---

[6]Important examples include Liu (1960), Leamer (1983), Dijkstra (1988), Manski (1995), McKim and Turner (1997), and Berk (2003). See also Lucas (1976); Cox (1977); Copas and Li (1997); Lang, Rothman, and Cann (1998); and Scharfstein, Rotnitzky, and Robins (1999). Within political science, work that reflects this broader statistical perspective includes Achen (1986, 2000, 2002), Bartels (1991), and Wallerstein (2000). Within sociology, relevant examples are Lieberson (1985), Goldthorpe (2001), and Ní Bhrolcháin (2001).

[7]Campbell and Stanley (1966); Campbell and Ross (1968); Cook and Campbell (1979).

[8]The authors of *DSI* (102 n. 13) state that they adopt a "philosophical Bayesian" approach; yet Bayesian analysis plays no discernible role in the book's recommendations.

the data are not a random sample from a larger universe may not be justified. As Freedman, Pisani, and Purves (1998: 558) put it, "[i]f a test of significance is based on a sample of convenience, watch out." While significance tests can be an appropriate way to handle forms of randomness other than sampling error, Greene (2000: 147) argues that standard interpretations of statistical significance tests in such situations require that the test statistic be random. When the data are a random sample, this requirement is automatically satisfied; it may not be met under other circumstances. Overall, scholars should heed Freedman and Lane's (1983) warning against using conventional significance tests as a general tool for estimating uncertainty.

Bayesian statistics definitely cannot solve all the problems of making descriptive and causal inferences with a nonrandom sample. Yet these tools do provide a framework for evaluating uncertainty that may sometimes allow researchers to incorporate more kinds of uncertainty, and more detailed information about the sampling process, than do traditional significance tests. Thus, while *DSI*'s emphasis on estimating uncertainty is laudable, this goal might be better accomplished using insights based on a Bayesian perspective.

Another reason a Bayesian perspective may be relevant for thinking about small-N research is that it systematizes a research strategy noted briefly by *DSI* (211): overcoming the small-N problem by situating small-N findings within a larger research program. Bayesian ideas help in reasoning about the relation between the findings of prior research and the insights generated by any given small-N study. As we have argued above, Bayesian analysis also provides tools for evaluating arguments about necessary and sufficient causation (218 this volume), and thus specifically for improving the practice of qualitative research. In some of these situations, a full Bayesian framework, including formalization of prior beliefs about all parameters, may be quite useful. More generally, however, informal applications of the central Bayesian insight—that is, that inferences should be evaluated in light of the data *and* of prior knowledge—can provide a useful corrective to the sometimes inappropriate use of significance tests in causal inference.

Overall, from this wider perspective of statistical theory, the tools emphasized by *DSI* are properly seen as just one option—an option that perhaps needs to be approached with greater recognition of its limitations and of available alternatives. In order to further illustrate why such caution is needed, we now discuss two additional distinctions: between determinate and indeterminate research designs, and between data mining and specification searches.

Determinate versus Indeterminate Research Designs

In discussing the challenge of eliminating rival explanations, *DSI* distinguishes between "determinate" and "indeterminate" research designs.[9] The book designates as "determinate" those designs that meet the standards of: (a) having a sufficient N in relation to the number of explanatory parameters being estimated, and (b) avoiding the problem that two or more explanatory variables are perfectly correlated—that is, perfect multicollinearity (*DSI* 119, 150; see also 120).[10] Meeting these standards gives the researcher stronger tools for adjudicating among rival hypotheses. By contrast, designs that fail to meet these standards are called "indeterminate" (118–24, 145, 228). Such designs do not consider enough data[11] to distinguish the causal impact of alternative independent variables, which is one aspect of the problem of unidentifiability (*DSI* 118 n. 1).[12] As a consequence, the data under consideration are compatible with numerous interpretations. *DSI* goes so far as to state: "[a] determinate research design is the sine qua non of causal inference" (116).[13] By contrast, for research designs that are indeterminate, "virtually nothing can be learned about the causal hypotheses" (118).

---

[9] This distinction, of course, involves quite different issues from the contrast between deterministic and probabilistic causation discussed in chapter 12.

[10] *DSI* (122) uses the term "multicollinearity" in discussing this problem. The definition of multicollinearity that *DSI* offers is, however, stronger than most definitions of the term in statistics (see, e.g., Vogt 1999: 180). Therefore, we have used the term "perfect multicollinearity" in discussing this issue.

[11] Perfect multicollinearity is a problem of insufficient data, in the sense that the analyst lacks data that can distinguish between the effects of two (or more) explanatory variables. Adding such data by finding cases in which the explanatory variables are not perfectly correlated would, of course, eliminate the perfect multicollinearity.

[12] Unidentifiability also involves other important issues that *DSI* does not discuss. In structural equation modeling, problems of unidentifiability arise in several different situations. This problem arises if all the variables are endogenous because they appear as both independent and dependent variables within the same system of equations. In this case everything affects everything else, and there is no way of finding a "prime mover" to pin down causal relationships. It also arises if, for a particular endogenous variable of interest, there is no exogenous (i.e., truly independent) variable that affects only the endogenous variable directly (and there is no other identifying information). In this case the researcher has no way to isolate the endogenous variable's impact on the other endogenous variables. These aspects of unidentifiability are key challenges in using statistical tools to address endogeneity and selection bias (Achen 1986: 38–39; Greene 2000: 663–76).

[13] At a later point, *DSI* (150) does soften this statement by discussing ways in which a determinate research design can produce invalid inferences.

The distinction between a determinate and an indeterminate research design relies on the standard idea of the power of statistical tests. Discussions about the power of a test are useful for focusing on the degree to which the analysis is capable of rejecting the null hypothesis when that hypothesis is in fact false, under the assumption that the model is correct and only random error is at stake. This is a useful, but narrow, idea.

Correspondingly, we find the distinction between determinate and indeterminate research designs somewhat misleading. It is true that researchers must think carefully about the size of the N, given that it is the principal source of leverage in dealing with the issue of sampling error. Yet the size of the N is hardly the only source of inferential leverage, and sampling error is certainly not the only challenge to causal inference. Correspondingly, *DSI*'s distinction gives these specific concerns too much weight.

Further, it seems particularly inappropriate to argue that a determinate research design in this sense is the sine qua non of causal inference, whereas an indeterminate design contributes little. This claim can be seen as reifying the small-N problem, in the specific sense that it establishes a vivid dichotomy, in relation to which the small-N researcher is always on the wrong side.

The strong contrast that *DSI* draws between determinate and indeterminate research designs runs the risk of obscuring the broader, and much more important, contrast between experimental and observational studies discussed above. From this broader point of view, all inferences drawn from observational data share fundamental problems of alternative explanations and misspecified models. These problems pose a much greater challenge to the validity of causal inference than the problem of insufficient data—above all the small-N problem—emphasized by the idea of a determinate research design. In the realm of observational studies, the conclusions drawn from research are always partial, uncertain, and dependent on meeting underlying analytical assumptions, as *DSI* (passim) at various points acknowledges.

To put this another way, we find it problematic to suggest that any observational study can ever be "determinate," given this term's questionable implication that the "inferential monsters" to which Leamer refers can definitively be ruled out. We doubt they can. Further, if no observational research design is ever really determinate, then the concept of an indeterminate research design is also misleading when applied to observational studies. All such studies can be understood as involving indeterminate research designs. For this reason, we suggest avoiding the distinction between determinate and indeterminate research designs, while recognizing the issues raised as an unavoidable aspect of the larger problem of identifiability in research design.

In addition, we are concerned that *DSI*'s use of the label "determinate research design" focuses attention on issues of identifiability to an extent that implicitly advocates an inversion of what we see as the most productive relationship between theory and testing. Avoiding multicollinearity and large numbers of explanatory variables vis-à-vis the N are obviously important for regression analysis, and such issues should be a concern in small-N analysis as well. However, an excessive focus on these objectives may push analysts toward redesigning theory to be conveniently testable, instead of searching for more rigorous tests of the theories that scholars actually care about.

We would argue that, in situations where researchers are trying to test well-developed theories against clear alternative explanations, adopting an approach to testing that first requires modifications of the theories in question gives up a lot. In such circumstances, it is usually best to establish the testing requirements in light of the theory and the relevant alternative explanations: only in this way can we effectively adjudicate among these alternatives. If a hypothesis is difficult to test against the relevant alternative hypotheses with the existing data, then the best approach is to find new data and new approaches to testing, not to modify the hypotheses until it is easy to test them. Hence, to reiterate, the term "determinate" emphasizes the standards of identifiability and statistical power in a way that can distract analysts from testing the theories that often motivate research to begin with.

Rather than evaluating research designs as being determinate or indeterminate, it may be more productive to ask a broader question: are the findings and inferences yielded by a given research design *interpretable*,[14] in that they can plausibly be defended? The interpretability of findings and inferences can be increased by many factors, including a larger N, a particularly revealing comparative design, a rich knowledge of cases and context, well-executed conceptualization and measurement, or an insightful theoretical model. If the research question has been modified in order to make it more testable, then the findings may be less interpretable in relation to the original research question, and inferential leverage has probably been lost, not gained. This focus on interpretable findings broadens *DSI*'s idea of a determinate research design by recognizing multiple sources of inferential leverage.

Data Mining versus Specification Searches

Many researchers seek to evaluate competing explanations through intensive analysis of their data; however, this practice often raises the concern that researchers have engaged in "data mining" (*DSI* 174) or "data snooping" (Freedman, Pisani, and Purves 1998: 549) and have thereby exhausted the inferential leverage provided by the data. If researchers try out enough different combinations of explanatory variables, they will eventually find one that fits the data—even if the

---

[14]See, for example, Stone's (1985: 689) discussion of interpretability as a central characteristic of statistical models.

data are random.[15] Data mining is therefore seen as an undesirable research practice that weakens causal inference. Concerns about different forms of this problem recur in the guidelines, presented in chapter 2 above, that summarize *DSI*'s framework. Guideline no. 27 is concerned with the problem that researchers run "regressions or qualitative analyses with whatever explanatory variables [they] can think of" (*DSI* 174). no. 34, the injunction to test theory with data other than that used to generate the theory, and no. 35, the recommendation that theory should generally not be reformulated after analyzing the data, also address concerns related to data mining.

We find it striking that the related, partially inductive, econometric practice of "specification searches" is, by contrast, viewed favorably by methodologists as an unavoidable step in making causal inferences from observational data. The literature on specification searches has proposed systematic approaches to the iterated process of fitting what are inevitably incomplete models to data. The main ideas in this literature implicitly point to the dilemma that treating these inductive practices as a problem can be misleading, if not counterproductive, in establishing criteria for good research. Such a dilemma can be seen, first of all, in quantitative research that uses complex explanatory models. In the social sciences, such models are virtually never sufficiently detailed to tell us *exactly* what should be in the regression equation. Scholars who wish to test these models are forced to make decisions about the underspecified elements of the model and, in actual practice, they almost never stop after running the first regression that seems reasonable to them. It is the myth that these multiple tests do not occur that leads Leamer to worry about "the fumes which leak from our computer labs" (1983: 43). Rather than pretending that they do not occur, Freedman, Pisani, and Purves specifically urge analysts to report "how many tests they ran before statistically significant [results] turned up" (1998: 549).

Because we usually do not know the correct specification of a model, stopping with the first specification is methodologically problematic, just as it would be unjustified to stop with the specification that most favors the working hypothesis. The methodology of specification searches is concerned with systematic procedures for deciding where to start, when to stop, how to report the steps in between, and when we should believe the results of this overall process. Some scholars present elaborate justifications for beginning with the simplest plausible model and then engaging in "fragility testing" or "sensitivity analysis" by adding variables that may change the coefficients of interest (Leamer 1983: 40–42; 1994 [1986]; Levine and Renelt 1992). Other scholars work from the other side: they

---

[15]Thus, if a researcher who is running bivariate regressions successively regresses a purely random dependent variable on each of one hundred purely random independent variables, on average five of the resulting bivariate relationships will be statistically significant at the .05 level. This is true by the definition of significance tests.

begin with the most elaborate plausible model and eliminate elements of the model that prove to have little explanatory power (Hendry 1980; Hendry and Richard 1982; White 1994; see Granger 1990 for statements from both sides of this debate). These two approaches both use induction to test the plausibility of findings under divergent sets of methodological assumptions. The specification searches literature thus takes a position on induction that is radically different from the simple mandate not to reformulate theory after looking at the data.

The idea of specification searches is, of course, just one facet of a much larger concern with the inductive component of research. Both quantitative and qualitative researchers routinely adjust their theories in light of the data—often without taking the further step of moving to new data sets in order to test the modified theory. Whether this inductive component involves completely overturning previous models or refining them in the margins, such inductive practices are widely recognized as an essential part of research. For example, the chapters above by Ragin and Munck devote extensive attention to procedures for inductive analysis.

To conclude, data mining can certainly be a problem. Yet the misleading pretense that they are not routinely utilized, and even worse, the indiscriminate injunction against inductive procedures, is at least as big a problem in social research.

Conditional Independence or the Specification Assumption

Two alternative formulations of key assumptions underlying causal inference are the assumption of conditional independence and the specification assumption. The issue here is how to conceptualize and label the set of assumptions used to justify causal inference based on observational data. Rather than conceptualizing the most important of these several assumptions in terms of conditional independence—the concept employed by *DSI*—we find it productive to frame these issues in terms of the specification assumption. In discussing the choice between these alternative overarching concepts, it is essential to recognize that they are fundamentally similar. Given this similarity, this section conveys a suggestion, and simultaneously sounds a note of caution, about the focus and emphasis entailed in these alternative assumptions.

Our basic point in the discussion that follows is that, while the assumption of conditional independence is rooted in an analogy to experiments, the specification assumption more directly reflects the situation of a researcher seeking to analyze observational data. For this reason, we find the specification assumption to be more helpful—at the same time that we recognize the underlying similarities between the two assumptions.

As discussed in greater depth in chapter 2, the assumption of conditional independence builds on an analogy involving a counterfactual understanding of causation and treats every causal inference as a partial approximation of an ideal experiment. For the purpose of explicating the contrast with the specification assumption, in this section we briefly summarize conditional independence. We begin by discussing the basic thought experiment behind the idea of conditional independence, which serves as the foundation for introducing the assumption of "independence of assignment and (potential) outcomes." We use this assumption in defining *conditional* independence, and we then discuss why it is particularly relevant for observational studies. In comparison with the discussion in chapter 2, our goal here is particularly to discuss the range of issues that are highlighted by these conceptualizations, rather than to present the more general framework they represent.

The assumption of conditional independence posits that each case can be understood as having a value (which may or may not actually be observed—hence, this is in effect a hypothetical variable) on an outcome variable, Y_t, that reflects the outcome that case would experience if given an experimental *treatment*; and likewise a value (which, again, may or may not be observed) on a second variable, Y_c, that reflects the outcome the case would experience if it were the *control* in an experiment. The causal effect of the treatment relative to the control for this case is the (hypothetical) difference between its values on these two variables.

In the real world, even in randomized experiments, the value of only one of these variables can actually be observed for each case at any point in time. Through some process (i.e., through randomization in experiments, or, in an observational study, through a real-world process that may or may not be known to the researcher), any given case is, in effect, assigned either the treatment, or the control. A given case cannot simultaneously be assigned to both. For example, an individual can either be exposed to a political message, or not be exposed to it; or a democratic country can either use proportional representation to elect its officials, or use some other electoral method.

Because we cannot empirically observe what would have happened to the same individual or country at any one point in time both with and without the treatment, causal inference routinely relies on real-world comparisons of cases that receive the treatment with other cases that do not receive the treatment. The comparison of these observed treated cases with the observed control cases substitutes for the hypothetical comparison of each case with and without the treatment. Comparing two real-world groups of cases that do and do not receive the treatment yields a good causal inference, provided that these two groups are similar in the sense that both have the same mean values of the (hypothetical) variable Y_t, and also the same mean values of the (hypothetical) variable Y_c. With a large enough sample, randomization of assignment, as in a well-designed experiment, ensures that this condition will be met.

With observational data, however, this standard, which is called *independence* of assignment and outcome,[16] is usually not met. Furthermore, there is no way to test whether independence is satisfied—because only Y_t or Y_c, but not both, is observed for each case. Although we can calculate the mean value of Y_t for the cases that are actually assigned to the treatment, we cannot do so for the cases assigned to the control. Similarly, although we can calculate the mean value of Y_c for the cases assigned to the control, we cannot do so for the cases that are assigned to the treatment. Consequently, we cannot know if the treatment cases would have had the same average on Y_c (if they had been assigned to the control) as the cases that were actually assigned to the control. Further, we cannot establish whether the control cases would have had the same average on Y_t (if they had been assigned to the treatment) as the cases that were actually assigned to the treatment. In short, no test will allow us to establish whether the standard of independence holds for a given set of cases.

The assumption of conditional independence becomes relevant if this criterion of independence is not met. Conditional independence means that there is another variable or set of variables, which serve as "statistical controls," such that by controlling for—or *conditioning* on—these variables, the treatment group and the control group come to have the same mean values on both Y_t and Y_c. If the researcher uses quantitative techniques that control for these variables, such as stratification,[17] conditional independence is thereby satisfied and an important criterion for good causal inference has been met. In effect, by introducing statistical controls into the analysis and then assuming conditional independence, the researcher turns the observational study into something akin to an experiment. However, it is obviously vital to remember that the assumption of conditional independence, like the assumption of independence, is hard to test.

Unlike conditional independence, which is rarely mentioned in econometrics textbooks, the specification assumption is frequently discussed in econometric and statistical work on regression analysis.[18] The specification assumption has the ma-

---

[16]More precisely, as noted in chapter 2, this standard in fact involves mean independence of assignment and outcome, and the standard of conditional independence of concern here is mean conditional independence of assignment and outcome.

[17]Regression analysis employs assumptions that some readers may view as similar to the assumption of conditional independence, in that these assumptions stress the importance of control variables in causal inference. At a general level, this understanding is probably adequate; however, it is important to remember that analytic techniques (e.g., stratification versus regression) differ, sometimes substantially, in the details of the assumptions they depend on.

[18]See, e.g., Greene (2000: 219–20); Kennedy (1998: chaps. 3 and 5); Mirer (1995); Darnell (1994: 369–73); Gujarati (1988: 57–60, 166, 178–82); and Wonnacott and Wonnacott (1979: 413–19). Treatments by political scientists include Achen (1982: chap. 5; 1986: 12, 27); and Hanushek and Jackson (1977: 79–86). For a highly accessible state-

jor advantage that it starts with what is typically the actual situation of the researcher—that is, having an explanatory model of unknown usefulness—and then specifies the criteria that must be met to move in the direction of causal inference. The name of this assumption refers directly to this process of specification.

Thus, the starting point for the specification assumption is not the metaphor of an experiment, but rather the model that researchers use to organize their hypotheses. In the simplest case, this model consists of a dependent variable and a set of independent variables in a single regression equation. More generally, it may explicitly include an equation for the process of assignment to treatment, as well as for the outcome variable. The specification assumption focuses attention on what must be true—concerning the relationships between the included explanatory variables and the unobserved error terms in the model—in order to make unbiased inferences about the strength of the associations predicted by these relationships.

In the context of a regression model, the specification assumption is the claim that the included independent variables are statistically unrelated to the error term that derives from a (hypothetical) comparison between the regression model and the true causal equation.[19] One major threat to the specification assumption is omitting variables that ought to be included—and therefore relegating the effects of those variables to the error term, sometimes producing missing variable bias (the central, direct concern of conditional independence). A second major threat is including variables that are endogenous, that is, are statistically related to the part of the dependent variable that is not caused by the included variables. Including

---

ment, see Vogt (1999: 271–72). Stone (1993) discusses the relationships among the specification assumption (which he calls "no confounding"), conditional independence, and mean conditional independence (which he calls "no mean effect").

[19]The specification assumption as defined here is sometimes confused with the much weaker assumption that the expectation of the residuals in a regression analysis is zero, conditional on the included variables. This second assumption, which is *not* the specification assumption, focuses on whether the included right-hand side variables successfully capture all predictive information that these variables provide about the dependent variable. For example, the heights of sisters can provide an excellent prediction of their brothers' heights even though the correlation is causally spurious. Because no causal connection is implied by this assumption, researchers can always meet this standard without introducing additional right-hand side variables (although they may have to add nonlinear transformations of the included variables).

By contrast, the specification assumption means that there is no statistical relationship between the included independent variables and any excluded variables that causally affect the dependent variables. Often, meeting this assumption would require analysts to include more independent variables. Thus, in a regression equation that predicts brothers' heights from sisters' heights, the specification assumption fails because there is a correlation between the sisters' heights—the included independent variable—and the parents' heights, excluded variables that causally affect brothers' heights. Only by including these missing variables can the researcher meet the specification assumption.

such variables that have a direct connection with the error term yields endogeneity bias. When a model has either of these problems, the estimated causal effects of the included variables will be biased because the included variables will stand in for (or proxy for) either missing variables or the error term.

A further benefit of discussing these issues in terms of the specification assumption—in addition, as noted above, to focusing attention more directly on the actual situation of the researcher—is that this term is directly linked to other standard methodological labels: model specification, specification error, specification analysis, the specification problem, misspecification, and specification searches.

While we believe that the framework of the specification assumption brings basic issues of causal inference into sharper focus, it also has a major limitation—which it shares with the assumption of conditional independence. Both assumptions are hard to test, and no analyst can ever prove that an observational study meets either assumption. Leamer's inferential monsters may always be lurking beyond the researcher's immediate field of vision. This is one of the reasons why, in order to supplement correlation-based causal inference, scholars turn to alternative sources of inferential leverage such as experiments or causal-process observations.

To reiterate the point made at the start of this section, our argument here is neither that the assumption of conditional independence is misleading in any fundamental sense, nor that meeting the specification assumption solves all problems of causal inference. Rather, we believe that the analogy behind conditional independence may focus too much attention on control variables as a solution to problems of causal inference based on observational data. By contrast, the specification assumption focuses more directly on problems of endogeneity and misspecified relationships *among* measured variables, as well as other inadequacies of our causal models.

Taken together, our observations about these five distinctions considered in this section help to spell out the perspective on causal inference that we have adopted, which clearly differs from that of *DSI*. We now turn to some additional distinctions that help to develop further our overall argument about sources of leverage in causal inference: qualitative versus quantitative research, cases versus observations, and data-set observations versus causal-process observations.

Four Approaches to the Qualitative versus Quantitative Distinction

Debates about sources of leverage for eliminating rival explanations in causal inference—and obviously also about tools for descriptive inference—are routinely framed in terms of the relative strengths and weaknesses of qualitative and quantitative research. Yet this distinction needs to be disaggregated if it is to play a useful role in thinking about research design. In conjunction with this distinction, we do not find two neatly bounded categories, but rather four over-lapping categories (see table 13.1). However, notwithstanding this complexity, it is still useful for many purposes to use the dichotomous labels of qualitative versus quantitative.

Level of Measurement

One distinction concerns the level of measurement. Here we find ambiguity regarding the cut-point between qualitative and quantitative, and also contrasting views of the leverage achieved by different levels of measurement. Some scholars label data as qualitative if it is organized at a nominal level of measurement and as quantitative if it is organized at an ordinal, interval, ratio, or other "higher" level of measurement (Vogt 1999: 230). Alternatively, scholars sometimes place the qualitative-quantitative threshold between ordinal and interval data (Porkess 1991: 179). This latter cut-point is certainly congruent with the intuition of many qualitative researchers that ordinal reasoning is central to their enterprise (Mahoney 1999: 1160–64). With either cut-point, however, quantitative research is routinely associated with higher levels of measurement.

Higher levels of measurement are frequently viewed as yielding more analytic leverage, because they provide more fine-grained descriptive differentiation among cases. However, higher levels of measurement depend on complex assumptions about logical relationships—for example, about order, units of measurement, and zero points—that are sometimes hard to meet. If these assumptions are not met, such fine-grained differentiation can be illusory, and qualitative categorization based on close knowledge of cases and context may in fact provide more leverage. In any case, careful categorization is a valuable, indeed essential, analytic tool.

Size of the N

A second approach is to identify the qualitative-quantitative distinction with the contrast between small-N and large-N research. Here we will treat the question of the "N" as a relatively straightforward matter involving the number of observations on the main dependent variable that the researcher seeks to explain, understood at the level of analysis that is the principal focus of the research.[20] In a sub-

---

[20]Obviously, the unit of analysis, as well as the number of cases being studied, may change in the course of research.

Table 13.1. **Four Approaches to the Qualitative-Quantitative Distinction**

Approach	Defining Distinction	Comment
1. Level of Measurement	Cut-point for qualitative vs. quantitative is nominal vs. ordinal scales and above; alternatively, nominal and ordinal scales vs. interval scales and above.	Lower levels of measurement require fewer assumptions about underlying logical relationships; higher levels yield sharper differentiation among cases, provided these assumptions are met.
2. Size of the N	Cut-point between small N vs. large N might be somewhere between 10 and 20.	A small N and a large N are commonly associated with contrasting sources of analytic leverage, which correspond to the third and fourth criteria below.
3. Statistical Tests	In contrast to much qualitative research, quantitative analysis employs formal statistical tests.	Statistical tests provide explicit, carefully formulated criteria for descriptive and causal inference; a characteristic strength of quantitative research. Yet this again raises question of meeting relevant assumptions.
4. Thick vs. Thin Analysis[a]	Central reliance on detailed knowledge of cases vs. more limited knowledge of cases.	Detailed knowledge associated with thick analysis is likewise a major source of leverage for inference; a characteristic strength of qualitative research.

[a]This distinction draws on Coppedge's (1999) discussion of thick versus thin concepts. See also note 22 in the text below.

sequent section, we will explore the complex issues that can arise in establishing the N.

The N involved in a paired comparison of Japan and Sweden, or in an analysis of six military coups, would routinely be identified with the qualitative tradition. By contrast, an N involving hundreds or thousands of observations would routinely be identified with the quantitative tradition. Although there is no well-established cut-point between qualitative and quantitative in terms of the N, such a cut-point might be located somewhere between ten and twenty.

However, some studies definitely break the methodological stereotypes: that is, those with a larger N that in other respects adopt a qualitative approach; as well as those with a relatively small N that in other respects adopt a quantitative approach. Examples of qualitative studies which have a relatively large N include Rueschemeyer, Stephens, and Stephens's (1992) *Capitalist Development and Democracy* (N=36), Tilly's (1993) *European Revolutions, 1492–1992* (hundreds of cases), and R. Collier's (1999) *Paths toward Democracy* (N=27). Wickham-Crowley's (1992) *Guerillas and Revolution in Latin America* focuses on twenty-six cases: he carries out a qualitative/narrative analysis, based on detailed discussion of thirteen cases, and he analyzes thirteen additional cases using dichotomous/categorical variables and Boolean methods.

Some studies that rely heavily on statistical tests in fact have a smaller N than these qualitative studies. Examples are found in the literature on advanced industrial countries: a study with an N of eleven focused on the impact of partisan control of government on labor conflict (Hibbs 1987); and studies with an N of fifteen focused on the influence of corporatism and partisan control on economic growth (Lange and Garrett 1985, 1987; Jackman 1987, 1989; Hicks 1988; and Hicks and Patterson 1989; Garrett 1998). Likewise, quantitative research that seeks to forecast U.S. presidential and congressional elections routinely employs an N of eleven to thirteen (e.g., Lewis-Beck and Rice 1992; J. Campbell 2000; Bartels and Zaller 2001). Choices about the N are thus at least partially independent from choices about other aspects of a qualitative or quantitative approach.

Scholars decide on the N according to many different criteria, including the availability of analytically relevant data and a concern with the alternative sources of inferential leverage associated with a small N and a large N. The third and fourth criteria for qualitative versus quantitative, presented below, address these alternative sources of leverage.

Statistical Tests

The third approach focuses on the use of statistical tests.[21] An analysis is routinely considered quantitative if it employs statistical tests in reaching its descriptive and explanatory conclusions. By contrast, qualitative research typically does not employ such tests. While the use of statistical tests is generally identified with higher levels of measurement, the two are not inextricably linked. Quantitative researchers frequently apply statistical tests to nominal variables. Conversely, qualitative researchers often analyze data at higher levels of measurement without utilizing statistical tests. For example, in the area studies tradition, a qualitative country study may make extensive reference to ratio-level economic data.

Statistical tests are a powerful analytic tool for evaluating the strength of relationships and important aspects of the uncertainty of findings in a way that is more difficult in qualitative research. Yet, as with higher levels of measurement, statistical tests are only meaningful if complex underlying assumptions are met. If the assumptions are not met, alternative sources of analytic leverage employed by qualitative researchers may in fact be more powerful.

Thick versus Thin Analysis

Finally, we distinguish between "thick" and "thin" analysis.[22] Qualitative research routinely utilizes *thick analysis*, in the sense that analysts place great reliance on a detailed knowledge of cases. Indeed, some scholars consider thick analysis the single most important tool of the qualitative tradition. One type of thick analysis is what Geertz (1973) calls "thick description," that is, interpretive work that focuses on the meaning of human behavior to the actors involved. In addition to thick description, many forms of detailed knowledge, if utilized effectively, can greatly strengthen description and causal assessment.[23] By contrast,

---

[21]We intend the present usage of "statistical tests" somewhat broadly, including techniques of parameter estimation as well as tools of statistical inference.

[22]This distinction draws on Coppedge's (1999) discussion of thick versus thin concepts. Neither our distinction nor that of Coppedge should be confused with Geertz's (1973) distinction between "thick description," which focuses on the meaning of human behavior to the actors involved, as opposed to "thin description," which is not concerned with this meaning. With the expression "thick analysis," we mean research that focuses closely on the details of cases. These details may or may not encompass subjective meaning. In this sense, Geertz's thick description, and also constructionism, is a specific type of what we call thick analysis.

[23]This should not be taken to imply that researchers pursuing the goal of thick description must always use tools of thick analysis. For example, survey researchers may seek to gain insights into the subjective meaning of respondents' behavior, at the same

quantitative researchers routinely rely on *thin analysis*, in that their knowledge of each case is typically far less complete. However, to the extent that this thin analysis permits them to focus on a much larger N, they may benefit from a broader comparative perspective, as well as from the possibility of using statistical tests. Whereas the precision and specificity of statistical tests are a distinctive strength of quantitative research, the leverage gained from thick analysis is a characteristic strength of qualitative research.

The distinction between thick and thin analysis is closely related to Ragin's (1987) discussion of case-oriented versus variable-oriented research. Of course, qualitative researchers do think in terms of variables, and quantitative researchers do deal with cases. The point is simply that qualitative researchers are more often immersed in the details of cases, and they build their concepts, their variables, and their causal understanding in part on the basis of this detailed knowledge. Such researchers seek, through their in-depth knowledge of cases, to carefully rule out alternative explanations until they come to one that stands up to scrutiny. Detailed knowledge of cases does sometimes play a role in quantitative research. Indeed, some quantitative research employs thick analysis. However, in-depth knowledge is far more common in qualitative research and much less common among quantitative researchers, who tend to rely on statistical tests.

Drawing Together the Four Criteria

As this section illustrates, there is no single, sharp distinction that consistently differentiates qualitative and quantitative research—and that unambiguously sorts out the most important sources of inferential leverage. We would certainly classify as qualitative a study that places central reliance on nominal categories, focuses on relatively few cases, makes little or no use of statistical tests, and places substantial reliance on thick analysis. By contrast, a study based primarily on interval- or ratio-level measures, a large N, statistical tests, and a predominant use of thin analysis is certainly quantitative. Both types of study are common, which is why it makes sense, for many purposes, to maintain the overall qualitative-quantitative distinction.

However, an adequate discussion of inferential leverage requires careful consideration not only of these polar types, but also of the intermediate alternatives. For example, a particularly strong form of inferential leverage may be gained by combining statistical tests with thick analysis, bringing together their complementary logics in what may be called "nested inference."[24] This relationship between

---

time that they may have a selective and in some ways superficial overall level of knowledge about each respondent.

[24]This term is adapted from Coppedge's (2001) "nested induction" and from Lieberman's (2003a) "nested analysis."

qualitative and quantitative methods is very different from that proposed by *DSI*, because with nested inference the characteristic strengths of each approach supplement and enhance research based on the other approach.

Cases versus Observations

Well-understood definitions of "case" and "observation" are essential in discussing sources of inferential leverage in qualitative and quantitative research, yet finding adequate definitions of these terms is a serious challenge. Indeed, the question "what is a case?" is the title of an entire book (Ragin and Becker 1992).

Cases

We understand a case as one instance of the unit of analysis employed in a given study. Cases correspond to the political, social, institutional, or individual entities or processes about which information is collected. For example, the cases in a given study may be particular nation-states, social movements, political parties, trade union members, or episodes of policy implementation. The number of cases is conventionally called the "N."

It is productive to think about cases in relation to a "rectangular data set"— that is, a matrix or uniform array of data in which the rows correspond to cases and the columns correspond to variables. The pieces of data aligned in a single row in the data set pertain to a particular case, and the number of rows corresponds to the number of cases (the N). The pieces of data aligned in a single column in the data set pertain to a particular variable, and the number of columns corresponds to the number of variables. The information in a rectangular data set may be either quantitative or qualitative—that is, it may consist of scores on variables at any level of measurement.

Observations

We now present a definition of the term observation that serves to underscore the importance of this second, horizontal slice. "Observation," of course, has a commonsense meaning: it is an insight or piece of information recorded by the researcher about a specific feature of the phenomenon or process being studied. This usage is widespread, and it is found, for example, in *DSI* (57). In the language of variables, an observation in this sense is a single piece of data that constitutes the value of a variable for a given case. The commonsense meaning also includes other kinds of information that might not conventionally be thought of as a score on a variable—for example, information about context that makes the phenomenon under study intelligible and that helps the researcher avoid basic mistakes in interpreting it.

A fundamentally different meaning of observation, which is standard in quantitative analysis, refers to a row in a rectangular data set. According to this meaning, an observation is the collection of scores for a given case, on the dependent variable *and* all the independent variables (*DSI* 117; also 53, 209). In other words, an observation is "all the numbers for one case," that is, all the scores within any given row of the data set. In relation to this definition of observation, a "case," which also corresponds to a row in the data set, should be understood as the larger setting from which the numbers in each row are drawn.[25]

The second definition may initially seem counterintuitive for scholars not oriented toward thinking about rectangular data sets and matrix algebra. Whereas the commonsense meaning of observation refers only to one score, this second meaning involves two or more scores. A useful way of clarifying this second usage is to think about it as a "data point," which in a two-dimensional scatterplot corresponds to the scores of the independent and dependent variables. The data point is an observation whose meaning depends on simultaneously considering the scores for both variables.[26] The cluster of information contained in a data point plays a central role in causal inference by focusing our attention simultaneously on the scores for the independent and dependent variables. This same idea can be extended to the analysis of more than two variables (as in scatterplots with three or more dimensions), and the purpose of this second definition of observation is to highlight that central inferential role. As with the rectangular data set, the data entailed in an observation of this type may be either quantitative or qualitative.

This second meaning of observation serves a useful methodological purpose. For example, it can clarify the meaning of the well-known "many-variables, small-N problem" (Lijphart 1971: 685–91). In debates on methodology, increasing the number of observations is routinely understood as a basic solution to this problem. Obviously, the content of this recommendation depends on our definition of an observation. For instance, if we score the cases on an additional variable, we add observations in the sense of the ordinary language usage noted above—that is, we introduce one new piece of data for each case. However, adding a variable generally makes the many-variables, small-N problem worse, because it reduces the degrees of freedom. In this sense, increasing the number of observations does not help the problem concerning the degrees of freedom.

---

[25]*DSI* (52–53, 117–18, 217–18) makes a parallel distinction between case and observation. While the book mainly uses observation in the sense of data-set observation, see also *DSI* (57), which refers to observation as a score.

[26]The term "data point" is also sometimes used informally to mean the score for a given variable on a given case (Vogt 1999: 71). However, for any scholar who has worked with scatterplots, the meaning given in the text above more directly conveys the intuitive idea of a data point in a scatterplot.

By contrast, using the second definition of observation, it makes sense to say that increasing the number of observations addresses the many-variables, small-N problem. Adding observations—in the sense of adding "all the numbers" for one or more new cases—increases the number of rows in the matrix.

This usage thus clarifies a basic piece of methodological advice. At various points in the present volume, we argue that "increasing the number of observations," as *DSI* frequently recommends, may not always be a good idea. However, taking one position or the other on this issue makes little sense as long as there is ambiguity about whether one is referring to adding "pieces of data" or adding cases to the analysis.

Given that it is confusing when the same term carries two meanings, we adopt the following usage. When we mean observation in the first, commonsense usage discussed above, we refer to a score, or to a piece of data or information. To highlight the second meaning of observation, we propose the expression "data-set observation."

Data-Set Observations versus Causal-Process Observations

We thus introduce the label "data-set observation" to refer to observation in the sense of a row in a rectangular data set. At the same time, we do not want to lose sight of the critical role played in causal inference by information that is not part of a row in a data set. We therefore introduce the expression "causal-process observation" to emphasize the role such pieces of information play in causal inference (table 13.2). Whereas data-set observations lend themselves to statistical tests within the framework of what we have called "thin analysis," causal-process observations offer an alternative source of inferential leverage through "thick analysis," as discussed above.

A causal-process observation is an insight or piece of data that provides information about context or mechanism and contributes a different kind of leverage in causal inference. It does not necessarily do so as part of a larger, systematized array of observations. Thus, a causal-process observation might be generated in isolation or in conjunction with many other causal-process observations—or it might also be taken out of a larger data set. In the latter case, it yields inferential leverage on its own.[27] In doing so, a causal-process observation may be like a "smoking gun." It gives insight into causal mechanisms, insight that is essential to

---

[27]Knowledge about the place of a causal-process observation within a larger data set can certainly influence how a scholar interprets this observation. Yet that is a different matter from relying on covariation within the data set to make causal inferences. And of course, causal-process observations are routinely studied in conjunction with an analysis of data-set observations based on such covariation.

Table 13.2. Data-Set Observation versus Causal-Process Observation

	Data-Set Observation	Causal-Process Observation
Corresponding Root Meaning of "Observation"	Standard quantitative/statistical meaning. Thus, all the scores for a given case; a row in a rectangular data set.	Ordinary language meaning. Thus, a piece of data or information; a datum.
Contribution to Causal Inference	The foundation for correlation-based causal inference. Provides the basis for tests of overall relationships among variables.	The foundation for process-oriented causal inference. Provides information about mechanism and context.

causal assessment and is an indispensable alternative and/or supplement to correlation-based causal inference.

Part of the contrast between data-set observations and causal-process observations is that these two expressions utilize different root meanings of the term "observation" (table 13.2). Because the idea of "observation" is so closely tied in the minds of many quantitatively oriented scholars to data in a rectangular matrix, we might have chosen the expression "causal-process *information*." However, we deliberately introduce the expression "causal-process *observation*" to emphasize that this kind of evidence merits the same level of analytic and methodological attention as do "data-set *observations*."

While we can distinguish these two types of observations, we also find connections between them. For example, a scholar who has discovered a fruitful causal-process observation in one case—involving, for example, a causal mechanism that links two variables—might then proceed to systematically score many cases on this same analytic feature and add the new scores to an existing collection of data-set observations. Thus, the discovery of a causal-process observation can motivate the systematic collection of new data. Alternatively, a researcher who has done an analysis based on data-set observations may turn to causal-process observations to provide evidence about causal mechanisms. Thus, inference may be strengthened by movement in either direction.

The idea of causal-process observations is intended to make explicit the source of leverage in causal inference that lies at the heart of a long tradition of within-case analysis in qualitative research, a tradition discussed above in the chapters by Rogowski; Collier, Mahoney, and Seawright; Munck; McKeown; and Tarrow. As discussed in chapter 6 (93 this volume), this tradition dates back at least to the 1940s and has, over the years, employed a number of different labels in the effort to pinpoint the distinctive analytic leverage offered by this approach. Recent writing on "mechanisms" is a valuable extension of this tradition.[28]

Although the role of causal-process observations in qualitative research may be fairly obvious, their contribution to quantitative work should be underscored. Goldthorpe (2001), developing a line of argument that explicitly builds on the work of statisticians,[29] pinpoints this contribution in his important article "Causation, Statistics, and Sociology." He uses the label "generative process" in referring to the linkage mechanisms that play an essential role in giving causal interpretations to quantitative associations. Goldthorpe contrasts this focus on generative processes with attempts to demonstrate causation through experiments or regression models.

> This idea of causation [that] has been advanced by statisticians does not ... reflect specifically [quantitative] thinking. It would appear to derive, rather, from an attempt to specify what must be *added* to any [quantitative] criteria before an argument about causation can convincingly be made. (Goldthorpe 2001: 8)[30]

This procedure assumes that in quantitative analysis, an association

> is created by some "mechanism" operating "at a more microscopic level" than that at which the association is established. In other words, these authors would alike insist ... on tying the concept of causation to some process existing in time and space, even if not perhaps directly observable, that actually generates the causal effect of X on Y and, in so doing, produces the [quantitative] relationship that is empirically in evidence.... [This mechanism can] illuminate the "black boxes" left by purely [quantitative] analysis. ... (Goldthorpe 2001: 9)[31]

---

[28]Among many authors, see Elster 1999: chap. 1; McAdam, Tarrow, and Tilly 2001: chaps. 1–3; Tilly 2001.

[29]Goldthorpe (2001: 8–9) cites various authors who have embraced this perspective, including Hill (1991 [1937]); Simon and Iwasaki (1988); Freedman (1991, 1992a, b); Cox (1992); and Cox and Wermuth (1996). See also Rosenbaum (1984).

[30]In this and the following block quotation, the word "statistical" has been replaced (in brackets) by the word "quantitative." The goal is to make clear the extent to which Goldthorpe's argument converges with the argument of the present volume. Specifically, Goldthorpe is using ideas from statistical theory to argue that findings from the branch of applied statistics that we are calling mainstream quantitative methods analysis must be supplemented by qualitative insights.

[31]Goldthorpe goes on to point out that these efforts to establish causation "can never be taken as definitive" and must always be open to further empirical testing. "[F]iner-grained accounts, at some yet deeper level, will in principle always be possible" (2001: 9). Note that the quotation in the text above is in part Goldthorpe's summary of argu-

We see a sharp contrast between (a) Goldthorpe's assertion that inference based on causal-process observations does *not* involve the approach of what we are calling mainstream quantitative methods; and (b) *DSI*'s approach, which explicitly seeks to subordinate this form of causal inference to its quantitative framework. The authors of *DSI* argue, in discussing the inferences drawn from "process tracing" (226), "historical analysis," and "detailed case studies" (86), that these inferences must be treated through the framework for inference discussed throughout their book (85–87; see also 226–28). King, Keohane, and Verba reemphasize this point in chapter 11 above (181, 191–92 this volume). Yet *DSI*'s framework is designed for analyzing data-set observations and not causal-process observations, and the book's recommendations therefore effectively treat causal-process observations as if they were data-set observations.

Our point, by contrast, is that causal-process observations offer a *different* approach to inference. Causal-process observations are valuable, in part, because they can fill gaps in conventional quantitative research. They are also valuable because they are an essential foundation for qualitative research. One goal of the present discussion is to strengthen the methodological justification for that foundation. Because inferences based on data-set and causal-process observations are fundamentally different, one promising direction of research is to combine the strengths of both types of observation within a given study. In the present volume, Tarrow presents an invaluable inventory of practical suggestions for how this may be accomplished.[32] We would call attention to two of Tarrow's techniques, which he labels "sequencing qualitative and quantitative research" and "triangulation."[33] These utilize the distinctive strengths of alternative tools for data collection and inference. Tarrow (177 this volume) cites research on Poland's Solidarity Movement as an example of the kind of fruitful exchange that may take place between analysts using data-set observations and others relying on causal-process observations. Tarrow also points to the complementarities that result when elements of both approaches are combined in a given study.

In sum, both data-set observations and causal-process observations can play a role in both qualitative and quantitative research. The rich causal insights that qualitative researchers may gain from thick analysis can often be supplemented by systematic cross-case comparison using data-set observations, statistical tests, and thin analysis. Similarly, the correlation-based inferences that quantitative researchers derive from data-set observations can often be enhanced by causal-process observations.

---

ments made by these statisticians, but Goldthorpe clearly intends this as a statement of his own position.

[32]See also Bennett and George (1997a); Wallerstein (2001); and *APSA-CP* (2003).

[33]King, Keohane, and Verba (191–92 this volume) conclude their chapter by endorsing a related concept of triangulation.

Examples of Causal-Process Observations

Three brief, schematic illustrations of causal-process observations will help to clarify their contribution to causal inference. Because we seek to underscore the contrast with data-set observations, we present examples of studies in which both data-set and causal-process observations are employed.[34]

The first example focuses on the use of causal-process observations to discredit the findings of a time-series cross-sectional regression analysis, based on data-set observations. In an article that became an important part of the political debate after the 2000 U.S. presidential election, John R. Lott (2000) used regression to conclude that at least 10,000 votes for Bush were lost in the Florida panhandle because the media declared Gore the winner in Florida shortly before the polls had closed in this region, which, unlike the rest of the state, is on Central Standard Time. Brady (see appendix below) employs causal-process observations, focused on the actual events of election day, to demonstrate that this inference is implausible. Brady shows that the maximum number of votes that Bush could have lost was 224, and that the actual loss was probably just a few dozen votes. Brady's causal-process observations draw on diverse sources of data to establish several pertinent facts: the number of last-minute voters, the proportion of this group of voters exposed to the media, the further proportion who would specifically have heard media predictions of the outcome, and the likely impact of this prediction on their vote. Although he could have addressed this question through a broader analysis based on data-set observations, Brady is convinced that he got better answers using causal-process observations focused sharply on what actually happened that day in the Florida panhandle.

Another example is Susan Stokes's (2001) analysis of the dramatic economic policy shifts toward neoliberalism initiated by several Latin American presidents between 1982 and 1995. These presidents had campaigned strongly against neoliberalism. Yet, shortly after being elected, they abruptly embraced neoliberalism. Stokes's question is whether the presidents opted for neoliberalism on the basis of (a) considered views about the consequences for the economy and the functioning of the state in their countries if they failed to implement neoliberal reform, or (b) a narrower rent-seeking calculation regarding short-term economic or social payoffs from powerful market actors. Stokes systematically compares thirty-eight Latin-American presidents, some of whom switched and some of whom did not. She scores them on a series of explanatory variables, as well as on the outcome variable, that is, the adoption of neoliberal policies, thus using data-set observations. This approach, employing both a probit model (93–101) and more informal com-

---

[34]For other examples in which the contributions of these two kinds of observations are juxtaposed, see Tarrow's chapter above (especially 175–79 this volume). Of course, many case-study researchers carry out extended analyses based on causal-process observations without relying in any substantial way on data-set observations.

parative analysis, yields evidence favoring the first explanation, that is, that the choice was based on the conviction that neoliberalism would solve a series of fundamental national problems.

Stokes supplements this large-N analysis by examining a series of causal-process observations concerning three of the presidents, who abruptly switched from populist campaign rhetoric to neoliberal policies after winning the election. In this small-N analysis, her inferential leverage derives from the direct observation of causal links. In one of these analyses, Stokes offers an intriguing step-by-step account of how Peruvian President Fujimori decided to abandon the more populist rhetoric of his campaign and adopt a package of neoliberal reforms (2001: 69–73). Stokes shows that, just after Fujimori's electoral victory, a sequence of encounters with major international and domestic leaders exposed him to certain macroeconomic arguments, and these arguments convinced him that Peru's economy was headed for disaster if neoliberal reforms were not adopted. Causal-process observations thus provide valuable evidence for the argument that Fujimori's decision was driven by this conviction, rather than by the rent-seeking concerns identified in the rival hypothesis.

A final example of the distinctive contribution of causal-process observations comes from Nina Tannenwald's (1999) analysis of the role played by normative concerns in U.S. decisions about the use of nuclear weapons. Tannenwald hypothesizes that decisions about nuclear weapons have been guided by a "nuclear taboo," that is, a normative stigma against nuclear weapon use, which she hypothesizes to have to been a powerful influence on U.S. decision making during the decades since the invention of nuclear weapons. She frames her discussion around the important competing hypothesis that decisions about nuclear weapons were guided exclusively by considerations associated with deterrence theory.

Tannenwald uses a small-N, qualitative test based on data-set observations to evaluate the hypothesis that the nuclear taboo has had a causal impact on U.S. decision making. In comparing U.S. decisions about nuclear weapons during World War II, the Korean War, the Vietnam War, and the Gulf War, Tannenwald controls for deterrence, since none of these conflicts involved an opponent with the capacity for nuclear retaliation. Because nuclear weapons were only used during World War II, when the broad tradition of negative world public opinion about such weapons had not yet formed, Tannenwald's data-set observations are compatible with the nuclear taboo hypothesis. This comparison of four different wars thus provides some initial evidence in favor of Tannenwald's argument. However, the N is only four, so the comparison yields relatively little analytic leverage.

To gain additional leverage, Tannenwald devotes most of her analysis to the historical record, in search of evidence regarding the actual priorities of key political leaders during decisions about nuclear weapon use in each crisis. Since the nuclear taboo hypothesis implies that decision makers would be both aware of and explicitly concerned about such a taboo, causal-process observations focused on decision-making processes during each war can provide a useful test of the hypothesis. If the historical record shows that decision makers actually discussed constraining effects of a nuclear taboo, then Tannenwald has found important evidence in favor of the hypothesis.

In fact, Tannenwald finds many such statements in accounts of the relevant decision-making processes. To cite a few representative examples, when discussing the Korean War, Tannenwald presents documentary evidence that key U.S. decision makers thought the use of nuclear weapons would be a disaster in terms of world public opinion (1999: 444) and, in the words of one prominent decision maker, "offensive to all morality" (1999: 445). In parallel top-level debates on the potential use of nuclear weapons during the Vietnam War, one key meeting reached the conclusion that "use of atomic weapons is unthinkable" (1999: 454) for normative reasons.

Of course, this evidence could be accounted for in other ways than by the nuclear taboo hypothesis. For example, the statements she quotes might be strategic misrepresentations of political leaders' real agendas, or the beliefs and priorities of these leaders may in some way have been irrelevant to the decisions that they ultimately adopted. However, to the extent that researchers find alternative accounts such as strategic misrepresentation less plausible, Tannenwald's causal-process observations provide valuable support for her argument.

In discussing these three examples, we certainly do not claim to have discovered a new type of evidence for use in political and social research. Such evidence is obviously familiar to scholars who use process tracing, within-case analysis, and related techniques. Our goals in this discussion are, first, to argue that these many forms of analysis employ a similar kind of evidence; and, second, to give this type of evidence, based on causal-process observations, a methodological status parallel to that of data-set observations.

Further, these three examples illustrate an important complementarity between data-set observations and causal-process observations. In all three examples, the causal-process observations focus on ideas or priorities that must be held by actors in order for the hypothesis associated with the data-set observations to be correct. They identify indispensable steps in the causal process, without which the hypothesis does not make sense.

In the following section, we explore the analytic leverage that derives from these two types of observations.

Implications of Contrasting Types of Observations

The distinction between data-set observations and causal-process observations helps to clarify several methodological issues. These include differences between qualitative and quantitative research; the implications of adding different kinds of data for the N, for degrees of freedom, and for inferential leverage; the consequences of missing data; the tools of causal inference employed in quantitative analysis; and advice about increasing the number of observations. These issues will now be explored in turn.

**Table 13.3. Adding Different Forms of Data:
Consequences for Causal Inference**

	Consequences for Causal Inference		
Adding Data	**For the N**	**For Degrees of Freedom**	**For Inferential Leverage**
Adding Data-Set Obser-vations	Increases the N.	Increases degrees of freedom.	Greater degrees of freedom increase leverage; yet leverage may be reduced if the addition of new observations violates measurement and causal assumptions.
Adding Causal-Process Obser-vations	Usually does not affect the N.	Usually does not affect degrees of freedom.[a]	New information about causal patterns may increase leverage; and if observations are drawn from original set of cases, there is less risk of vio-lating assumptions under-lying measurement and causal inference.
Adding Variables	Does not affect the N.	Decreases degrees of freedom.	Fewer degrees of freedom reduce leverage; yet lever-age is increased if key mis-sing variables are added.

[a]There is no effect, unless focusing on causal-process observations leads the analyst to modify either the model being estimated, or the data set.

Qualitative versus Quantitative

Large-N quantitative researchers may routinely use large numbers of data-set observations and many fewer causal-process observations. By contrast, small-N qualitative researchers may use few data-set observations and a great many causal-process observations. These qualitative researchers use causal-process observations, as we put it above, to slowly but surely rule out alternative explanations until they come to one that stands up to scrutiny. This is a style of causal inference focused on mechanisms and processes, rather than on covariation among variables.

At the same time, we do not wish to narrowly identify the qualitative versus quantitative distinction with the causal-process versus data-set distinction. The two types of observations, used together, can provide strong inferential leverage in both traditions of research. For example, within the framework of Alexander George's "method of structured, focused comparison," which has played a central role in defining the comparative case-study tradition, researchers ask "a set of *standardized, general questions* of each case" (1979a: e.g., 62), producing a uniform collection of data-set observations based on qualitative data. Conversely, as Goldthorpe and others have argued (see above), causal-process observations can make a valuable contribution to mainstream quantitative research. The label "nested inference," noted above, is intended to highlight this two-way contribution.

Adding Observations and Adding Variables: Consequences for the N, Degrees of Freedom, and Inferential Leverage

The distinctions offered above may help refine the frequently repeated advice to add observations as a means of strengthening causal inference. We would frame this topic more generically as "adding data," which can include adding data-set observations, causal-process observations, and new variables. These three alternative ways of adding data have different consequences for the N, for degrees of freedom, and for inferential leverage (table 13.3).

Consequences for the N are summarized in the left-hand column of table 13.3. The N is the number of cases, which corresponds to the number of data-set observations, that is, the number of rows in a rectangular data set. As noted, this idea applies equally to quantitative and qualitative data. The key distinction here is that increasing the number of data-set observations increases the N— whereas adding causal-process observations often does not affect the N. Given the extensive discussion of "increasing the number of observations," this distinction is helpful. Finally, adding variables, which may incorporate many additional pieces of data into the analysis, adds columns to the rectangular data set but does not increase the N.

The second issue concerns the consequences of adding data for the degrees of freedom (see middle column in the table). Degrees of freedom merit attention, because to the extent they are greater, the researcher has more capacity to adjudi-ate among rival explanations, within the framework of analyzing data-set observa-tions.[35] Other things being equal, the more data-set observations (i.e., the larger the N) vis-à-vis the number of parameters to be estimated (which usually corresponds to the number of explanatory variables), the greater the degrees of freedom. Add-ing causal-process observations does not usually increase the N or affect the de-grees of freedom.[36] If the researcher adds data in the sense of adding variables, this typically reduces the degrees of freedom. This is because the N remains un-changed, while the number of parameters about which inferences are to be made has increased.

Another question concerns the overall consequence for inferential leverage of adding different forms of data (right column in table 13.3). Degrees of freedom is a useful concept, but it does not capture all relevant aspects of inferential leverage. For example, it is true that adding data-set observations—that is, adding cases—can often increase inferential leverage by increasing degrees of freedom. However, a loss of inferential leverage may occur if adding cases extends the analysis to new domains where prior conceptualizations are inappropriate, measurement proce-dures are invalid, or causal homogeneity is lacking.

Moving down the right column in the table, we see that if the researcher makes insightful use of causal-process observations, this can increase inferential leverage. Finally, adding variables decreases the degrees of freedom and can therefore decrease inferential leverage. However, if relevant missing variables are added to the model, inferential leverage thereby increases because missing-variable bias decreases.

As an example of how adding different forms of data affects inferential lever-age, let us consider a comparative study with an N of twenty-four, focused on ex-plaining change in electoral systems. One hypothesis is that such change occurs when (a) public protest over political corruption increases sharply, (b) electoral reform is seen as a salient response, and (c) legislators have the constitutional au-thority to rapidly introduce electoral reform (Shugart, Moreno, and Fajardo 2001: 3–5, 23–34). From this starting point, the researcher might add data-set observa-tions to the study by finding additional episodes of potential electoral change. The N and the degrees of freedom are thereby increased; other things being equal, the scholar has gained inferential leverage. However, other things are not equal if con-

---

[35] It is important to note that degrees of freedom, and also inferential leverage in general, are not properties of the data, but rather of the researcher's model in relation to the data. Adding a variable to an analysis decreases the degrees of freedom if the rest of the model is not changed. Yet, it could, for example, increase the degrees of freedom if it leads to a reconceptualization of the model as a sequence of causal steps in which the number of parameters estimated is smaller at each step.

[36] However, the degrees of freedom could, once again, change if these causal-process observations lead the researcher to modify the statistical model being tested.

cepts and indicators do not fit the new cases, or if causal homogeneity is violated. To the extent that these problems arise, leverage for causal inference may actually be reduced.

Alternatively, the researcher might add causal-process observations to strengthen causal inferences about the original four episodes of potential electoral reform. For example, the researcher might carefully examine critical moments in the crystallization or collapse of public protest, or turning points in the electoral reform process. Nonetheless, in terms of data-set observations, the N is still twenty-four. The degrees of freedom have not changed,[37] yet inferential leverage may have increased.

Finally, the investigator might add data by introducing new explanatory variables—for example, the structure of the party system—as part of the uniform array of scores on the dependent and independent variables. Clearly, the N has not increased, and, with more explanatory variables, the degrees of freedom will typically be reduced. On the other hand, if the original model was underspecified and the structure of the party system is, in fact, a key missing variable, then inferential leverage is strengthened by adding this variable, which may counteract the effect of the reduced degrees of freedom.

This example illustrates how adding data to an analysis can mean three different things, and that degrees of freedom, although a valuable concept, captures only one aspect of inferential leverage. This conclusion stands out clearly in table 13.3, where for all three rows the consequences for overall inferential leverage are different, and often more ambiguous, than they are for the degrees of freedom. In order to evaluate advice to "increase the number of observations" as a means of strengthening research design, we must adopt a multifaceted view of the types of data that may be added and of their varied contribution to improving inference.

Implications for Research Design

These arguments, as summarized in table 13.3, have implications for research design. *DSI* repeatedly makes a case for increasing the N, but we should recognize that researchers often have good reasons for focusing on a small N. Therefore, advice to increase the N may be misplaced. For instance, the researcher may have made an enormous investment in gaining expertise on a few cases. This expertise can provide the researcher with access to a broad array of causal-process observations, which in turn can sometimes yield greater leverage for valid inference than additional cases about which the investigator knows far less. Alternatively, this scholar may have serious doubts about whether the causal patterns in these cases will be found in other cases—that is, doubts about causal homogeneity and the generality of findings. In discussions of method and theory, the problem of generalization, and specifically of overextending findings, is both an old theme (Weber 1949: 72–76; Bendix 1963; Walker and Cohen 1985) and a recently renewed con-

---

[37]Except under the conditions specified in note 36 above.

cern (Elster 1999: chap. 1). Given this potential problem, along with the issues of measurement validity that can arise in moving to new contexts, the analyst might be well advised to stick to a small N.

By contrast, adding causal-process observations does not pose this problem of overextending the analysis, because the focus typically remains on the original cases. Such research seeks to deepen the knowledge of causal processes and mechanisms in these cases, rather than extend the study to additional cases. The challenge a researcher faces when adding causal-process observations is to know which details to collect, when enough details have been collected to make an inference, and how to increase the likelihood that this inference is valid. The literature on case studies and within-case analysis would do well to address these issues in greater depth.

To conclude, although the advice to increase the number of data-set observations is sometimes valuable, it may simply be distracting for researchers who have deliberately focused on explaining a small number of important outcomes. These researchers may find that collecting relevant causal-process observations is more helpful. Further, for quantitative researchers, causal-process observations can be a valuable supplement to large-scale data sets.

Missing Data

A distinction should also be made about the implications of missing data for these two types of observations. With data-set observations, missing data can be a serious issue. Indeed, the idea that data-set observations involve a uniform array should be understood as encompassing the norm that the data set should preferably be complete, and that a problem of missing data requires close attention (Griliches 1986; Greene 2000: 259–63).

Almost by definition, the issue of missing data does not arise in the same way for causal-process observations. The inferential leverage derived from causal-process observations does not depend on having complete data across a given range of cases and variables. Thus, one or a few causal-process observations may provide great leverage in making inferences. For example, Stokes's analysis of presidential policy switches, discussed above, derives analytic leverage from observations of the decision-making processes involved in only three of the thirty-eight cases that she considers. Her close analysis of these three cases obviously does not "prove" her hypothesis for all thirty-eight episodes, but it does increase the plausibility of her overall conclusions by offering telling evidence about three episodes. Likewise, data-set observations can potentially compensate for gaps or inadequacies in causal-process observations.

Standard Quantitative Tools versus Careful Analysis of
Causal-Process Observations

The distinction between data-set observations and causal-process observations offers a new basis for thinking about the application of standard quantitative tools to different kinds of research. We have elaborate quantitative procedures for evaluating inferences made with data-set observations. By contrast, causal-process observations force us to make complex judgments about inference and probability without explicit guidance from quantitative tools. It is precisely the emphasis on standard quantitative tests that leads *DSI* to make what we view as a major mistake: subordinating causal-process observations to a conventional quantitative framework (see again 85–87, 226–28).

A small number of causal-process observations, that seek to uncover critical turning points or moments of decision making, can play a valuable role in causal inference. Making an inference from a smoking gun does not require a large N in any traditional sense. However, it does require careful thinking about the logic of inference and a rich knowledge of context, which may in turn depend on many additional causal-process observations. The several chapters in the present volume that discuss tools for qualitative analysis have suggested points of departure for reasoning about how these inferences take place.

Conclusion: Drawing Together the Argument

In chapters 12 and 13, we have expressed reservations about *DSI*'s positions on causal inference, descriptive inference, and related methodological questions. *DSI* in effect treats causal inference as fairly straightforward, provided the researcher follows the quantitative template.[38] We would instead argue that adequate causal inference is difficult. To the extent that *DSI* addresses challenges to causal inference, it treats these issues as in effect depending on the power of quantitative tests. Thus, the book focuses on increasing the number of observations, estimating uncertainty, and the closely related and misleading idea that— as *DSI* puts it—determinate research designs (i.e., designs with a sufficiently large N and a lack of perfect multicollinearity) are the "sine qua non" of causal inference.

This emphasis on determinate research designs obscures basic challenges in making what we prefer to call "interpretable" causal inferences: the challenges of ruling out an unknown number of alternative explanations and dealing with hard-to-test assumptions. Effective causal inference requires bringing to bear as many different kinds of evidence as possible, including evidence from qualitative research. Yet in *DSI*'s approach, the contribution of qualitative evidence is undervalued because it is inappropriately assessed in terms of the size of the N and quantitative tests, which misrepresents its distinctive contributions.

With regard to descriptive inference, *DSI* devotes a chapter to this topic. However, the book's discussion focuses primarily on relatively straightforward questions, such as how to generalize from a sample to a population and how to

---

[38]See again the cautionary observation in chapter 1 above (9 n. 3 this volume).

productively organize and summarize descriptive detail. Yet descriptive inference raises broader, more complex issues that require far more attention. Causal inferences are only reasonable if measurement is valid. Measurement validity, in turn, depends on careful attention to conceptualization—a topic for which *DSI*'s advice points in the wrong direction—and on the plausibility of each decision taken in the measurement process. Issues of conceptualization and measurement are more fundamental than the conventional problem of generalizing from a sample to a population; indeed, such issues must be addressed even if researchers make no attempt to generalize their claims.

For many other methodological questions, we are again convinced that *DSI* adopts positions that are somewhat simplistic: for example, the book's arguments about appropriate techniques for case selection and against testing deterministic causal models, along with the failure to recognize that techniques of within-case analysis yield a different kind of evidence than do conventional quantitative data. These are complex issues and must be addressed within a methodological framework that extends well beyond that of *DSI* and of mainstream quantitative methods.

In the present volume, we have sought to develop this broader framework and have argued that it yields a more positive perspective on qualitative tools for descriptive and causal inference. Part of this argument derives from what we have called the statistical rationale for qualitative research. Specifically, we have invoked the statistical idea that important gaps in causal inference based on the quantitative analysis of data-set observations can be filled by evidence derived from qualitative, causal-process observations. Inference based on qualitative data routinely employs different assumptions than quantitative inference, and correspondingly it provides an alternative source of analytic leverage. Such leverage can serve to improve not only qualitative research, but also quantitative research.

Similarly, with regard to descriptive inference, we have argued that reasoning about measurement found in psychometrics and mathematical measurement theory points to concerns to which qualitative researchers are routinely more attentive—such as the foundational role of paired comparisons in the logic of measurement, as well as concern with issues of domain and context. The present volume has sought to show how these qualitative and statistical traditions can help lay a stronger methodological foundation for progress in the social sciences.

Running through this discussion have been the themes of diverse tools and shared standards. From one perspective, these ideas might seem contradictory: a strong set of shared standards might rule out all but a single, best package of tools. We are convinced that this contradiction does not arise in the social sciences for a simple reason. In light of the current state of methodological knowledge, scholars face many trade-offs in pursuing good descriptive and causal inference. Given these trade-offs, there is no such thing as a universally best set of tools. Rather, the existence of trade-offs requires a sustained recognition that diverse analytic tools are needed in social research.

Balancing Methodological Priorities:
Technification and the Quest for Shared Standards

In concluding this volume, we would like to reflect on the overall mix of concerns and priorities that are most productive in advancing both methodology and substantive research. We find ourselves in a period when increasingly technical approaches to methodology and theory have growing influence in the social sciences. Whether they involve new procedures for statistical estimation or new tools for deductive inference, these innovations unquestionably help us to understand political and social reality.

Yet this trend toward technification can impose substantial costs. It can lead to replacing a simple and appropriate tool with an unnecessarily complex one. It can sometimes distance analysts from the detailed knowledge of cases and contexts that is an invaluable underpinning for any inference, whether derived through complex research procedures or simpler tools. Technification can also devolve into a form of intellectual obscurantism in which research ceases to be driven by important substantive questions and interesting intellectual agendas.

In some circumstances a sophisticated, technical solution is indeed more powerful. However, at other times it is better to adopt an alternative solution based on simpler tools. As qualitative methodologists routinely emphasize, these simpler tools can place scholars in closer contact with the cases being studied, sometimes enabling analysts to discover unanticipated causal patterns. Further, when highly technical tools are employed, they cannot be a substitute either for careful thinking about the process that produced the data, or for crafting good—and often elegantly simple—research designs that allow one to rule out alternative explanations. This careful thinking often relies on simple forms of data analysis—employing, perhaps, a scatterplot, or a two-by-two table—and on crafting a parsimonious model that undergirds the research design.[39]

Scholars should recognize that simpler analytic tools can sometimes contribute more to achieving the shared standards of valid descriptive and causal inference and refining theory. We believe that the greatest promise for progress in social science lies in an eclectic view of methodology that recognizes the potential contributions of diverse tools to meeting these shared standards.

---

[39]See Achen (2000, 2002) and also Diaconis (1998). For a broader statement on these tensions in the discipline of political science, see Keohane 2003.

Data-Set Observations versus Causal-Process Observations:
The 2000 U.S. Presidential Election

Henry E. Brady

The outcome of the 2000 presidential election in Florida produced major political, legal, and scholarly disputes. This appendix addresses one of these disputes, first by summarizing a time-series cross-sectional regression analysis based on data-set observations, and then by challenging these findings through analyzing a string of causal-process observations.[1]

The approach I adopt is a form of detective work. It uses Fenno's (1977: 884) "soaking and poking" to gather information, as well as George's (1979b: 113–14) "process tracing," to establish the "physical and social processes through which purported causes affect outcomes" (Bennett and George 1997: 3).

---

[1]For definitions of these two types of observations, see chapter 13 and the glossary in the present volume.

The Option of Regression Analysis

John R. Lott argues that, in the 2000 U.S. presidential election, at least 10,000 votes were lost for George W. Bush in the ten panhandle counties of Florida.[2] The votes were lost because the networks declared Al Gore the winner in Florida after the polls had closed in eastern Florida but before the polls had closed in the panhandle counties, which are on Central Standard Time. Lott's conclusion was widely discussed in the aftermath of the 2000 election and led to a series of congressional hearings.

To get his result, Lott employed a "difference-in-differences" form of regression analysis, based on data-set observations.[3] He obtained turnout data on all sixty-seven Florida counties for four presidential elections (1988, 1992, 1996, and 2000), and he estimated a time-series cross-sectional regression with fixed county and time effects and with a "dummy variable" for the ten panhandle counties. In effect, Lott looked at the difference between one set of counties that got a "treatment" in the year 2000 (the ten panhandle counties whose polls were still open when the election was "called") and those that did not (the remaining fifty-seven Florida counties in the eastern time zone), while controlling for differences reflected in the data from previous elections. Lott (2000) concluded that:

> By prematurely declaring Gore the winner shortly before polls had closed in Florida's conservative western Panhandle, the media ended up suppressing the Republican vote.... An examination of past Republican presidential votes by county in Florida from 1988 to 2000 shows that while total votes declined, the Republican voting rate in the western panhandle was significantly suppressed relative to the non-Republican vote. The 4 percent greater reduction in Republican votes averages about 1,000 votes per county, [yielding] 10,000 Republican votes for all 10 counties in the western Panhandle. This holds true even after accounting for the average differences in voting rates across counties as well as the changes in voting rates from one election to another.

---

[2]This discussion is based on three sources. The first is Lott's article in the November 14, 2000, *Philadelphia Inquirer* (Lott 2000) in which he provides a general description of his methodology and claims that 10,000 votes were lost. Second, Lott's econometric analysis is described in Mason, Frankovic, and Jamieson (2001: 77–78). Third, Congressman Billie Tauzin subsequently held hearings on the elections and collected different analyses and interpretations of the vote. Congressman Tauzin's office provided me with an annotated computer printout of Lott's analysis, which reflects a methodology identical to that described both in Lott's article and in Mason et al.

[3]"Difference-in-differences" estimators are widely used in economics, and they are now a staple of introductory econometrics textbooks such as Stock and Watson (2003: 385–88) and Wooldridge (2000: 414–19).

Turning to Causal-Process Observations

A researcher accustomed to the exclusive use of data-set observations might stop at this point, convinced that an adequate inference had been made. However, researchers oriented toward the use of causal-process observations would ask whether the result makes any sense. Is Lott's estimate reasonable, given the number of voters who had not yet voted when the media called the election for Gore? How many of these voters heard the call? Of these, how many decided not to vote? And of those who decided not to vote, how many would have voted for Bush? Researchers can obtain answers to these questions by consulting diverse data sources and constructing a more intricate characterization of events on election day.

An inquiry to the networks established that the media calls were made ten minutes before the panhandle polls closed at 7:00 p.m.—twelve hours after the opening time of 7:00 a.m. If we assume that voters go to the polls at an even rate throughout the day, then only 1/72nd (ten minutes over twelve hours) of the voters had not yet voted when the media call was made. Alternatively, an analysis of Census data from 1996 on time of voting suggests that no more than about one-twelfth of the voters in Florida come to the polls in the last hour. If we assume that voters go to the polls at an even rate in this last hour, then (once again) only 1/72nd (one-sixth of one hour times one-twelfth) of the voters had not yet voted when the media call was made. Of the 379,000 voters in the panhandle, about 20 percent were absentee voters—leaving about 303,000 voters who voted on election day. One seventy-second of this figure is, in round numbers, 4,200 voters. The major assumption in this calculation is that voters come to the polls uniformly during the day or during the last hour. Interviews with Florida election officials and a review of media reports suggest that, typically, no rush to the polls occurs at the end of the day in the panhandle.

Only 4,200 people could have been swayed by the media call of the election, if they heard it. How many heard it? Research on media exposure suggests that an audience of 20 percent of adults for all media outlets would be very large. To be very conservative, I will assume that 20 percent of the 4,200 voters who intended to vote in the last ten minutes, or 840 people, heard the early call—though this is undoubtedly an overestimate because not all media were reporting the elections. Moreover, many of these prospective voters were Democrats or Independents who would not have voted for George W. Bush. In the panhandle, the Bush vote was about two-thirds of the total. If we assume the same proportion among those who were still to vote, it yields a total of 560 Bush voters who might have been affected.

Of these 560 Bush voters who might have heard the media call, how many decided not to vote? A review of past work on the impact of early calls (Jackson 1983) and a general knowledge of voting behavior suggests a figure of 10 percent for the fraction of voters who decided not to vote once they knew the call was made for the presidential election. After all, voters select other officials as well, and they vote for reasons other than the likelihood that their vote will be decisive.

Ten percent of 560 yields fifty-six Bush voters who might have been deterred from voting.

This estimate of Bush's vote loss still probably exceeds the actual net effect. It seems just as likely that a Gore voter, rather than a Bush voter, might have decided not to vote. After all, for both candidates, the vote is no longer relevant to the presidential election once the call has been made. If 10 percent of the 280 Gore voters did not vote, then the net effect would be 28 Bush votes—56 Bush voters minus 28 Gore voters. This suggests a range of 28 to 56 Bush votes lost depending upon whether Gore voters were affected by the call. Even if we forget the offset for Gore voters and quadruple the estimate of 56 Bush voters who might have decided not to vote, the resulting upper-bound estimate of 224 voters is far short of the 10,000 that Lott claims.

My detective work leads to the inference that the approximate upper bound for Bush's vote loss was 224 and that the actual vote loss was probably closer to somewhere between 28 and 56 votes. Lott's figure of 10,000 makes no sense at all. This simple case-study analysis based upon information that goes beyond the turnout data used in the difference-in-differences model suggests a figure that is two orders of magnitude smaller than Lott's result.

Although this case study of late voting uses quantitative data, it employs inferential tools typically associated with qualitative research. It draws upon multiple sources of information, utilizing inferences based on common sense, to establish an argument. It tries to approach the problem in several different ways, cross-checking information at every turn, and asking if the posited causal effect is probable, or even possible, given what we know from many different sources. In short, it investigates causal processes in close detail, and it tries to get beyond the results of an elaborate quantitative analysis of data-set observations.

Where Did Lott Go Wrong?

The difference-in-differences method is widely used in economics and other social science disciplines as a way to adjust observational data for confounding factors that can lead to incorrect inferences. In this case, the method assumes that turnout in 2000 can be predicted by turnout in past years after adjusting for idiosyncratic factors of two types: those factors that affect each county in the same way over the entire time period but vary from county to county (county fixed effects), and those factors that affect all counties in a given year but vary over years (time fixed effects).

This method does badly when idiosyncratic factors vary both by county and over time. For example, in 2000, organized labor put significant effort into increasing turnout in Florida, and it seems likely that it put its effort into mobilizing Democratic voters. As a result, turnout would be increased, compared to prior years, in counties with more Democrats (namely those outside the panhandle). The difference-in-difference method would not control for this. In fact, it would presume that the higher turnout outside the panhandle in 2000 should be translated into higher turnout inside the panhandle as well. To the extent that this higher turnout was not realized, Lott's equation would pick it up as a negative coefficient on his dummy variable for the panhandle counties that he interpreted as the effect of the early media call. Instead, his coefficient might simply reflect labor's success in mobilizing voters outside the panhandle.

In addition, quantitative methods are most believable when researchers are conservative about their inferences. Instead of using the standard .05 level of significance, Lott chose to use a .10 level, and he chose to employ a one-sided test that made his t-statistic of 1.285 just significant at this 10 percent level. This lenient approach to hypothesis testing allowed him to claim that his regression detected a significant effect. However, if Lott had decided to provide a 10 percent one-sided confidence interval for his estimate instead of a point estimate of 10,000, his confidence interval would have gone from zero to 20,000, thus providing little confidence in his assertions.

Even if these problems in Lott's analysis were cleaned up by getting data on labor union activity and other factors, the analysis of such data would not necessarily supercede the inference based on causal-process observations. Even after putting aside the practical problems of collecting suitable data, it would be hard to collect data that could rule out all of the possible confounding effects. Consequently, rather than seeking additional data-set observations, in my judgment it would be more productive to do further in-depth analysis of causal-process observations drawn from these ten Florida panhandle counties, finding out what happened there, for example, by interviewing election officials and studying media reports.

Conclusion

Causal-process observations demonstrate that it was highly implausible for the media effect suggested by Lott's analysis to have occurred. Thus, what from a technical perspective could be seen as a less sophisticated tool of analysis demonstrates that his quantitative conclusions based upon regression analysis cannot be valid.

In this sense, I have sought to demonstrate the value of causal-process observations in what could be seen as a "least-likely case," that is, a data-rich domain of mass political behavior. Even in this domain, this strategy of causal assessment provides valuable inferential leverage that supplements, and in this instance contradicts, the conclusions based on the analysis of data-set observations. Indeed, the lesson for quantitative researchers is the necessity of paying attention to the causal processes underlying behavior. Otherwise, regression analysis is likely to go off the rails.

Glossary

Jason Seawright and David Collier

This glossary defines methodological terms employed in this book. The core definition is presented in the initial paragraph of each entry, and additional paragraphs are included for terms that require more elaboration. Some definitions are drawn directly from the text.[1]

For entries that extend beyond one paragraph, the initial paragraph is intended to provide a self-contained definition that may be sufficient for many readers. Cross-references to related terms are identified in boldface, with the exception of a few terms used so frequently that the repeated bolding would be distracting. Page references to the corresponding discussion in the text are noted in the index.

---

[1]While in general we do not use bibliographic citations in the glossary, we do acknowledge particular authors in certain instances. For definitions of methodological terms, Schwandt (1997) is a useful reference for the qualitative tradition, and Darnell (1994) and Kennedy (1998) are good sources for econometric terms. Van Evera (1997), Vogt (1999), and Gerring (2001) give many useful definitions relevant to both the qualitative and quantitative traditions. Some of our definitions parallel the usage in the text of King, Keohane, and Verba's *Designing Social Inquiry* (hereafter *DSI*). For a discussion of their use of terms, see chapter 2 in the present volume.

antecedent variable. A type of **independent variable** that stands causally prior to another **explanatory variable**, which may be called an **intervening variable**. A variable's categorization as antecedent or intervening is not a permanent status, but is understood in relation to a particular causal model. See **endogenous variable**, **exogenous variable**.

assumption. An underlying premise about the characteristics of a model being estimated, of the data being analyzed, and/or of the contexts from which the data are drawn. Although such premises are often difficult to test, they play a central role in descriptive and causal inference. To the degree that the assumptions made in a particular analysis are not met, inferences drawn from the analysis are questionable. Assumptions are sometimes misunderstood as relevant only to quantitative analysis, but in fact all forms of research depend on assumptions. See **causal homogeneity**, **conditional independence**, **constant causal effects**, **independence of observations**, **specification assumption**.

autocorrelation. A failure of the assumption of **independence of observations**, due to patterns of influence among observations that are either temporally or spatially proximate.

Bayesian inference. Procedures for statistical inference in which the researcher's preexisting knowledge and beliefs are quantified as a prior probability that is used as a baseline to be adjusted on the basis of empirical evidence.

This approach contrasts with more traditional **significance tests**, which evaluate a **null hypothesis** (typically of "no relationship") against an alternative hypothesis (typically of "some relationship"). Empirical data are then used to either reject or fail to reject the null hypothesis. While many scholars believe that the strict application of a Bayesian framework is inappropriate in much social science research, several ideas underlying Bayesian inference serve as a valuable point of reference.

bias. Systematic error in inference. With bias, successive **errors** cannot be expected to cancel each other out, and inferences will therefore be faulty, even with extremely large samples. Contrast with **random error**. See **selection bias**, **missing variable bias**.

Boolean algebra. A mathematical representation of formal logic. In Ragin's (1987) **qualitative comparative analysis**, Boolean algebra is used to formalize arguments about causal relations among dichotomous variables.

Campbell's checklist of threats to validity. An inventory of threats to validity in causal inference presented in Donald Campbell's classic work[2] on experimental and quasi-experimental research.

Campbell's perspective is especially relevant to inferences based on time-series data, and it represents a valuable supplement to the perspective on causal inference conventionally offered by regression analysis and **econometrics**. Examples of these threats to valid inference are history, maturation, instrumentation, selection, and mortality.

case-oriented research. Research in which the center of attention is the close analysis of one or a few cases.

This approach contrasts with **variable-oriented research** (Ragin 1987). Case-oriented researchers certainly think in terms of variables, but their attention is strongly focused on detailed contextual knowledge of specific cases and on how variables interact within the context of these cases. See **case**; **causation, multiple and conjunctural**; **comparative method**.

cases. The units of analysis in a given study. Cases are the political, social, institutional, or individual entities or phenomena about which information is collected and inferences are made. Examples of cases are nation-states, social movements, political parties, trade union members, and episodes of policy implementation.

In a **rectangular data set** the rows correspond to the cases, that is, to what we are calling **data-set observations**. In a given study, the scholar may shift to a different **level of analysis**, so the definition of a case may change. However, if the goal of this shift is to provide greater analytic leverage at the original level of analysis, as in **within-case analysis**, then the original definition of "case" still corresponds to the predominant focus of the analysis.

case selection. Identification of cases for analysis in a given study. This is a fundamental task in **research design**. See **sample, universe of cases**.

case-study. A **research design** focused on one (N=1) or a few cases, typically analyzing the case(s) in great detail through **cross-case** or **within-case analysis**. Ragin's (1987) **case-oriented research**, with its emphasis on contextually specific patterns of causation, is one version of the case-study method. See **qualitative-quantitative distinction**.

causal effect. The impact of a given **explanatory variable** on a particular outcome. More specifically, other things being equal, the causal effect is the differ-

[2]Campbell and Stanley (1966); Campbell and Ross (1968); Cook and Campbell (1979).

ence between the two values of the dependent variable that arise according to whether an independent variable assumes one of two specific values. **Causal inference** seeks to estimate such causal effects. This definition is understood as applying both to quantitative and qualitative analysis.

causal heterogeneity. Presence of contrasting causal patterns. Thus, it is the absence of **causal homogeneity**.

causal homogeneity. The assumption that, other things being equal, a given set of values for the **explanatory variables** always produces the same **expected value** for the dependent variable within a given set of cases. The causal homogeneity assumption is met if the scores on the dependent variable for all the cases included in the analysis are produced in accordance with one shared causal model. Thus, if all cases were, counterfactually, assigned the same values on the independent variables, they would have the same expected value on the dependent variable.

If this assumption is not met, yet a researcher analyzes the data as if it were met, the inferences will be misleading because they will average together different patterns of causation among subgroups of cases. In such situations, researchers may either divide the sample of cases and make inferences within each causal subset, or develop a more complex causal model that incorporates the differences between the subsets. Given these two possibilities, causal homogeneity may be seen as a property of the data *in relation to* a given causal model.

In the statistical literature on causation (e.g., Rubin 1974; Holland 1986), a stronger version of this assumption is presented, which is called **unit homogeneity**. According to this version, different units are presumed to be *fully identical* to each other in all relevant respects except for the main independent variable and, potentially, the dependent variable. Unit homogeneity is sufficient to allow causal inference without the assumption of **conditional independence**, but it is also unlikely that this strong homogeneity assumption holds in typical social science applications, even in experiments. This assumption is generally violated by the fact that no two individuals share identical life histories.

Although *DSI* uses the label **unit homogeneity** in discussing assumptions, its framework in fact relies on the idea of causal homogeneity. Hence, in discussing *DSI*'s arguments, we use the label "causal homogeneity." See **constant causal effects**, **expected value**.

causal inference. The process of reaching conclusions about causation on the basis of observed data. See **descriptive inference**, **inference**.

causal inference, fundamental problem of. The major problem of causal inference, according to many philosophers of science. Given a **counterfactual definition of causation**, the problem is that—for a given case at a given point in time—the researcher can observe either the *presence* of the cause (and of its presumed effect), or the *absence* of the cause (and hence potentially the absence of its presumed effect), but not both. Therefore, the researcher can never make the comparisons that directly meet the criteria of the counterfactual definition, and must instead turn to imperfect real-world comparisons among cases. *DSI* (79–80) devotes central attention to this problem.

causal mechanism. A link or connection in a **causal process**. In the relationship between a given independent variable and a given dependent variable, a causal mechanism posits additional variables, sometimes called **intervening variables**, that yield insight into how the independent variable actually produces the outcome, including the sequence through which this occurs. Compared to the original causal relationship that the scholar is considering, the causal mechanism is often located at a more fine-grained level of analysis.

causal model. A framework of concepts and insights that provides a theoretical rationale for a set of hypothesized explanatory relationships. This term is most often used in referring to a "specified" form of a causal model that posits specific variables and particular relationships among those variables.

A causal model draws on, and is part of, a **theory**. Causal models are not necessarily expressed in equations, but they can be. Quantitative researchers routinely formalize such models, for instance, with regression equations. Qualitative researchers generally do not, though Ragin (1987, 2000) has used tools of Boolean algebra and fuzzy-set logic to formalize some kinds of qualitative analysis.

Several distinctions used to characterize particular types of variables or data sets (for example, independent versus dependent variable, higher versus lower degrees of freedom, or causal homogeneity versus heterogeneity) are only meaningful in relation to a particular causal model. A causal model may be derived from, or linked to, other forms of models, such as a game-theoretic model, but the concern in the present volume is with causal models as particular specifications of causal relations among variables. The ideas of **causal sequence**, **causal process**, and **causal mechanism** are elements of a causal model.

causal process. A sequence of events or steps through which causation occurs. A causal process is often understood as the real-world phenomenon of causation.

causal-process observation. An insight or piece of data that provides information about context, process, or mechanism, and that contributes distinctive leverage in causal inference. A causal-process observation sometimes resembles a "smoking gun" that confirms a causal inference in qualitative research, and is frequently viewed as an indispensable supplement to correlation-based inference in quantitative research as well.[3]

A causal-process observation typically is not initially treated as a cell in a **rectangular data set**. However, insights generated by this observation may lead the researcher to collect additional observations that become part of a rectangular data set. Thus, in the course of research, causal-process observations may generate **data-set observations**. See **causal mechanism, process tracing**.

causal sequence. Two or more steps in a causal chain that generally correspond to a chronological sequence. Similar to **causal process**, but with more emphasis on the idea of discrete causal steps. See **intervening variable, causal mechanism**.

causation, multiple and conjunctural. A causal pattern in which (a) alternative (i.e., multiple) combinations of factors can produce a given outcome, and (b) any one of these causal paths may involve the interaction (i.e., conjunction) of two or more explanatory factors. Ragin (1987) has formalized this perspective on causation with **Boolean algebra**.

cause. A factor that helps to bring about the occurrence of an outcome. Specific types of causes include deterministic, necessary, probabilistic, sufficient. See causal homogeneity, causal inference, causal mechanism, causal model, causal process, causal sequence.

censoring. See truncation.

classification. As a verb, the process of sorting cases into the categories of a conventional nominal or ordinal scale, or **typology**. As a noun, a conceptual schema consisting of an organized set of analytic categories that may be used in making theoretical distinctions and categorizing cases.

comparative-historical analysis. Research combining: (1) a sustained comparative analysis of a well-defined set of national cases; (2) a focus on the unfolding of causal processes over time; and (3) the use of systematic comparison to generate and/or evaluate explanations of outcomes. Specific studies may be identified with this tradition even though they do not have all of these attributes.

comparative method. The systematic analysis of a relatively small number of cases. It involves a smaller N than most statistical studies, but a larger N than a case study. Tools associated with the comparative method include procedures for **concept formation**, standard practices for looking at **matching** and **contrasting cases**, and using theory to identify **most-likely** and **least-likely cases**.

---

[3]For parallel arguments in quantitative research, see Freedman 1991, 1992a,b; Goldthorpe 2001: 8–10; see also Elster 1999: chap. 1.

complexification based on extreme cases. The tendency of research focused on cases with extreme values on the dependent variable to yield new, but potentially idiosyncratic, explanations. Such complexification may provide insight, yet may also distract from identifying causal patterns that are easier to detect in the full range of cases. This issue arises in discussions of **selection bias**.

concept. Variously understood as an abstract idea that offers a point of view for understanding some aspect of our experience; an idea of a phenomenon formed by mentally combining its attributes; a mental image that, when operationalized, helps to organize the analysis of data. The word employed to label any particular concept is often called a **term**.

It is productive to distinguish the "classical" and the "frame" views of concepts. The classical view focuses on defining attributes and understands **concept formation** as centrally concerned with making careful choices about the **intension**, that is, the set of meanings associated with the concept itself; and the **extension**, that is, the range of cases seen as instances of the concept. By contrast, the frame perspective treats a concept as one component in a stylized scenario, or idealized cognitive model that constitutes a point of view for thinking about some domain within the real world. Here concept formation is centrally concerned with reasoning about the relationships among different components of this scenario or model and about their implications for the particular concept.

Though this distinction between the classical and the frame views of concepts is useful, these two perspectives in some respects overlap, and many scholars hold elements of both. Qualitative and quantitative analysts may combine elements of the two perspectives in **concept formation**, in the **operationalization** of concepts, and in establishing **measurement validity**.

concept formation. The process of specifying and refining **concepts** employed in empirical research.[4] Concepts may be provided by the observer (the etic approach), by the actors being studied (the emic approach), or by a combination of the two. Analyzing the concepts of the actors being studied involves **interpretation**.

conceptualization. See concept formation.

conceptual stretching. A form of measurement error that arises when scholars inappropriately apply established concepts and theories to new contexts. Prior assumptions about the meaning of some components of the concept, and about the interrelations among these components, are not met in these new contexts.

---

[4]Political theorists may of course engage in concept formation for other purposes, but our concern here is with the empirical application of concepts.

concreteness (as a property of theory). Precisely stated, and making specific predictions. Such a theory is, in principle, easier to **falsify**.

conditional independence. An assumption used to justify causal inferences based on observational data, that is, in the absence of a true experiment.

In an experiment, "independence" is achieved when the assignment of cases to the treatment and control groups is statistically unrelated to other characteristics of those cases that may influence the dependent variable in the study. **Random assignment** meets this criterion. With **observational data**, scholars seek to approximate independence by using tools such as **stratification** to control for, or "condition" on, relevant control variables—thereby achieving "conditional independence." The assumption of conditional independence is similar in meaning to, although different in emphasis from, the **specification assumption**.

confounder. A theoretically relevant variable that, if added to a causal model, improves the causal inference. It is also called a **missing variable** or **omitted variable**. Adding **intervening variables** to a model may change the estimates of the direct effects of some explanatory variables, but not the estimates of total effects; intervening variables are not considered confounders.

constant causal effects. The assumption that, other things being equal, a given increment in the explanatory variable always produces a fixed magnitude of change in the dependent variable. This standard is in effect equivalent to the assumption that the relationship between the independent and the dependent variable is linear, and that the independent variable does not appear in an **interaction term** with any other variables.

This differs from the **causal homogeneity** assumption, which requires that, other things being equal, all cases have the same **expected value** of the dependent variable for given values of the independent variables.

constructivism. A research tradition focused on how social and psychological processes influence the way people view, and in part create, reality. It is the study of how human beings, individually and collectively, constitute their world. Some usages also encompass the idea of a "reflexive" perspective, involving a concern on the part of researchers with the implications of their own social position for the focus and findings of their research. See **interpretation**.

context. The political, social, and historical setting within which the phenomenon under study is located. In **descriptive inference**, detailed knowledge of context may lead the scholar to recognize the need for **contextualized comparison**; in **causal inference**, such knowledge may lead to the refinement of the **causal model**. Human understanding inevitably draws selectively on the context, which is typically too complex to be entirely understood.

contextualized comparison. Measurement procedures that take into account differences in **context**. The goal is to establish the appropriateness of concepts and the equivalence of measurement across contexts. These procedures acknowledge that the interpretation of indicators, or even the indicators themselves, may need to vary across contexts if they are to validly measure a given concept.

contrasting cases. A set of cases that have very different scores on a variable of concern. For example, with a dichotomous variable, cases that have positive scores and cases that have negative scores; with a continuous variable, cases that have high scores and low scores. See **matching cases**.

contrast space. The analytic frame that establishes the range of a variable, based on identifying conceptually relevant **positive** and **negative cases**. The idea of contrast space is closely associated with the question, "as opposed to what?"

control. A key element in the evaluation of causal effects. One may distinguish between experimental control and statistical control.

In *experiments,* "control group" refers to the cases to which the experimental treatment is not applied. Comparing the treatment group with the control group is the basis for assessing the direction and magnitude of the causal effect.

In social science discussions of observational studies, a "control" is a variable that is introduced *statistically* (as opposed to experimentally) into the analysis with the goal of removing its effect on the relationships among two or more other variables. While the meaning of "control" might appear to be parallel in research based on experimental and observational data, in fact it is not. Statistical control with observational data is concerned with eliminating one or more rival explanations.[5] By contrast, in experiments, rival explanations are eliminated not merely through the fact of having experimental and control groups, but rather through **random assignment** to these groups. Thus, in experiments, randomization is the equivalent of perfect statistical control in observational studies.

Further, in observational studies, "to control" for a variable (as a verb) means to statistically remove its effect from the relationship among two or more other variables.

controlled comparison, method of. Small-N analysis based on the careful matching of cases on selected variables. Depending on the variables selected for matching, this method may correspond either to the **method of agreement** or to

---

[5]It is sometimes believed that adding more control variables always improves inference. In fact, the addition of a particular control may improve inference, may not affect it, or may make it worse. The key issue is whether adding the control brings the analysis closer to meeting the specification assumption.

the **method of difference**. This usage of "control" is related to, but different from, the ideas of experimental and statistical **control**.

correlation. A measure of the association between two or more variables.

counterfactual analysis. Reasoning about phenomena that did not occur. In causal assessment, this involves considering how outcomes would have changed if a prior event had not occurred, or had occurred in a different way. Also called a **thought experiment**.

counterfactual definition of causation. An influential understanding of **causation** as the difference between what actually happened and what would have happened if some prior circumstance(s) had been different in a particular way. Thus, the **causal effect** of a given explanatory factor on a particular outcome for a specific case at one point in time is defined on the basis of a comparison between the observed outcome and the hypothetical outcome that would have occurred in the same case at the same point in time if the explanatory factor had not been present. See **counterfactual analysis**; **causal inference, fundamental problem of**.

covariance structure models. Statistical models that explicitly incorporate assumptions about measurement and about causation. When applied to empirical data, these models yield inferences about unobserved parameters involving both the measurement relationships between observed variables and latent variables, and also the causal relationships among unmeasured **latent variables**.

These models combine aspects of regression analysis, factor analysis, and measurement modeling. Also called LISREL-type models, MIMC (multiple-indicator, multiple-causes) models, and structural equation models with latent variables.

critical juncture. A specific historical period in which particular political choices, or the emergence of a particular historical alternative, strongly dispose a given case to follow one path of change, and not others. The critical juncture can alternatively be viewed as involving a high degree of agency, or strong structural determinism. See **path dependence**.

cross-case analysis. The systematic comparison of **cases**. In discussions of small-N, case-study research, this term usefully points to the contrast vis-à-vis **within-case analysis**. Quantitative researchers would routinely assume that they do cross-case analysis. Cross-case analysis in both qualitative and quantitative research typically involves **data-set observations**.

cross-sectional analysis. Research that focuses on multiple cases at one point in time. Contrast with **longitudinal analysis**.

crucial case. A case that is seen as especially likely to make a valuable contribution to causal inference. For example, crucial cases may be strongly expected to confirm (**most-likely case**) or reject (**least-likely case**) a prior hypothesis. New causal insight may result if these expectations are *not* met. These ideas were developed by Harry Eckstein (1975).

data. Information collected by a researcher. In particular, data is typically information organized for analysis and used as a basis for inference. See **experimental data**, **observational data**.

data mining. In data analysis, the practice of trying out many different explanatory variables without theoretical justification, in the hope of finding one that explains an outcome. This is also called "data dredging," "data snooping," and "ransacking." These terms often convey a negative evaluation of inductive research practices; the econometric term **specification search** is a more neutral label.

data, piece of. The value of a variable for a given case. Also called a datum or a score, and sometimes informally called an observation. See **data-set observation**, **causal-process observation**.

data point. In a two-dimensional scatterplot, the point that corresponds to the scores of the two variables for a particular case. A data point is an observation whose meaning crucially depends on simultaneously considering the scores for both the independent and the dependent variable. A data point can also be located in a multidimensional scatterplot, in which instance it corresponds to the scores for several variables.[6] See **data-set observation**.

data set. A collection of scores for one or more variables across a given set of cases. Also called a **rectangular data set**.

data-set observation. All the scores in a given row, in the framework of a **rectangular data set**. It is thus the collection of scores for a given case on the dependent variable *and* all the independent variables. This includes **intervening** and **antecedent variables**. Put another way, it is "all the numbers for one case."[7] A data point in a two- or multidimensional scatterplot is a data-set observation.

Although this definition is presented in the language of quantitative research, it is fully as useful for qualitative researchers as for quantitative researchers. A

---

[6]The term data point is also sometimes used informally to mean the score for a given variable on a given case.

[7]For a nominal or ordinal variable, it is all the scores on the relevant categories for each case.

piece of data that begins as an isolated **causal-process observation** can subsequently be incorporated into a rectangular data set. Thus, through the collection of additional data, it can become part of a data-set observation.

deductive analysis. In empirical social science, the use of theories and hypotheses to make empirical predictions, which are then routinely tested against data.

degrees of freedom. A basic tool in quantitative analysis, used in establishing whether an analyst has sufficient information to make a given inference. Usually, it is the number of independent observations used in making a causal inference, minus the number of **parameters** in the model being estimated. Thus, the greater the number of **data-set observations** vis-à-vis the number of parameters—of which there is usually one per explanatory variable—the greater the degrees of freedom, other things being equal.

Degrees of freedom is not a property of the causal model by itself, or of the data set by itself, but rather of the causal model in relation to the data set. In estimating more complex models that may include both causal and measurement components, degrees of freedom may also refer to the number of variances and covariances among observed variables in relation to the number of parameters being estimated. Increasing the degrees of freedom is generally seen as desirable and is a rationale for arguments in favor of increasing the N, because **inferential leverage** will be greater. See **determinate research design**, **identifiability**.

dependent variable. What the researcher seeks to explain. It is hypothesized to be caused by, or "dependent" on, one or more independent variables. It is also called an outcome variable.

description. A statement about what has occurred. Description differs from **explanation**, which in a commonsense understanding is concerned with why something occurred. The relationship between description and explanation is complex, yet this distinction remains fundamental in political and social research.

descriptive inference. The process of reaching descriptive conclusions on the basis of observed data. This may involve using what is inevitably partial or imperfect information about the real world to make inferences about a concept, or it may involve using such information to characterize a broader set of cases. We find *DSI*'s distinction between descriptive inference and **causal inference** to be valuable, and we follow it in the present volume.

In standard statistical usage, related terms are assigned somewhat different meanings. "Descriptive statistics" is concerned with numerically or graphically summarizing a data set. "Inferential statistics," by contrast, is concerned with reaching conclusions about a larger population on the basis of a sample, or with estimating parameters in a model. Tests of statistical significance would be considered part of inferential statistics. Both descriptive statistics and inferential statistics are sets of tools that can contribute to the goals of descriptive and **causal inference**, as conceptualized in the present volume.

determinate research design. A design with a sufficient number of **data-set observations** to estimate each **parameter** of interest, and to avoid situations of perfect **multicollinearity**. This is a key concept in *DSI* (116, 118–24). Chapter 12 in the present volume recommends the alternative concept of **interpretable**. Contrast with **indeterminate research design**. See **degrees of freedom**.

deterministic. A **measurement model** or a **causal model** that contains no random elements and is not **probabilistic**. In the case of a causal model, it posits an invariant relationship between cause and effect.

In common statistical usage, a deterministic model is, by assumption, deliberately designed without a random component or an **error term**. In the vocabulary of qualitative methodologists, by contrast, "deterministic causation" often refers to models of necessary and/or sufficient causation, which represent a subset of the causal models that are deterministic according to the statistical definition. Contrast with **stochastic**.

deterministic cause. See **deterministic**.

deviant case. A case that is an **outlier** with respect to a given empirical relationship. In standard regression analysis, a deviant case is a case with an exceptionally large value for the residual. Analysis of a deviant case may lead researchers to reconceptualize concepts, revise indicators, or rethink causal hypotheses.

dichotomy. A categorical variable that classifies cases into two groups. A dichotomy may be measured on a **nominal scale** (male/female) or on an **ordinal scale** (rich/poor). Behind dichotomies, of course, one routinely finds finer differentiation that would be associated with higher **levels of measurement**.

diffusion. A form of causation in which the value of a given variable in one case influences the value of that same variable in other cases. Diffusion can be a methodological problem in that the assumption of **independence of observations** may be violated. Diffusion is also treated as a substantive topic in its own right.

disturbance term. See **error term**.

econometrics. The methodological subfield within the discipline of economics, which has contributed major refinements to **regression analysis** and **time-series analysis**.

efficiency. The extent to which a given analytic procedure fully utilizes available evidence to maximize inferential leverage. The concept is used in the present volume in evaluating alternative procedures for assessing **necessary** and/or **sufficient causes**. In statistical usage, this term specifically refers to an estimator whose sampling distribution has a smaller variance than another estimator, or a test that has greater inferential power than another test.

elaboration model. Procedures for data analysis and causal inference that build up larger models from bivariate relationships by successively introducing control variables. The terms **intervening variable** and **antecedent variable** are identified with this approach, which is strongly associated with the work of the sociologist Paul Lazarsfeld. Compare with **stratification**.

empirical. Based on observation and evidence.

endogeneity. A problem that arises when one or more **endogenous variables** in a given causal model are treated as **exogenous**.

Endogeneity occurs when a researcher tests a causal model in which one of the explanatory variables is correlated with the **error term**. Specific examples of endogeneity include **missing variable bias** and reciprocal causation. If a variable in a causal model is endogenous and the analyst does not adopt an appropriate technique to correct this problem, the resulting causal inferences are invalid. Endogeneity is a failure to meet the **specification assumption**.

endogenous variable. A variable caused by other variables within a given causal model; or, a variable correlated with the **error term** (i.e., it could be caused by a missing variable). A variable that is *not* caused by other variables in the model is called an **exogenous variable**.

error. A discrepancy between the estimated value of a parameter and its "true" value; alternatively, in causal inference, a discrepancy between the predicted and observed values of a given case on a given dependent variable. Error may be due to systematic mistakes in data collection or analysis, or to random factors. See **bias**, **random error**, **systematic error**, **uncertainty**.

error term. In a regression model, an unobserved variable that consists of the differences between the observed values of the dependent variable for each case and the theoretically expected values, given the scores on a set of independent variables.

The residuals in a regression equation, which consist of the difference between the observed values of the dependent variable and its *estimated* expected value, may be used to estimate the error term, but they are not themselves the error term. The difference between the true error term and these errors of prediction (which is sometimes called the disturbance term) in any particular regression analysis may be due to an incorrectly specified model, measurement error, or random factors. The variance of the residuals is a good estimate of the variance of the error term only if certain assumptions are met: for example the **specification assumption**, **causal homogeneity**, and the assumption that errors across cases are independent and identically distributed (IID).

estimation. The process of finding the most appropriate value for a **parameter** in a given model, based on the analysis of data. Estimation may be carried out using a statistical technique or a qualitative tool of descriptive or causal inference.

estimator. A procedure or formula used to find the most appropriate value for a **parameter** in a given statistical model, using the evidence provided by a particular set of cases. Formulas for calculating means, correlations, and slopes are estimators.

ethnographic research. Analysis based on sustained, direct observation of and interaction with the individuals or groups being studied, often involving participant observation.

exogenous variable. A variable not caused by other variables within a given causal model and not correlated with the error term. Whereas the pairing of exogenous and **endogenous** is fairly straightforward, the relationship of these terms to independent variable requires clarification. A strict understanding of "independent" could lead to the conclusion that an independent variable is necessarily an exogenous variable. However, the expression independent variable is commonly used more broadly for any explanatory variable, exogenous or endogenous.

expected value. The mean value of the theoretical sampling distribution of any statistic. Statistical reasoning is centrally concerned with the expected value, as opposed to any particular observed value. In statistical procedures that seek to predict the values of a dependent variable using one or more independent variables, the predictions are typically estimated expected values, conditional on the independent variables included in the analysis.

experiment. Research in which the investigator introduces a treatment or stimulus in order to evaluate its causal effect. Compared to an **observational study**, an experiment far more effectively eliminates rival explanations.

In general, the treatment is applied to one set of cases, but not to a **control** group, and the effects are then evaluated. In more complex research designs, more than two groups, with more than two levels of the treatment, may be employed. Assignment to the groups should be random, in order to isolate the causal effect of the treatment from the effects of other potential causes. See **natural experiment, quasi-experiment**.

experimental data. Data generated using a research design in which the investigator assigns particular values on one or more independent variables to the cases being studied. Contrast with **observational data**.

explanation. A statement about why an outcome has occurred. A given variable may be called an explanation, but the term is also applied to the larger framework of causal understanding within which a particular independent (i.e., explanatory) variable or variables are located.

Explanation differs from **description**, which in a commonsense understanding is concerned with what has occurred. The relationship between explanation and description is complex, yet this distinction remains fundamental in political and social research.

explanatory variable. See independent variable.

ex post facto **hypothesis formation.** Formation of new hypotheses after examination of the data.

Whereas in some traditions of research this is seen as a mistake, many qualitative researchers view the **iterated refinement of hypotheses** in light of the data to be essential. Within the quantitative tradition, the term **data mining** implies an inappropriate search for statistically significant relationships within a given data set, whereas **specification search** is intended to refer to a disciplined approach to this task.

extension. The range of cases to which a concept applies. This idea is particularly relevant to dichotomous concepts, for which the idea of empirical membership or nonmembership in the category suggested by the concept is especially meaningful. See **intension**.

external validity. The degree to which descriptive or causal inferences for a given set of cases can be generalized to other cases. It is also called generalizability. Contrast with **internal validity**.

falsifiable. The potential of a claim, **hypothesis**, or theory to be proven wrong.

field research. The collection of data from a real-life setting, as opposed to a library or laboratory. It commonly involves direct observation of, and sometimes interaction with, the political and social actors being studied. Collecting data through archival research would often be considered an aspect of field research. Field experiments, including experiments embedded within public opinion surveys, are a special type of field research that utilizes experimental intervention by the investigator.

goals. Objectives in the conduct of research. See **overarching** and **intermediate goals**.

goals, intermediate. Methodological norms for the application of research **tools** in pursuit of **overarching goals**. In carrying out description, intermediate goals include precision, reliability, and sensitivity to context. In causal assessment, alternative intermediate goals include generality, parsimony, and accuracy.

The pursuit of intermediate goals raises the issue of **trade-offs**, which may lead scholars to embrace some intermediate goals and reject others. In promoting the idea of **shared standards** as a basic theme in the present volume, our purpose is to encourage recognition that these varied choices at the level of intermediate goals may constitute legitimate, alternative means of achieving the overarching goals.

goals, overarching. Broad, shared goals that motivate diverse research practices. In the framework of the present volume, the overarching goals are to (1) strive for valid descriptive and causal inference, and (2) refine theory in the effort to improve these inferences and to strengthen our understanding of political and social reality.

Overarching goals are central to the idea of **shared standards** for evaluating research. We do not intend these goals to be construed narrowly, and some scholars may use a different vocabulary in discussing these goals. For example, Ragin (124 this volume) suggests that "inference" can also be understood as "making sense of cases." Of course, scholars make different choices about how they pursue overarching goals, and such choices are usefully understood at the level of **intermediate goals**.

guidelines. Norms for the conduct of research. The guidelines in chapter 2 of the present volume summarize *DSI*'s methodological advice.

hermeneutics. The epistemology and methodology of **interpretation**.

heteroskedasticity. The situation in which the error term in a regression model does not have a constant variance across all observations, conditional on the explanatory variables.

hypothesis. A tentative answer to a **research question**. In causal analysis, a hypothesis is a conjecture about the relationship between one or more independent variables and a dependent variable. Typically, a hypothesis is connected to a larger conceptual framework/theory.

identifiability. A characteristic of a statistical model, in relation to a particular data set, that makes it possible to estimate the parameters.

A parameter is identifiable if different values for the parameter produce different distributions for some observable aspect of the data. In a regression model, two variables are not separately identifiable if there is **perfect multicollinearity** between them. A model is likewise not identifiable with too few **degrees of freedom**. The issue of identifiability is sometimes referred to as the **identification problem**. See **determinate research design**.

identification. The process of demonstrating that the researcher has sufficient information (typically involving the number of **data-set observations**) to produce estimates of the parameters in a given causal model.

identification problem. The dilemma that, in general, the researcher does *not* have sufficient information to fully identify a model without making restrictive assumptions about some of the relationships among variables in the model. See **identification**.

independence of observations. The assumption that for each observation, a given outcome occurs independently (conditional on the included explanatory variables) from its occurrence or nonoccurrence in other observations.

To the extent that outcomes do not occur independently, for example, due to **diffusion** across observations, each new observation provides less new information for the purpose of causal inference. Interdependence among observations does not bias the causal inference, but it does bias tests of significance that depend on the N, in that such tests tend to overestimate the amount of new information provided by each observation. The issue of independence of observations is a completely different matter from the question of **conditional independence**.

For some readers, a familiar alternative label for this assumption, which is appropriate for discussing cross-sectional analysis, is "independence of cases." However, this same assumption plays a major role in **time-series analysis**, in which the researcher analyzes multiple observations over time for each case. Hence, the broader idea of independence of these observations becomes a central issue, and it is useful to employ this more general label.

independent variable. A variable that influences, or is hypothesized to influence, another variable. This other variable is called the dependent, or outcome, variable. The term **explanatory variable** is often used interchangeably with independent variable.

Although "independent" might be understood to give this term the same meaning as **exogenous variable**, the term "independent variable" is routinely used more broadly to refer to all the explanatory variables in a model. Thus, in quantitative analysis, all the right-hand side variables in a regression equation are independent variables, including **intervening** and **antecedent variables**.

indeterminate research design. A design that lacks a sufficient number of **dataset observations** in relation to the number of **parameters** to be estimated, and/or may suffer from perfect **multicollinearity**. This is a key concept in *DSI* (118–24).

Within the framework of standard statistical techniques, an indeterminate research design can leave the analyst with insufficient information to adjudicate among rival explanations. However, these problems can sometimes be overcome through techniques such as the analysis of **causal-process observations**. Contrast with **determinate research design**. See **degrees of freedom**, **interpretable**.

indicator. A procedure for measuring or **operationalizing** a concept. It may be a quantitative procedure that generates numerical scores, or an operational definition employed in qualitative research to classify cases.

inductive analysis. A method that employs data about specific cases to reach more general conclusions. Contrast with **deductive analysis**.

inference. The process of using data to draw broader conclusions about concepts and hypotheses that are the focus of research.

This definition is specifically intended for the present discussion of empirical research; in other contexts, including mathematics, formal logic, and game theory, scholars are concerned with logical inferences, rather than with inferences from data. Descriptive inference employs data to reach conclusions about what happened; causal inference employs data to reach conclusions about why it happened. See **nested inference**.

inferential leverage. The capacity to make valid inferences, given a particular measurement model or causal model and a specific data set. Some methodological tools serve to increase inferential leverage.

intension. The core meaning or defining attributes of a concept. See **extension**.

interaction term. An element in a regression equation that reflects the joint, multiplicative effect of two or more independent variables on the dependent variable. With an interaction term, the influence of each independent variable depends in part on the value of the other independent variable.

intermediate goals. See goals, intermediate.

Glossary

internal validity. The degree to which descriptive or causal inferences from a given set of cases are correct for those cases. Contrast with **external validity**.

interpretable. A characterization of findings or inferences that can plausibly be defended. The interpretability of findings or inferences can be increased by many factors, including a large N, an ingenious comparative design, a rich knowledge of cases and context, well-executed conceptualization and measurement, and an insightful theoretical model.

The present volume recommends this concept as an alternative to *DSI*'s idea of a **determinate research design**. This usage of the term interpretable involves different issues from the tradition of **interpretation**.

interpretation. A description or characterization of the meaning of human behavior from the standpoint of the individuals whose behavior is being observed. It is sometimes used interchangeably with **thick description** (following Geertz) and *Verstehen* (following Weber). See **constructivism**.

interpretivism. See **interpretation**.

interrupted time-series design. An **observational study** in which the researcher examines time-series data before and after a major event (for instance, a policy switch) that is hypothesized to affect the dependent variable. In some cases, this major event may be the principal explanatory variable; in other cases, it may be one of several explanatory variables. See **quasi-experiment**.

interval scale. See level of measurement.

intervening variable. A variable that stands causally between a given explanatory variable and the outcome being explained. The status of being an intervening variable should be understood in relation to a particular causal model. An **antecedent variable** (also called a background variable) stands prior to an intervening variable.

iterated refinement of hypotheses. Movement back and forth between hypotheses and data to refine hypotheses and take advantage of new insights that can be gained from the data. See **data mining**, *ex post facto* **hypothesis formation**, **specification search**.

large N. A large number of cases. Contrast with **small N.**[8] There is no well-established cut-point between a large and a small N, but it might be located somewhere between ten and twenty cases.

latent variable. An attribute or characteristic observed through indicators that measure it indirectly.

least-likely case. A case that is not expected to conform to the prediction of a particular theory.

A least-likely case often has extreme values on variables associated with rival hypotheses, such that we might expect these other variables to negate the causal effect predicted by the theory. If the case nonetheless conforms to the theory, this provides evidence against these rival hypotheses and, therefore, strong support for the theory. This contrasts with a **most-likely case**, which is strongly expected to conform to the prediction of the theory. See **critical case**.

level of analysis. The level of aggregation on which a given study is focused. This should be understood within the framework of a hierarchy of levels. Examples of levels in such a hierarchy are individual actors, subnational units (cities, states, or provinces), national organizations (nation-states, or components of nation-states such as national legislatures or national political regimes), and the international system (relations among nations and international institutions).

At any given level of analysis, research may focus on different **units of observation**. For example, at the level of contemporary nation-states, it can focus on individuals (e.g., on top decision makers within the state), on characteristics of national institutions, or on aggregated features of the national population.

level of measurement. The generic label for the logical relations entailed in nominal, ordinal, interval, and ratio scales (as well as various other scale types). Different types of scales constitute successive levels of measurement, in that they sequentially incorporate into the scale (in the case of the four types just noted) the ideas of equal/nonequal, order, unit of measurement, and a mathematically meaningful zero. See also **typology**.

According to one major approach to measurement theory, measurement must ultimately be understood in terms of pairwise comparison among specific cases. Thus, a given level of measurement (or particular scale type) is based on: (1) a set of logical relations among cases located within a specified domain, logical relations which, in principle, must ultimately be validated by pairwise compari-

---

[8]Some confusion arises because large N and small N are hyphenated when they serve as a compound adjective, as in "large-N (or large-N) research"; but are not hyphenated when used as a noun, as in "they focused on a small N (or a large N)."

son of cases; and (2) the claim that these logical relations can validly be employed to compare those cases with respect to a given variable.

LISREL. A computer program (acronym for "Linear Structural Relations") that estimates causal models which explicitly incorporate the researcher's assumptions about measurement relations and causal relations. The more generic label is LISREL-type models or **covariance structure models**.

longitudinal analysis. Analysis of change over time, focused on one or more variables or cases. It is also called **time-series analysis**. See **cross-sectional analysis**.

mainstream quantitative methods. An approach to methodology strongly oriented toward regression analysis, econometric refinements on regression, and the search for statistical alternatives to regression models in contexts where specific regression assumptions are not met.

These refinements and alternatives include logit and probit models for categorical variables; corrections to regression models in the context of time-series analysis; methods for dealing with measurement error in regression analysis; and techniques that attempt to address, within the regression framework, problems such as simultaneity, **heteroskedasticity**, **autocorrelation**, and **causal heterogeneity**. Mainstream quantitative methods in this sense constitute a major corpus of methodological research that has developed and refined many widely used research tools, within what is basically the framework of regression models.

In relation to this research tradition of mainstream quantitative methods, the concerns expressed in the present volume are threefold. First, when researchers within this tradition address violations of basic regression assumptions, they usually consider only one or two assumptions at a time. They rarely give adequate attention to the possibility that simultaneously violating multiple assumptions may undermine the credibility of any given statistical inference. Second, the analytic procedures introduced to address the potential violation of assumptions in turn require making additional, generally untested assumptions, thereby possibly compounding the problem. Third, this research tradition sometimes becomes the basis for advocating the inherent superiority of quantitative methods, a position that, in light of the first two concerns, requires serious reflection. We argue that such concerns are more thoroughly considered in work on **statistical theory**.

matching cases. Cases that all have the same score on a particular dichotomous variable, or that all have similar scores on a continuous variable. See **contrasting cases**.

measurement. The process of making empirical observations in relation to a given concept. This includes, in addition to quantitative measurement, the scoring of cases carried out by qualitative researchers on the basis of categorical variables. An **indicator** is a specific procedure for measurement.

measurement error. Failure to perfectly operationalize a concept, due to the use of indicators that lack **reliability** and/or **validity**. See **measurement**.

measurement model. A set of understandings or hypotheses concerning the relationship between one or more **concepts** and one or more **indicators** of those concepts. This relationship may or may not be formalized mathematically.

measurement theory. A body of literature, associated with **psychometrics** and mathematical measurement theory, which has developed logical foundations and empirical tools for measurement.

measurement validity. The extent to which the scores produced by a given measurement procedure meaningfully reflect the concept being measured.

One view is that measurement validity is concerned with nonrandom error (or **bias**), and that **reliability**, which concerns **random error**, is a separate issue. However, according to other definitions, reliability is a requisite for **validity**. Measurement validity is an issue in both quantitative measurement and qualitative classification.

method of agreement. A research design that compares cases which are matched (i.e., in *agreement*) on one of the main variables of concern (either an independent or a dependent variable), and which *differ* on other variables understood to be potential causes or effects of that variable. However, in current usage, this label is generally employed more specifically for designs in which cases are matched on the dependent variable and differ from one another on many explanatory variables. The method was proposed by J. S. Mill.[9] Contrast with **method of difference**.

method of difference. A research design that compares cases which *differ* on one of the main variables of concern (either an independent or a dependent variable), but that are *similar* on other variables understood to be potential causes or effects of that variable. However, in current usage, this label is generally employed more specifically for designs in which cases differ on the dependent variable and are matched (i.e., in agreement) on many explanatory variables. This method was proposed by J. S. Mill. Contrast with **method of agreement**.

---

[9]Mill (1974b [1843]). It is well known that Mill (1974a [1843]) argued that the methods of agreement and difference are not applicable in the social sciences, yet they remain an important point of reference in social science methodology.

The expression "most similar systems design," introduced by Przeworski and Teune (1970), refers to essentially this same research design. With Przeworski and Teune's label, the term *similar* refers to the matching of cases with respect to alternative explanations. With both approaches, the key step in causal inference is to find, along with the many explanatory variables on which the cases are matched, one on which they differ—which is thus congruent with the difference on the dependent variable.[10] This congruence is then used as the basis for a causal inference.

Mill's methods of agreement and difference. See method of agreement, method of difference.

missing variable. A theoretically relevant variable that, if added to a causal model, would change estimates of the effects of other explanatory variables. A model with no missing variables in this sense still may not explain all the variance in the dependent variable. Rather, other things being equal, the expected values of the causal estimates for a model with no missing variables will be nearly correct. Also called an **omitted variable** or **confounder**.

missing variable bias. Bias introduced in causal inference when a theoretically relevant explanatory variable is missing. As a consequence of missing variable bias, the causal estimate for any given variable that is included may be too large, in which case the causal effect attributed to the included variable is at least partially spurious. Alternatively, the estimate may be too small, in which case the missing variable is a suppressor variable; or the estimate may have the wrong sign, in which case the missing variable is a distorter variable. See **missing variable**.

model. A framework of concepts, descriptive claims, and causal hypotheses, through which the analyst seeks to abstract understanding and knowledge from

---

[10]In characterizing the most similar systems design, Przeworski and Ţeune state that "common systemic characteristics are conceived as 'controlled for,' whereas intersystemic differences are viewed as explanatory variables. The number of common characteristics sought is maximal and the number of not shared characteristics sought, minimal" (1970: 33). However, they go on to point out that "although the number of differences among similar countries is limited, it will almost invariably be sufficiently large to 'overdetermine' the dependent phenomenon" (34); they then characterize this design as based on "concomitant variation," which is in fact another one of Mill's methods. By contrast, Przeworski and Teune's "most different systems" design (1970: chap. 2) begins with the cross-national analysis of individual-level data. If the researcher discovers that individual-level patterns are not homogeneous across national units, then the focus shifts to analyzing the differences among the national units (1970: 34–35). Thus, it is in fact not parallel to Mill's method of agreement.

the complexities of the real world. A model is often seen as a more systematized version of a **theory**. See **causal model**, **measurement model**.

model, causal. See causal model.

most-likely case. A case that is strongly expected to conform to the prediction of a particular theory. If the case does not meet this expectation, there is a basis for revising or rejecting the theory. This contrasts with a **least-likely case**, which is strongly expected not to conform to the prediction of the theory. See **critical case**.

multicollinearity. A problem of statistical estimation and inference, in which high correlations among independent variables make it difficult to separate, and hence to estimate, their individual effects. Sometimes also called collinearity.

This problem is related to the issue of **degrees of freedom**, in that the larger the number of independent cases in relation to the number of parameters to be estimated, the easier it is to deal with multicollinearity. With perfect multicollinearity, there is a perfect linear relationship among two or more independent variables, and the coefficients cannot be separately estimated. See **determinate** and **indeterminate research design**, **identification**.

multiple conjunctural causation. See causation, multiple and conjunctural.

N. The number of cases in a given study. The N also corresponds to the number of rows in a **rectangular data set**, that is, to the number of **data-set observations**.

natural experiment. A specific type of **quasi-experiment** in which the researcher can present compelling evidence that the treatment is uncorrelated with rival explanatory variables.

The treatment and control groups in a natural experiment are viewed as similar in all relevant respects except for the hypothesized cause. Frequently, this means specifically that deliberate human choices are not involved in determining which individuals or social units experience the treatment and which do not. Although a natural experiment still involves observational data, the researcher has additional leverage, in comparison with conventional observational studies, for adjudicating among rival explanations.

necessary cause. A cause whose presence is required for the outcome to occur. Correspondingly, its absence definitively prevents the outcome. It is also called a necessary condition. See **sufficient cause**.

negative cases. Theoretically or substantively relevant cases in which an outcome of concern does not occur. This label is sometimes used more broadly with a nondichotomous dependent variable in referring to cases in which, to a substantial degree, the outcome does not occur. See **contrast space**, **positive cases**.

nested inference. A causal inference that draws on both **data-set observations** and **causal-process observations**, sometimes at different levels of analysis. Such inference takes advantage of the distinctive contribution offered by each type of observation.[11] See **triangulation**.

Neyman-Rubin-Holland model. A counterfactual theory of causation. According to this view, we cannot observe causation directly, but must make inferences about it in other ways, ideally with randomized experiments. Alternatively, and much more problematically, researchers may address causation in **observational studies**, using statistical tests and other analytic tools that approximate the procedures followed in experiments.

According to this account, the idea that "X causes Y" in any given unit of analysis raises the hypothetical question of how the outcome on Y would have differed if X had been prevented from occurring in that unit. Given that it is impossible to observe both the occurrence and nonoccurrence of X for any given unit at one point in time, causal inference in effect involves comparing something that did occur with something that did not occur. This is the source of the **fundamental problem of causal inference**. While this is sometimes called the Rubin-Holland model, the central influence of Neyman makes it more appropriate to designate this as the Neyman-Rubin-Holland model (see, for example, Neyman 1923 [1990]; Rubin 1990).

Neyman, Rubin, and Holland embrace a "hypothetical manipulationist" view of causation, closely identified with the experimental tradition, in which a given factor can only be viewed as a potential cause if it can in principle be subjected to experimental manipulation. While respecting this view, and adopting other important components of the Neyman-Rubin-Holland framework, both *DSI* and the present volume see the strict hypothetical manipulationist position as sometimes being too limiting for the social sciences.

nominal scale. See level of measurement.

nonconforming cases. See **deviant cases**.

no-variance design. A research design with no variance (or little variance) on the main dependent variable. See **method of agreement**.

null hypothesis. A hypothesis against which the main hypothesis is tested. It is often, but not always, the hypothesis that there is no relationship.

---

[11]This term is adapted from Coppedge (2001) and Lieberman (2003a).

observable implications. Empirical observations suggested by a given hypothesis. To the extent that such observations are found, this is routinely treated as evidence in support of the hypothesis.

observation. Information about the world that is collected in a given study. See **causal-process observation**, **data-set observation**.

observational data. Data in which the values of all variables are produced by real-world events and processes not subject to the direct control of the investigator. Contrast with **experimental data**.

observational study. A study based on **observational data**, in which the values of all variables are produced by real-world events and processes not subject to the direct control of the investigator. Contrast with **experimental data**.[12]

omitted variable. See missing variable.

omitted variable bias. See missing variable bias.

operationalization. The process of using **indicators** to measure concepts.

ordinal scale. See level of measurement.

outcome variable. The phenomenon that the researcher seeks to explain. It is hypothesized to be caused by one or more other variables. The term outcome variable is often used interchangeably with dependent variable. Independent variable (or explanatory variable) is the standard label for the hypothesized cause.

outlier. A **deviant case** in the relationship among two or more variables. It is sometimes also used to mean an extreme value on a given variable.

overarching goals. See goals, overarching.

parameter. A characteristic of a **causal model** that the researcher seeks to estimate. In **regression analysis**, the parameters that usually receive the most attention are the coefficients associated with each of the independent variables. Another major usage of the term parameter is to identify any feature of a population that the researcher seeks to estimate on the basis of a sample statistic.

---

[12]Rosenbaum (2002: 1–2) uses the term "observational study" much more narrowly. In his usage, it must involve a treatment, manipulation, or intervention that is applied to some cases and not to others. The distinction between an observational study in this sense and an experiment is simply that the experiment uses random assignment, while the observational study does not. To date, this usage has not become standard in the social sciences, and in the present volume we follow the more conventional usage.

parameter estimation. The use of available data to make inferences about a given characteristic or trait. In a typical regression analysis, parameter estimation involves finding values for the coefficients associated with each independent variable, as well as any other parameters included in the model.

Tools used in conjunction with parameter estimation allow researchers to carry out tests of statistical significance for specific parameters, as well as some tests that may help them improve or reject the model as a whole. Nevertheless, because statistical tools for parameter estimation rely on the assumption that the model is in fact correct, parameter estimation does not fully test the model.

parsimony. The use of few explanatory variables in a theory or **explanation**.

path dependence. A pattern of causation in which events or processes at one point in time strongly constrain subsequent events or processes. See **critical juncture**.

population. See universe of cases.

positive cases. Cases in which an outcome of concern does occur. This label is sometimes used more broadly with a nondichotomous dependent variable in referring to cases in which, to a substantial degree, the outcome occurs. See **contrast space**, **negative cases**.

power of a statistical test. The probability that a test will reject the **null hypothesis** when it is in fact false.

A test with greater power more effectively adjudicates between the null hypothesis and the hypothesis of interest. Increasing statistical power is one tool, although hardly the only tool, for strengthening causal inference. See **degrees of freedom**, **determinate research design**, **parameter estimation**, **significance test**.

probabilistic. Containing an element of randomness. Generally used interchangeably with **stochastic**. Contrast with **deterministic**.

probabilistic cause. A cause that makes a given outcome more likely (or less likely), but not inevitable. See **deterministic**.

probability theory. A body of mathematical theory concerned with analyzing the odds that uncertain events will occur.

process tracing. Analysis of processes of change that seeks to uncover **causal mechanisms** and **causal sequences**. A basic tool of qualitative methods. See **case study**, **intervening variable**.

psychometrics. The subfield of psychology concerned with **measurement theory** and tools for measurement.

The name of this subfield might lead some qualitative researchers in political science and sociology to conclude that its concerns are remote from their own. However, this subfield has been an area of considerable innovation in addressing the challenges of measuring difficult concepts and the idea that measurement is inherently context specific.

qualitative. See **qualitative-quantitative distinction.**

Qualitative Comparative Analysis (QCA). A systematization of small-N comparative analysis and **analytic induction** developed by Ragin (1987), based on Boolean algebra.

qualitative-quantitative distinction. A common heuristic distinction usefully understood in terms of four overlapping dimensions: level of measurement, size of the N, statistical tests, and thick versus thin analysis.

Although some studies are unambiguously qualitative or quantitative according to these criteria, mixed types are equally important, given the wide interest in combining tools of qualitative and quantitative analysis. However, the simple qualitative-quantitative dichotomy has productively structured much of the current debate.

a. Level of measurement. Some scholars label **data** as qualitative if it is organized at a nominal level of measurement, and as quantitative if it is organized in terms of ordinal and higher levels of measurement. Alternatively, the threshold is sometimes placed between ordinal data and data that are at least at the interval level.

b. Size of the N. The qualitative-quantitative distinction is sometimes identified with the contrast between small-N and large-N research, involving the number of observations analyzed by the investigator. It is certainly not meaningful to insist on a specific cut-point between these alternatives, but it might be placed somewhere between 10 and 20.

c. Statistical tests. An analysis may be considered quantitative—even if it focuses on nominal scales—if it utilizes explicit statistical tests in reaching its descriptive and explanatory conclusions. By contrast, qualitative research employs a "verbal" style of analysis, often involving narrative treatment of the material. Adopting a verbal style of analysis does not mean that qualitative researchers work only with nominal variables; indeed, they employ variables at all levels of **measurement**. Moreover, they compare alternative indicators in the course of constructing composite measures and assessing **measurement validity**, and they may assess hypotheses through examining covariation among variables.

Thus, they perform research operations that are in some respects analogous to standard statistical tests, yet they do not actually employ such tests.

d. Thick versus thin analysis. Qualitative researchers are more inclined toward thick analysis that relies on detailed knowledge of specific cases. By contrast, quantitative researchers are more strongly oriented toward thin analysis, which relies on a more limited knowledge of each case and typically depends instead on a larger N for inferential leverage.[13]

quantitative. See mainstream quantitative methods, qualitative-quantitative distinction.

quantitative methods, mainstream. See mainstream quantitative methods.

quasi-experiment. An **observational study** that in some respects resembles an experiment. Specifically, the researcher observes one or more cases after (and often before) what may be thought of as a "treatment," involving a change in an explanatory variable at a given point in time. This treatment can be a major policy change or some other large-scale political event, such as a revolution, or an individual choice, for example, a decision that a child will go to an integrated or segregated school. Thus, the treatment involves real-world events produced by the unfolding of political and social processes. See, **natural experiment**, **interrupted time-series design**.

An important intellectual legacy of research on quasi-experiments is **Campbell's checklist of threats to validity**, which offers an important alternative to conventional discussions of the threats to validity encountered in observational studies.

random assignment. See **randomization.**

random error. Error that is not attributable to any systematic relationship. Contrast with **systematic error**.

randomization. Assignment of values (e.g., treatment or control) on an independent variable to different cases according to an impartial chance procedure. See **experiment**.

---

[13]This distinction draws on Coppedge's (1999) discussion of thick versus thin concepts. Neither our distinction nor that of Coppedge should be confused with Geertz's (1973) distinction between "thick description," which focuses on the meaning of human behavior to the actors involved, as opposed to "thin description," which is not centrally concerned with this meaning. With the expression "thick analysis," we mean research that focuses closely on the details of cases. These details may or may not encompass subjective meaning. In this sense, Geertz's thick description is one tool for what we call thick analysis.

random sample. A sample selected in such a manner that all cases from the relevant **universe of cases** have a known probability of being selected.

ratio scale. See level of measurement.

rectangular data set. An array or matrix of data in which the rows correspond to cases and the columns to variables. The variables in the columns include all dependent and independent variables. A rectangular data set may contain either quantitative or qualitative data. It is often called a **data set**.

regression analysis. An extension of correlation analysis, which makes predictions about the value of a dependent variable using data about one or more independent variables. A key **parameter** estimated in a regression analysis is the magnitude of change in the dependent variable associated with a unit change in an independent variable. This parameter is referred to as the slope or the regression coefficient.

reliability. The stability of an indicator over (potentially hypothetical) replications of the measurement procedure. Reliability involves the magnitude of **random error**. Repeated application of a reliable measure to a subject who has not changed regarding the trait being measured produces results that cluster in a narrow range. See **measurement validity**.

replication. An attempt to reproduce the findings of a given study. Two different research practices are both called replication: a narrow version, which involves reanalyzing the original data, and a broader version based on collecting and analyzing new data.

research cycle. The sequence of steps typically undertaken in research. These commonly include defining the **research problem**, **specifying the theory**, selecting cases, carrying out descriptive and causal inference, and sometimes the **iterated refinement of hypotheses**, based on movement back and forth between data and hypotheses. The later steps in this cycle routinely provide insight that may lead the researcher to revise the earlier steps, and in practice, researchers may move in many different ways among these steps.

research design. A plan for carrying out a given study, commonly involving a sequence of research steps such as those listed under **research cycle**.

research problem. See research question.

research program. A coordinated effort to address a given set of research questions.[14] Whereas a **research design** is a plan for carrying out a specific study, a research program encompasses a number of studies and the work of many scholars.

research question. The theoretical or empirical puzzle that motivates a given study. It is also called a research problem.

Rubin-Holland model. See Neyman-Rubin-Holland model.

sample. The set of cases on which the analysis is focused, and which are often selected from a larger **universe of cases**. Selecting cases is a fundamental task of **research design**, and scholars in different research traditions have approached this task in a variety of ways. See **random sample**.

sampling error. Random error in inferences from a **sample** to a **universe of cases**. This error occurs because the sample, although randomly drawn, is imperfectly representative of the universe. Sampling error is sometimes contrasted with sampling **bias**, which involves **systematic error**. Sampling error can affect the **validity** or **reliability** of descriptive and causal inference. See **sample**.

scientific. A normative view of the theoretical, methodological, and empirical goals of research.

Alternative definitions of "scientific" express different normative views. For example, *DSI* (8–9) presents a four-part definition of "scientific research" that is fundamental to the book's framework: Scientific research is based on **inference**, it makes its procedures public, it views conclusions as inherently uncertain, and its findings are judged in light of the method employed. Some other definitions, by contrast, place central emphasis on building theory and accumulating knowledge. Scientific research is thus a prominent example of a contested concept.

scope conditions. Criteria that specify the appropriate range of cases (i.e., the **universe of cases**) to which a theory applies.

score. The value assumed by a variable for a given case. This includes not only quantitative scores, but also the results of qualitative classification. A score is sometimes informally called an **observation**.

selecting on the dependent variable. Any pattern of case selection that overrepresents cases at one end of the dependent variable. That is to say, the researcher tends to select cases that consistently have higher, or lower, values on the de-

---

[14]The term is thus often used in a broad sense, and not with the relatively specific meaning intended by Lakatos (1970).

pendent variable. The form of selecting on the dependent variable that receives most attention in the present volume is **truncation**.

Selecting on the dependent variable is routinely viewed as a source of **selection bias**. In regression analysis, truncation does indeed produce such bias. However, some modes of selecting on the dependent variable do not yield selection bias. For example, if the analyst selects on the dependent variable indirectly by choosing cases that have high scores on a key independent variable, this will yield cases with high scores on the dependent variable, but will not produce selection bias—because it does not constrain the error term.

"Selecting on the dependent variable" sometimes has an alternative meaning, in that it is used to designate the deliberate selection of cases that reflect the full range of that variable. In this instance, the mode of selection may not be correlated with the dependent variable.

selection bias. Systematic error that arises either when cases are selected according to an unrepresentative sampling rule, or when some (often unknown) nonrandom process assigns causes to cases. Such bias can result from selection procedures employed by the investigator, from self-selection of individuals or other units of analysis into the sample, or from self-selection of the cases under study into the categories of a major independent variable. In this last situation, causes may in effect be assigned to cases in a way that reinforces preexisting differences among the cases. Under any of these conditions, tests of explanatory hypotheses routinely suffer from systematic error.

The source of selection bias of primary concern in the present volume is deliberate **truncation** by the investigator, which yields bias due to the interplay among three elements. Thus, truncation on (1) the dependent variable produces selection bias by creating a **correlation** between (2) the independent variable and (3) the **error term**. This correlation yields bias because it flattens the slope of the regression line in the truncated sample. Alternative sources of selection bias are real-world political or social processes that "select" cases into the sample or into key analytic categories in ways that confound the impact of a hypothesized cause with the selection mechanism. These processes may include self-selection by the individuals being studied.

Selection bias is generally treated as an issue in regression analysis. **Within-case analysis** in the qualitative tradition, which employs different tools of causal inference, may not be subject to this form of bias.

shared standards. Commonly accepted methodological norms for the conduct of research. The **overarching goals** of valid descriptive and causal inference and of building theory are central to the idea of shared standards.

The present volume argues that scholars face basic **trade-offs** in selecting research **tools** and also in choosing **intermediate goals**. The idea of shared standards centrally involves the search for common criteria in evaluating and managing these trade-offs.

significance test. A tool for addressing the concern that an observed relationship could be due to **sampling error** or other hypothesized forms of random error. It thus provides a set of rules for deciding when empirical evidence suggests a relationship that is not simply due to chance.

In contemporary social science, significance tests are often treated much more broadly as a general-purpose test for the **validity** and **reliability** of causal inferences, a practice that extends these tests beyond the uses for which they were designed and raises serious concerns among some statisticians.

small N. A small number of cases. Contrast with **large N.**

specification. The construction or revision of a **causal model.**[15] Specification is the process of establishing the variables to be included, the functional form of the model, and the assumptions relevant to making inferences with the model. See **specification assumption, specification search, underspecified model.**

specification assumption. An assumption used to justify causal inferences based on observational data, that is, in the absence of a true experiment.[16] If the specification assumption is met, researchers can expect to achieve estimates that are unbiased.

Two major threats to this assumption are: (1) excluding a variable that should be included in the analysis, which can produce **omitted variable bias;** and (2) including an **endogenous variable** without using an analytic technique that successfully corrects for the endogeneity, so that endogeneity bias is likely.

---

[15]The process of specification is also important in noncausal statistical models, such as forecasting models.

[16]To define the specification assumption formally, in a context where the true causal relation is $Y = X\beta + W\gamma + \varepsilon$ and where the analyst wishes to estimate a regression model that posits the relationship $Y = Xb + e$, the specification assumption requires that $E(e|X) = 0$. By comparison with the true causal model, we see that $e = W\gamma + \varepsilon$. Therefore, in order to meet the specification assumption, each explanatory variable in X must be statistically unrelated to W and ε. A variable that is statistically unrelated to W and ε is exogenous, whereas one that is related to any variable in W or to ε is endogenous. It should be clear from this discussion that the specification assumption involves many issues beyond those assessed through residual plots and other standard tools of regression diagnostics. To clarify the notation, Y, ε, and e are vectors with one value per case, β, γ, and b are vectors with one value per relevant variable, and W and X are matrices with one column per relevant variable and one row per case.

Meeting the specification assumption is a requirement for valid causal inference, but it is not by itself sufficient. Scholars must also know enough about the structure of the **error term** to judge the amount of independent information contributed by each observation. Further, scholars must present evidence that makes it appropriate to treat the statistical inference as causal. The clearest and most common example of how this step may be taken is found in studies that employ **natural experiments**, where evidence is used to show that variation in the hypothesized cause is due to exogenous manipulation. The specification assumption encompasses several issues of causal inference that are also addressed through the assumption of **conditional independence**.

specification search. An iterated process of fitting a model to data. The literature on specification searches has sought to develop a disciplined approach to this task that considers where such a search should start, where it should stop, and how to report the steps in between. By contrast, **data mining** often implies carrying out this task in an undisciplined manner that inappropriately increases the likelihood of finding a model that fits the data.

specifying the theory. Clarifying theoretical arguments to the point where they can generate specific hypotheses. This is one step in a **research cycle**.

spurious correlation. A relationship in which two or more variables are statistically related (i.e., correlated), but are not causally linked. Rather, the statistical relationship occurs because a third variable causes both of them. See **confounder, missing variable bias**.

standardized slope. A regression coefficient that has been adjusted to make it comparable with the coefficients for other independent variables with different ranges and variances. Thus, all variables are standardized to have a mean of zero and a variance of one. Contrast with **unstandardized slope**.

standards, shared. See shared standards.

statistical control. See **control**.

statistical power. See **power of statistical tests**.

statistical theory. A broad framework for reasoning about evidence and inference, employing mathematical probability theory to address tasks such as measurement, selecting estimators for causal inference, and inference from samples to populations.

The present volume devotes central attention to the distinction between important ideas drawn from statistical theory and **mainstream quantitative methods**. A well-established tradition of thinking in statistical theory, dating back to the emergence of statistics as an academic discipline, expresses serious doubts about the applicability of the assumptions behind regression analysis and related tools to **observational data** in the social sciences.[17] Correspondingly, this statistical tradition sometimes advocates techniques that allow researchers to draw more delimited inferences that depend on fewer untested assumptions about the data. By contrast, mainstream quantitative methodologists sometimes strongly advocate regression-based tools.

Statistical theory is understood here as a multidisciplinary body of work that encompasses, in addition to research by statisticians, other lines of research in **econometrics**, **psychometrics**, and **measurement theory**, as well as some methodological contributions by scholars in disciplines such as political science and sociology.

Although work in statistical theory is sometimes thought of as distinctively linked to quantitative analysis, it may also offer a rationale for some practices of qualitative investigation. For example, this statistical tradition provides part of the justification for **causal-process observations**.[18]

stochastic. A model or process containing an element of randomness or error. It is used interchangeably with **probabilistic**. Contrast with **deterministic**.

stratification. An approach to causal inference that controls for alternative explanations by using categorical measures of independent variables to create subgroups of the data that effectively hold these rival explanatory factors constant. Causal inferences are then made within each subgroup. This involves multivariate cross tabulation, and is a standard form of hypothesis testing in experiments.[19] Compare with **elaboration model**.

---

[17]This statistical tradition grows out of debates among statisticians on causal inference in experiments and observational studies. It may be dated to Karl Pearson's 1896 critique of G. Udny Yule's causal assessment, based on a regression analysis of observational data, of the relation between welfare policy and poverty in Britain (Stigler 1986: 351–53, 358). For a recent statement about this tradition, see Freedman (1999).

[18]The distinction between statistical theory and mainstream quantitative methods is not intended to imply that these are sharply bounded categories. Many scholars are located between these alternatives, and all work by any given scholar will not always fall in the same category. Indeed, it is likely that some statistical theorists become mainstream quantitative methodologists when they turn to applied work. Further, analytic tools that are sometimes called "quantitative tests" may also be called "statistical tests," and this choice about labeling should not be seen as reflecting a position vis-à-vis the larger distinction between mainstream quantitative methods and statistical theory.

[19]The assumptions relevant to different tools of causal inference merit brief comment here. The conditional independence assumption, which employs the experimental tradition as a metaphor, is directly relevant to causal inference based on stratification. Other inferential tools, such as regression analysis, employ related assumptions, including the specifica-

subtype. A concept or category derived from a broader concept, with the goal of introducing finer differentiation. Subtypes are often formed by adding an adjective to the noun that designates the original concept, as in "parliamentary democracy."

sufficient cause. A cause whose presence inevitably produces an outcome. This is also called a sufficient condition. See **necessary cause**.

systematic error. Error whose direction and magnitude can in principle be predicted, as opposed to **random error**. With systematic error, the expected value of a given statistic is **biased**, because the errors do not cancel one another out.

term. A word that designates a **concept**. Other more specialized usages are also found in this volume, as in **error term**.

test of significance. See **significance test**.

theory. The conceptual and explanatory understandings that are an essential point of departure in conducting research, and that in turn are revised in light of research. Different analytic traditions have divergent norms about the appropriate structure and content of these understandings. A **causal model** draws on, and is part of, a theory.

thick analysis. See thick versus thin analysis.

thick description. A description or characterization of the meaning of human behavior from the standpoint of the individuals whose behavior is being observed (Geertz 1973). This is not to be confused with detailed description, which may or may not be thick in this sense. This term is often used interchangeably with **interpretation** and *Verstehen*.

thick versus thin analysis. A distinction that captures different styles of research and sources of analytic leverage. Some investigators utilize thick analysis, in the sense that they have a rich knowledge of cases.[20] If this knowledge is utilized effectively, it can greatly strengthen descriptive and causal inference. By contrast, researchers who deal with large numbers of cases more frequently rely on thin

---

tion assumption. For many purposes, such as helping analysts focus on the potential problem of missing variable bias in causal inference, it is productive to emphasize the similarities between these two assumptions. However, the distinctive strengths of different research tools (e.g., stratification versus regression) often depend on the contrasts among the many different sets of assumptions that serve to justify these tools.

[20]This usage is adapted from Coppedge (1997). A related distinction is made by *DSI* (154) in contrasting the "descriptive richness" of nominal categories with the "facilitation of comparison" at higher levels of measurement.

analysis, in the sense that they depend not on detailed knowledge of cases, but rather on the inferential leverage that derives from statistical tools applied to a large N. Whereas the capacity to use statistical tests is a distinctive strength of quantitative research, the leverage gained from thick analysis is a characteristic strength of qualitative research. **Thick description**, which is concerned with interpreting meaning, should be seen as one tool of thick analysis, as defined here.

thin analysis. See thick versus thin analysis.

thought experiment. Reasoning about phenomena that have not been observed. See **counterfactual analysis**.

time-series analysis. Analysis focused on change over time. It is also called **longitudinal analysis**. Contrast with **cross-sectional analysis**.

tipping point. A discontinuity or inflection in a process of change over time. Thus, it is a point at which a previous trend ends and a new one begins.

tool. A specific research procedure or practice. Some tools are highly systematized and have elaborate mathematical underpinnings: **probability theory**, **regression analysis**, **significance tests**, and **covariance structure models**. Increasing the number of observations is likewise a tool that has routinely been justified on the grounds that it increases **inferential leverage.** Other tools involve practices and procedures that are not explicitly rooted in statistics or mathematics. This second group of tools includes **within-case analysis**, **process tracing**, **triangulation**, procedures for avoiding **conceptual stretching**, qualitative **validity** assessment, and strategies for the comparison of **matching** and **contrasting cases**. Methods of data collection are also tools, such as public opinion research, focus groups, participant observation, event scoring, content analysis, archival research, the construction of unobtrusive measures, and systematic collection of secondary data. See **goals, trade-off**.

trade-off. Incompatibility among desired objectives.

triangulation. Research procedure that employs empirical evidence derived from more than one method or from more than one type of data. Triangulation can strengthen the **validity** of both descriptive and causal inference.[21] See **nested inference**.

---

[21]The idea of triangulation and of multimethod triangles can be dated to Campbell and Fiske (1959: 38–39), who in turn cite the philosopher Feigl (1958) as the source of this concept.

truncation. A selection process that omits cases located in some specific part of the distribution of values for a given variable. Omitting cases above or below a given value is the form of truncation of concern in the present volume.[22]
The difference between truncation and "censoring" is that with truncated samples, no data are available on any of the omitted cases. By contrast, some data are available for the cases subject to censoring. See **selection bias**.

typology. A coordinated set of categories or types that establishes theoretically relevant analytic distinctions. It is often formed by cross-tabulating two or more nominal or ordinal variables, with the cells in the resulting table becoming the categories in the typology. Each category commonly has a name. A typology is usually, but not always, a nominal (or occasionally an ordinal) scale. See **level of measurement**.

uncertainty. Lack of complete knowledge.

underspecified model. A model with the problem of **missing variable bias.** More specifically, theoretically relevant variables are missing which, if added to the model, would change the estimates of causal effects for the already-included variables. See **specification**.

unidentifiability. See **identifiability**.

unit homogeneity. The strong assumption for causal inference that the units in an analysis are completely identical in all relevant respects except for the dependent and independent variables of interest. A somewhat weaker assumption is defined above as **causal homogeneity**. Although *DSI* uses the label "unit homogeneity," its framework instead relies centrally on the idea of causal homogeneity. Hence, in discussing their arguments, we use the label "causal homogeneity."

units of analysis. See **units of observation**.

units of observation. The individuals, institutions, entities, or objects about which data are collected. In studies based on **data-set observations**, each unit typically receives a score on each variable. This should not be confused with **level of analysis**, in that, at any given level of analysis, researchers may make different choices about units of observation. Also called cases or **units of analysis**.

universe of cases. The set of cases about which the analyst seeks to make inferences. Research may focus on a **sample** of cases from within this universe, with the goal of making inferences to the universe. Alternatively, in some studies the

---

[22]This is sometimes called "outer" truncation. By contrast, "inner" truncation omits cases within a given range of values but includes cases above and below that range.

set of cases under analysis is the universe. Identifying a conceptually and theoretically appropriate definition of the universe is a basic task of research. Universe of cases is often used interchangeably with **population**. See **scope conditions**.

unstandardized slope. A regression coefficient that is not adjusted to account for
the differing means and variances of the variables entered into the analysis. The
unstandardized slope has the advantage that it is not affected by the variance of
the independent variables; it has the disadvantage that the unstandardized slopes
associated with different explanatory variables are typically not expressed in the
same measurement units, and hence may be hard to compare. Contrast with
standardized slope.

validity. The adequacy of descriptive and causal inference. See **external validity**,
internal validity, **measurement validity**, **reliability**.

value. The **score** assumed by a variable for a particular case.

variable. A systematized understanding of similarities and differences among
observed phenomena. Different levels of measurement reflect some of the alternative logical forms that this systematized understanding can take.

The term variable is sometimes used interchangeably with **concept** and with
indicator. See: **antecedent, background, dependent, endogenous, exogenous,
explanatory, independent, intervening, latent, missing, omitted**, and **outcome variable**. See also **missing variable bias, level of measurement**, and
thick versus thin analysis.

variable-oriented research. Analysis that typically focuses on a large number of
cases and on systematically analyzing a well-defined set of variables for these
cases. This term is identified with Ragin (1987). Variable-oriented researchers
may engage in fine-grained examination of cases, but their attention is centered
more strongly on understanding the cases in terms of this set of variables. Contrast with **case-oriented research**.

Verstehen. A description or characterization of the meaning of human behavior
from the standpoint of the individuals who are being observed. Often used interchangeably with **interpretation** and **thick description**.

within-case analysis. The internal analysis of one or a few cases. Within-case
analysis takes two principal forms, the first of which is of central concern in the
present volume.

The first type, especially identified with the qualitative tradition, focuses on
internal evidence about patterns of causation connected with an overall outcome

distinctively associated with the particular case or cases. Familiar examples include in-depth studies of macrolevel events such as wars, revolutions, and regime change, although the focus may be at other levels of analysis as well. In such within-case analysis, scholars work with only one observation on the dependent variable (e.g., war broke out, revolution was averted, or democracy collapsed). Correspondingly, new evidence is introduced, but the number of observations (i.e., the N) is not increased. The additional evidence added by such within-case analysis contributes to evaluating explanations of this single outcome on the basis of **causal-process observations**.

In the second type of within-case analysis, researchers collect observations on the dependent variable and all the independent variables for multiple (spatial or temporal) subunits of the original case. In this instance, the number of observations (i.e., the N) increases, and this can be seen, within the framework of *DSI*, as an important example of increasing the number of observations as a means of gaining inferential leverage. When scholars study subunits in this way, within-case analysis in effect becomes **cross-case analysis** and focuses on **data-set observations**.

within-case control. A procedure that uses predictions about causal mechanisms to distinguish between systematic and random aspects of a given outcome within a single case. Researchers achieve within-case control by exploring causal processes to determine which aspects of a decision or an outcome were influenced by a set of hypothesized systematic variables, and which were influenced by other, idiosyncratic factors.

Bibliography

Abbott, Andrew. 1988. "Transcending General Linear Reality." *Sociological Theory* 6, no. 2: 169–86.

———. 1992. "From Causes to Events: Notes on Narrative Positivism." *Sociological Methods and Research* 20, no. 4: 428–55.

———. 2001. *Time Matters: On Theory and Method.* Chicago: University of Chicago Press.

Achen, Christopher H. 1977. "Measuring Representation: Perils of the Correlation Coefficient." *American Journal of Political Science* 21, no. 4 (November): 805–15.

———. 1982. *Interpreting and Using Regression.* Beverly Hills, Calif.: Sage Publications.

———. 1983. "Toward Theories of Data: The State of Political Methodology." In Ada W. Finifter, ed., *Political Science: The State of the Discipline.* Washington, D.C.: American Political Science Association.

———. 1986. *The Statistical Analysis of Quasi-Experiments.* Berkeley: University of California Press.

———. 2000. "Warren Miller and the Future of Political Data Analysis." *Political Analysis* 8, no. 2: 142–46.

———. 2002. "Toward a New Political Methodology: Microfoundations and ART." *Annual Review of Political Science,* vol. 5, 423–50. Palo Alto, Calif.: Annual Reviews.

Achen, Christopher H., and Duncan Snidal. 1989. "Rational Deterrence Theory and Comparative Case Studies." *World Politics* 41, no. 2 (January): 143–69.

Achinstein, Peter. 1983. *The Nature of Explanation*. New York: Oxford University Press.

Adcock, Robert, and David Collier. 2001. "Measurement Validity: A Shared Standard for Qualitative and Quantitative Research." *American Political Science Review* 95, no. 3 (September): 529–46.

Alker, Hayward R. 1996. *Rediscoveries and Reformulations: Humanistic Methodologies for International Studies*. New York: Cambridge University Press.

Allen, William Sheridan. 1965. *The Nazi Seizure of Power: The Experience of a Single German Town, 1930–1935*. Chicago: Quadrangle Books.

Allison, Graham T. 1971. *Essence of Decision: Explaining the Cuban Missile Crisis*. Boston: Little, Brown.

Almond, Gabriel A., and Stephen J. Genco. 1977. "Clouds, Clocks, and the Study of Politics." *World Politics* 29, no. 4 (July): 489–522.

Alvarez, R. Michael, Geoffrey Garrett, and Peter Lange. 1991. "Government Partisanship, Labor Organization, and Macroeconomic Performance." *American Political Science Review* 85, no. 2 (June): 539–56.

Andrich, David. 1988. *Rasch Models for Measurement*. Newbury Park, Calif.: Sage Publications.

APSA-CP. 1996. "Replication Debate." APSA-CP, Newsletter of the APSA Organized Section in Comparative Politics 7, no. 1 (Winter): 5–13.

———. 2003. "Symposium on Bridging the Quantitative-Qualitative Divide." *APSA-CP, Newsletter of the APSA Organized Section in Comparative Politics* 14, no. 1 (Winter): 8–24.

Arendt, Hannah. 1958. *The Origins of Totalitarianism*. Cleveland, Ohio: World.

Aronson, Jerrold L., Rom Harré, and Eileen Cornell Way. 1994. *Realism Rescued: How Scientific Progress Is Possible*. London: Duckworth.

Arrow, Kenneth J. 1951. *Social Choice and Individual Values*. New Haven: Yale University Press.

Axelrod, Robert, ed. 1976. *Structure of Decision: The Cognitive Maps of Political Elites*. Princeton: Princeton University Press.

Babbie, Earl R. 2004. *The Practice of Social Research*. 10th edition. Belmont, Calif.: Wadsworth.

Bailey, Kenneth D. 1994. *Typologies and Taxonomies: An Introduction to Classification Techniques.* Beverly Hills, Calif.: Sage Publications.

Bartels, Larry M. 1991. "Instrumental and 'Quasi-Instrumental' Variables." *American Journal of Political Science* 35, no. 3 (August): 777–800.

———. 1995. "Symposium on *Designing Social Inquiry*, Part 1." *The Political Methodologist* 6, no. 2 (Spring): 8–11.

———. 1996. "Pooling Disparate Observations." *American Journal of Political Science* 40, no. 3 (August): 905–42.

———. 1997. "Specification Uncertainty and Model Averaging." *American Journal of Political Science* 41, no. 2 (April): 641–74.

Bartels, Larry M., and Henry E. Brady. 1993. "The State of Quantitative Political Methodology." In Ada W. Finifter, ed., *Political Science: The State of the Discipline II*. Washington, D.C.: American Political Science Association.

Bartels, Larry M., and John Zaller. 2001. "Presidential Vote Models: A Recount." *PS: Political Science & Politics* 34, no. 1 (March): 9–20.

Barton, Allen H., and Paul F. Lazarsfeld. 1969 [1955]. "Some Functions of Qualitative Analysis in Social Research." In G. J. McCall and J. L. Simmons, eds., *Issues in Participant Observation*. Reading, Mass.: Addison-Wesley. Originally published in the Frankfurter Beitrage zur Soziologie, vol. 1. Frankfurt: Europaische Verlagsanstalt.

Bates, Robert H. 1981. *Markets and States in Tropical Africa: The Political Basis of Agricultural Policies*. Berkeley: University of California Press.

———. 1983. *Essays on the Political Economy of Rural Africa*. New York: Cambridge University Press.

Bates, Robert, Avner Greif, Margaret Levi, Jean-Laurent Rosenthal, and Barry Weingast. 1998. *Analytic Narratives*. Princeton: Princeton University Press.

Beck, Nathaniel, and Jonathan N. Katz. 1995. "What to Do (and Not to Do) with Time-Series Cross-Section Data in Comparative Politics." *American Political Science Review* 89, no. 3 (September): 634–47.

Beck, Nathaniel, Jonathan N. Katz, R. Michael Alvarez, Geoffrey Garrett, and Peter Lange. 1993. "Government Partisanship, Labor Organization, and Macroeconomic Performance: A Corrigendum." *American Political Science Review* 87, no. 4 (December): 945–48.

Bendix, Reinhard. 1963. "Concepts and Generalizations in Comparative Sociological Studies." *American Sociological Review* 28, no. 4 (August): 532–39.

Bennett, Andrew, and Alexander L. George. 1997a. "Case Study Methods and Research on the Democratic Peace." Paper presented at the American Political Science Association Conference, Washington D.C., August.

———. 1997b. "Process Tracing in Case Study Research." Paper presented at the MacArthur Foundation Workshop on Case Study Methods, Belfer Center for Science and International Affairs (BCSIA), Harvard University, October 17–19.

Berelson, Bernard R., Paul F. Lazarsfeld, and William N. McPhee. 1954. *Voting: A Study of Opinion Formation in a Presidential Campaign*. Chicago: University of Chicago Press.

Berk, Richard A. 2003. *Regression Analysis: A Constructive Critique*. Newbury Park, Calif.: Sage Publications.

Blalock, Hubert M., Jr. 1982. *Conceptualization and Measurement in the Social Sciences*. Beverly Hills, Calif.: Sage Publications.

Boix, Charles. 1998. *Political Parties, Growth and Equity: Conservative and Social Democratic Economic Strategies in the World Economy*. New York: Cambridge University Press.

Bollen, Kenneth A. 1989. *Structural Equations with Latent Variables*. New York: Wiley.

———. 1993. "Liberal Democracy: Validity and Method Factors in Cross-National Measures." *American Journal of Political Science* 37, no. 4 (November): 1207–30.

Bollen, Kenneth A., and Richard Lennox. 1991. "Conventional Wisdom on Measurement: A Structural Equation Perspective." *Psychological Bulletin* 110, no. 2: 305–15.

Brady, Henry E. 1995. "Symposium on Designing Social Inquiry, Part 2: Doing Good and Doing Better." *The Political Methodologist* 6, no. 2 (Spring): 11–19.

Brady, Henry E., and Stephen Ansolehebere. 1989. "The Nature of Utility Functions in Mass Publics." *American Political Science Review* 83, no. 1 (March): 165–92.

Braumoeller, Bear. 1999. "Small-N Logic and Large-N Research: Statistical Tests of Multiple Causal Path Theories." Paper prepared for presentation at the American Political Science Association (APSA) 1999 Annual meeting, Atlanta, September 2–5.

Braumoeller, Bear F., and Gary Goertz. 2000. "The Methodology of Necessary Conditions." *American Journal of Political Science* 44, no. 4 (October): 844–58.

———. 2002. "Watching Your Posterior: Bayes, Sampling Assumptions, Falsification, and Necessary Conditions." *Political Analysis* 10, no. 2 (Spring): 198–203.

Brody, Baruch A., and Richard E. Grandy, eds. 1989. *Readings in the Philosophy of Science*. 2nd edition. Englewood Cliffs, N.J.: Prentice-Hall.

Bueno de Mesquita, Bruce, and David Lalman. 1992. *War and Reason: Domestic and International Imperatives*. New Haven: Yale University Press.

Bunce, Valerie. 1981. *Do New Leaders Make a Difference? Executive Succession and Public Policy under Capitalism and Socialism*. Princeton: Princeton University Press.

Burger, Thomas. 1976. *Max Weber's Theory of Concept Formation: History, Laws, and Ideal Types*. Durham, N.C.: Duke University Press.

Cain, Bruce, John Ferejohn, and Morris Fiorina. 1987. *The Personal Vote: Constituency Service and Electoral Independence*. Cambridge, Mass.: Harvard University Press.

Campbell, Donald T. 1975. "'Degrees of Freedom' and the Case Study." *Comparative Political Studies* 8, no. 2 (July): 178–93.

———. 1988. *Methodology and Epistemology for Social Science*. Chicago: University of Chicago Press.

Campbell, Donald T., and Robert F. Boruch. 1975. "Making the Case for Randomized Assignment to Treatments by Considering the Alternatives: Six Ways in Which Quasi-Experimental Evaluations in Compensatory Education Tend to Underestimate Effects." In Carl A. Bennett and Arthur A. Lumsdaine, eds., *Evaluation and Experiment: Some Critical Issues in Assessing Social Programs*. New York: Academic Press.

Campbell, Donald T., and Donald W. Fiske. 1959. "Convergent and Discriminant Validation by the Multitrait-Multimethod Matrix." *Psychological Bulletin* 56, no. 2 (March): 81–105.

Campbell, Donald T., and H. Laurence Ross. 1968. "The Connecticut Crackdown on Speeding: Time-Series Data in Quasi-Experimental Analysis." *Law and Society Review* 3, no. 1 (August): 33–53.

Campbell, Donald T., and Julian C. Stanley. 1966. *Experimental and Quasi-Experimental Designs for Research*. Chicago: Rand McNally.

Campbell, James E. 2000. *The American Campaign: U.S. Presidential Campaigns and the National Vote*. College Station, Tex.: Texas A&M University Press.

Caporaso, James A. 1995. "Research Design, Falsification, and the Qualitative-Quantitative Divide." *American Political Science Review* 89, no. 2: 457–60.

Chehabi, H. E., and Juan L. Linz. 1998. *Sultanistic Regimes*. Baltimore: Johns Hopkins University Press.

Clarke, Kevin A. 2002. "The Reverend and the Ravens: Comment on Seawright." *Political Analysis* 10, no. 2 (Spring): 194–97.

Cohen, Bernard P. 1989. *Developing Sociological Knowledge: Theory and Method*. 2nd edition. Chicago: Nelson-Hall.

Cohen, Michael D., and Robert Axelrod. 1984. "Coping with Complexity: The Adaptive Value of Changing Utility." *American Economic Review* 74, no. 1 (March): 30–42.

Collier, David. 1993. "The Comparative Method." In Ada W. Finifter, ed., *Political Science: The State of the Discipline II*. Washington, D.C.: American Political Science Association.

———. 1995a. "Translating Quantitative Methods for Qualitative Researchers: The Case of Selection Bias." *American Political Science Review* 89, no. 2 (June): 461–66.

———. 1995b. "Trajectory of a Concept: 'Corporatism' in the Study of Latin American Politics." In Peter H. Smith, ed., *Latin America in Comparative Perspective: New Approaches to Methods and Analysis*. Boulder, Colo.: Westview Press.

———. 1998. "Comparative Method in the 1990s." *APSA-CP: Newsletter of the APSA Organized Section in Comparative Politics* 9, no. 1 (Winter): 1–2, 4–5.

———. 1999. "Data, Field Work and Extracting New Ideas at Close Range." *APSA-CP: Newsletter of the APSA Organized Section in Comparative Politics* 10, no. 1 (Winter): 1–2, 4–6.

Collier, David, and Robert Adcock. 1999. "Democracy and Dichotomies: A Pragmatic Approach to Choices about Concepts." *Annual Review of Political Science*, vol. 2. Palo Alto: Annual Reviews.

Collier, David, and Steven Levitsky. 1997. "Democracy with Adjectives: Conceptual Innovation in Comparative Research." *World Politics* 49, no. 3 (April): 430–51.

Collier, David, and James E. Mahon. 1993. "Conceptual 'Stretching' Revisited: Adapting Categories in Comparative Analysis." *American Political Science Review* 87, no. 4 (December): 845–55.

Collier, David, and James Mahoney. 1996. "Insights and Pitfalls: Selection Bias in Qualitative Research." *World Politics* 49, no. 1 (October): 56–91.

Collier, Ruth Berins. 1999. *Paths Toward Democracy: The Working Class and Elites in Western Europe and South America*. New York: Cambridge University Press.

Collier, Ruth Berins, and David Collier. 1991. *Shaping the Political Arena: Critical Junctures, the Labor Movement, and Regime Dynamics in Latin America*. Princeton: Princeton University Press. Reprinted, 2002, Notre Dame, Ind.: University of Notre Dame Press.

Commins, Margaret M. 1992. "From Security to Trade in U.S.–Latin American Relations: Explaining U.S. Support for a Free Trade Agreement with Mexico." Paper presented at the 17th International Congress of the Latin American Studies Association, Los Angeles, September 24–27.

Cook, Thomas D., and Donald T. Campbell. 1979. *Quasi-Experimentation: Design and Analysis for Field Settings*. Boston: Houghton Mifflin.

Coombs, Clyde H., Robyn M. Dawes, and Amos Tversky. 1970. *Mathematical Psychology: An Elementary Introduction*. Englewood Cliffs, N.J.: Prentice-Hall.

Copas, John B., and H. G. Li. 1997. "Inference for Non-Random Samples." *Journal of the Royal Statistical Society* 59 (Series B): 55–77.

Coppedge, Michael. 1999. "Thickening Thin Concepts and Theories: Combining Large-N and Small in Comparative Politics." *Comparative Politics* 31, no. 4 (July): 465–76.

———. 2001. "Explaining Democratic Deterioration in Venezuela Through Nested Induction." Paper presented at the annual meeting of the American Political Science Association, San Francisco, September 2–5.

Costigliola, Frank. 1995. "Kennedy, the European Allies, and the Failure to Consult." *Political Science Quarterly* 110, no. 1 (Spring): 105–23.

Cowden, Jonathan A., and Thomas Hartley. 1993. "Complex Measures and Sociotropic Voting." In John R. Freeman, ed., *Political Analysis*, vol. 4. Ann Arbor: University of Michigan Press.

Cox, D. R. 1977. "The Role of Significance Tests." *Scandinavian Journal of Statistics* 4: 49–70.

———. 1992. "Causality: Some Statistical Aspects." *Journal of the Royal Statistical Society* 155 (Series A): 291–301.

Cox, David R., and N. Wermuth. 1996. *Multivariate Dependencies*. London: Chapman Hall.

Cronbach, Lee J., and Paul E. Meehl. 1955. "Construct Validity in Psychological Tests." *Psychological Bulletin* 52, no. 4: 281–302.

Cyert, Richard M., and James G. March. 1963. *A Behavioral Theory of the Firm*. Englewood Cliffs, N.J.: Prentice-Hall.

Darnell, Adrian C. 1994. *A Dictionary of Econometrics*. Cheltenham, U.K.: Elgar.

Dessler, David. 1991. "Beyond Correlations: Toward a Causal Theory of War." *International Studies Quarterly* 35: 337–55.

Diaconis, Persi. 1998. "A Place for Philosophy? The Rise of Modeling in Statistical Science." *Quarterly of Applied Mathematics* 56, no. 4 (December): 797–805.

Diesing, Paul. 1991. *How Does Social Science Work? Reflections on Practice.* Pittsburgh: University of Pittsburgh Press.

Dijkstra, Theo K., ed. 1988. "On Model Uncertainty and Its Statistical Implications." Proceedings of a workshop held in Groningen, the Netherlands, September 25–26, 1986. *Lecture Notes in Economics and Mathematical Systems,* no. 307. Berlin, New York: Springer.

Dion, Douglas. 1998. "Evidence and Inference in the Comparative Case Study." *Comparative Politics* 30, no. 2 (January): 127–45.

Doner, Richard F. 1992. "Limits of State Strength: Toward an Institutionalist View of Economic Development." *World Politics* 44, no. 3 (April): 398–431.

Dreze, Jean, and Amartya Sen. 1989. "China and India." Chapter 11 in *Hunger and Public Action.* Oxford: Clarendon Press.

Duncan, Otis Dudley. 1984a. *Notes on Social Measurement: Historical and Critical.* New York: Russell Sage Foundation.

———. 1984b. "Measurement and Structure: Strategies for the Design and Analysis of Subjective Survey Data." In Charles F. Turner and Elizabeth Martin, eds., *Surveying Subjective Phenomena.* New York: Russell Sage Foundation.

Eckstein, Harry. 1975. "Case Study and Theory in Political Science." In Fred I. Greenstein and Nelson W. Polsby, eds., *Handbook of Political Science,* vol. 7. Reading, Mass.: Addison-Wesley.

Ekeland, Ivar. 1988. *Mathematics and the Unexpected.* Chicago: University of Chicago Press.

Ekiert, Grzegorz. 1996. *The State against Society: Political Crises and Their Aftermath in East Central Europe.* Princeton: Princeton University Press.

Elster, Jon. 1983. *Explaining Technical Change: A Case Study in the Philosophy of Science.* New York: Cambridge University Press.

———. 1999. *Alchemies of the Mind: Rationality and the Emotions.* New York: Cambridge University Press.

Epstein, Lee, and Gary King. 2002. "The Rules of Inference." *The University of Chicago Law Review* 69, no. 1 (Winter): 1–133.

Ericsson, K. Anders, and Herbert A. Simon. 1984. *Protocol Analysis: Verbal Reports as Data.* Cambridge, Mass.: MIT Press.

Ertman, Thomas. 1997. *Birth of the Leviathan: Building States and Regimes in Medieval and Early Modern Europe.* New York: Cambridge University Press.

Fearon, James D. 1991: "Counterfactuals and Hypothesis Testing in Political Science." *World Politics* 43, no. 2 (January): 169–95.

Feigl, Herbert. 1958. "The Mental and the Physical." In Herbert Feigl, Michael Scriven, and Grover Maxwell, eds., *Minnesota Studies in the Philosophy of Science,* vol. 2. *Concepts, Theories and the Mind-Body Problem.* Minneapolis: University of Minnesota Press.

Fenno, Richard F. 1977. "U.S. House Members in Their Constituencies: An Exploration." *American Political Science Review* 71, no. 3 (September): 883–917.

————. 1978. *Home Style: House Members in Their Districts*. Boston: Little, Brown.

Feynman, Richard Phillips. 1965. *The Character of Physical Law*. Cambridge, Mass.: MIT Press.

Fish, M. Steven. 1995. *Democracy from Scratch: Opposition and Regime in the New Russian Revolution*. Princeton: Princeton University Press.

Fisher, Sir Ronald Aylmer. 1935. *The Design of Experiments*. Edinburgh: Oliver & Boyd.

Freedman, David A. 1983. "A Note on Screening Regression Equations." *American Statistician* 37, no. 2 (May): 152–55.

————. 1991. "Statistical Models and Shoe Leather." In Peter Marsden, ed., *Sociological Methodology*. San Francisco: Jossey-Bass.

————. 1992a. "As Others See Us: A Case Study in Path Analysis." In J. P. Shaffer, ed., *The Role of Models in Nonexperimental Social Science: Two Debates*. Washington, D.C.: American Educational Research Association and American Statistical Association.

————. 1992b. "A Rejoinder on Models, Metaphors and Fables." In J. P. Shaffer, ed., *The Role of Models in Nonexperimental Social Science: Two Debates*. Washington, D.C.: American Educational Research Association and American Statistical Association.

————. 1999. "From Association to Causation: Some Remarks on the History of Statistics." *Statistical Science* 14: 243–58.

Freedman, David A., and David Lane. 1983. "A Nonstochastic Interpretation of Reported Significance Levels." *Journal of Business and Economic Statistics* 1: 292–98.

Freedman, David A., Robert Pisani, and Roger Purves. 1998. *Statistics*. 3rd edition. New York: Norton.

Garrett, Geoffrey. 1998. *Partisan Politics in the Global Economy*. New York: Cambridge University Press.

Geddes, Barbara. 1991. "How the Cases You Choose Affect the Answers You Get: Selection Bias in Comparative Politics." In James A. Stimson, ed., *Political Analysis*, vol. 2. Ann Arbor: University of Michigan Press.

————. 1999. "What Do We Know about Democratization after Twenty Years?" *Annual Review of Political Science*, vol. 2, 115–44. Palo Alto, Calif.: Annual Reviews.

————. 2003. *Paradigms and Sand Castles: Research Design in Comparative Politics*. Ann Arbor: University of Michigan Press.

Geertz, Clifford. 1973. "Thick Description: Toward an Interpretive Theory of Culture." In C. Geertz, ed., *The Interpretation of Cultures*. New York: Basic Books.

Gelman, Andrew, and Gary King. 1994. "A Unified Method of Evaluating Electoral Systems and Redistricting Plans." *American Journal of Political Science* 38, no. 2 (May): 514–54.

George, Alexander L. 1979a. "Case Studies and Theory Development: The Method of Structured, Focused Comparison." In Paul Gordon Lauren, ed.,

Diplomacy: New Approaches in History, Theory and Policy. New York: Free Press.

————. 1979b. "The Causal Nexus between Cognitive Beliefs and Decision-Making Behavior: The 'Operational Code' Belief System." In Lawrence S. Falkowski, ed., *Psychological Models in International Politics*. Westview Special Studies in International Relations. Boulder, Colo.: Westview Press.

George, Alexander L., and Andrew Bennett. Forthcoming. *Case Studies and Theory Development*. Cambridge, Mass.: MIT Press.

George, Alexander L., and Timothy J. McKeown. 1985. "Case Studies and Theories of Organizational Decision Making." In Robert F. Coulam and Richard A. Smith, eds., *Advances in Information Processing in Organizations*, vol. 2. Greenwich, Conn.: JAI Press.

Gerring, John. 2001. *Social Science Methodology: A Criterial Framework*. New York: Cambridge University Press.

Gibbs, David N. 1994. "Taking the State Back Out: Reflections on a Tautology." *Contention* 3, no. 3 (Spring): 115–37.

Gigerenzer, Gerg. 1991. "From Tools to Theories: A Heuristic of Discovery in Cognitive Psychology." *Psychological Review* 98, no. 2: 254–67.

Glaser, Barney G., and Anselm L. Strauss. 1967. *The Discovery of Grounded Theory: Strategies for Qualitative Research*. Chicago: Aldine.

Glymour, Clark, Richard Scheines, Peter Spirtes, and Kevin Kelly. 1987. *Discovering Causal Structure: Artificial Intelligence, Philosophy of Science, and Statistical Modeling*. Orlando, Fla.: Academic Press.

Goertz, Gary. 2003. "The Substantive Importance of Necessary Condition Hypotheses." In Gary Goertz and Harvey Starr, eds., *Necessary Conditions: Theory, Methodology, and Applications*. Lanham, Md.: Rowman & Littlefield.

Goertz, Gary, and Harvey Starr, eds. 2003. *Necessary Conditions: Theory, Methodology, and Applications*. Lanham, Md.: Rowman & Littlefield.

Goldstone, Jack A. 1991. *Revolution and Rebellion in the Early Modern World*. Berkeley: University of California Press.

Goldthorpe, John H. 1991. "The Uses of History in Sociology: Reflections on Some Recent Tendencies." *British Journal of Sociology* 12, no. 2 (June): 211–30.

————. 1997. "Current Issues in Comparative Macrosociology: A Debate on Methodological Issues." *Comparative Social Research*, vol. 16. Greenwich, Conn.: JAI Press.

————. 2001. "Causation, Statistics, and Sociology." *European Sociological Review* 17, no. 1: 1–20.

Gooding, David. 1992. "The Procedural Turn; or, Why do Thought Experiments Work?" In Ronald N. Giere, ed., *Cognitive Models of Science*, vol. 15. Minnesota Studies in the Philosophy of Science. Minneapolis: University of Minnesota Press.

Gourevitch, Peter Alexis. 1978. "The International System and Regime Formation: A Critical Review of Anderson and Wallerstein." *Comparative Politics* 10, no. 3 (April): 419–38.

Granger, Clive W. J., ed. 1990. *Modelling Economic Series: Readings in Econometric Methodology*. Oxford: Clarendon.

Greene, Kenneth F. 2002. "Defeating Dominance: Opposition Party Building and Democratization in Mexico." Doctoral dissertation, Department of Political Science, University of California, Berkeley.

Greene, William H. 2000. *Econometric Analysis*. 4th edition. Upper Saddle River, N.J.: Prentice-Hall.

Griffin, Larry J. 1992. "Temporality, Events, and Explanation in Historical Sociology: An Introduction." *Sociological Methods and Research* 20, no. 4: 403–27.

Griffin, Larry J., Christopher Caplinger, Kathryn Lively, Nancy L. Malcom, Darren McDaniel, and Candice Nelsen. 1997. "Comparative-Historical Analysis and Scientific Inference: Disfranchisement in the U.S. South as a Test Case." *Historical Methods* 30, no. 1 (Winter): 13–27.

Griffin, Larry J., and Marcel van der Linden, eds. 1999. *New Methods for Social History*. Supplement 6 of the *International Review of Social History*. New York: Cambridge University Press.

Griliches, Zvi. 1986. "Economic Data Issues." In Z. Griliches and Michael Intriligator, eds., *Handbook of Econometrics*, vol. 3. Amsterdam: North Holland.

Gujarati, Damodar N. 1988. *Basic Econometrics*. 2nd edition. New York: McGraw-Hill.

Haggard, Stephan, and Robert R. Kaufman. 1995. *The Political Economy of Democratic Transitions*. Princeton: Princeton University Press.

Hall, Peter A. 2003. "Aligning Ontology and Methodology in Comparative Research." In James Mahoney and Dietrich Rueschemeyer, eds., *Comparative Historical Analysis in the Social Sciences*. New York: Cambridge University Press.

Hanushek, Eric A., and John E. Jackson. 1977. *Statistical Methods for Social Scientists*. Orlando, Fla.: Academic Press.

Heberle, Rudolf. 1963. *Landbevölkerung und Nationalsozialismus: Eine soziologische Untersuchung der politischen Willensbildung in Schleswig-Holstein 1918 bis 1932*. Revised edition. Stuttgart: Deutsche Verlags-Anstalt.

———. 1970. From Democracy to Nazism: A Regional Case Study on Political Parties in Germany. New York: Grosset & Dunlap.

Heckman, James J. 1976. "The Common Structure of Statistical Models of Truncation, Sample Selection and Limited Dependent Variables and a Simple Estimator for Such Models." *Annals of Economic and Social Measurement* 5 (Fall): 475–92.

———. 1979. "Sample Selection Bias as a Specification Error." *Econometrica* 47 (January): 153–61.

———. 1990a. "Selection Bias and Self-Selection." In John Eatwell, Murray Milgate, and Peter Newman, eds., *Econometrics*. New York: Norton.

———. 1990b. "Varieties of Selection Bias." *American Economic Review* 80, no. 2: 313–18.

———. 1992. "Randomization and Social Policy Evaluation." In Charles F. Manski and Irwin Garfinkel, eds., *Evaluating Welfare and Training Programs.* Cambridge, Mass.: Harvard University Press.

Hekman, Susan J. 1983. *Weber, the Ideal Type, and Contemporary Social Theory.* Notre Dame, Ind.: University of Notre Dame Press.

Hempel, Carl G. 1965. *Aspects of Scientific Explanation and Other Essays in the Philosophy of Science.* New York: Free Press.

———. 1966. *Philosophy of Natural Science.* Englewood Cliffs, N.J.: Prentice-Hall.

———. 1970 [1952]. *Fundamentals of Concept Formation in Empirical Science.* Chicago: University of Chicago Press.

Hendry, David F. 1980. "Econometrics—Alchemy or Science." *Economica* 47, no. 188 (November): 387–406.

Hendry, David F., and Jean-François Richard. 1982. "On the Formulation of Empirical Models in Dynamic Econometrics." *Journal of Econometrics* 20, no. 3: 3–33. Also in Granger, 1990.

Hibbs, Douglas A. 1987. "On the Political Economy of Long-Run Trends in Strike Activity." In Hibbs, *The Political Economy of Industrial Democracies.* Cambridge, Mass.: Harvard University Press.

Hicks, Alexander. 1988. "Social Democratic Corporatism and Economic Growth." *Journal of Politics* 50, no. 3 (August): 677–704.

Hicks, Alexander, and William David Patterson. 1989. "On the Robustness of the Left Corporatist Model of Economic Growth." *Journal of Politics* 51, no. 3 (August): 662–75.

Higley, John, and Richard Gunther, eds. 1992. *Elites and Democratic Consolidation in Latin America and Southern Europe.* Cambridge: Cambridge University Press.

Hill, Austin Bradford. 1991 [1937]. *Principles of Medical Statistics.* 12th edition. London: Arnold.

Hodges, Joseph L., and Erich L. Lehmann. 1964. *Basic Concepts of Probability and Statistics.* San Francisco: Holden-Day.

Holland, Paul W. 1986. "Statistics and Causal Inference." *Journal of the American Statistical Association* 81, no. 396 (December): 945–60.

Jackman, Robert W. 1987. "The Politics of Growth in the Industrial Democracies, 1974-80: Leftist Strength or North Sea Oil?" *Journal of Politics* 49, no. 1 (February): 242–56.

———. 1989. "The Politics of Economic Growth, Once Again." *Journal of Politics* 51, no. 3 (August): 646–61.

Jackman, Simon, and Gary N. Marks. 1994. "Forecasting Australian Elections: 1993 and All That." *Australian Journal of Political Science* 29: 277–91.

Jackson, John E. 1983. "Election Night Reporting and Voter Turnout." *American Journal of Political Science* 27, no. 4 (November): 615–35.

———. 1996. "Political Methodology: An Overview." In Robert E. Goodin and Hans-Dieter Klingemann, eds., *A New Handbook of Political Science*. New York: Oxford University Press.

Janoski, Thomas, and Alexander Hicks, eds. 1994. *The Comparative Political Economy of the Welfare State*. New York: Cambridge University Press.

Kahler, Miles. 1985. "European Protectionism in Theory and Practice." *World Politics* 37, no. 4 (July): 475–502.

Kapstein, Ethan B. 1992. "Between Power and Purpose: Central Bankers and the Politics of Regulatory Convergence." *International Organization* 46, no.1 (Winter): 265–87.

Katzenstein, Peter J. 1985. *Small States in World Markets: Industrial Policy in Europe*. Ithaca, N.Y.: Cornell University Press.

Kennedy, Peter. 1998. *A Guide to Econometrics*. Cambridge, Mass.: MIT Press.

Keohane, Robert O. 2003. "Disciplinary Schizophrenia: Implications for Graduate Education in Political Science." *Qualitative Methods* 1, no. 1 (Spring): 9–12.

Kerlinger, Fred N. 1979. *Behavioral Research: A Conceptual Approach*. New York: Holt, Rinehart, and Winston.

Key, V. O., Jr. 1984 [1949]. *Southern Politics in State and Nation*. Knoxville: University of Tennessee Press.

Kim, Jae-On, and Charles W. Mueller. 1978. *Introduction to Factor Analysis: What It Is and How to Do It*. London: Sage Publications.

King, Gary, Robert O. Keohane, and Sidney Verba. 1994. *Designing Social Inquiry: Scientific Inference in Qualitative Research*. Princeton: Princeton University Press.

———. 1995. "The Importance of Research Design in Political Science." *American Political Science Review* 89, no. 2 (June): 475–80.

Kitschelt, Herbert. 1994. *The Transformation of European Social Democracy*. New York: Cambridge University Press.

Kittel, Bernhard. 1999. "Sense and Sensitivity in Pooled Analysis of Political Data." *European Journal of Political Research* 35: 225–53.

Kohli, Atul. 1987. *The State and Poverty in India*. New York: Cambridge University Press.

Kornhauser, William. 1959. *The Politics of Mass Society*. Glencoe, Ill.: Free Press.

Krantz, David L., R. Duncan Luce, Patrick Suppes, and Amos Tversky. 1971, 1989, 1990. *Foundations of Measurement*, vols. 1, 2, and 3. New York: Academic Press.

Kriesi, Hanspeter, et al. 1995. *New Social Movements in Western Europe: A Comparative Analysis*. Minneapolis: University of Minnesota Press.

Kubik, Jan. 1994. *The Power of Symbols against the Symbols of Power: The Rise of Solidarity and the Fall of State Socialism in Poland*. University Park, Penn.: Pennsylvania State University Press.

Kuhn, Thomas. 1962. *The Structure of Scientific Revolutions*. Chicago: University of Chicago Press.

Laba, Roman. 1991. *The Roots of Solidarity: A Political Sociology of Poland's Working-Class Democratization*. Princeton: Princeton University Press.

Laitin, David D. 1995. "Disciplining Political Science." *American Political Science Review* 89, no. 2 (June): 454–56.

Lakatos, Imre, and Alan Musgrave, eds. 1970. *Criticism and the Growth of Knowledge.* Cambridge: Cambridge University Press.

Lane, Robert E. 1962. *Political Ideology: Why the American Common Man Believes What He Does.* New York: Free Press.

Lang, Janet, Kenneth J. Rothman, and C. L. Cann. 1998. "That Confounded P-Value." *Epidemiology* 9:1 (January): 7–8.

Lange, Peter, and Geoffrey Garrett. 1985. "The Politics of Growth: Strategic Interaction and Economic Performance in the Advanced Industrial Democracies, 1974–1980." *Journal of Politics* 47 (August): 792–827.

———. 1987. "The Politics of Growth Reconsidered." *Journal of Politics* 49 (February): 257–74.

Lave, Charles, and James G. March. 1975. *An Introduction to Models in the Social Sciences.* New York: Harper & Row.

Lazarsfeld, Paul F. 1940. "Introduction." In Mirra Komarovsky, *The Unemployed Man and His Family.* New York: Dryden.

———. 1955. "Interpretation of Statistical Relations as a Research Operation." In Paul F. Lazarsfeld and Morris Rosenberg, *The Language of Social Research.* New York: Free Press.

Lazarsfeld, Paul F., and Morris Rosenberg. 1955. *The Language of Social Research.* Glencoe, Ill.: Free Press.

Leamer, Edward E. 1978. *Specification Searches: Ad Hoc Inference with Nonexperimental Data.* New York: Wiley.

———. 1983. "Let's Take the Con Out of Econometrics." *American Economic Review* 73, no. 1 (March): 31–43.

———. 1994 [1986]. "A Bayesian Analysis of the Determinants of Inflation." In Edward E. Leamer, *Sturdy Econometrics.* Aldershot, U.K.: Edward Elgar.

———. 1994. *Sturdy Econometrics.* Aldershot, U.K.: Edward Elgar.

Lederer, Emil. 1940. *State of the Masses: The Threat of the Classless Society.* New York: W. W. Norton.

Levi, Isaac. 1984. *Decisions and Revisions: Philosophical Essays on Knowledge and Value.* New York: Cambridge University Press.

Levine, Ross, and David Renelt. 1992. "A Sensitivity Analysis of Cross-Country Growth Regressions." *The American Economic Review* 82, no. 4 (September): 942–63.

Lewis-Beck, Michael, and Tom W. Rice. 1992. *Forecasting Elections.* Washington, D.C.: Congressional Quarterly.

Lieberman, Evan. 2003. "Nested Analysis in Cross-National Research." *APSA-CP: Newsletter of the APSA Comparative Politics Section* 14, no. 1 (Winter): 17–20.

Lieberson, Stanley. 1985. *Making It Count: The Improvement of Social Research and Theory.* Berkeley: University of California Press.

———. 1991. "Small N's and Big Conclusions: An Examination of the Reasoning in Comparative Studies Based on a Small Number of Cases." *Social Forces* 70, no. 2 (December): 307–20.

———. 1994. "More on the Uneasy Case for Using Mill-Type Methods in Small-N Comparative Studies." *Social Forces* 72, no. 4 (June): 1225–37.

———. 1997. "The Big Broad Issues in Society and Social History: Application of a Probabilistic Perspective." In Vaughn R. McKim and Stephen P. Turner, eds., *Causality in Crisis? Statistical Methods and the Search for Causal Knowledge in the Social Sciences*. Notre Dame: University of Notre Dame Press.

Lijphart, Arend. 1971. "Comparative Politics and the Comparative Method." *American Political Science Review* 65, no. 3 (September): 682–93.

———. 1975. "The Comparable-Cases Strategy in Comparative Research." *Comparative Political Studies* 8, no. 2 (July): 158–65.

———. 1975 [1968]. *The Politics of Accommodation: Pluralism and Democracy in the Netherlands*. Berkeley: University of California Press.

Linz, Juan J. 1964. "An Authoritarian Regime: Spain." In Erik Allardt and Yrjö Littunen, eds., *Cleavages, Ideologies and Party System: Contributions to Comparative Political Sociology*. Helsinki: Academic Bookstore.

———. 1975. "Totalitarianism and Authoritarian Regimes." In Fred Greenstein and Nelson W. Polsby, eds., *Handbook of Political Science*, vol. 3. *Macropolitical Theory*. Reading, Mass.: Addison-Wesley Press.

Linz, Juan J., and Alfred Stepan. 1996. *Problems of Democratic Transition and Consolidation: Southern Europe, South America, and Post-Communist Europe*. Baltimore, Md.: Johns Hopkins University Press.

Lipset, Seymour M., and Stein Rokkan. 1967. "Cleavage Structures, Party Systems, and Voter Alignments: An Introduction." In Seymour M. Lipset and Stein Rokkan, eds., *Party Systems and Voter Alignments: Cross-National Perspectives*. New York: Free Press.

Lipton, Michael. 1976. *Why Poor People Stay Poor: Urban Bias in World Development*. Cambridge, Mass.: Harvard University Press.

Little, Daniel. 1991. *Varieties of Social Explanation: An Introduction to the Philosophy of Social Science*. Boulder, Colo.: Westview.

Liu, Ta Chung. 1960. "Under-Identification, Structural Estimation, and Forecasting." *Econometrica* 28: 855–65.

Locke, Richard M., and Kathleen Thelen. 1995. "Apples and Oranges Revisited: Contextualized Comparisons and the Study of Comparative Labor Politics." *Politics and Society* 23, no. 3 (September): 337–67.

Lott, John R., Jr. 2000. "Gore Might Lose a Second Round: Media Suppressed the Bush Vote." *Philadelphia Inquirer*, Tuesday, 14 November 2000, p. 23A.

Lucas, Robert E., Jr. 1976. "Econometric Policy Evaluation: A Critique." In K. Brunner and A. Meltzer, eds., *The Phillips Curve and Labor Markets*, vol. 1. Carnegie-Rochester Conferences on Public Policy, Supplementary Series to the *Journal of Monetary Economics*. North-Holland, Amsterdam: North-Holland.

Luebbert, Gregory M. 1991. *Liberalism, Fascism, or Social Democracy: Social Classes and the Political Origins of Regimes in Interwar Europe*. New York: Oxford University Press.

Maddala, G. S. 1983. *Limited-Dependent and Qualitative Variables in Economics*. Cambridge: Cambridge University Press.

Magee, Stephen P. 1980. "Three Simple Tests of the Stolper-Samuelson Theorem." In Peter Oppenheimer, ed., *Issues in International Economics*. London: Oriel.

Mahoney, James. 1999. "Nominal, Ordinal, and Narrative Appraisal in Macro-causal Analysis." *American Journal of Sociology* 104, no. 4 (January): 1154–96.

———. 2000a. "Strategies of Causal Inference in Small-N Research." *Sociological Methods and Research* 28, no. 4 (May): 387–424.

———. 2000b. "Path Dependence in Historical Sociology." *Theory and Society* 29, no. 4 (August): 507–48.

Mahoney, James, and Dietrich Rueschmeyer, eds. 2003. *Comparative Historical Analysis in the Social Sciences*. Cambridge: Cambridge University Press.

Manski, Charles F. 1995. *Identification Problems in Social Sciences*. Cambridge, Mass.: Harvard University Press.

Martin, Lisa L. 1992. *Coercive Cooperation: Explaining Multilateral Economic Sanctions*. Princeton: Princeton University Press.

Mason, Linda, Kathleen Frankovic, and Kathleen Hall Jamieson. 2001. "CBS News Coverage of Election Night 2000." Accessed 5 November 2003 at www.cbsnews.com/htdocs/c2k/pdf/REPFINAL.pdf.

McAdam, Doug. 1988. *Freedom Summer*. New York: Oxford University Press.

McAdam, Doug, Sidney Tarrow, and Charles Tilly. 2001. *Dynamics of Contention*. New York: Cambridge University Press.

McDonald, Terrence J., ed. 1996. *The Historic Turn in the Human Sciences*. Ann Arbor: University of Michigan Press.

McKeown, Timothy J. 1999. "Case Studies and the Statistical Worldview: Review of King, Keohane, and Verba's *Designing Social Inquiry*: Scientific Inference in Qualitative Research." *International Organization* 53, no. 1 (Winter): 161–90.

McKim, Vaughn R., and Stephen P. Turner, eds. 1997. *Causality in Crisis? Statistical Methods and the Search for Causal Knowledge in the Social Sciences*. Notre Dame, Ind.: Notre Dame Press.

McMichael, Philip. 1990. "Incorporating Comparison within a World-Historical Perspective: An Alternative Comparative Method." *American Sociological Review* 55, no. 3: 385–97.

Messick, Samuel. 1989. "Validity." In Robert L. Linn, ed., *Educational Measurement*. 3rd edition. New York: Macmillan.

Michell, Joel. 1990. *An Introduction to the Logic of Psychological Measurement*. Hillsdale, N.J.: Lawrence Erlbaum Associates.

Michels, Robert. 1915. *Political Parties: A Sociological Study of the Oligarchical Tendencies of Modern Democracy*. London: Jarrold & Sons.

Migdal, Joel S. 1988. *Strong Societies and Weak States: State-Society Relations and State Capabilities in the Third World.* Princeton: Princeton University Press.

Miles, Matthew B., and A. Michael Huberman. 1994. *Qualitative Data Analysis.* 2nd edition. Thousand Oaks, Calif.: Sage Publications.

Mill, John Stuart. 1974a [1843]. "Of the Chemical, or Experimental, Method in the Social Science." In book 6, chapter 7, *A System of Logic, Raciocinative and Inductive.* Toronto: University of Toronto Press.

———. 1974b [1843]. "Of the Four Methods of Experimental Inquiry." In book 3, chapter 8, *A System of Logic, Raciocinative and Inductive.* Toronto: University of Toronto Press.

Miller, Richard W. 1987. *Fact and Method: Explanation, Confirmation, and Reality in the Natural and the Social Sciences.* Princeton: Princeton University Press.

Mirer, Thad W. 1995. *Economic Statistics and Econometrics.* 3rd edition. Englewood Cliffs, N.J.: Prentice-Hall.

Mitchell, J. Clyde. 1984. "Case Studies." In R. F. Ellen, ed., *Ethnographic Research: A Guide to General Conduct.* Orlando, Fla.: Academic Press.

Mjøset, Lars, Fredrik Engelstad, Grete Brochmann, Ragnvald Kalleberg, and Arnlaug Leira. 1997. "Methodological Issues in Comparative Social Science." *Comparative Social Research*, vol. 16. Greenwich, Conn.: JAI Press.

Moore, Barrington, Jr. 1967. *Social Origins of Dictatorship and Democracy: Lord and Peasant in the Making of the Modern World.* Boston: Beacon.

Moss, Pamela A. 1992. "Shifting Conceptions of Validity in Educational Measurement: Implications for Performance Assessment." *Review of Educational Research* 62 (Fall): 229–58.

———. 1995. "Themes and Variations in Validity Theory." *Educational Measurement: Issues and Practice* 14 (Summer): 5–13.

Munck, Gerardo L. 1998. "Canons of Research Design in Qualitative Analysis." *Studies in Comparative International Development* 33, no. 3 (Fall): 18–45.

———. 2001. "Game Theory and Comparative Politics: New Perspectives and Old Concerns." *World Politics* 53, no. 2 (January): 173–204.

Neyman, Jerzy Splawa, with D. M. Dabrowska, and T. P. Speed. 1990 [1923]. "On the Application of Probability Theory to Agricultural Experiments. Essay on Principles. Section 9." *Statistical Science* 5, no. 4 (November): 465–72. Originally published by Neyman in Polish in the *Annals of Agricultural Sciences.*

Ní Bhrolcháin, Máire. 2001. "'Divorce Effects' and Causality in the Social Sciences." *European Sociological Review* 17, no. 1: 33–57.

Perrot, Michelle. 1986. "On the Formation of the French Working Class." In Ira Katznelson and Aristide Zolberg, eds., *Working Class Formation: Nineteenth Century Patterns in Western Europe and the United States.* Princeton: Princeton University Press.

Peters, B. Guy. 1998. *Comparative Politics: Theory and Methods.* New York: New York University Press.

Pierson, Paul. 1993. "When Effect Becomes Cause: Policy Feedback and Political Change." *World Politics* 45, no. 4 (July): 595–628.

———. 2000. "Increasing Returns, Path Dependence, and the Study of Politics." *American Political Science Review* 94, no. 2 (June): 251–67.

Piore, Michael. 1979. "Discovering Qualitative Research." *Administrative Science Quarterly* 24 (December): 560–69.

Pitkin, Hanna. 1967. *The Concept of Representation*. Berkeley: University of California Press.

Polanyi, Karl. 1944. *The Great Transformation: The Political and Economic Origins of Our Time*. New York, Toronto: Farrar & Rinehart.

Popper, Karl. 1959. "Prediction and Prophecy in the Social Sciences." In Patrick Gardiner, ed., *Theories of History*. Glencoe, Ill.: Free Press.

———. 1968. *The Logic of Scientific Discovery*. New York: Harper & Row.

Porkess, Roger. 1991. *The HarperCollins Dictionary of Statistics*. New York: HarperCollins.

Porter, Michael E. 1990. *The Competitive Advantage of Nations*. New York: Free Press.

Powell, Robert. 1999. *In the Shadow of Power: States and Strategies in International Politics*. Princeton: Princeton University Press.

Pratt, J. W., and Robert Schlaifer. 1984. "On the Nature and Discovery of Structure." *Journal of the American Statistical Association* 79, no. 385 (March): 9–21.

PS: Political Science & Politics. 1995. "Symposium on Verification/Replication." In *PS: Political Science & Politics* 28, no. 3 (September): 443–99.

Przeworski, Adam. 1995. Contribution to a symposium on "The Role of Theory in Comparative Politics." *World Politics* 48, no. 1 (October): 16–21.

Przeworski, Adam, Michael E. Alvarez, José Cheibub, and Fernando Limongi. 2000. *Democracy and Development: Political Institutions and Well-Being in the World, 1950–1990*. Cambridge: Cambridge University Press.

Przeworski, Adam, and Henry Teune. 1970. *The Logic of Comparative Social Inquiry*. New York: Wiley.

Putnam, Hilary. 1981. *Reason, Truth, and History*. Cambridge: Cambridge University Press.

Putnam, Robert D. 1993. *Making Democracy Work: Civic Traditions in Modern Italy*. Princeton: Princeton University Press.

Ragin, Charles C. 1987. *The Comparative Method: Moving Beyond Qualitative and Quantitative Strategies*. Berkeley: University of California Press.

———. 1992. "'Casing' and the Process of Social Inquiry." In Charles C. Ragin and Howard S. Becker, eds., *What Is a Case? Exploring the Foundations of Social Inquiry*. New York: Cambridge University Press.

———. 1994. *Constructing Social Research: The Unity and Diversity of Method*. Thousand Oaks, Calif.: Pine Forge.

———. 1997. "Turning the Tables: How Case-Oriented Research Challenges Variable-Oriented Research." *Comparative Social Research*, vol. 16. Greenwich, Conn.: JAI Press.

———. 2000. *Fuzzy-Set Social Science*. Chicago: University of Chicago.

Ragin, Charles C., and Howard S. Becker. 1992. *What Is a Case? Exploring the Foundations of Social Inquiry*. New York: Cambridge University Press.

Ragin, Charles C., Dirk Berg-Schlosser, and Gisèle de Meur. 1996. "Political Methodology: Qualitative Methods." In Robert E. Goodin and Hans-Dieter Klingemann, eds., *A New Handbook of Political Science*. New York: Oxford University Press.

Ragin, Charles C., and David Zaret. 1983. "Theory and Method in Comparative Research: Two Strategies." *Social Forces* 61, no. 3 (March): 731–54.

Rasch, Georg. 1980 [1960]. *Probabilistic Models for Some Intelligence and Attainment Tests*. Chicago: University of Chicago Press.

Rescher, Nicholas. 1970. *Scientific Explanation*. New York: Free Press.

Ringer, Fritz. 1997. *Max Weber's Methodology: The Unification of the Cultural and Social Sciences*. Cambridge, Mass.: Harvard University Press.

Roberts, Fred S. 1976. *Discrete Mathematical Models, with Applications to Social, Biological, and Environmental Problems*. Englewood Cliffs, N.J.: Prentice-Hall.

Rogowski, Ronald. 1995. "The Role of Theory and Anomaly in Social-Scientific Inference." *American Political Science Review* 89, no. 2 (June): 467–70.

Rosenbaum, Paul R. 1984. "From Association to Causation in Observational Studies: The Role of Tests of Strongly Ignorable Treatment Assignment." *Journal of the American Statistical Association* 79, no. 385 (March): 41–48.

———. 2002. *Observational Studies*. 2nd edition. New York: Springer.

Rosenberg, Morris. 1968. *The Logic of Survey Analysis*. New York: Basic Books.

Rubin, Donald B. 1974. "Estimating Causal Effects of Treatments in Randomized and Nonrandomized Studies." *Journal of Educational Psychology* 66, no. 5 (October): 688–701.

———. 1978. "Bayesian Inference for Causal Effects: The Role of Randomization." *Annals of Statistics* 6, no.1 (January): 34–58.

———. 1980. "Discussion of 'Randomization Analysis of Experimental Data: The Fisher Randomization Test' by D. Basu." *Journal of the American Statistical Association* 75, no. 351 (September): 575–82.

———. 1990. "Comment: Neyman (1923) and Causal Inference in Experiments and Observational Studies." *Statistical Science* 5, no. 4 (November): 472–80.

Rueschemeyer, Dietrich, Evelyne Huber Stephens, and John D. Stephens. 1992. *Capitalist Development and Democracy*. Chicago: University of Chicago Press.

Russell, Bertrand. 1969. *The Autobiography of Bertrand Russell, 1914–1944*. New York: Bantam Books.

Salmon, Wesley C. 1984. *Scientific Explanation and the Causal Structure of the World*. Princeton: Princeton University Press.

Sartori, Giovanni. 1970. "Concept Misformation in Comparative Politics." *American Political Science Review* 64, no. 4 (December): 1033–53.

———. 1984. "Guidelines for Concept Analysis." In Giovanni Sartori, ed., *Social Science Concepts: A Systematic Analysis*. Beverly Hills, Calif.: Sage Publications.

———. 1991. "Comparing and Miscomparing." *Journal of Theoretical Politics* 3, no. 3: 243–57.

Scharfstein, Daniel O., Andrea Rotnitzky, and James M. Robins. 1999. "Adjusting for Non-Ignorable Dropout Using Semi-Parametric Non-Response Models." *Journal of the American Statistical Association* 94: 1096–146.

Schwandt, Thomas A. 1997. *Qualitative Inquiry: A Dictionary of Terms*. Thousand Oaks, Calif.: Sage.

Sciubba, Roberto, and Rossana Sciubba Pace. 1976. *Le comunità di base in Italia*. Rome: Coines.

Scriven, Michael. 1975. "Causation as Explanation." *Nous* 9: 3–10. *Methods and Research* 20, no. 4: 428–55.

Seawright, Jason. 2002a. "Testing for Necessary and/or Sufficient Causation: Which Cases Are Relevant?" *Political Analysis* 10, no. 2:178–93.

———. 2002b. "What Counts as Evidence? Reply." *Political Analysis* 10, no. 2: 204–7.

Sewell, William. 1996. "Three Temporalities: Toward an Eventful Sociology." In Terrence J. McDonald, ed., *The Historic Turn in the Human Sciences*. Ann Arbor: University of Michigan Press.

Shepard, Lorrie. 1993. "Evaluating Test Validity." *Review of Research in Education* 19: 405–50.

Shugart, Matthew, Erika Moreno, and Luis E. Fajardo. 2001. "Deepening Democracy through Renovating Political Practices: The Struggle for Electoral Reform in Colombia." Paper presented at the conference on Democracy, Human Rights, and Peace in Colombia, Kellogg Institute, University of Notre Dame, March 26–27.

Shultz, Kenneth S., Matt L. Riggs, and Janet L. Kottke. 1998. "The Need for an Evolving Concept of Validity in Industrial and Personnel Psychology: Psychometric, Legal, and Emerging Issues." *Current Psychology* 17 (Winter): 265–86.

Signorino, Curtis S. 1998. "Statistical Analysis of Finite Choice Models in Extensive Form." Paper presented at the 94th Annual Meeting of the American Political Science Association, Boston, September 2–6.

Sil, Rudra. 2000. "The Division of Labor in Social Science Research: Unified Methodology or 'Organic Solidarity'?" *Polity* 32, no. 4 (Summer): 499–531.

Simon, Herbert A., and Y. Iwasaki. 1988. "Causal Ordering, Comparative Statistics, and Near Decomposability." *Journal of Econometrics* 39: 149–73.

Skocpol, Theda. 1979. States and Social Revolutions: A Comparative Analysis of France, Russia, and China. New York: Cambridge University Press.

———, ed. 1984. *Vision and Method in Historical Sociology*. New York: Cambridge University Press.

————. 1994. *Social Revolutions in the Modern World*. New York: Cambridge University Press.

Skocpol, Theda, and Margaret Somers. 1980. "The Uses of Comparative History in Macrosocial Inquiry." *Comparative Studies in Society and History* 22, no. 2 (October): 174–97.

Smelser, Neil J. 1968. "The Methodology of Comparative Analysis of Economic Activity." In Neil J. Smelser, ed., *Essays in Sociological Explanation*. Englewood Cliffs, N.J.: Prentice-Hall.

————. 1973. "The Methodology of Comparative Analysis." In Donald P. Warwick and Samuel Osherson, eds., *Comparative Research Methods*. Englewood Cliffs, N.J.: Prentice-Hall.

————. 1976. *Comparative Methods in the Social Sciences*. Englewood Cliffs, N.J.: Prentice-Hall.

Snyder, Jack. 1984/85. "Richness, Rigor, and Relevance in the Study of Soviet Foreign Policy." *International Security* 9, no. 3 (Winter): 89–108.

Snyder, Richard C., H. W. Bruck, and Burton Sapin. 1954. *Decision-making as an Approach to the Study of International Politics*. Foreign Policy Analysis Series No. 3. Princeton, N.J.: Organizational Behavior Section, Princeton University.

Stark, David. 1992. "Path Dependence and Privatization Strategies in East Central Europe." *East European Politics and Society* 6, no. 1 (Winter): 17–51.

Stepan, Alfred. 1978. *The State and Society: Peru in Comparative Perspective*. Princeton: Princeton University Press.

Stevens, S. S. 1946. "On the Theory of Scales of Measurement." *Science* 103: 677–80.

————. 1951. "Mathematics, Measurement, and Psychophysics." In S. S. Stevens, ed., *Handbook of Experimental Psychology*. New York: Wiley.

Stigler, Stephen M. 1986. *The History of Statistics: The Measurement of Uncertainty Before 1900*. Cambridge, Mass.: Belknap Press of Harvard University Press.

Stinchcombe, Arthur L. 1968. *Constructing Social Theories*. New York: Harcourt, Brace & World.

————. 1978. *Theoretical Methods in Social History*. New York: Academic Press.

Stock, James H., and Mark W. Watson. 2003. *Introduction to Econometrics*. Boston: Addison-Wesley.

Stokes, Susan Carol. 2001. *Mandates and Democracy: Neoliberalism by Surprise in Latin America*. New York: Cambridge University Press.

Stolzenberg, Ross M., and Daniel A. Relles. 1990. "Theory Testing in a World of Constrained Research Design: The Significance of Heckman's Censored Sampling Bias Correction for Nonexperimental Research." *Sociological Methods and Research* 18, no. 4: 395–415.

Stone, Charles J. 1985. "Additive Regression and Other Nonparametric Models." *Annals of Statistics* 13, no. 2 (June): 689–705.

Stone, Richard. 1993. "The Assumptions on Which Causal Inferences Rest." *Journal of the Royal Statistical Society* 55, no. 2 (Series B): 455–66.

Stouffer, Samuel A., et al. 1949. *The American Soldier*. Princeton: Princeton University Press.

Strauss, Anselm, and Juliet Corbin. 1994. "Grounded Theory Methodology: An Overview." In Norman K. Denzin and Yvonna S. Lincoln, eds., *Handbook of Qualitative Research*. Thousand Oaks, Calif.: Sage Publications.

Sundquist, James L. 1973. *Dynamics of the Party System: Alignment and Realignment of Political Parties in the United States*. Washington, D.C.: The Brookings Institution.

Taber, Charles S. 1992. "POLI: An Expert System Model of U.S. Foreign Policy Belief Systems." *American Political Science Review* 86, no. 4 (December): 888–904.

Tannenwald, Nina. 1999. "The Nuclear Taboo: The United States and the Normative Basis of Nuclear Non-Use." *International Organization* 53, no. 3 (Summer): 433–68.

Tanner, Wilson P., Jr., and John A. Swets. 1954. "A Decision-Making Theory of Visual Detection." *Psychological Review* 61, no. 6 (November): 401–9.

Tarrow, Sidney G. 1988. "Old Movements in New Cycles of Protest: The Career of an Italian Religious Community." In B. Klandermans, Hanspeter Kriesi, and Sidney Tarrow, eds., *From Structure to Action: Comparing Social Movements Across Cultures*. International Social Movement Research Series, vol. 1. Greenwich, Conn.: JAI Press.

———. 1989. *Democracy and Disorder: Protest and Politics in Italy, 1965–1975*. New York: Oxford University Press.

———. 1994. *Power in Movement: Social Movements, Collective Action, and Politics*. New York: Cambridge University Press.

———. 1995. "Bridging the Quantitative-Qualitative Divide in Political Science." *American Political Science Review* 89, no. 2 (June): 475–81.

Tetlock, Philip E., and Aaron Belkin, eds. 1996. *Counterfactual Thought Experiments in World Politics: Logical, Methodological, and Psychological Perspectives*. Princeton: Princeton University Press.

Thompson, E. P. 1963. *The Making of the English Working Class*. New York: Vintage Books.

Tilly, Charles. 1984. *Big Structures, Large Processes, Huge Comparisons*. New York: Russell Sage Foundation.

———. 1990. *Coercion, Capital, and European States, 990–1990 A.D.* Cambridge, Mass.: Blackwell.

———. 1993. *European Revolutions, 1492–1992*. Oxford: Blackwell.

———. 1994. "States and Nationalism in Europe, 1492–1992." *Theory and Society* 23, no. 1: 131–46.

———. 2001. "Mechanisms in Political Processes." *Annual Review of Political Science*, vol. 4. Palo Alto: Annual Reviews.

Tintner, Gerhard. 1952. *Econometrics*. New York: Wiley.

Toulmin, Stephen E. 1972. *Human Understanding*. Princeton: Princeton University Press.

Truman, David Bicknell. 1951. *The Governmental Process: Political Interests and Public Opinion*. New York: Knopf.

Valenzuela, J. Samuel. 1998. "Macro Comparisons without the Pitfalls: A Protocol for Comparative Research." In Scott Mainwaring and Arturo Valenzuela, eds., *Politics, Society, and Democracy: Latin America*. Boulder, Colo.: Westview.

van Deth, Jan W. 1995. "Comparative Politics and the Decline of the Nation-State in Western Europe." *European Journal of Political Research* 27: 443–62.

Van Evera, Stephen. 1997. *Guide to Methods for Students of Political Science*. Ithaca: Cornell University Press.

Verba, Sidney. 1971. "Cross-National Survey Research: The Problem of Credibility." In Ivan Vallier, ed., *Comparative Methods in Sociology: Essays on Trends and Applications*. Berkeley: University of California Press.

Verba, Sidney, Kay Lehman Schlozman, and Henry E. Brady. 1995. *Voice and Equality: Civic Voluntarism in American Politics*. Cambridge, Mass.: Cambridge University Press.

Vogt, W. Paul. 1999. *Dictionary of Statistics & Methodology: A Nontechnical Guide for the Social Sciences*. 2nd edition. Thousand Oaks, Calif.: Sage Publications.

Walker, Henry A., and Bernard P. Cohen. 1985. "Scope Statements: Imperatives for Evaluating Theory." *American Sociological Review* 50, no. 3 (June): 288–301.

Wallerstein, Immanuel Maurice. 1974. *The Modern World-System*, vol. 1. New York: Academic.

Wallerstein, Michael. 2000. "Trying to Navigate Between Scylla and Charybdis: Misspecified and Unidentified Models in Comparative Politics." *APSA-CP: Newsletter of the APSA Comparative Politics Section* 11, no. 2 (Summer): 1–2, 4, 21.

———. 2001. "Bridging the Quantitative/Non-Quantitative Divide." *APSA-CP: Newsletter of the APSA Comparative Politics Section* 12, no. 2 (Summer): 1–2, 23.

Walton, John. 1992. "Making the Theoretical Case." In Charles C. Ragin and Howard Becker, eds., *What Is a Case? Exploring the Foundations of Social Inquiry*. New York: Cambridge University Press.

Warwick, Donald P., and Samuel Osherson. 1973. "Comparative Analysis in the Social Sciences." In Donald P. Warwick and Samuel Osherson, eds., *Comparative Research Methods*. Englewood Cliffs, N.J.: Prentice-Hall.

Weber, Max. 1949. *The Methodology of the Social Sciences*. Glencoe, Ill.: Free Press.

Western, Bruce, and Simon Jackman. 1994. "Bayesian Inference for Comparative Research." *American Political Science Review* 88, no. 2 (June): 412–23.

White, Halbert. 1994. *Estimation, Inference, and Specification Analysis*. Cambridge: Cambridge University Press.

Wickham-Crowley, Timothy P. 1992. *Guerrillas and Revolution in Latin America: A Comparative Study of Insurgents and Regimes Since 1956.* Princeton: Princeton University Press.

Wieviorka, Michel. 1993. *The Making of Terrorism.* Chicago: University of Chicago Press.

Wonnacott, Ronald J., and Thomas H. Wonnacott. 1979. *Econometrics.* New York: Wiley.

Wooldridge, Jeffrey M. 2000. *Introductory Econometrics.* Cincinnati: South-Western College.

Zelditch, Morris, Jr. 1971. "Intelligible Comparisons." In Ivan Vallier, ed., *Comparative Methods in Sociology: Essays on Trends and Applications.* Berkeley: University of California Press.

Zuckerman, Alan S. 1997. "Reformulating Explanatory Standards and Advancing Theory in Comparative Politics." In Mark Irving Lichbach and Alan S. Zuckerman, eds., *Comparative Politics: Rationality, Culture, and Structure.* New York: Cambridge University Press.

Subject Index

anomaly, theoretical. *See* theory
assumptions, 4, 6, 10, 11, 14, 15, 28–36, 39, 42, 46, 246 (table 13.1), **274**
    causal homogeneity, 12, 28–30, 39, 88, 89, 107, 108 (table 7.1), 110, 111, 111n6, 113, 210, **276**
    conditional independence, 31–36, 59–61, 230, 232, 240–44, **280**
    constant causal effects, 29n10, **280**
    independence of observations, 28, 28n8, 30–31, 31n13, **290**
    specification assumption, 240–44, **306**
    unit homogeneity, 29–30, 29n9, 29–30n11, **311**

Bayesian inference, 9, 141 (table 9.1), 159–62, 167, 217, 218, 234–35, **274**
bias. *See* error
Boolean algebra, 108 (table 7.1), 110, 134–35, **274**

cases, 39, 76n6, 124n1, 141 (table 9.1), 250, **275**
    cases versus observations, 39, 250–52
case selection, 22–23, 27, 39–41, 85–102, 108 (table 7.1), 112–14, 125, 126 (table 8.1), 127–29, 136, 141 (table 9.1), 159–60, 163, 167, 188–90, **274**
    selecting on the dependent variable, 79, 80, 80n8, 83, 85–102, 186–88, 190, **305**
case studies, 8, 16, 77–83, 85, 86, 94, 98, 101, 102, 105–121 passim, 123–38, 139–67, 186–88, **275**
    case-oriented versus variable-oriented research, 120, 123–38, **275**
    constitution of cases, 125–28
    contrasting cases, 8, 114, **281**
    cross-case analysis, 12, 16, 91(figure 6.1), 92–95, 100–106, 116–19, 198n2, 210, 212, **283**
    crucial case, 87, 116, 141 (table 9.1), 145, 159, 163, 214, **283**
    deviant case, 108 (table 7.1), 118, 120, 216, **285**
    least-likely case, 8, 271, **293**
    matching cases, defined, **295**
    most-likely case, 8, 77, 201, **297**
    negative case, 17, 101, 111n6, 119, 126 (table 8.1), 130–33, **297–98**
    non-conforming case, 124, 126 (table

8.1), 136–38
positive case, 17, 50, 111n6, 126
    (table 8.1), 130–34, **300**
within-case analysis, 8, 12, 16, 86,
    92–102, 106, 110, 112–14, 116–
    19, 210, 212, **312–13**
    See also constructivism; critique of
    subordinating causal-process ob-
    servations, process tracing, and
    case studies to norms of main-
    stream quantitative methods;
    interpretation
causality, 56–62
    causal effect, 26, 32, 33, 41, 43, 44,
        58, 59n10, 60, 61, 80n8, 86, 88,
        96, 97, 99, 100, 101, **275–76**
    causal heterogeneity, 30, 88, 106,
        110, 111 (table 7.1), 111n6, 113,
        135, **276**
    causal homogeneity. *See* assump-
        tions
    causal inference. *See* inference
    causal mechanism, 58, 112, 114, 141
        (table 9.1), 143, 153, 156, 163,
        165, 174 (table 10.1), 253, 254,
        277
    causal model, 24, 29–30, 107,
        117n19, 213, 214, 217, 222n23,
        277
    causal process, 30, 51, 96, 97, 110,
        111, 118, 120, 141 (table 9.1),
        164–66, 218, 219n20, 225, 261,
        267, 270, 271, **277**
    causal-process observations. *See*
        observations
    causation, multiple and conjunctural,
        124–25, 126 (table 8.1), 136, **278**
    constant causal effects. *See* assump-
        tions
    cause, 25, 57, 57n7, 108 (table 7.1), 118,
        213–20, **278**
    counterfactual definition of causa-
        tion. *See* counterfactual analysis
    deterministic cause, 24, 108 (table
        7.1), 116, 117n19, 136–38, 213–
        20, 226, **285**
    necessary cause, 99n18, 117n19,
        213–20, 215 (table 12.1), **297**
    probabilistic cause, 213–20, 215

(table 12.1), 219n20, **301**
    sufficient cause, 117n19, 213–20,
        215 (table12.1), **324**
cognitive mapping, 155–56
comparative method, 4n1, 105n1, 113n11,
    278–79. *See also* cases
    comparative-historical analysis, 92,
        100, 110, 126, 127, 176, 218, **278**
    contextualized comparison, 107, 115,
        281
    critical juncture, 110, 117, 117n18,
        282
    method of agreement, 8, 99, 130,
        131, 133, 163, 214, **295**
    method of difference, 8, 163, 214,
        295
    path dependence, 108 (table 7.1),
        110, 117, **300**
    Qualitative Comparative Analysis,
        108 (table 7.1), 110, 116, **301**
    tipping point, 174 (table 10.1), 175,
        179, **310**
    within-case control, 117–19, **313**
concepts, 8, 42, 50, 62–63, **279**
    conceptual stretching, 106, 113, 204,
        280
    contrast space, 111n6, **281**
    extension of concepts, 221n21, **288–
        89**
    formation of concepts, 51, 54n1, 62,
        63, 66, 125, 127, 202–9, **279**
    ideal types, 153, 158
    intension of concepts, 221n21, **292**
conditional independence. *See* assump-
    tions
constant causal effects. *See* assumptions
constructivism, 4n1, 248, 257–58, **280**.
    See also interpretation
context, 8, 42, 48, 107–12, **280–81**
counterfactual analysis, 57, 67, 141 (table
    9.1), 149, 157, 163–64, 167, 184,
    282
    counterfactual definition of causa-
        tion, 25, 31, 36, 57, 232, 240, **280**
creativity in research, 200–202
critical juncture. *See* comparative method
critique of distinction between determi-
    nate and indeterminate research
    designs, 236–38

Name Index

347

348 *Name Index*

Brody, Baruch A., 57n6, 58n8
Bruck, H. W., 155
Bueno de Mesquita, Bruce, 156
Bunce, Valerie, 178
Burger, Thomas, 153, 158

Cain, Bruce, xxii, 58
Campbell, Donald T., 60, 60n13, 61,
   62, 63, 93, 112n10, 184, 184n2,
   201, 231, 231n3, 234, 234n7, 275,
   275n2, 302, 310n21
Campbell, James F., 247
Cann, C. L., 234n6
Caplinger, Christopher, 130, 131
Caporaso, James A., 153, 181n1, 183,
   184, 184n2, 188n5, 231, 233,
   361n1
Cardona, Christopher, xxii
Carruthers, Bruce, 123
Chehabi, H. E., 35n18
Cheibub, José, 212n15
Clarke, Kevin A., 219
Cohen, Bernard P., 110, 221n21, 222,
   224, 262
Cohen, Michael D., 158n10
Collier, David, 14, 16, 18, 19, 45, 47,
   48, 70, 87, 88, 93, 98, 100, 105n1,
   106nn1–2, 110, 111n6, 112n10,
   113, 113nn13–14, 114n15, 115,
   117n18, 120, 123, 139, 171, 181n1,
   183, 186, 188, 188n5, 190, 195,
   199, 201, 203, 204, 205n4, 206n8,
   208, 210, 253
Collier, Jennifer, xxii
Collier, Ruth Berins, xxii, 100, 105n1,
   110, 117n18, 203, 247
Collier, Stephen, xxii
Commins, Margaret M., 160
Cook, Thomas D., 60, 61, 62, 231,
   234n7, 275n2
Coombs, Clyde H., 206n7, 208
Copas, J. B., 234n6
Coppedge, Michael, xxi, xxii, 221n21,
   246, 248n22, 249n24, 298n11,
   302n13, 309n20
Corbin, Juliet, 200
Costigliola, Frank, 112n7
Cowan, Rubette, xxii
Cowden, Jonathan A., 73

Cox, D. R., 234n6, 254n29
Cronbach, Lee J., 145n3
Cyert, Richard M., 155

Dabrowska, D. M., 25, 207, 232, 298
Darnell, Adrian C., 242n18, 273n1
Dawes, Robyn M., 206n7, 208
de Meur, Gisèle, 106n2, 110, 112
Descartes, René, 166
Dessler, David, xxii, 93, 139
Diaconis, Persi, 266n39
Diesing, Paul, 143, 144, 144n2, 166
Dijkstra, Theo K., 234n6
Dion, Douglas, 113n14, 116, 216, 217,
   218
Domínguez, Jorge, xxii
Doner, Richard F., 112n7
Dosh, Paul, xxii
Downs, George, 139
Dreze, Jean, 92, 93, 94n14, 100
Duncan, Otis Dudley, 63

Eckstein, Harry, 76n2, 77, 105n1, 114,
   116, 120, 145, 159, 163, 200, 214,
   282
Eden, Lynn, 139
Ekeland, Ivar, 157
Ekiert, Grzegorz, 117n18
Elman, Colin, xxi
Elster, Jon, 158, 254n28, 263, 278n3
Engelstad, Frederik, 106n1
Epstein, Lee, 22n1
Ericsson, K. Anders, 155, 161
Ertman, Thomas, 118, 119
Espach, Ralph, xxii
Etchemendy, Sebastián, xxii

Fajardo, Luis E., 261
Fearon, James D., 139, 149, 148, 152
Feigl, H., 310n21
Fenno, Richard F., 70, 172, 267
Ferejohn, John, 58
Feynman, Richard Phillips, 76, 185,
   185n3
Fiorina, Morris, 58
Fish, M. Steven, 64–65
Fisher, Sir Ronald Aylmer, 182
Fiske, D. W., 63, 66, 310n21
Frankovic, Kathleen, 268n2

Contributors

Larry M. Bartels is Donald E. Stokes Professor of Public and International Affairs and director of the Center for the Study of Democratic Politics at Princeton University. His methodological writing has appeared in the *American Journal of Political Science*, *Political Methodology*, and *Political Analysis*. He has also written extensively on electoral politics, public opinion, and the mass media. Bartels is author of *Presidential Primaries and the Dynamics of Public Choice* (1988), which won the Woodrow Wilson Foundation Award of the American Political Science Association, and coeditor of *Campaign Reform: Insights and Evidence* (2000). A fellow of the American Academy of Arts and Sciences, Bartels has served as president of the Political Methodology Section, American Political Science Association, as well as chair of the board of overseers of the National Election Studies.

Henry E. Brady is Robson Professor of Political Science and Public Policy at the University of California, Berkeley, and director of the Berkeley Survey Research Center. He received his Ph.D. in economics and political science from MIT. His current research focuses on political participation in America, Estonia, and Russia, the dynamics of public opinion and political campaigns, the evaluation of social welfare programs, and the impact of computers on social policy making. Brady has coauthored *Letting the People Decide: Dynamics of a Canadian Election* (with Richard Johnston, André Blais, and Jean Crête, 1992), which won the Harold Adams Innis Award for the best book in the social sciences published in English in Canada in 1992 and 1993. His book *Voice and Equality: Civic Voluntarism in American Politics* (with Sidney Verba and Kay Schlozman, 1995) was the subject of a review symposium in the *American Political Science Review* (1997). Brady has also authored numerous articles on political participation, political methodology, and public opinion. Within the American Political Science Association, he has served as president of the Political Methodology Section and as program cochair of the APSA annual meeting. He is a fellow of the American Academy of Arts and Sciences.

David Collier is Professor of Political Science at the University of California, Berkeley, where he has served as department chair and as chair of the Center for Latin American Studies. His research focuses on democracy and authoritarianism, Latin American politics, comparative-historical analysis, and methodology. His books include *The New Authoritarianism in Latin America* (1979) and *Shaping the Political Arena* (with Ruth Berins Collier, 1991, reissued in 2002), which won the Best Book Prize of the APSA Comparative Politics Section. Collier's articles include work on regime change, corporatism, international diffusion, comparative method, and concept analysis. He has been a Guggenheim Fellow and a fellow at the Center for Advanced Studies in the Behavioral Sciences. Within the American Political Science Association, he has served as president of the Organized Section for Comparative Politics (1997–1999), vice president of the Association (2001–02), and founding transitional president of the Organized Section for Qualitative Methods (2002–2003). He is a fellow of the American Academy of Arts and Sciences.

Robert O. Keohane is James B. Duke Professor of Political Science at Duke University. His book, *After Hegemony: Cooperation and Discord in the World Political Economy* (1984), won the Grawemeyer Award for Ideas Improving World Order. Keohane also wrote *International Institutions and State Power* (1989) and *Power and Governance in a Partially Globalized World* (2002). He is coauthor of *Power and Interdependence* (with Joseph S. Nye, 1977, third edition 2001) and of *Designing Social Inquiry: Scientific Inference in Qualitative Research* (with Gary King and Sidney Verba, 1994). Keohane has also taught at Swarthmore College, Stanford University, Brandeis University, and Harvard University. He is former president of the International Studies Association and of the American Political Science Association, and a fellow of the American Academy of Arts and Sciences.

Gary King is David Florence Professor of Government at Harvard University. He is director of the Harvard-MIT Data Center and senior science advisor to the World Health Organization. King has published widely in the field of methodology, including innovative books on maximum likelihood estimation and on ecological inference, as well as numerous articles. He is author of *Unifying Political Methodology: The Likelihood Theory of Statistical Inference* (1989), *Designing Social Inquiry: Scientific Inference in Qualitative Research* (with Robert O. Keohane and Sidney Verba, 1994), and *A Solution to the Ecological Inference Problem: Reconstructing Individual Behavior from Aggregate Data* (1997). King is former president of the Organized Section for Political Methodology of the American Political Science Association, and he is a fellow of the American Academy of Arts and Sciences.

James Mahoney is Associate Professor of Sociology at Brown University. His book, *The Legacies of Liberalism: Path Dependence and Political Regimes in Central America* (2001), won the Barrington Moore, Jr., Prize of the Comparative-Historical Sociology Section, American Sociological Association. He is coeditor and coauthor of *Comparative Historical Analysis in the Social Sciences* (with Dietrich Rueschemeyer, 2003). Mahoney has also published many articles on path dependence, causal inference in small-N analysis, theories of regime change, and the historical development of political regimes in Central America. In 2001 he received a career award from the National Science Foundation to pursue research on development and the legacy of colonialism in Spanish America, and an article from that project, "Long-Run Development and the Legacy of Colonialism in Spanish America," is forthcoming in the *American Journal of Sociology* (2003).

Timothy J. McKeown is Associate Professor of Political Science at the University of North Carolina, Chapel Hill. His research focuses on international political economy and foreign policy decision making. He is coauthor and coeditor of *Organizing Business: Trade Associations in the U.S. and Japan* (1993) and *Diplomacy, Force and Leadership* (1993). McKeown has published numerous articles on foreign policy, international trade, and security issues, and he is coauthor of the landmark statement on the case-study method, "Case Studies and Theories of Organizational Decision-Making" (with Alexander L. George, 1985). His current research focuses on foreign-aid decision making in the United States during the Cold War. In 1998 he won the Charles Robson Award for Outstanding Graduate Instructor in Political Science, UNC-Chapel Hill.

Gerardo L. Munck is Associate Professor in the School of International Relations, University of Southern California. His research focuses on political regimes and democratization, Latin American politics, and research methods. He is author of *Authoritarianism and Democratization: Soldiers and Workers in Argentina, 1976–83* (1998) and numerous articles and book chapters, including "Game Theory and Comparative Politics: New Perspectives and Old Concerns," published in *World Politics* (2001). In 2002 he contributed the lead article (coauthored with Jay Verkuilen) to a symposium on "Conceptualizing and Measuring Democracy: Evaluating Alternative Indices," published in *Comparative Political Studies*. This article subsequently won the Award for Conceptual Innovation in Democratization Studies of the Committee on Concepts and Methods, International Political Science Association. Munck's *Theorizing Action: Game Theory and Comparative Politics* is forthcoming with Cambridge University Press (2003). He is Chief Technical Advisor for the UNDP *Report on Democratic Development in Latin America*.

Charles C. Ragin is Professor of Sociology and Political Science at the University of Arizona, and he also teaches at the University of Oslo, Norway. He publishes in the fields of methodology, political sociology, and comparative-historical analysis, with a substantive focus on the welfare state, ethnic political mobilization, and international political economy. Ragin is author of *The Comparative Method* (1987), which won the Stein Rokkan Prize for Comparative Research of the International Social Science Council. Other books include *What Is a Case? Exploring the Foundations of Social Research* (with Howard S. Becker, 1992) and *Fuzzy-Set Social Science* (2000). Ragin has developed two software packages for set-theoretic analysis of social data: Qualitative Comparative Analysis (QCA) and Fuzzy-Set/Qualitative Comparative Analysis (fs/QCA). He received the Donald Campbell Award for Methodological Innovation of the Policy Studies Association in 2001.

Ronald Rogowski is Professor and former chair of Political Science at the University of California, Los Angeles. He was educated at the University of Nebraska (B.A. in political science and mathematics, 1964), the Free University of Berlin, and Princeton University (Ph.D. in politics). Rogowski has held research appointments at Harvard University and the Center for Advanced Study in the Behavioral Sciences, and he has also taught at Princeton, Duke, and the University of Minnesota (Visiting Stassen Professor). He is author of *Rational Legitimacy* (1974) and *Commerce and Coalitions* (1989), and is currently engaged in work on economic consequences of electoral systems. Rogowski has served as vice president and program cochair of the American Political Science Association and as president of the APSA Comparative Politics Section. He is a fellow of the American Academy of Arts and Sciences.

Jason Seawright is a Ph.D. candidate in political science at the University of California, Berkeley, specializing in comparative party systems, Latin American politics, and methodology. He is author of "Testing for Necessary and/or Sufficient Causation: Which Cases are Relevant?" and "What Counts as Evidence?" in *Political Analysis* (2002). He has presented conference papers on "Democracy and Growth: A Case Study in Failed Causal Inference" (2002) and "Economic Voting and Party System Collapse in Latin America" (2003). Seawright is country coordinator for Venezuela within a four-country comparative survey project on the comparative infrastructure of representation in Latin America. He holds an undergraduate degree in computer science from Brigham Young University and is a National Science Foundation Graduate Research Fellow.

Sidney Tarrow is Maxwell M. Upson Professor of Government and Professor of Sociology at Cornell University, where he teaches comparative European politics, political sociology, political parties, and collective action. Tarrow's numerous books on social movements and European politics include *Democracy and Disorder: Protest and Politics in Italy, 1965–1975* (1989), which received the Best Book on Collective Action and Social Movements Award of the American Sociological Association. He has also published *Power in Movement: Social Movements, Collective Action, and Politics* (1998); *Dynamics of Contention*, a fifteen-country qualitative comparative study (with Doug McAdam and Charles Tilly, 2001); and *Contentious Europeans: Protest and Politics in an Emerging Polity*, a quantitative time-series analysis of protest events linked to the politics of European integration (with Doug Imig, 2001). Tarrow is a fellow of the American Academy of Arts and Sciences.

Sidney Verba is Carl H. Pforzheimer University Professor at Harvard University and director of the Harvard University Library. His research focuses on political participation, electoral politics, participatory democracy, civic culture, and methodology. Verba's most recent book is *The Private Roots of Public Action* (with Nancy Burns and Kay Lehman Schlozman, 2001), which won the Woodrow Wilson Foundation Award of the American Political Science Association. His many coauthored books include *Elites and the Idea of Equality: A Comparison of Japan, Sweden, and the United States* (1987), *Voice and Equality: Civic Voluntarism in American Politics* (1995), *Equality in America: The View from the Top* (1995), and *Designing Social Inquiry: Scientific Inference in Qualitative Research* (1994). Verba is former president of the American Political Science Association, a member of the National Academy of Sciences, and a fellow of the American Academy of Arts and Sciences. In 2002 he received the Johan Skytte Prize for Distinguished Contribution to Political Science, awarded by Uppsala University.

Acknowledgment of Permission to Reprint Copyrighted Material

In the present volume, chapters 1, 12, 13, the appendix, and the glossary are entirely new material, and chapters 2, 6, and 7 are largely new material, although they draw on previously published articles. Chapters 3, 4, 5, 8, 9, and 10 are essentially reprints of earlier articles; three of these chapters have new summary tables, some have revised headings and/or new titles, and some have undergone substantial editing. Chapter 11, by King, Keohane, and Verba, is a reprint of their response to a symposium devoted to *Designing Social Inquiry*.[1]

We wish to thank several publishers for permission to reprint:

Chapters 2 and 7 are greatly expanded and revised versions of different sections drawn from Gerardo L. Munck, "Canons of Research Design in Qualitative Analysis," *Studies in Comparative International Development* 33, no. 3 (Fall 1998): 18–45, copyright Transaction Publishers, reprinted with permission of the publisher.

Chapters 3 and 4 were originally published as Larry M. Bartels, "Symposium on *Designing Social Inquiry*, Part 1," and Henry E. Brady, "Symposium on Designing Social Inquiry, Part 2: Doing Good and Doing Better," both in *The*

---

[1] We would like to call attention to two additional articles in the 1995 symposium on King, Keohane, and Verba's book, published in the *American Political Science Review* and edited by Mark Lichbach: Laitin (1995) and Caporaso (1995). These valuable contributions are cited at various points in the present volume.